French London

MANCHEStER
1824

Manchester University Press

New Ethnographies

Series editor
Alexander Thomas T. Smith

Already published

French London

A blended ethnography of a migrant city

Saskia Huc-Hepher

MANCHESTER UNIVERSITY PRESS

The right of Saskia Huc-Hepher to be identified as the author
of this work has been asserted by them in accordance with
the Copyright, Designs and Patents Act 1988.

Published by Manchester University Press
Altrincham Street, Manchester M1 7JA

www.manchesteruniversitypress.co.uk

British Library Cataloguing-in-Publication Data
A catalogue record for this book is available from the British
Library

ISBN 978 1 5261 4333 4 hardback

First published 2021

The publisher has no responsibility for the persistence or
accuracy of URLs for any external or third-party internet
websites referred to in this book, and does not guarantee that
any content on such websites is, or will remain, accurate or
appropriate.

Typeset by
Servis Filmsetting Ltd, Stockport, Cheshire

Contents

Figures

Series editor's foreword

When the *New Ethnographies* series was launched in 2011, its aim was to publish the best new ethnographic monographs that promoted interdisciplinary debate and methodological innovation in the qualitative social sciences. Manchester University Press was the logical home for such a series, given the historical role it played in securing the ethnographic legacy of the famous 'Manchester School' of anthropological and interdisciplinary ethnographic research, pioneered by Max Gluckman in the years following the Second World War.

New Ethnographies has now established an enviable critical and commercial reputation. We have published titles on a wide variety of ethnographic subjects, including English football fans, Scottish Conservatives, Chagos islanders, international seafarers, African migrants in Ireland, post-civil war Sri Lanka, Iraqi women in Denmark and the British in rural France, among others. Our list of forthcoming titles, which continues to grow, reflects some of the best scholarship based on fresh ethnographic research carried out all around the world. Our authors are both established and emerging scholars, including some of the most exciting and innovative up-and-coming ethnographers of the next generation. *New Ethnographies* continues to provide a platform for social scientists and others engaging with ethnographic methods in new and imaginative ways. We also publish the work of those grappling with the 'new' ethnographic objects to which globalisation, geopolitical instability, transnational migration and the growth of neoliberal markets have given rise in the twenty-first century. We will continue to promote interdisciplinary debate about ethnographic methods as the series grows. Most importantly, we will continue to champion ethnography as a valuable tool for apprehending a world in flux.

Alexander Thomas T. Smith
Department of Sociology, University of Warwick

Introduction

When London's minority migrant communities are referred to in political, media and everyday discourses, the French tend not to be the people that spring to mind. Despite being significant in number, historic impact and their cultural contribution to the capital, they remain largely overlooked in both societal and academic fields. Not conforming to the disadvantaged, invasive stereotype we are routinely fed through mass media and right-wing political rhetoric, particularly in a post-EU-membership referendum era, the French, as a minority, escape the public gaze (Favell and Nebe, 2009). Having observed my partner's trajectory from France to London, since the early months of his arrival in 1991 to his (factual but not yet official) 'settled status' today, accompanying him on spells of return migration to France, interacting with the social and filial networks in both locales, and participating in the cultural rituals of such circles, this elusive quality is not applicable to my own experience. The decision to dedicate years of ethnographic study and subsequently this book to the French presence in London was, therefore, to a large extent a fait accompli.

Michael Peter Smith contends that migrants are 'classed, raced and gendered bodies in motion in specific historical contexts' (2005: 238) and should hence be apprehended within these situated and embodied time–space frameworks. Placing my own experiential knowledge of the community on a historic backdrop, it is clear why recent studies refer to the French, like the Italians, as 'valuable', '"old" EU migrants' (Lulle *et al.*, 2018: 2). The tangible legacy of the French diaspora in London since at least the seventeenth century is substantial (Kelly and Cornick, 2013). From the engineering feats of London Huguenots, such as Labelye's Westminster Bridge, Bazalgette's sewage system and Brunel's Rotherhithe Tunnel, 'the first to be built under a river' (Randall, 2013: 36), to the culinary delights of 'the patisserie Maison Bertaux in Greek Street, Soho, reputedly founded by exiled Communards' (Kelly, 2016: 7), the vestiges of French migration to the British capital are omnipresent and enduring. The impact of French settlers on the City's financial institutions cannot be forgotten either: the first Governor of the Bank of England, in 1694, was the Huguenot, Sir John Houblon, while the Bosanquet and Minet families ran several insurance firms throughout the eighteenth and nineteenth centuries (Janvrin and Rawlinson, 2013), deploying the then innovative probability theory of fellow Huguenot, Abraham de Moivre (Randall, 2013). Today, building on the accomplishments of Bazalgette, the French company Veolia, headed by Antoine Frérot, is investing £1 billion in innovative waste, water and sustainable energy infrastructure in the UK (Veolia, 2016a).[1] Similarly, the 'artisanal skills: from joinery to exquisite paint finishes or hand-crafted furniture' (Jean Michel Brun Ltd, no date) of contemporary French interior design firms recall the craftmanship of seventeenth-century religious exiles, including Jean Tijou, responsible for the ornate ironwork at St Paul's Cathedral and Hampton Court Palace, and Louis Laguerre, painter of the frescoes at Hampton Court and Buckingham Palaces (Janvrin and Rawlinson, 2013: 81). The same artistry – panelling, paintwork, carpentry, furnishings, fashion and gastronomy – held in high esteem in the powerful circles of London's past, persist as symbolic markers of social and cultural distinction today (Bourdieu, 1979a; Kelly, 2016).

This multifarious contribution to the fabric of British society and infrastructure has granted contemporary French migrants a select status, meaning they appear more 'entitled to privileged treatment than others' (Lulle *et al.*, 2018: 3) and effortlessly 'integrated' in London's multicultural mix (Kelly, 2013).[2] This 'positive invisibilisation' process has resulted in a lack of attention in migration literature, the population's perceived prestige masking its demographic complexity. Isolated studies from David Block (2006), Helen Drake (Drake and d'Aumale, no date; Huc-Hepher and Drake, 2013), Adrian Favell (2008a), Jon Mulholland and Louise Ryan (Ryan and Mulholland, 2013, 2014a, 2014b; Mulholland and Ryan, 2014, 2015, 2017; Ryan *et al.*, 2014), and more recently Bénédicte Brahic and Maxime Lallement (2018, on the French in Manchester) and Fabrice Lyczba (Huc-Hepher and Lyczba, forthcoming), are welcome exceptions to the rule, but tend to focus either on the high-flying 'Eurostars' alluded to by Favell or on youth mobility, which consequently precludes 'the messy middle ground' (Conradson and Latham, 2005a; Scott, 2006: 1,107; Walsh, 2012).

The ethnography I present here aims to address precisely that shortfall, bringing into relief the sociocultural nuances of London's 'superdiverse' (Vertovec, 2007; Wessendorf, 2018) French diaspora, whose historic legacy, geographic proximity, demographic and socioeconomic heterogeneity, and symbolic potency arguably distinguish them from other forms of privileged, predominantly white, 'expatriate' (Fechter, 2005; Farrer, 2010; Leonard, 2010b; Walsh, 2018; Leonard and Walsh, 2019) or 'lifestyle'

(Scott, 2004, 2006; Oliver and O'Reilly, 2010; Benson, 2011; Korpela, 2014; Benson and O'Reilly, 2016) migrant populations. Although there are clear synergies between these varying forms of privileged migration, the equivalence of French and English imperial histories and combined membership of the European Union (until 2020) afford the French in London a somewhat different status than, for example, expatriate communities in Hong Kong, Africa or the Middle East. The balances of power, postcolonial legacies and reduced propensity of onward migration are all distinguishing factors. For French Londoners of Colour, often first- or second-generation migrants in France from former colonial or current overseas' 'territories', London is a superdiverse, multicultural city which allows a freedom and anonymity denied in France. For others, London is a 'home away from home', its proximity giving rise to a practical and politically enabled transnationalism that 'expatriation' or 'emigration' further afield inhibits.

In this interdisciplinary book, which draws on expertise from sociology, anthropology, geography and semiotics, my intention is to paint portraits that fully exploit the vibrant colours of participants' narratives (originally in French) that stem from observational and linguistic sensibilities I have honed over a lifetime studying the French language, literature, culture and people. A primary objective is to give readers a deeper understanding of the motivations underpinning London-French mobilities, questioning preconceived ideas about the agentive deployment of post-Maastricht free movement for purely economic or lifestyle reasons, and instead draw attention to the simultaneous plurality and commonality of lived experiences, including implicit forces at play in the 'sending society'. While recognising the increasing 'liquidity' of contemporary life-trajectories and the widespread development of a 'migrancy habitus' (Lulle *et al.*, 2018: 2), I argue that simply accounting for French migration to London through the lure of its buoyant labour market, dynamic youth culture and the fluidity of present-day settlement processes is an oversimplification.

In addition to the multi-scalar and morally charged spatialities to which Mulholland and Ryan astutely allude (2015, 2017) and to the affective pull of London (Conradson and Latham, 2007), some implicit ideological determinants that are traceable back to the premigration social space have hitherto been largely ignored. These underlying mobility drivers generally surface when participants consider their trajectories retrospectively and often contradict their initial, cognisant migration 'choices', which casts doubt over the very agency of the decision-making process (Murphy-Lejeune, 2001; Fechter and Walsh, 2010; McGhee *et al.*, 2017; Ryan, 2018) and sheds as much light onto twenty-first-century French society as it does onto diasporic life in London. These subtle, yet pervasive, societal pressures add to the complexity of the migration, making it difficult to shoehorn into a single typology or taxonomy (Brahic and Lallement, 2018). Neither labour nor lifestyle migration is an ideal fit, with 'ideological' migration more apposite for some (Huc-Hepher and Drake, 2013), despite the geographic, historic and 'moral' proximity of France and Britain. However, with the result of the 2016 EU membership referendum creating a 'rupture' (Hörschelmann, 2011, cited in Lulle *et al.*, 2018: 1) which threatens the durability of London-French mobility in unprecedented ways, such ideological stimuli are subject to erosion, as are migrants' long-term settlement practices. This revalidates the conception of migration as a continuum (Kelly and Lusis, 2006), ongoing (Benson, 2011), just one part of 'the non-linear transitions' (Lulle *et al.*, 2018: 3) that make up contemporary living, albeit a transition imposed by external political circumstances.

Based on years of ethnographic immersion, on-land and online,[3] I draw on Bourdieusian theory in order to understand the processes at play in both pre- and postmigration contexts. As well as identifying implicit mobility drivers and framing them within symbolic violence (Bourdieu and Wacquant, 1992; Bourdieu *et al.*, 1993; Huc-Hepher, 2019), I sub-divide Bourdieu's concept of habitus ([1972] 2000) into habitat, habits and habituation. My triadic construct accounts for the objective (external/material) and subjective (internal/affective) dimensions of homemaking and settlement, together with the dynamic space in between. It also allows me to provide a detailed account of how the migrants (re)construct home, the extent to which they are *at* home and how that sense of place and belonging maps onto the digital 'diasberspace'. In *The British in Rural France: Lifestyle migration and the ongoing quest for a better way of life* (2011), Michaela Benson introduces several key themes whose pertinence unexpectedly remerges in relation to my own ethnography of an antithetical population. Specifically, the multiple ambivalences and the processual nature of the migration experience, affirmations of cultural distinction and the relocation of class structures are shared concerns. Despite this common ground, there are unequivocal differences, with my respondents' explicit and implicit motivations, individual experiences and homemaking practices representing a peculiar and spatio-temporally situated set of characteristics. Given the unique relationship between the UK and France, 'that sweet enemy' (Tombs and Tombs, 2007), there is a need to acknowledge the existence of specificities 'within the category of "Western expatriates", problematising any assumption that they are a homogenous group fitting neatly into one position in a city or global class hierarchy' (Fechter and Walsh, 2010: 1,200). Equally, there is a need to recognise '[d]ifferences in integration and identification … observed both between and within national groups' (Duchêne-Lacroix and Koukoutsaki-Monnier, 2016: 138).

Functioning as a counterpoint to Benson's work, this volume therefore acknowledges the micro-level cultural intricacies and ambivalent personal (hi)stories of individuals representing the London-French diaspora, revealing the messy reality of their lived experience. It does not seek to provide solutions to perceived social injustice or inequalities in France, nor does it seek to portray London as a multicultural world city par excellence, particularly given the disquieting sociopolitical transformations afoot. Rather, by considering the opinions and attitudes of a carefully selected group of French Londoners, who characterise the socio-economic and demographic diversity of this diaspora in the years preceding the EU membership referendum, the book aims to provide readers with a first-hand perspective on their mobility and embedding, drawing attention to their ambivalent relationship with France (Roudaut, 2009) and their reasons for, and ways of, making London home.

Additional themes central to the book, which have been under-scrutinised in other studies on the London French, include identity/habitus transformation, community practices, symbolic violence as a mobility driver, the relevance of the local within the transnational, and the interrelationship between 'life lived offline' and 'online life' (Adami and Kress, 2010: 189). In her edifying study of British mobility to Dubai, Walsh (2012; 2018) explores the intimate dimensions of migration, considering the role of friendship, family and communities in 'the texture of everyday space' (Walsh, 2018: 15). Mulholland and Ryan convincingly problematise the affective pull of London and the 'moral geographies' (2017: 135) mapped out by their respondents, who spontaneously compare it with Paris. But transformation of embodied affective dispositions over time and how such dispositions influence place-making practices and perceptions are neglected. Conradson and Latham are keen to underline the importance of the affective in contemporary (antipodean) mobility to London, describing the deliberate 'resubjectification' opportunities of an overseas' experience, which 'is not meant to leave the individual the same' (Conradson and Latham, 2007: 234). It is a compelling conceptual framework, particularly regarding the notion of 'cosmopolitanisation', but their analysis is somewhat limited regarding the specifities of self-transformation.

By breaking down Bourdieu's conception of habitus into a multifaceted triad that straddles the physical and phenomenological, and studying on-land narratives in conjunction with online material, I reveal the practical and internalised particularities of my participants' self-reinvention and sense of emplacement in multiple spaces (Glick Schiller and Çaglar, 2013). Drawing on Massey (1995), Appadurai (1995, 1996) and Smith (2001, 2005), Gieles recommends adopting a 'place lens' (2009: 276) that foregrounds the 'translocal'. I contribute to this 'placial turn' (2009: 277), demonstrating the ways in which the local (neighbourhood) and intimate places (houses/flats) my participants inhabit within the global city are imbued with equally localised elements from a sub-national, originary home setting. Within this necessarily situated context, I also demonstrate how respondents' relationship with – or not – the more abstract (and loaded) notion of 'community' affects their identity and repertoires of belonging. Confirming Gieles's claim that much attention has been placed on networks in order to overcome 'the problem of methodological nationalism' (2009: 274, citing Wimmer and Glick Schiller, 2003), Beaverstock (2005) and Ryan and Mulholland devote much attention to relationships and social networks within the diasporic space (Ryan, 2011, 2018; Ryan and Mulholland, 2014b; Ryan *et al.*, 2014), but overlook the notion of community per se and the establishment of online networks. Duchêne-Lacroix and Koukoutsaki-Monnier's (2016) enlightening mixed-methods study on the French in Berlin acknowledges community as an integration variable but does not drill down into its implications. Yet, since the idea of community is key to understanding the London-French population's sense of self and diasporic positioning, its relevance should not be underestimated. The London French are a 'distinctive' migrant group – partly because of their status within the British social space, linked to their role in both nations' shared histories, and partly because of their socio-demographic and motivational heterogeneity. This distinctiveness, coupled – crucially – with their own negation of a collective 'community' identity (Huc-Hepher and Drake, 2013), compounds their simultaneously visible and invisible presence, which in turn compounds the ambivalence of their emplacement and imperviousness to typological and *community* classification.

Indeed, I contend that the migrants are in a perpetual state of ambivalence or paradox, simultaneously rejecting France/French 'mentalities', yet reasserting their Frenchness through their homemaking practices. They consciously embrace local habits and identify with individuated selfhoods, yet form a sense of community through their shared 'originary' habits, or coincidental 'common-unity' of practices. Their integration into/of the local culture is therefore only ever partial, with the habitus of origin, as Bourdieu states, proving resistant to complete transformation (Bourdieu, 1980a). In contemporary society, this ambivalence is increased by the proportion of people's lives spent online, which means the migrants are not only suspended between two nations, cultures, homes and identities, but between physical and digital realities, hence the need for ethnographic acknowledgement of this digital presence alongside the on-land research. As a means of triangulation, therefore, my online analysis tests the extent to which my on-land observations about symbolic violence in French society, the community-building scope of shared practices and habitus transformation over time are re-presented in digital environments. In a 'blended' ethnographic turn (Androutsopoulos, 2008; Dyke, 2013; Tagg *et al.*, 2016), the following chapters explore all these themes in depth, based on migrant (hi)stories recorded in the physical field and on digital diasporic representations collected from the internet. At a time when a 'hostile environment' (Fox *et al.*, 2012; Looney, 2017; Brahic and Lallement, 2018; Lulle *et al.*, 2018) for migrants is openly part of public and political discourse, and the appeal of the UK as a migratory destination is threatened like never before in the country's recent history, it is of unprecedented relevance, urgency and value to understand what it is about London that has appealed so much to our closest European neighbours and how they positioned themselves in this global city prior to the so-called 'Brexit' referendum, and – in the form of a detailed Epilogue – their feelings of belonging since.

Measuring, mapping and defining the 'French' in London

A fundamental premise of the European Union is free movement within member states. Indeed, it was this liberal principle that underpinned much of the Vote Leave referendum campaign and has rendered attempts to establish the precise number of London-French inhabitants almost futile (Favell, 2008b), with many states – France and the UK in particular – not formally monitoring or recording intra-EU migratory flows. However, since a declaration made by former French president, Nicolas Sarkozy, during a state visit to London in 2008 and more recently by the current president, Emmanuel Macron, in his 2017 presidential campaign, the media on both sides of the Channel have repeatedly reported London's French population as quantitatively equivalent to that of France's fifth or sixth largest city (Huc-Hepher and Drake, 2013). Although rightly testifying to the significance of the French presence in London, these claims are both unreliable and misleading; first, because the initial estimate is based on speculation, according to a vague and arguably inflated consular approximation (Ryan and Mulholland, 2013). Second, French city population numbers include only *intramuros* residents and exclude all those residents inhabiting the outer municipalities, who, in the example of Bordeaux, increase its population from 239,399 to a more realistic 1.18 million (Population Data, 2014). This would consequently place London's French community (assuming the consulate's estimations are deemed accurate) on a par with the populations of small towns such as Pau or Annecy, in other words, France's forty-fourth largest 'city' (*La Tribune*, 2014).

French consulate estimates place the figure at 300,000, although there are but 120,000 French residents throughout the UK officially registered

(Consulat Général, 2013). The 2011 ONS census, on the other hand, recorded French-passport holders as the fourth highest-ranking non-British group in London (after Poland, Ireland and India), yet in terms of numbers of French-born citizens, only 66,654 were recorded, ranking the population ninth (Krausova and Vargas Silva, 2013). Mulholland and Ryan (2017) noted a considerable rise in the number of French people living in the UK between the 2001 and 2011 censuses, up from 38,000 to 129,804. None of these figures match the inflated media claims, but all could be underestimates, as most French migrants fail to register at the embassy unless or until administrative formalities require it (Ledain, 2010; Huc-Hepher and Drake, 2013; Duchêne-Lacroix and Koukoutsaki-Monnier, 2016). Furthermore, there is currently no formal obligation for household members to respond to the national census and many French migrants live in shared accommodation for the initial months or years of their migration. Therefore, rather than dwell on an intrinsically dubious quantitative assessment of the French presence in London, it is far more valuable here to consider the demographic and geographic dimensions.

In 2012, the results of the London-French vote in the presidential elections for the first time mirrored those of France as a whole. By 2017, the trend was accentuated, Macron winning with over 51 per cent of the vote in the first round (compared to 24 per cent in France), against under 3 per cent for far-right Marine Le Pen (compared to 21 per cent in France) and over 11 per cent for far-left Jean-Luc Mélenchon (against almost 20 per cent in France) (Consulat Général de France). The move away from the right-leaning patterns of previous presidential elections in London reflects the current diversity of the London-French diaspora, an observation supported by Ryan and Mulholland (2013). Meanwhile, the considerable share of the vote in favour of Macron and derisory numbers voting for Le Pen arguably reflects the forward-thinking, open-minded and (neo)liberal characteristics of London that so appeal to its French residents (Mulholland and Ryan, 2017). Thus, the stereotypical image of the French diplomat, investment banker or tax-avoiding entrepreneur living in South Kensington and sending his progeny to the Lycée Français no longer tallies with the voting practices or places of abode of the French on the ground.

Indeed, the physical spaces inhabited by my research participants (Figure 1) demonstrate that all of London's cardinal points have been chosen as places to set down roots, hence dispelling the South Kensington community myth. Similarly, their socio-professional profiles, ages, geographical and ethnic origins bear witness to this diversity (see Appendix). The age range of my respondents was from 16 to 80; their professions included 'highly skilled' scientists, medics and researchers, as well as teachers, white-collar city workers and middle management, together with staff

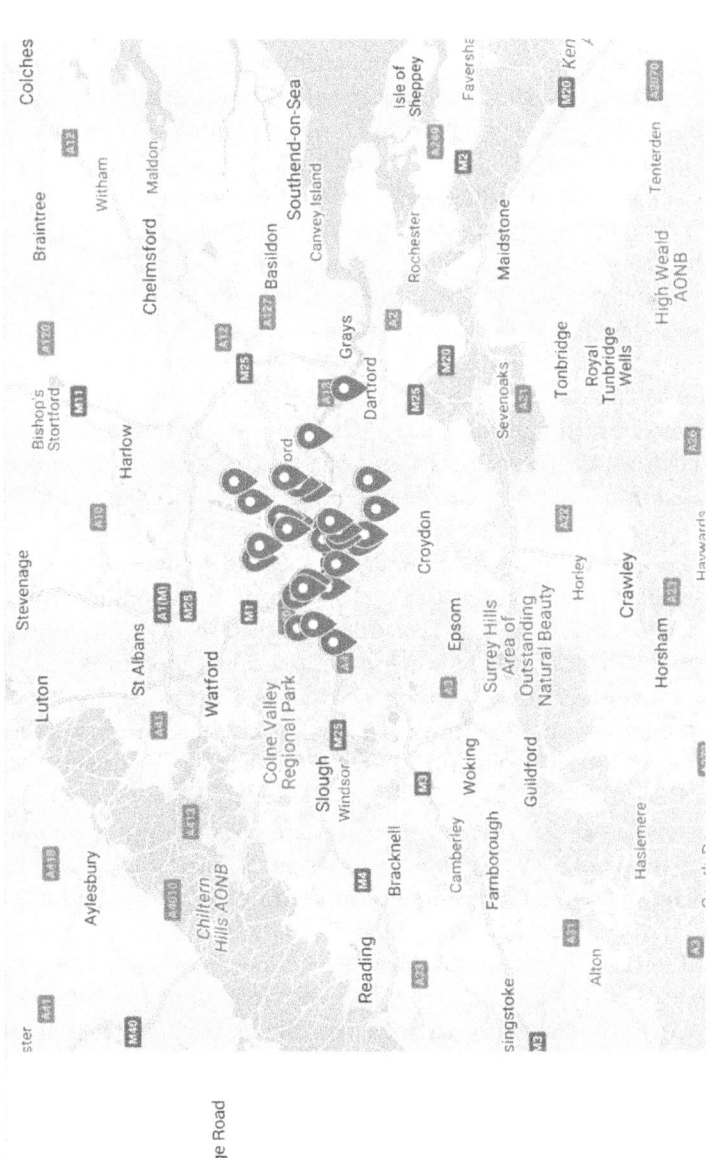

West Norwood
Bromley
Greenwich
Docklands
Crystal Palace
Archway
Wandsworth Bridge Road
Beckenham
Tower Hamlets
Richmond
Bethnal Green
Dartford
Abbey Wood
Leyton
Arsenal Station
Peckham
Camberwell
North Dulwich
South Woodford
Acton
East Dulwich
W11
Clapham South

Figure 1 Map of interviewees' places of residence in London

from the hospitality and creative industries, and sixth-form students. Their origins spanned the length and breadth of France, urban and rural areas alike, as well as French overseas' regions, such as Reunion or other French-speaking countries, like Canada. In terms of heritage, several participants were second-generation migrants from France's former colonies, including Algeria, Benin and Senegal, in search of what Shahrokni (2019) has termed a 'third space', beyond the antagonism of the postcolonial settings. Yet, the important point here is that the diversity of my participants reflects that of the contemporary French-speaking community in London as a whole. No longer can a single profile be considered to dominate, and no single location in France emerges as a distinctly prominent 'sending' area. In keeping with Benson's British expats in France, therefore, and the multiple typologies of middle-class British migrants in Paris identified by Sam Scott, the migrant narratives brought to bear in this book each tell differentiated, individuated stories. A shared trait among them, however, is their choice of inner-London boroughs as their destination, in common with post-2009 middle-class Italian migrants in Paris (Dubucs *et al.*, 2017).

This brings us back to the map (Figure 1). Given the importance of space and place when assessing the settlement of migrant communities (Brettell, 2008), it is necessary to consider the physical placement of my respondents in more depth, particularly because 'transnational literature ... all too often fails to consider scale, context and place' (Hardwick, 2008: 171) and '[m]ost ethnographic reportage seems oddly lacking in physical location' (Atkinson, 2005: 9). The map confirms that most informants live in central boroughs, inside the North-/South-Circular periphery, with one alone nearing the definitive M25 boundary. This distribution is supported by the 2011 census statistics (Office for National Statistics, 2012), wherein a total of 45,669 French-born residents are recorded in inner-London local authorities and less than half that amount (20,985) in outer-London boroughs, with fewer still choosing to live in the 'home' counties. The preference for urbanised London, as opposed to its circumferential countryside or market towns, is demonstrated unequivocally by the 2011 census rankings, in which Oxford, Elmbridge and Canterbury are the local authorities accounting for the highest concentrations of French-born residents outside London, but where the said communities are placed in 14th, 29th and 31st numeric position respectively. By comparison, French-born inhabitants constitute the most populous community in Kensington and Chelsea (representing 4.2 per cent of the local population, that is, 6,659 individuals), the second-largest in Hammersmith and Fulham (with a 2.7 per cent share or 4,977), third in Westminster (2.6 per cent) and fourth in the City of London (2 per cent). While these figures appear modest in relation to media depictions, the consistency of the relatively high distribution of French-born citizens *across* the capital is significant, with the inner-London boroughs of Camden, Islington, Lambeth, Tower Hamlets, Wandsworth, Southwark and Hackney all recording proportions of French-born citizens between 1 per cent and 1.7 per cent, and Lewisham, Haringey and Newham between 0.5 per cent and 0.8 per cent.

To put these French sub-communities into perspective, the largest concentrations of other founder-member EU communities struggle to approach the French numbers, with Italian residents representing the next highest (with 2.7 per cent in Kensington and Chelsea), then the Portuguese (2.3 per cent in Lambeth), German (1.7 per cent, again in Kensington and Chelsea) and Spanish (1.4 per cent *again* in Kensington and Chelsea) communities.[4] These figures not only reveal the quantitative significance of French migrants compared to their EU founder-state counterparts, with over 50 per cent more inhabitants than London's Italian diaspora, but they also highlight that the borough of Kensington and Chelsea is not the sole preserve of the French community, since it accommodates the largest concentrations of (undoubtedly affluent) Germans, Italians and Spanish alike. Thus, while the borough is indeed the local authority where the French community is at its densest, the phenomenon is not peculiar to the French community, as Kensington and Chelsea is equally popular among other well-heeled migrants, just as other boroughs are popular among the – less affluent – French.

Setting the French-community figures against statistics for inner-London populations born in EU-accession countries brings them further into relief.[5] For instance, according to the 2011 census, the largest community of Romanians is found in Newham and represents only 1.6 per cent of the local population (compared to 4.2 per cent French residents in Kensington and Chelsea), with Lithuanians constituting 2.7 per cent in the same borough. The Polish inner-London community in Haringey is the sole European group that equals that of the French in a single local authority, just surpassing it at 4.3 per cent. This gives a more concrete impression of the significance of French population numbers in relation to media portrayals of London's migrant communities more generally, and by extension the (pre/mis)conceptions of the collective 'host' imagination, in addition to reasserting the French preference for cosmopolitan London life, as opposed to the suburban existence to which many 'locals' aspire. The 2011 census stratifications for French communities in outer-London local authorities substantiate this point further, with the French ranked 127th in Bexley and 207th in Havering.

It is evident, therefore, that relatively few choose to settle among 'non-Londoners' in the outer boroughs and 'counties [which] exist in apposition to London' (Engel, 2014: xx), precisely because such areas are *not*

London, however proximate and filled with London's workforce they may
be. David Block refers to his respondents' conceptualisation of 'London as
an un-English island' (2006: 132), which echoes the sentiment of another
Frenchwoman in London some two hundred years earlier: 'Flora Tristan
saw London as a very separate spatial entity, governed principally but not
uniquely by a climate that created types of people' (Cross, 2013: 145).
Favell encountered the same 'London typology' among his high-skilled EU
migrant participants, who referred to the loneliness and isolation experienced in the Capital's commuter belt, where they had (re-)migrated in
search of a better quality of life, only to discover that it 'was difficult to
make contact' (Favell, 2008a: 177) and that 'cool Britannia isn't in fact
very multicultural, global, or international *at all*, once you get outside of
zones 2 or 3 of London' (2008a: 177, original emphasis), a point reiterated by the diverging London/Home Counties 2016 referendum and 2019
election results. Furthermore, if French migrants, like the New Zealanders
in Conradson and Latham's (2007) study and the Germans in King *et al.*'s
(2014), are moving to London precisely to escape the boredom of their
habitual provincial lifeworld, attracted by the dynamism and 'agency' of
the city itself (Scott, 2006; Mulholland and Ryan, 2017), it comes as little
surprise that parochial suburbia does not meet their expectations. This
might explain why the French outside London seem to favour those small
cities pervaded by 'Londonishness' (Engel, 2014: XX), such as Oxford and
Canterbury, rather than 'the leafy avenues of Respectable Street, Surrey'
(Favell, 2008a: 176). For French migrants drawn to London as a super-
diverse, global city and seeking new opportunities in the swirl of activity,
London does not equate to England, nor does it restrict itself to South
Kensington.

Dispelling the South Kensington myth further are the physical spaces
frequented by London's French-speaking members, brought to light (quite
literally) by a map of Twitter languages (Figure 2) produced by Ed Manley
and James Cheshire (Department of Geography, UCL), which shows that
French is the third most-tweeted language in London, with 28,226 French-
language tweets recorded (Cheshire, 2012b), and, of greater pertinence to
this mapping of the French presence, that there are significant concentrations
of French usage in locations considered atypical, such as Lewisham in the
south east. In Cheshire's words, the 'geography of the French tweets (red)
is perhaps most surprising as they appear to exist in high density pockets
around the centre and don't stand out in South Kensington' (2012a).

Perplexed by this distribution, the cartographers accounted for them
in technical rather than demographic, terms: 'It may be that as a proportion of tweeters in this area they are small so they don't stand out, or it
could be that there are prolific tweeters (or bots) in the highly concentrated

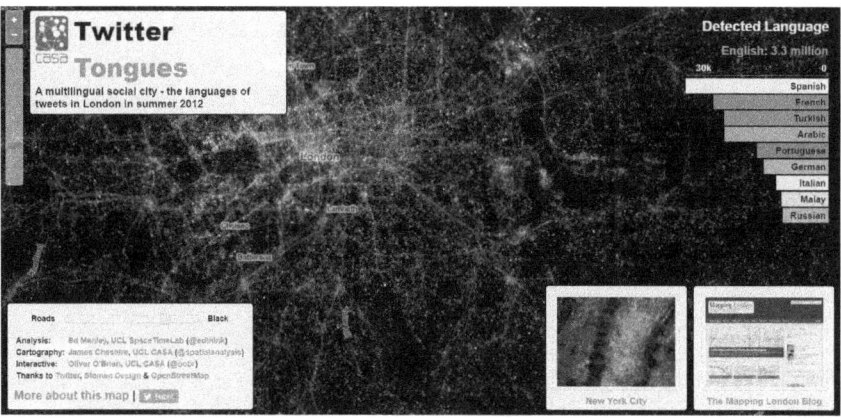

Figure 2 Twitter language communities in London, summer 2012

areas' (Cheshire, 2012a). However, in view of the participants' abodes illustrated in Figure 1, and my having observed many French and French-speaking families, with postcolonial links to the language and culture, in the Lewisham area during my field research, these findings are far from unexpected.[6] It is also noteworthy that this cluster coincides with the findings of the Annual School Census 2008 on the languages state-school pupils speak at home (Greater London Authority, 2011) in which the London boroughs of Lambeth (2.9 per cent) and Lewisham (2.1 per cent) recorded higher proportions of French-speakers among its schoolchildren than Ealing (0.8 per cent) or Richmond (0.9 per cent), districts typically associated with large numbers of French residents.[7] This is undoubtedly due to the density of francophone African populations in Lewisham and Lambeth boroughs, as I have previously suggested (Huc-Hepher and Drake, 2013) and von Ahn *et al.* (2010) confirm.[8] They assert, through cross-analysis of the Annual School Census language and ethnicity data, that '57% of French speakers are 'black' [and that] [w]hite French speakers tend to reside in West London, black French speakers in East London' (2010: 6). Despite being an oversimplification, as my empirical findings demonstrate, this claim testifies to the diversity and geographical spread of the French community in London.

A final map (Figure 3), produced by Oliver O'Brien (Department of Geography, UCL) on the basis of the 2011 census metric on language use, reveals that, while French is expectedly the foreign language most commonly spoken within a 200-metre radius of many underground stations in south-west London, South Kensington in particular, there are also several other less predictable concentrations. For example, French is dominant at almost

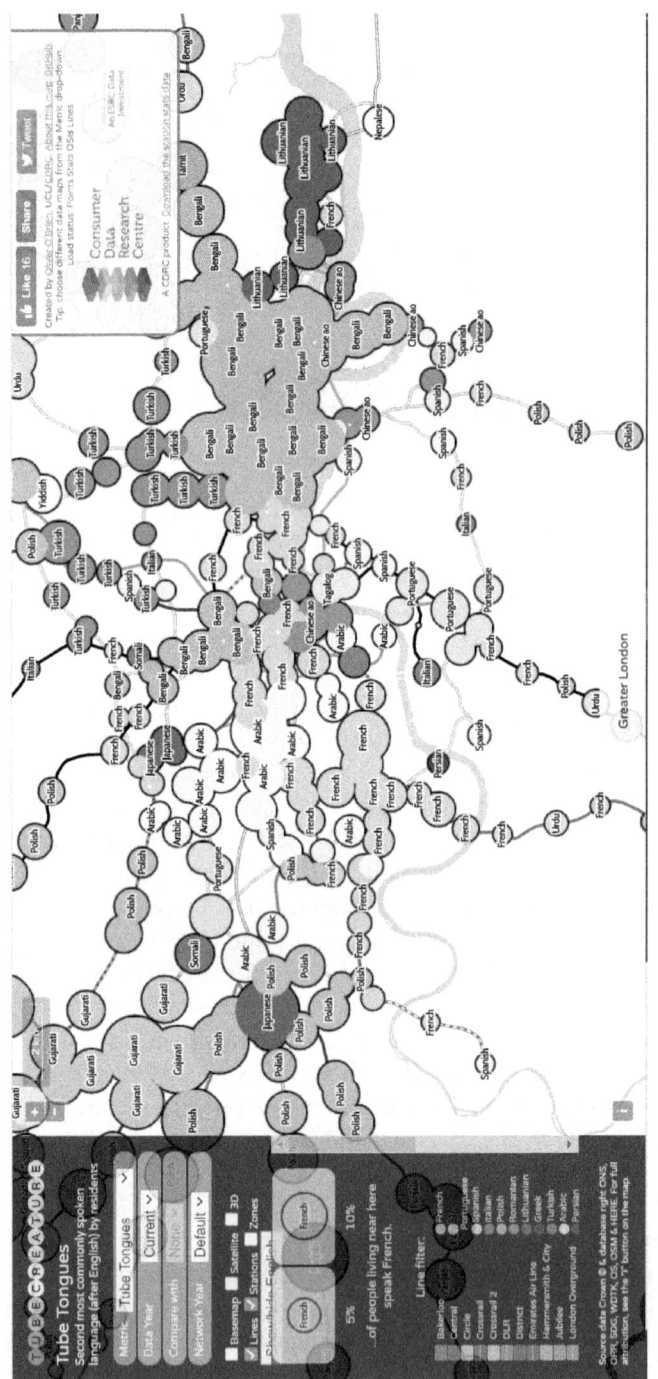

Figure 3 Tube tongues

all the stations in the square mile of the City of London (probably because a significant number of French highly skilled migrants work, like their forefathers, in the finance and banking sector), and at stations such Brockley and Deptford Bridge (both of which are in the London Borough of Lewisham) and Pontoon Dock (perhaps because of its closeness to Docklands' financial hub). This is also true of Hampstead, Hampstead Heath, Finchley Road and Frognal, Belsize Park and Tufnell Park, all of which are significant as they correspond to areas where many members of the French Jewish community migrated in the first half of the 2010s, subsequent to growing persecution in France (McLaren, 2015; Pollard, 2014) and to the burgeoning French community around the Collège Français Bilingue de Londres in Kentish Town (NW5), which opened in September 2011.

Clearly, the 'French' concentrations identified in this map may be subject to the same demographic influences as those discussed here, with the visualisation skewed to an even greater extent by the dearth of underground stations in southeast London. It is noteworthy, however, that in addition to French being the language most commonly spoken in the locations indicated on this image, when clicking on individual stations via the live web, it becomes apparent that French is in the top five at the vast majority of stations across the capital, often coming second, for instance in Mile End, Bermondsey and Shoreditch High Street, which again serves to confirm the consistency of the French presence across London.

In short, while the South Kensington community undeniably carries statistical and symbolic weight, it has tended to overshadow other French sub-communities in London owing to its historical influence on the physical environment. The French presence there has developed significantly since the opening of the Lycée Français Charles de Gaulle in 1915 (Faucher *et al.*, 2015), and today, in addition to the 2000-strong school, the neighbourhood accommodates numerous *librairies, cafés, épiceries* and *pâtisseries*, alongside the French Institute and the edifices of the French diplomatic corps. Paradoxically, this *visible* concrete legacy[9] obscures the topologically extensive physical habitats chosen as home by London's French 'community' more broadly and therefore *invisibilises* the 'middling' majority (Conradson and Latham, 2005a; Walsh, 2012: 43), who consequently feel disenfranchised from the 'community'. It is also misguided to condense the habitat of London's French community to the reductionist and erroneous Black–white binary alluded to by von Ahn *et al.* (2010), as the linguistic and geographical mapping, together with my own empirical evidence, bears witness. Moreover, in the same way that the Lycée Français Charles de Gaulle was perhaps the single most significant factor in determining South Kensington as the established heart of the contemporary French community in London, so new French/international schools in Greenwich, Clapham,

Figure 4 French café/bakery in Clapham Common

Wembley, Marylebone, and Kentish Town, are contributing to the development of alternative community hubs, with the physical cityscape undergoing a process of transformation reflective of the changing demographic (Figure 4).

When focusing on the physical spaces occupied by the London French, something of a paradox emerges. The migrants are initially drawn to London by its vibrancy, openness and popular culture, or its Londonishness, but as the French sub-communities establish and mobility steadily transforms into settlement, a process of Francisation of the local environment takes place: communitarianism materialised. High-street shops and eateries become French, British state schools offer tailored classes for their French-speaking students, extra-curricular provisions follow suit outside schools, council-run local libraries are equipped with dedicated French-language sections, Catholic churches hold regular services in French, parks and commons host French community picnics and so on; slowly the area is infused with Frenchness. So, while imagining that it is Englishness they seek and Frenchness they are escaping, and rejecting the notion of community per se, French-community building is quite literally cemented in the material space. Thus, the ambivalence alluded to by Benson (2011) emerges as a key factor of the French experience in London. As shown, they are simultaneously visible and invisible in the public consciousness and material space;

simultaneously here and there, embedded in London culture, yet reproducing French culture in various London places; simultaneously negating a community and creating one through their shared practices; simultaneously individual agents, in charge of their own individualised destinies and following well-trodden London-French paths; simultaneously on-land and on-line; simultaneously the embodiment of French and English languaging; and simultaneously French and Londoners (occasionally European, but never English). All these facets of the inherently ambivalent French migrant experience are developed in the following chapters, but I first discuss my ethnographic research methods, drawing attention to concerns of a pragmatic, conceptual and ethical nature.

Situating the study, situating the self: matters of methods and ethics

This study began formally in 2010 with a short, qualitative pilot survey distributed to approximately 200 French Londoners (10 per cent of whom returned the completed questionnaire), predominantly parents of French-speaking children attending the Grenadine supplementary school in Blackheath, southeast London. The research, however, less formal but equally compelling, extends considerably further back in time. Precisely because of my insider–outsider, or 'outsider within' (Ingram and Abrahams, 2016: 154) positioning in relation to my research 'object', it is impossible to pinpoint a specific moment when the research began. I am an insider owing to my profound and sustained affiliations with French community 'members' (wife, mother, god-daughter, friend and teacher) and an outsider because of my status as an external observer, possessing the 'intellectualising bias' (Bourdieu and Wacquant, 1992: 34)[10] that the scholarly gaze brings, but also as a London-born 'Englishwoman',[11] never feeling completely integrated in the London-French circles I have penetrated. Being a woman and a mother has provided me with an empathetic 'social bias' (Bourdieu and Wacquant, 1992: 34) vis-à-vis the French mothers I have encountered in various educational and social contexts, but approaching such contexts with an observer's eye, albeit a *participating* observational one, has at times filled me with a 'feeling of having committed a sort of disloyalty, by establishing myself as an observer of a game which I was still playing' (Bourdieu and Wacquant, 1992: 225). As Bourdieu accurately describes, being a researcher on and in a community has the drawback of injecting a degree of pretence into both the epistemic and ontological activities.

Similarly, conducting my interviews in (near-native) French had the intended advantage of encouraging spontaneity, enabling participants to

consider issues in an intuitive, 'French' frame of mind, and arguably generated more candid responses to questions concerning the 'host' culture and
their own positioning within it than if the conversations had taken place in
English. However, it simultaneously had the disadvantage of heightening
the sensation of disloyalty to which Bourdieu refers and of instilling in me
a tangible sense of betrayal vis-à-vis my respondents, who had so willingly
and deeply confided in me. They believed they were sharing their innermost
thoughts with a compatriot 'sister', only to discover, often at the end of
the interview, once the recorder had been switched off and the questioning
power balance with it, that I was in fact not equal but 'Other': other than
them as French Londoners, and other than what they believed I had led
them to believe, simply through my own embodiment of Frenchness.

These reflexive qualms aside, I now retrace my methodological journey.
In order to contain the potentially vast scope of this project, I limited my
fieldwork to French residents of Greater London. Some participants had
spent significant periods of time trialling life in other parts of England,
such as Miranda, Sadia, Charles, Robert and Suzanne, only to re-migrate
to London, lured back by its super-diverse, fast-paced atmosphere brought
into relief by exposure to the small-minded attitudes of parochial Britain,
as seen earlier and in opposition to Benson's migrants in the Lot, who
apprehended such dynamism in hostile, oppressive terms (2011). Although
focusing on a London-wide population negates the thousands of French
people who dwell outside the capital, given the numeric dominance of the
community in London (Ash, 2012), its historic presence and the bounded
character of ethnographic research, London was to be the physical anchor
of my study.

Having narrowed down the object of my study to French residents
of London, establishing the research participants who corresponded to
the 'French' epithet proved more challenging, particularly regarding the
semantic reach of the term. Should my research focus solely on French-
passport holders, in line with the ONS definition, or should all native
French speakers be deemed 'French'? The former *excludes* those who were
born in Britain to a French father and British mother, who hold British
passports by default, and older French Londoners, forced to relinquish their
French nationality when becoming British citizens (through marriage) in a
pre-EU era (as was the case for my 80-year-old interviewee). Conversely,
the latter *includes* individuals from countries geographically, historically,
and potentially ethnically and ideologically, removed from France, such as
Algeria, Belgium, Canada, Congo, Mauritius, Tahiti, and so on. Defining
Frenchness according to a postcolonial legacy, however, serves to perpetuate prejudicial supremacy structures. To relieve the moral burden of whom
to include/exclude and mitigate the risk of unintended essentialisation,

I therefore opted for a process of self-identification, which also placed potential research participants in an agentive position and minimised the researcher–researched power imbalance.

This self-profiling method had the added benefit of 'randomising' the sample. Thus, in addition to so-called '*Français de souche*'[12] and francophones from geographic locations outside France, my research participants included those who could be termed 'double' migrants: French passport holders, who had initially *migrated to* France from countries or territories further afield or who were second-generation migrants in France, subsequently deciding to *re-migrate* to the UK as unrecorded EU free movers. Within and beyond this self-selecting framework, I deployed a purposive method of sampling to reflect the demographic heterogeneity of the community. In total, I conducted twenty in-depth, semi-structured interviews, some of which resulted from articles on my research in community publications and others from a targeted approach. The latter was particularly important given the potential skewing effect of using only 'official' community recruitment channels, such as the French consulate website and *Ici Londres* magazine. I therefore invited members of the community whom I encountered in my day-to-day activities and close circles to take part in face-to-face interviews, in addition to the self-selected participants and those who had volunteered to be interviewed in the initial paper survey. Finally, snowballing was used to recruit individuals from sub-groups previously absent from the sample.

Moving beyond the problematisation of Frenchness and interview sampling, I was then confronted with the notion of sources and what should or should not qualify as valid ethnographic material. Bourdieu calls for 'a total social science' (Bourdieu and Wacquant, 1992: 30), in which theory and methods carry equal weight, and the research object is positioned in its spatio-temporal and social context. The approach also involves using a variety of methods for the sake of triangulation, scientific rigour and empirical holism (O'Reilly, 2012). Consequently, the ethnographic research presented in this book draws on a Bourdieusian conception of ethnography, using multiple sources, from audio-recorded interview and focus group narratives to autobiographies written by members of the French community, the original pilot questionnaire, official documentation transmitted to me by the French consulate, observational fieldnotes, photographic evidence of the London-French habitat and digital data collected from the internet, which is, by definition, inherently multimodal (including moving/still images, text and other semiotically meaningful affordances).

In addition to my one-to-one interviews, each lasting between one and half to two hours, three-quarters of which were conducted face-to-face and a quarter by telephone, I also held two focus groups. In an alteration to the original plan, as is often the case (Hine, 2015; Bourdieu and

Wacquant, 1992), they stemmed from a chance encounter with the head teacher of Newham Sixth Form College, whose student body contained a high proportion of mother-tongue French speakers, and from the unexpected predominance of education in the interviews. Wishing to pursue the theme further, while gaining insights from a younger demographic (16- to 18-year-olds), I opted for a comparative approach requiring focus groups at institutions at polar ends of the geographic and socio-economic spectrum: Newham Sixth Form College and the Lycée Français Charles de Gaulle (South Kensington). Thirteen students took part altogether: seven in Newham, all from ethnic minorities, their parents having migrated to Europe from such countries as Ivory Coast, Martinique and Mauritius, and six in South Kensington, five of whom conformed to the white, Franco-French-heritage profile. To inspire conversation and provide me with a permanent record of their individual thoughts, the persuasive influence of peers being particularly potent during adolescence, I asked the students to complete a short, illustrated questionnaire, after which they engaged in lively conversation around the issues raised.

Complementing these formalised research methods and ensuring against the 'part-time' approach decried by Hammersley (2005: 6), my fieldwork involved sustained interactions with the community in a variety of contexts. I was invited to evening meals with French mothers, aperitifs with others, and I celebrated New Year's Eve twice with different households. Through my children's enrolment at supplementary French nurseries and schools, I regularly held conversations with parents, made playground observations, met for coffee, volunteered for the schools in and outside the classroom, took part in extra-curricular events, like the yearly *kermesse* and Mardi Gras festivities, the AGM or the termly *représentations*. I attended formal community events organised by the French Institute and the French consulate, such as the French Associations Fair, Bastille Day celebrations, the 18 June and Lycée Charles de Gaulle centenary commemorations and the inauguration ceremony for the Lycée Winston Churchill. I was also invited to meetings at the French consulate to discuss my research with the Consul Général and Vice Consul.

These varied immersive experiences increased the scope of my ethnographic understanding of the community, from the inside. Being invited into research participants' homes enabled a more nuanced understanding of how their '*dispositions*' (Bourdieu [1972] 2000: 235; original emphasis) were transposed to their material surroundings, supporting Bourdieu's (habitus) theory that sociocultural 'structures [are] incorporated into appropriated physical space' (Bourdieu, 1996: 15). It also at times prompted comments and guided the conversation, with 'fractal habitus' (Rowsell, 2011: 333) elements triggering thoughts, memories and serving as concrete examples. This allowed me to enrich my text with thick descriptions (Geertz, 1973; Atkinson, 2005) of participants' domestic spaces and to situate them diasporically and socially (Bourdieu, 1996; Gieles, 2009; Walsh, 2018), before turning my attention to their online presence. Having discovered that the data collected in these research sites, during the focus groups and initial round of interviews was coinciding at multiple points, I concluded that saturation had been achieved (Fusch and Ness, 2015), which signalled the launch of the online data collection phase.

Christine Hine describes her approach to studying practices on the web as 'ethnography *for* the Internet' (2015: 5; original italics) to distinguish it from a necessarily over-ambitious ethnography *of* the internet. Meanwhile, Miller and Horst refer to 'digital anthropology' (2012: 3–4), Kozinets (2010) to 'netnography' and several commercial market research groups to 'blognography' (Rubenstein, 2011). The multiplicity of terms reflects the methodological uncertainty and sense of experimentation present in the field of online ethnographic research in the 2010s, as the internet was becoming increasingly 'embedded into people's lives' (Hine, 2015: 14). Despite the day-to-day omnipresence of the digital, however, studies incorporating web (archive) data as a means of understanding how people act, interact, feel, believe and express themselves remain under-represented and out of kilter with the dominant position the internet now plays in our lives (Murthy, 2008; Winters, 2017). My deployment of the web as a source of qualitative data differs from the methodological (and terminological) paradigms cited here. Rather than focus on people's on-land interactions with the internet (Miller and Slater, 2000), or study the communicational practices of internet users in specific on-line contexts (Elgesem, 2002; Hine, 2015; Vaisman, 2016; Miller and Sinanan, 2017) through participant observation (Kozinets, 2010), my exploitation of online data is a single strand of the overarching ethnographic spread of my study. Although my online research was observational, its exclusive analysis of 'found data' (Hine, 2015: 161) and limited online interaction nonetheless required 'moving between sites and developing an emergent understanding of the field' (2015: 187). It necessitated an ethical stance adapted to each situation, from discussion boards found in the historic JISC archive 1996–2010 to school websites and blog-specific archives on the live web, or images contained in web resources preserved in curated corpora. Each discrete context involved a rethinking of the ethical implications (McKee and Porter, 2009) and resultant parameters, as prescribed by the Association of Internet Research, recommending it to 'remain flexible, be responsive to diverse contexts, and be adaptable to continually changing technologies' (Markham and Buchanan, 2012: 5).

Although my online research was 'unobtrusive' (Hine, 2015: 160) and the data generated 'non-reactive' (Hine, 2015: 161), it followed a practice-based methodology, the findings of which served to triangulate the on-land data (O'Reilly, 2012). The practical aspect of the web-data-collection process consisted of my becoming the curator of an Open Access corpus of web resources (the London French Special Collection) for the UK Web Archive (UKWA), hosted by the British Library, who provided training on the web curator tool, selection rationale and metadata application. Curating a collection dedicated to the French community in London corresponded to the UKWA's mission to contain 'sites that reflect the rich diversity of lives and interests throughout the UK' (UKWA, no date). It would not only ensure the long-term preservation of an otherwise ephemeral London-French online presence for the benefit of future generations, but would provide a secure, reliable and ethically sound environment in which to analyse the data.

Although the field of ethics in internet-mediated research is in its infancy and remains a contested area, informed consent often constitutes the biggest hurdle (Hine, 2015; Flick, 2016), one that my reliance on data contained in the permissions-based London French Special Collection (LFSC) overcame. Ultimately, the curation process produced a stable platform for iterative consultation, but crucially, the act of repeatedly searching and selecting web objects, and being hyperlinked to other interconnected websites, was in itself an immersive one. Far from being an editorial top-down exercise, the web curation process allowed me to discover previously unfamiliar aspects of the London-French community and gain in-depth knowledge of the *on-land* sub-communities through my immersion in their networked *on-line* diasberspace. By first embedding the study in a physical context, as opposed to conducting it in a 'placeless "cyberspace"' (Miller and Slater, 2000: 1), my approach was effectively 'outside–in', with my extensive on-land field research preceding penetration of the on-line environment, to deliver a blended ethnographic whole (Androutsopoulos, 2008; Tagg *et al.*, 2017).

Chapter overview

This book is structured to retrace the methodological route described, taking the reader on a journey from the on-land to the on-line, and the geographical mobility of my participants, from their premigration habitus/field memories and motivations, through their current diasporic experience, to their digitised representations of the London-French migratory space. In Benson's study of British migrants in rural France (2011: 70), she refers to the 'simultaneous repulsion of and attachment to' the homeland. Christian Roudaut's book on French outward mobility captures the same contradiction in its title, *France: je t'aime, je te quitte* (France: I love you,

I leave you), and it is precisely this ambivalent relationship that underpins the overall framework of this book. The 'repulsion' dimension is explored in Chapter 1, with respondents' memories of painful, if at times subtle and not initially or explicitly acknowledged, memories of the originary field explored. The 'attachment' aspect is the focus of Chapters 2, 3 and 4, which respectively investigate the ways in which the homeland is reconstructed materially, mentally and practically in the diasporic context, while Chapters 5 and 6 deal with the inherent ambivalence brought about by the centrality of the internet to our everyday lives. Themes addressed in the preceding 'on-land' chapters, such as symbolic violence and habitus, are revisited via the close examination of digital representations, exploring how on-land and on-line lives overlap and permeate the diasporic experience.

According to Burke (2016), field and capital are often overlooked in contemporary Bourdieusian research, with habitus (defined in Chapter 2) being considered in isolation. This is at odds with Bourdieu's three-stage field analysis paradigm (Bourdieu and Wacquant, 1992; Grenfell, 2012), as well as with his repeated underscoring of the dynamic nature of lived experience, realities necessarily fashioned by the interplay between external, objective social field structures and internal(ised), subjective individual habitus. Thus, in Chapter 1, attention is placed on the educational, professional and social *fields* of origin and how social, symbolic and institutionalised *capital* is operationalised in such contexts to the advantage of some and the consequent disadvantage of others, and, in the case of those unwilling to accept their lot, serves as a migration driver. The chapter is set on the conceptual backdrop of symbolic violence in France (Bourdieu *et al.*, 1993; Bourdieu and Wacquant, 1992) and explores how these embedded practices, from discrimination in a purportedly egalitarian education system to misogynistic and xenophobic microaggressions in professional and social premigration spaces, underlie much mobility decision-making.

Given the ethnographic aspirations of this book, Chapter 2 focuses on the migration experience at the individuated habitus level. It is situated squarely in the diasporic context and examines how 'attachment' to the homeland manifests itself through reconstructions of originary materialities. Concentrating on objectivated homemaking manifested through the habitat dimension of habitus, I examine the intimate physical spaces inhabited by participants (Levin, 2016; Walsh, 2018), describing how they reflect a continued attachment to the homeland, despite assertions to the contrary. I reveal how transferring artefacts from the originary culture to the London space recreates a sense of the familiar, a sense of belonging, and how this reconstruction of Frenchness is intensified through the use of French broadcasting channels, with participants creating mediascapes (Appadurai, 1990) and soundscapes (Schafer, [1977] 1994) to mediate their migratory positioning (Gieles, 2009). I also posit that this intertwining of the material with the remembered or re-embodied homeland (Hardwick, 2008) emerges as a common trait among participants, and consequently bears witness to their shared and distinctive cultural positioning in the diasporic field.

In Chapter 3, I examine the second, habituation component of the habitus triad. The emphasis is oriented further towards the subjective dimensions of the migratory experience, revealing how participants' perspectives, attitudes and sense of belonging have evolved, imperceptibly, through sustained immersion in the London field. In addition to exploring the role of early encounters with the Other in subconscious migration decision-making (Findlay and Li, 1997), I examine how a pre-reflexive sense of security (Skulte-Ouaiss, 2013; Hopkins *et al.*, 2019), conceived as the 'securiscape', is central to homemaking and ultimately settlement (Leavey *et al.*, 2004; Ryan, 2018). I identify various aspects of the participants' embodied dispositions that have imperceptibly evolved during their London sojourn, from politeness codes, to sartorial expression and political views. However, taking humour as an example, I demonstrate that habituation can play a simultaneously divisive and cohesive role in the migratory space. Losses and gains in culturo-linguistic capital affect how participants negotiate their embodied Frenchness/Englishness in the transnational space, and clashes between the habitus and external(ising) field structures can cause a disquieting 'hysteresis effect' (Bourdieu, 1972[2000]; Hardy, 2012) or 'cleft habitus' (Bourdieu, 2004; Thatcher and Halvorsrud, 2016). I demonstrate how humour can serve as a mechanism to exclude participants from culturally cryptic interactions, while uniting them through a common appreciation of shared points of reference inherited from the originary field. Habituation, I posit, is therefore implicitly instrumental in the community-making process, as well as confirming the ultimate limits of habitus transformation.

Moving to the final 'habits' dimension of habitus, Chapter 4 bridges the gap between the objectivated habitat and subjective habituation facets of the triad. Drawing a physical connection to the habitats observed in Chapter 2, I specifically discuss practices relating to participants' everyday corporeal experiences, namely eating, drinking and healthcare. Despite the espousing of the cosmopolitan eating habits of London, I argue that the 'gustative acculturation' process is more complex as regards dining rituals and that participants' rhetoric reinvigorates the English 'malbouffe' stereotype as a means of social and cultural distinction. Acknowledging Bourdieu's call for holistic methods, I also draw on secondary online sources to understand how France's influence as the culinary super-power is today being challenged by our globalised, networked world, and how return migrants' evolved eating habits might in turn be transforming practices in France.

Conversely, regarding drinking habits, participants are seen to agentively resist 'acculturation' and instead perpetuate originary attitudes and behaviours. I contend that they aim to distinguish themselves from the dominant culture through their civilised act of restraint (Benson, 2011), particularly in relation to British women, whose stereotypical image of excessive alcohol consumption is not considered a form of liberation, but is held in contempt.

I conclude the chapter by exploring local therapeutic habits, concentrating on the unexpected finding that most participants appreciate the 'demedicalised' practices favoured in the diasporic field, despite tropes in France portraying the NHS as a 'third-world' system. I argue that, over time, healthcare habits are performed in a manner that empowers. Women and homosexual participants are seen to take back control of their bodies and, as such, play out third-wave xenofeminism (Hester, 2018). Their rejection of the over-medicalised, stubbornly patriarchal practices of France therefore serve to embed them within the diasporic space.

In Chapter 5, having, up to this point, concentrated on mobility motivations in the premigration field and habitus subjectivities in the postmigration context, I turn my attention to the *digital* London-French presence. Following several years of internet-based participant observation brought about by my curation of the LFSC, in this chapter I move towards a 'blended ethnographic' approach, bringing on-land and on-line material into dialogue with each other, but sourcing and analysing each discretely. Readdressing themes discussed at the beginning of the book, notably education and the hypocrisy some respondents' claim is at the heart of the French education system in relation to the perceived positive traits of the British model, I return to the notion of symbolic violence. The first half of the chapter is dedicated to on-land experiences and perceptions of education in France and/or French schools in London and state/independent London schools, while in the second half, I analyse on-line representations of three London-based institutions cited in my interviews: a French state-funded school, a UK maintained sixth-form college and a UK independent school. By conducting a granular multimodal analysis of their homepages, I demonstrate how participants' criticisms of, and praise for, different aspects of each educational model, such as the discriminatory universalism and overly academic positivist French educational epistemology (Lea *et al.*, 2003), or the practice-based, student-centred constructivist English methods (Lea *et al.*, 2003), are substantiated semiotically through the multimodal orchestrations of the websites. I also demonstrate how the websites function as microcosms of the wider migratory experience and how education plays an important part in settlement processes (Ryan and Sales, 2013).

Chapter 6 fully embraces the blended ethnosemiotic paradigm (Fiske, 1990) by taking on-line data as the analytical starting point and deploying on-land data for triangulation. Taking a comparative, multi-archival approach, I investigate habitus transformation over time as portrayed socio-semiotically in five migrant blogs selected for the LFSC. My fine-grained multimodal analysis teases out sociocultural meanings pertaining to migrant belonging, identity and 'community' practices, again through the prism of the habitus triad: habitat, habits and habituation. I compare snapshots taken of the 'same' blog pages between 2009 and 2014 to reveal subtle changes that would be undetectable on the live web and which bear witness to evolving blogger subjectivities. The securiscapes described in my on-land fieldwork rematerialise in highly stylised digital form, with the blog iconography developing in tandem with the bloggers' growing sense of feeling 'at home' in the diasporic space (Levin, 2016). Meanwhile, the bloggers' changing linguistic and typographical practices provide insights into their increasing cultural hybridisation, as well as demonstrating the conceptual limitations of hybridity (Anthias, 2018; Hutnyk, 2018), with translanguaging acting as a 'Thirdspace' beyond bilingual dualisms (Li, 2018) and the repurposing of blogs (Hester, 2018) expressing growing agency and self-assurance. By apprehending the meanings trapped in the materiality of the blogs, as opposed to the surface-level messages (Vaisman, 2011), I uncover important evidence pertaining not only to the bloggers' identities, but to their relationships within the women-dominated London-French blogging community and wider local and transnational audience(s). In this way, the blogs serve as 'gendered avatars' (Vaisman, 2016: 293), while simultaneously speaking of the migrants' on-land lived experience and the continued territorialisation of a purportedly 'world-wide' web. Overall, the chapter underlines the value of web archives in ethnographic research, given the inherent ephemerality of internet objects and their unpredictable rate of obsolescence.

The general Conclusion, which summarises my key findings, revisits the book's core themes and suggests future avenues for research, is followed by an Epilogue bringing the monograph to its close. Owing to my formal fieldwork ending prior to the 2016 EU membership referendum, this short chapter captures the sentiment of participants in a fundamentally altered diasporic landscape, between March and December 2019. Based on verbal and written testimonies collected at my original on-land and on-line research sites, as well as through email, telephone and face-to-face exchanges with existing and new participants, the Epilogue provides readers with an understanding of the pain, shock and incomprehension generated by the referendum result. Like the studies of Lulle *et al.* (2018), Brahic and Lallement (2018) and Benson (2019), it focuses on the affective implications of the referendum. Specifically, I ask participants to reflect on their feelings within three distinct timeframes: directly after the vote in 2016, at the present time in 2019 and in the future. Based on their responses, I argue that the 'rupture' (Hörschelmann, 2011, cited in Lulle *et al.*, 2018: 1) to their everyday existence caused by the symbolic violence of the referendum result challenges the optimistic notion of 'liquid migration' (Hörschelmann, 2011, cited in Lulle *et al.*, 2018: 1), but, unlike other EU-migrant groups, has not yet forced them into a state of 'undeliberate determinacy' (McGhee *et al.*, 2017). Rather, their coping strategies suggest a desire for prolonged fluidity, with apathy and denial taking precedence over the humiliating and uncomfortably conclusive act of 'settled status', or 'worse' still, British citizenship. I argue that the referendum result imposed an unsolicited set of external field structures on participants which disrupted their formally settled negotiations of belonging overnight and profoundly destabilised their sense of self (Ingram and Abrahams, 2016). As a result, they undergo an inverse form of hysteresis, feeling out of place in the city they had assumed was home.

Notes

1 Significantly, the well-known Veolia brand conceals the firm's French state origins, founded in 1853, by imperial decree under Napoleon III, as the *Compagnie Générale des Eaux*, in the same way that the acronym EDF obscures the origins of *Électricité de France* (Veolia, 2016b).

2 See, however, my article on anti-French xenophobic microaggressions for a more nuanced assessment (Huc-Hepher, 2019).

3 I favour this terminology over the usual 'online/offline' dichotomy, which, I consider, illogically prioritises digital practices.

4 This is somewhat unexpected given the visible presence of well-established Italian (see Scotto, 2010 and Sprio, 2013) and Spanish communities in London. The figures may, therefore, be suggestive of a phenomenon of first-generation return migration (the intent of many), coinciding with euro-zone growth at the turn of the twenty-first century (leading to increased youth employment in Italy and Spain prior to the 2009 financial crash and reducing the 'need' to migrate). Moreover, being based on country of *birth*, second and third generations would systematically be absent from the census figures.

5 A migrant population greatly publicised, exaggerated and ostracised in the national media, the negative tone of which doubtless contributed to the 'Brexit' outcome of the 2016 EU membership referendum.

6 The timing of the study is also likely to have skewed the results, since many French Londoners escape the city during the summer months, as is common practice in France.

7 More recent raw data has proved elusive. The Department for Education's 2014–15 School Census nevertheless indicates that ethnicity and language data continue to be collected (Dent, 2014: 38–40).

 8 The figures could also be skewed by the number of French residents in Ealing and Richmond who send their children to French or bilingual fee-paying schools, thereby precluding them from the British state-school statistics.

 9 The South Kensington legacy is far more recent than that of previous waves of French migration, whose mark has been eternalised in London districts and street names, such as Petty France, Garrick Street and Fournier Street.

10 As a qualified translator, I have translated all quotations from French primary and secondary sources myself.

11 In 2019, as a direct consequence of the 2016 EU membership referendum and keen to maintain my European identity and freedoms, I acquired full French citizenship.

12 The use of this term, which literally refers to the stump of a tree and hence French ancestry, has been the subject of fierce debate in France. It was adopted by Marine Le Pen's *Front National* and now carries nativist connotations linked to whiteness which are not intended here. I use the term in its metaphorical sense to refer to rootedness, that is, inhabitants of France over several generations, regardless of ethnicity.

1

Looking back:
the underlying push of symbolic violence in France

Introduction

Taking a retrospective view, this chapter marks the beginning of my analysis of participants' affective motivations. As Aldridge (1995) postulates, when speaking to migrants about their everyday lived experience, one often learns more about the people, places and selves left behind than their current reality (cited in Benson, 2011: 30). Accordingly, in this chapter, we learn of my participants' uneasy relationship with the 'homeland' and consequent domain-specific embedding practices (Wessendorf and Phillimore, 2018), driven by negative experiences in France. To appreciate how these negative forces operate in the premigration fields of education, employment and the wider social space, and consequently influence participant mobility and emplacement, I draw on Bourdieu's theory of symbolic violence.

Much of the originality of Bourdieu's thinking lies in his emphasis on revealing the unseen, be it the internalisation of external structures central to his habitus theory or his acknowledgement of the symbolic power tacitly governing our social systems and interactions. Accordingly, the muted weight of symbolic capital, domination and violence that encumbers society in usually invisible, or at least unobserved yet remarkably potent ways, constitutes a leitmotif of the Bourdieusian œuvre, from his early writings (Bourdieu and Passeron, 1964) to those published late in life (1997, 1998). Such barely perceptible forces, elsewhere referred to as 'inert violence', 'little miseries' and 'soft violence' (Bourdieu et al., 1993: 1,453), are also gaining increasing cross-disciplinary recognition in contemporary academic discourse and wider society in the form of implicit or unconscious bias (Saul, 2013; Maddox and Perry, 2017) and microaggressions (Sue et al., 2007). Like '(un)conscious bias' (Tate and Page, 2018), 'symbolic violence takes place through an act of knowledge and unacknowledgement, which lies beneath the controls of consciousness and willpower, in the darkness of the workings of habitus' (Bourdieu and Wacquant, 1992: 146). It is a subtle dynamic reliant on a binary negation. The perpetrator is supposedly unaware of any injury caused and the victim is caught in a silent paradox: if they 'say nothing, they risk becoming resentful [... and] may inadvertently encourage further microaggressions from the same person. In contrast, if they say something, the deliverer may deny having engaged in prejudice and accuse them of being hypersensitive or paranoid' (Lilienfeld, 2017: 141–2). In this way, symbolic violence thrives on the premise of victim complicity (Landry, 2006) and 'voluntary servitude' (Dubet, 2014: 19).

I conceptualise microaggressions as articulations of the broader and more emphatic umbrella construct of symbolic violence (Huc-Hepher, 2019), and as an implicit mobility vector. Although many of my research participants cognisantly foregrounded the attractiveness of London in terms of salient migration *pull* factors, highlighting its 'freedom', 'opportunity' and 'openness', equally forceful *push* factors emerged in their narratives, albeit less wittingly. One of the most surprising and recurrent findings emerging from my research was their spontaneous underlining of education and its power to influence mobility. In this chapter, and in greater detail in Chapter 5, I scrutinise participants' reflections on France's education system, seeking to understand the ways in which it influences their feelings of unease vis-à-vis France. The notion of implicitness is again important here, as it corresponds to the sub-surface potency informing my argument that many migrants' 'decision' to relocate is not as agentive as might first appear (Findlay and Li, 1997; Murphy-Lejeune, 2002; McGhee *et al.*, 2017; Mulholland and Ryan, 2017; Ryan, 2018). As Dubucs *et al.* posit, 'work-related motives are not crucial in determining the decision to move abroad' (2017: 583); in fact, rationalised reasoning, such as London's buoyant labour market or improving English language competence (Ledain, 2010), obfuscates deeper-seated affective drivers in educational, professional and social spaces (Wang, 2013a).

However, bar the growing body of literature specifically dedicated to international student mobility and academic migration (for example, Murphy-Lejeune, 2002; King and Raghuram, 2013; Beech, 2014; Bilecen and Van Mol, 2017; and Huc-Hepher and Lyczba, forthcoming), education remains under-researched in intra-EU migration studies more generally. Similarly, the deployment of Bourdieu's concept of symbolic violence, whether regarding education, the workplace or wider social field is operationalised in migration literature far less frequently than other Bourdieusian concepts, such as social and cultural capital. There are, however, some exceptions: Lozanovska (2008) examines symbolic violence against an ethnic aesthetic of taste in suburban migrant homes in Australia, and Grill's (2018) and Phillimore's (2019) work on racialised and gendered forms of symbolic violence suggests a growing – and sociopolitically fitting – interest in the concept. Equally, Cornejo Torres and Rosales Ubeda's (2015) paper demonstrates the construct's relevance in the twofold setting of schooling and migration, arguing that anti-immigrant symbolic violence has become structuralised in the Chilean education system, deemed overly rigid and insufficiently mindful of migrant children's disparities in cultural and institutionalised capital. While this resonates with the criticisms of the French model described by my own participants, a significant difference is that these studies relate to symbolic violence in the postmigration context rather than premigration. By apprehending the social space of the 'sending society' and participants' remembered affective encounters within it as mobility/settlement drivers, I build on the existing literature and begin to address de Haas's contention that there is an overemphasis on social networks in migration studies and 'a limited theorisation of second-order, contextual feedback mechanisms, which operate more indirectly' (de Haas, 2010: 1,590–1; original emphasis).

Embracing the holistic documentary approach endorsed by Bourdieu (1994) and O'Reilly (2012), alongside my own empirical findings, I draw on the educational experiences recounted in the autobiographical works of London-French migrants, Hamid Senni (2007) and Vladimir Cordier (2005). I argue that London-French migrants' premigration internalisation of negative labels and expectations contributes to pessimistic outlooks, leaving them with a choice to concede failure or to challenge the habitus (Friedmann, 2005) through their act of migration. Whereas this decision is often hidden beneath reasoning that foregrounds the fluidity and 'escalator effect' of the London workplace (Conradson and Latham, 2005a; Favell, 2008a: 87), the affective subjectivities shared by my participants belie such pragmatic agency. Their accounts of the symbolic power of institutionalised, social and cultural capital in the French employment field reveal a perceived obsession with qualifications (Roudaut, 2009), the continued influence of the 'ultra-elite *grande école* system' (Favell, 2008a: 88), together with normalised nepotistic practices (King *et al.*, 2014; Wang, 2013a) and racialised microaggressions (Pierce, 1970; Sue *et al.*, 2007) as forms of symbolic violence conducive to migration. I also describe how 'microaggression – considered a unique practice of invisible boundaries – classifies spaces' (Abutbul-Selinger, 2018: 3), solidifying prejudice and hierarchies in the material working environment, and again contrasting the purportedly more meritocratic and transparent conditions experienced in the London professional field.

Turning towards the wider social space in the final subsection, we find that memories of xenophobic, gendered (Owen *et al.*, 2010; Lilienfeld, 2017) and homophobic microaggressions (Nadal, 2013) dominate. I argue, like Simon (2006), Beaman (2018), Wolfreys (2018) and Escafré-Dublet (2019), that the French authorities' failure to openly acknowledge race effectively authorises discrimination and is experienced as an unequivocal act of universalist symbolic violence. France's structural efforts to homogenise its citizens in the name of equality and fraternity, in practice, results in the rejection of its third founding principle: liberty. It is precisely this sense of freedom that respondents' migration both enacts and sustains (Dhoest, 2018). For them, London represents an escape route from the conformist mentalities of the originary field and, quite simply, the freedom to be different. I uncover unsettling feelings of sexual objectification within the French social space, recollected in a pre-#MeToo era. The morally tinged sartorial standards French women feel pressured to maintain are, I contend, the incarnation of gendered discrimination brought about by the dominant male gaze (Bourdieu, 1998). Conversely, London is seen to embody women's rights (Wang, 2013a; Mulholland and Ryan, 2017), a place where homosexuality can be performed freely and fully, beyond the imposed shame (Chauvin, 2005) of the originary social field. Confirming Fortier's contention that 'queer migrants often have to "get out in order to come out"' (2002: 190), I argue that London affords them 'the right to invisible visibility' (Bourdieu, 1998: 165) through its cosmopolitanism and openness to intersectional difference (Dhoest, 2018).

As Favell asserts, migrants' 'stories can be moments of reflection; of catharsis when they step back and summarize what has happened to them … in comparison to the lives they left behind, or the paths they didn't take' (Favell, 2008a: 212). Based on these, sometimes painful, self-discoveries, in this chapter I reveal social injustices present, but not immediately obvious, in the structures and practices of the 'homeland'. Instead of envisaging France and the UK as relatively alike in broad socio-economic, demographic and cultural terms, I highlight the fundamental social and moral differences (Mulholland and Ryan, 2017) perceived between the two nations from the bottom up (Duchêne-Lacroix and Koukoutsaki-Monnier, 2016), factoring them into the mobility process, and hence acknowledging significant meso- and micro-level migration and settlement drivers.

Formative triggers: negotiating inequality in an egalitarian education system

It is arguably an 'awakening of consciousness' (Bourdieu, 1990: 116, cited by Jenkins, 2002: 83) that motivates some to migrate to London, and this sensation can begin at or shortly after school. Akin to the 'better education' imagined as part of a wider 'quest for a better way of life' (Benson, 2011: 32, 15) among some British migrants in the Lot, several of my informants chose the UK precisely for the educational opportunities it offered. For others, the memories explored in our interviews revived painful experiences of education in France when set against experiences in London. Theirs is therefore a reverse process to that experienced by Benson's respondents, for whom the idealised premigration imagining of the French education system, lauded in British media and political discourse, remained elusive post-migration (2011).[1] Vladimir Cordier's (2005) negative experience in France's higher education sector epitomises the sentiment: the profoundly pessimistic tone of the graduation speech delivered by one of his 'eminent professors, bedecked with qualifications' (2005: 13), caused the dismal inevitability of his future life-trajectory to appear before him. Like other French migrants I encountered in the field, he 'had had enough of a particular sort of "French mentality"', deciding 'it would be London or nothing' (2005: 20). The engrained pessimism fostered in the education system pushed him from France, while the prospect of sociocultural transformation, a reinvention of the self, pulled him to London (Conradson and Latham, 2007).

The disadvantage at which students from deprived backgrounds are inevitably placed, being taught and assessed on a necessarily equal basis as their economically – and culturally – affluent counterparts, illustrates how the habitus and familial entourage compound the imbalance from within. When (migrant) parents lack the wherewithal to challenge a system whose inner workings elude them (Cornejo Torres and Rosales Ubeda, 2015), they unintentionally convert educational shortcomings into innate deficiencies or 'individual destiny' (Bourdieu and Passeron, 1964: 109), which increases their children's sense of inevitable failure. The legitimising authority of the system therefore deepens 'social inequalities because the most disadvantaged classes, too conscious of their own destiny and too unconscious of the mechanisms through which it is realised … contribute to making it reality' (1964: 109). It is this cycle, whose persistence is confirmed by the 2018 OECD PISA results – rating France one of the most inequitable education systems worldwide (UNSA, 2019) – that some attempt to defy through their mobility. For those who have already migrated, education acts as an unintended embedding mechanism (Ryan and Sales, 2013; Ryan and Mulholland, 2015; McGhee *et al.*, 2017).

Some thirty years after Bourdieu's observations, City entrepreneur, Hamid Senni's (2007) experience of being educated in France is a case in point: 'Are we inferior beings, condemned to stay at the bottom of the ladder? At any rate, that's what the education system wants us to believe' (2007: 37–8). So commonplace are the negative tropes associated with the Maghrebi community of which Senni is a member – systematically branded a 'thief, liar, violent, ruffian' (2007: 76) – that he is habituated to the 'discrimination … It was simply a sort of inevitability' (2007: 77). Compounding the microaggression, the advice of a well-meaning teacher to change his forename to Lionel or George, since with a surname like Senni he ran the fortuitous risk of being (mis)taken for an Italian (2007: 18), demonstrates the pervasiveness of the discrimination. Unconscious of the violence of her words (Sue, 2010), the teacher believed she was acting in the name of equality (Dubet, 2004). It is noteworthy that Sadia, a research participant whose father was an Algerian migrant to France, recounted an analogous phenomenon:

> My dad called me Nicole so I'd integrate ... Although the name he'd chosen for me was Sadia ... that's the name I would've wanted actually. And it's funny because that name ... it's as if I won't give it to myself. Because I could ... When I arrived in England, I could've gone 'my name's Sadia', but I never did ... And whenever I start something new, I could say 'my name's ...'. But I don't. It's as if I won't allow myself to.

Sadia's unwitting complicity in her self-denial of the patronymic embodiment of her Algerian heritage aligns with Bourdieu's symbolic violence paradigm and supports Fechter and Walsh's (2010) contention that postcolonialism is central to contemporary mobility, despite the differences in flows and power dynamics. It illustrates how systemic xenophobia in France has been embodied as a predictability, part of her habitus. While the good intentions of Sadia's father might have been legitimate, the effect of such abnegation has been profoundly hurtful (Garratt, 2016). Moreover, such microaggressions are not restricted to early life-stages. During Senni's application to the prestigious Ecole supérieure des affaires, the oral examination proved a humiliating experience owing to the examiner's sardonic reliance on racial stereotypes. The condescension is evoked in tellingly tangible terms, her comments described as more painful than the blow of a baseball bat (Senni, 2007: 84) and her smirks 'unbearable, like razor blades' (2007: 83–4). The metaphors demonstrate the intensity of the hurt, comparable in its effects to physical violence (Schubert, 2012), yet largely ignored by society (Garratt, 2016).[2] Not being explicitly racist, the grounds for formal complaint are weak, as the microaggression catch-22 dictates (Lilienfeld, 2017). It is precisely these pernicious characteristics, within the wider societal framework of symbolic violence, that allow microaggressions to thrive unchallenged.

The internalisation of negative tropes and limited aspirations among France's young ethnic minorities is conducive to a spiral of failure, exacerbated by their parents' powerlessness to combat the 'education machine' (Senni, 2007: 37). Unacquainted with the *doxa* of the educational field (Bourdieu and Wacquant, 1992; Thomson, 2012), they become 'victims because they are unskilled in the subtle hierarchical games between institutions, pathways and careers advice, all those small differences that ultimately lead to big discrepancies' (Dubet, 2004: 8). Multiple studies demonstrate the persistence of a correlation between disadvantaged social background and underachievement at school, despite efforts to reverse the trend in the UK (Francis and Wong, 2013). Importantly, France has been even less effective in introducing change due to the power of student and teaching unions, whose systematic opposition to even the most 'minuscule reforms' (Dubet, 2004: 6) maintains the status quo, disguising it under a mantle of revolution (Dubet, 2004: 6). This enables the perpetuation of an intrinsically hypocritical system, founded on 'equality for all', but 'far from favouring equal opportunities, the education system contributes to the reproduction of social inequality and legitimises it through meritocratic discourse' (Jourdain and Naulin, 2011: 41). Consequently, initiatives such as the *loi du 8 juillet 2013* for the *refondation de l'école de la République* have been unsuccessful in bringing genuine reform or inhibiting the system's reproductive tendencies and 'incontestable ethnic segregation' (Dubet, 2004: 42).

During my fieldwork, Loïc, a returnee (who lived in London from 2001–2 as an au pair), described an almost identical scenario to Senni's. Although not from an ethnic minority, Loïc's socio-economic background is perceived to be incompatible with the bourgeois model typifying France's Ecoles des Beaux Arts, which is why he opted for 'plastic arts at uni instead'. Loïc is – or *was* – ambitious: the most qualified of all his family, he left school with the institutionalised capital of a *baccalauréat*, subsequently studying art to MA and setting his sights on a career in secondary education.[3] Loïc passed his written and practical art teaching exams with an impressive 17/20, only to fail at the last hurdle: the oral. Estimating a score of only 2/20 for the oral, given his strong marks elsewhere, Loïc's explanation for the discrepancy was 'institutional prejudice or corruption', or perhaps both. Yet, such allegations are again difficult to verify: 'I don't have any proof of this *concours* malfunctioning, which is exactly what makes this rigged system work so well in France. It exists at every level.'

The meritocratic principles of the CAPES *concours* served Loïc well in the anonymised assessments, but his social background functioned as a detrimental 'handicap' (Bourdieu and Passeron, 1964: 105) in the symbolically loaded oral, causing him to fail by a mere half point overall. Although the *concours* system 'ensures formal equality between candidates' (1964: 104), it can also 'transform privilege into merit, since it allows the action of social origin to continue to operate, but in more secret ways' (1964: 104). Such secrecy enables the perpetuation of positions of social dominance and subordination. Senni's and Loïc's oral examiners and their students from privileged backgrounds, rich in cultural (and social?) capital, maintain their superiority through mutually recognised symbolic articulations of dominance, since they cannot 'but apprehend reality indirectly and symbolically ... through the veil of rhetorical illusion' (Bourdieu and Passeron, 1964: 75). It is thus a symbolic cycle which reinforces the 'limits of capital gains' (Friedman, 2016: 107) and restricts social mobility, hence paving the way for international mobility.

In this light, while Loïc's oral examination 'failure' may have been due to a deliberate, if secretive, act of nepotistic symbolic violence, it could also issue from the examiners' insufficient awareness of their own prejudicial positioning. Being the products of the education system, they pre-reflexively embody its inherent value systems, leading to 'unintended' discrimination against those in possession of less cultural capital (Ingram and Abrahams, 2016). Loïc, however, was unequivocal about the nepotistic grounds of his 'failure': a form of corruption considered endemic by many informants, resulting in a quest for new, more equitable opportunities abroad (Wang, 2013a). Block's research on French teachers in London corroborates my findings. He alludes to the 'relative flexibility of the British education system, in particular the *transparent* and relatively straightforward progression from first degree to teacher qualifications to teaching post' (Block, 2006: 132; my emphasis), and to 'the fact that in Britain there is no CAPES' (2006: 132). The references to transparency and the comparative rigidity of the French educational field are telling, and both are defined as direct migration triggers.

Other field-research examples include preclusion from a high-performing school in central Paris, recounted by a woman informant with Mauritian heritage, which confirms Patrick Simon's contention that France's minorities are often disqualified from certain 'établissements' (2006: 168). Symbolic violence was also noted by students at the Lycée Français Charles de Gaulle (LFCG): 'in France, if you're of African or Arabic descent, you're a lot less likely to get into a school than if you're of French descent ... er truly French ... white'. The student's testimony confirms Beaman's assertion that full belonging to French society is dependent on whiteness and that such phenotypical paradigms in 'France are continually produced and reproduced' (Beaman, 2018: 2). Another student in Focus Group Two provided evidence of normalised intimidation from LFCG teachers against pupils not epitomising the '*archetypal* traditional student' (Bourdieu and Passeron, 1964: 75–6; original emphasis): 'they create clans. They say, "if you feel uncomfortable in this school" and that "your marks are super bad", or "you're going to be kicked out", and all that. They say "why are you disengaged?", "you need to do better", and stuff like that.' The staff are perceived to mobilise collectively, projecting their frustrations onto students. Rather than seeking a solution or questioning their own teaching methods, they repeatedly discredit pupils.

In other fields, such microaggressions might be considered harassment, but the subtle nature of habitus and symbolic violence, together with the inherent power dynamics of the teacher–pupil relationship, places such discrimination outside UK jurisdiction.[4] Legally, the student who made the statement above is compelled to accept this 'microinvalidation' (Sue *et al.*, 2007: 274), his only self-defence being *not* to submit to the negative characterisation of failing at school and 'becoming a thug in line with their prejudiced expectations' (Senni, 2007: 84). These examples suggest that Bourdieu's defence of teachers as *unintentionally* complicit in the reproduction of inequality in France's education system is overly assuasive, although the connivance of society as a whole, as demonstrated through its imbalanced harassment legislation in the field of education, is patent.[5]

Parallels with other EU migrants validate my contention that symbolic violence in the premigration education setting serves as a migration vector. Italian migrants repeatedly referred to endemic favouritism as a push factor (King *et al.*, 2014: 21), resulting in 'profound disenchantments … a kind of "rejection" of Italy … almost a "disidentification" with the country of their birth, upbringing and education' (2014: 21). The sentiment is strikingly analogous to Loïc's, whose CAPES 'failure' left him utterly disillusioned by the inner workings of France's public institutions. For him, the underhand exploitation of the system 'is a means of tackling the applicant surplus and choosing who they want, where they want. That's not the principle behind the *concours* system. Actually, they've succeeded in putting me off altogether.' The despondency has engendered a fundamentally ambivalent relationship with France (Benson, 2011). Loïc is simultaneously grateful for the educational opportunities granted him, but deeply resentful that the system subsequently denied him the chance to convert his institutionalised capital (Bourdieu, 1979b) into a profession. Instead, he spent the following decade earning a meagre living as a manual labourer, 'put off' to the extent of casting aside his talents as both painter and pedagogue, and fatalistically following the blue-collar pathway (and the concomitant symbolic/social humiliation) projected for him by his secondary-school teachers and the inevitability of his habitus.

Consistent with the symbolic violence paradigm, Loïc could be deemed complicit in his own underachievement, for rather than take the agentive step to sabotage his 'social destiny' (Bourdieu and Passeron, 1964: 109), he relinquished his aspirations in favour of a reliable – if derisory – wage, knowing 'deep down, that his school career [was] over' (Bourdieu *et al.*, 1993: 126) and relying on the professional achievements of his partner. Cynics may postulate that this is precisely the aim of the system: to encourage those from less advantaged backgrounds to play the educational game until the hardship of being judged on an ostensibly equal but inherently inequitable basis (Dubet, 2014) becomes too difficult to overcome and they surrender to the symbolic forces, leaving the holders of inherited cultural capital to fill that social space. In this sense, symbolic violence operates as a powerful societal tool, capable of greater harm and tangible effects, on individuals and social groups, than more explicit forms of violence (Bourdieu and Wacquant, 1992). One of its serendipitous by-products, however, is that it affords France an advantageously over-qualified workforce, just as the 'initial downward mobility' (Erel, 2010; Tzeng, 2012: 125) experienced by London-French migrants benefits the local labour market. It is not, however, a win-win situation. The frustration experienced by those unable to see their education bear fruit or for whom '[l]osing a job means [they] then go through one of the longest periods of unemployment in any developed nation' (Wolfreys, 2018: 16), and who ultimately reject France, contribute to a damaging brain-drain phenomenon (Bellion, 2005; Roudaut, 2009).

This was borne out by both Sarkozy (Kelly, 2013) and Macron, who brought their respective presidential campaigns to London to mitigate the brain-drain effect. In 2007, Sarkozy appealed '[t]o all those expatriates unhappy with the situation in France … to "come home". We need your work, your intelligence, your imagination and your enthusiasm' (*L'Express*, 2007). Whereas in 2017, Macron asked them to 'come back to be entrepreneurial and make things happen in France, to innovate, research, create and [crucially] teach. Because I want a country where we can do all that again' (En Marche, 2017). My findings therefore concur with de Haas's assertion that migration impacts 'on inequality, social stratification, economic growth, entrepreneurship and cultural change' in both 'sending *and* receiving communities and societies' (de Haas, 2010: 1,591), but, as evidenced in the migrant narratives described, it remains in the interests of the symbolically and materially dominant to maintain society's invisible structures, despite President Macron's efforts to revitalise them.

By uncovering several of the subtle symbolic forces present in the French educational field, I have demonstrated the extent to which habitus and field interact dynamically, with students' primary habitus impacting their educational trajectories and ability to negotiate the complexities of the educational field. I have also revealed the inherently complicit nature of symbolic violence, itself intrinsically linked to habitus, and how it can result in social discrimination and/or racism. These institutionally and socially 'accepted' practices ultimately push some individuals away from a system where the mantra of 'l'égalité des chances' (Dubet, 2004: 6) appears little more than a myth and towards an alternative set of social structures whose appeal lies in their perceived meritocracy.

Employment barriers: escaping 'diplomitis', discrimination and exclusivity in the French workplace

What's profoundly annoying is the gulf between the egalitarian Republican discourse (if you *play the game* of the Republic you'll succeed) and the reality, whereby *discrimination in recruitment and employment is an everyday occurrence*. Of course, there are people who practise discrimination here [in London], but watch out, they'll be in trouble for it later.

These are the words of Charles, a correspondent with a national French media group, who has settled in Crystal Palace, where we meet in a characterless high-street cafe for a two-hour conversation. Perhaps as a result of his critical, journalistic eye, coupled with the clarity with which the originary field comes into focus when seen from the perspective of the detached migrant (Parisot, 2007: 12), Charles's account is remarkably perceptive. The symbolic value placed on qualifications and their relevance to a specific career were cited frequently by my respondents as mobility drivers. Christian Roudaut goes as far as labelling the phenomenon a national illness: diplomitis (Roudaut, 2009: 103), while Patrick Simon refers to French society as 'completely locked by its elites, saturated in selection, from school to the workplace' (Simon, 2006: 167–8). Robert, a 40-year-old (white, gay) French teacher/lecturer living in East Dulwich, also acknowledges the national affliction: here 'people gave me a chance on the basis of my performance. Whereas in France, … if I didn't have the qualification to prove my level, I wouldn't have been given the professional opportunity.' According to the 'mythical system' (Bourdieu, 1996: 17), migration causes Robert's qualifications and professional profile to undergo two processes of 'social alchemy' (Bourdieu, 1979b: 5). In France, where the exchange rate is low, his institutionalised capital is discredited. Conversely, in London, he profits professionally from high symbolic-economic exchange rates (Bourdieu, 1979b: 6). Importantly, as Robert explains, such symbolic forces are commonplace in France, which reinforces the appeal of London:

> of all the people who studied languages with me at uni, only one uses their English … One friend is in telemarketing, just to pay the bills. Another has become a hairdresser. One girl had to carry on in higher education to launch her career in a supermarket chain.

This routine undervaluation of young people's personal investment in their tertiary education (Block, 2006) gives rise to a sentiment of workplace symbolic violence conducive to mobility. Arthur, a 34-year-old, born in Reunion, and now in a managerial position in Docklands, provides further illustration. Trained in electronics, he was only able to secure a basic catering job in Paris, after a year of unemployment and rejection from the army. Similarly, Séverine, a lawyer also with minority-ethnic heritage, notes that 'when you have a law qualification in England, people welcome you with open arms, whereas in France people say "you don't have exactly the qualification or specialisation we're looking for"'. The narrow-minded rigidity (Roudaut, 2009) leads to a sense of frustration. Institutionalised capital is convertible on the London labour market to positions of value, thus allowing individuals to feel valued. Meanwhile, in France, the disproportionately low symbolic and economic worth of employment degrades academic accomplishments, naturally leading to a sense of *personal* degradation and hence serving as a migration trigger.

The perversity of the paradox of simultaneously demanding and disparaging institutionalised academic capital is heightened by the symbolic value of *social* capital (Bourdieu, 1980b). Succinctly defined by Kelly and Lusis as 'networks and connections that can be mobilised to generate advantages or benefits ... [i]n the labour market' (2006: 834), the machinations of social capital are so prevalent in France that there is a dedicated term: *pistonnage*. Derived from the physical piston, that is a mechanism for upward mobility, it involves recommendation to achieve an advantage (*Larousse*). However, as King *et al.* (2014) assert, like *raccomandazione*, it 'is so much more than being "recommended" for a job; it is a culture of power brokering, nepotism and "favours" in which the best candidates frequently fail to get the post they rightfully deserve' (2014: 21). It is precisely these power dynamics and the pervasive 'culture' that *pistonnage* encompasses and that English translations (e.g. string-pulling or cronyism) bypass. The lexical void in everyday English arguably reflects the comparative socio-professional irrelevance of the term, or at least its reduced presence in the collective consciousness.[6]

Robert clarifies the practice during our conversation: 'the sons of doctors become doctors, and the same goes for lawyers. Very few people from disadvantaged backgrounds are able to change social status.' Curiously, given the empirical differences in our studies, Cangbai Wang's research on Chinese migrants in Hong Kong uncovered equivalent dynamics; his interviewee '"felt" Hong Kong was a "fairer" society and therefore a better choice for her as she did not have strong family background ... If you have a father in a powerful position, you could easily have a bright future' (Wang, 2013a: 392). In other words, having considerable amounts of social capital at one's disposal results in the 'reproduction of directly usable social ties' (Bourdieu, 1980b: 2). More often than not, therefore, 'influential people come from influential families' (Bourdieu, 1994: 194) and those with limited or negative social capital and insignificant family status find themselves chronically excluded from high-ranking positions. Furthermore, the system of inherited social capital was, until 2015 with the introduction of the *loi Macron*, enshrined in French law. The structures of privilege are thus concretised in France's institutional structures.

Bruno, a 37-year-old head chef in a central London eatery, who moved to London in 1991, is explicit regarding the omnipresence of nepotism in the originary field: 'in France, *pistonnage* is common currency: it's considered normal. Whereas in England it doesn't even occur to people.' It is meaningful here that Bruno chooses an economic metaphor (currency) to refer to *pistonnage*, thereby exemplifying the intrinsic *value* and *convertibility* of social ties to the detriment of institutionalised capital. While the formal qualification serves as the transparent, legitimised currency for access – or denial – to professional positions of proportionate responsibility or specialism, it is often used as a means of 'laundering' covertly transacted *social* capital gains. By emphasising the power of social capital in France, I do not, however, claim that such insidious systems of favour do not exist in London, rather that my participants fail to see them here, having been granted professional opportunities denied in France.

This duplicitous process of selection is rendered more powerful by its ex officio credibility and societal acknowledgement in France, consistent with the complicity inherent in symbolic violence. Importantly, Bourdieu's notion of social capital is, as Deschenaux and Laflamme (2009) maintain, conceptualised as networks of 'inter-knowledge and inter-acknowledgement' (Bourdieu, 1980b: 2). It is this mutual recognition that distinguishes social capital from social networks per se, injecting the requisite tacit connivance that qualifies it as symbolic violence (Moore, 2012). Such endemic disingenuousness leaves worthy job-seekers – yet deficient in social capital or inappropriately qualified – formally 'de-graded or dis-qualified' (Cordier, 2005: 111). This calls into question the integrity of the entire French recruitment structure and the political system governing it, described by Simon as '"le modèle français de discrimination"' (Simon, 2006: 176), which turns a blind eye to its colonial and institutionally xenophobic past (2006: 176). It also explains why some see migration as an escape route and a means of subverting the habitus.

In *Enfin un boulot!* (A job at last!), Cordier epitomises the complicated and damaging system of paradoxes surrounding 'diplomitis' and *pistonnage*. The inequitable intricacies of the professional game are accentuated further by the symbolic role played by France's prestigious institutions:

> a qualification alone is no longer enough ... [D]on't expect to land the job of your dreams on the wages you're supposedly worth because of your qualifications, unless you've done an exemplary course at a prestigious university or a fee-paying *grande école*, or have benefited from a serious *coup de piston*. And even with all that ... you still might have to become an immigrant to find elsewhere what you couldn't find at home (Cordier, 2005: 19).

Cordier's reference to the symbolic worth of the highly stratified *grandes écoles* (Bourdieu, 1989; Albouy and Wanecq, 2003: 31) is a theme that emerged repeatedly from my interviews and proved as detrimental in the professional field as France's 'diploma dictatorship' (Roudaut, 2009: 103). Robert's first-hand experience of the *grande-école* system corroborates this: 'I was rejected because I was from a working-class background. My parents were … my mum was a cleaner, but I was with students whose parents were doctors.' Robert bears witness to 'class racism' (Puwar, 2009: 376), whereby his lack of symbolic capital causes exclusion from the tight-knit circles of France's 'grandes familles bourgeoises' (Bourdieu, 1994: 194). Chantal, who attended Sciences Po, confirms the persistence of these impervious networks: 'there's an aristocracy that remains very closed, and they only socialise with each other, except it's actually never spoken about. So, people act as though it didn't exist.' Class therefore plays out as 'an absent presence' (Lawler, 2008: 126): absent from the values and rhetoric of the *République*, but present in practice. This initiates a process of homegrown *displacement*, which counters the emplacement practices of the diasporic field (Wessendorf and Phillimore, 2018), because 'the opportunities of "a better life"' intrinsic to belonging are negated (Levin, 2016: 26), and hence render the move to London self-evident, a fait accompli brought about by socio-professional dis-integration in France and 'disruption to a sense of home' (Blunt and Dowling, 2006: 2).

Intensifying the inequity of this *grande-école* system, statistics reveal that the more prestigious the institution, the wider the social divide (Albouy and Wanecq, 2003). According to a Focus Group Two student, the invisible boundary is not restricted to class (Abutbul-Selinger, 2018): 'there are only French people in the *grandes écoles* in Paris, like central ones, but here, at Imperial, it's full of people from different backgrounds; it's a lot more diverse.' Whether 'French' refers to whiteness here is not made explicit (Beaman, 2015, 2018), but bearing in mind that many students from the socio-ethnically homogeneous group identified in Paris's *grandes écoles* will later hold positions in public office, the question of whether this pattern will be replicated on the labour market is pertinent. François suggests it is:

> in France … ninety per cent of [civil service] positions are occupied by …
> (I think it's more like ninety-five per cent in high public office) white Catholics,
> Protestants or Jews. And knowing the proportion of North Africans, Asians
> and Africans in the normal population, they're not there. It goes to show that
> the population on the ground isn't represented.

Given that France's Muslim community is calculated at 2.1 million for the 18–50 age bracket alone (Beauchemin *et al.*, 2010) and that '[i]mmigrants and second-generation minorities make up 20.9 per cent of the total population in France' (Reitz *et al.*, 2017: 2,477), the perceived absence is edifying. Through comparison with the UK, Séverine confirms François's observation: 'there's been a whole movement so that civil servants represent the citizens they are supposed to be serving, in terms of region, accent ... people from less advantaged backgrounds'. Nevertheless, Puwar challenges the underlying diversity of the UK civil service, evoking a negative form of cultural 'erasure': '[d]ifferent bodies can exist in the senior civil service so long as they mimic ... the norm, whilst the norm itself is not problematised' (Puwar, 2004: 117). It is important to recognise that the presence of a variety of phenotypes and regional representatives within the ranks of high public office, irrespective of whether they conform to the 'white', unproblematised norm, is nonetheless a step closer to equality than in the French model, where the *concours* process functions as a convenient 'filter'.[7]

The potency of this selection process lies in the very *legitimacy* of the meritocratic tenets on which it is seemingly based (Simon, 2006). That is, the *concours* system deployed in France's *grandes écoles* and subsequently replicated as a sifting mechanism for admission into public office, is the direct product of the founding universal values of the Republic: 'All citizens are equally admissible to ... public office on the basis of their ability and without any other distinction than that of their virtues and their talents' (Declaration of the Rights of Man, 1789). Yet social and ethnic distinctions have been noted, as has a failure to recognise individual attributes, unlike in London, where Marie, a 63-year-old return migrant, feels 'the abilities of the individual are recognised more'. Thus, while public authorities apply an idealistically equitable recruitment process based on 'impersonality through the *concours* [which means] the State chooses its "servants" thanks to a process devoid of favouritism – or at least one that cannot be criticised for it' (Percebois, no date: 6), the majority of successful applicants nonetheless proceed from *grandes écoles*. This not only casts doubt over the effectiveness of the egalitarian paradigm, but over the good faith of the Republican edifice (Simon, 2006). Acting as a universally instituted and universally embraced myth (Wolfreys, 2018), the power of the French state to exert symbolic violence imperceptibly, lies precisely in its worthiness in the minds of the people (characteristically complicit in the process). For, as 52-year-old architect, Antoine declares, 'saying that you work for local government is something you can be proud of in France. Maybe this is a fantasy of culture, but it is of much more value than here [in London].' Consequently, because the state and its ideologies are in the name of the public good, the public are blind to those practices which are bad.

'In London, people don't see my colour'

Echoing the words of Roma migrants interviewed by Jan Grill, '"In England, they don't call you black!"' (2018: 1,136) and those of a mixed-heritage participant in Conradson and Latham's study: 'I don't stand out in London, whereas at home I've always felt that I was noticeably not white' (Conradson and Latham, 2007: 241), this sentiment is as much testament to the colour-sensitive gaze of the originary spaces as to perceived colour-blindness in London. The simultaneous recognition of phenotypical difference and non-recognition of French identity, by definition oblivious to ethnic difference in the name of equality, is a phenomenon that has been gaining academic scrutiny (Simon and Tiberj, 2016; Wolfreys, 2018; Escafré-Dublet, 2019). I argue that an outside-in denial of Frenchness is experienced as a microaggression that serves an exclusionary role in the workplace, thereby driving migration and 'resubjectification' (Conradson and Latham, 2007: 234).

The empirical basis of this subsection draws on the experiences of two French-born, Black interviewees: Paulette, a 35-year-old logistics manager with Beninese heritage, and Moses, a 24-year-old commercial exports representative with Senegalese parentage. Germain and Larcher postulate that French scholarship, even in its feminist forms, has typically ignored 'how racism, colonialism, (transnational) migration, and xenophobia structured French society, consequently dismissing the experiences of women of colour, particularly black women' (Germain and Larcher, 2018: xiii). While there is growing recognition of the institutionalised blindness to matters of colour, the specificities of Black French women's experiences of intra-EU migration are relatively unscrutinised. The testimony provided by Paulette is therefore all the more timely and important.

Although initially reluctant to leave France, Paulette's everyday exposure to racialised symbolic violence, most detrimentally manifested through chronic unemployability, cemented her resolve to test the waters elsewhere: 'To begin with, I came against my will ... I was finding it really, really hard to get a job in France, and ... with all my academic achievements, I was wasting my time hanging around there, doing one futile training-course after another.' This confirms Larcher's assertion that the French education system 'benefits the daughters of sub-Saharan immigrants more than the sons' (Larcher, 2018: 84), but the non-conversion of her institutionalised capital into employment of any kind compounded the personal frustration and sense of societal rejection. Later, I discover how Paulette's French identity is encumbered by her Blackness, with Frenchness being so entangled with 'whiteness and maleness ... [she] was both hypervisible and invisible in [its] definitions' (Mitchell, 2018: 185). As she explains, 'I was born in France … But, in France, when people ask where you're from, you instantly say Benin. Whereas here, they might expect you to say you're French because of the French accent, but it doesn't ring true to me to say I'm French, so I say I'm French with Beninese heritage … Actually, in London, people don't see my colour.'

In London, Paulette's embodiment of Frenchness is perceived to transcend her phenotype, whereas according to Oberon Garcia, 'Color will always trump all other attributes, even individuality, in the eyes of white French people' (Garcia, 2018: 225). Despite being French-born, Paulette feels unentitled to assert her Frenchness in France, ricocheting the prejudice and otherness routinely projected at her (Escafré-Dublet and Simon, 2014). She bears witness to a structurally imposed disidentification with Frenchness that is so engrained it has become part of her habitus, such that it is transferred to the diasporic space (Benson, 2019). The disingenuousness she feels at the idea of self-identifying as French is accentuated by her use of the impersonal pronoun 'on', which detaches her from the account and thus complies with symbolic violence's intrinsic complicity (Bourdieu, 1994).[8] There is an emerging sense of a reinvented self, but Paulette's resubjectification remains incomplete (Conradson and Latham, 2007): 'it's always shocked me to see a Black person say they're British, but they say it here. It's strange actually because I see the perception of others but it's also my perception.' With considerable insight into her own insider-outsider positioning, Paulette recognises the tension at the core of her identity and her intractably French outlook. French society has rejected her due to her African heritage, recruiters repeatedly denied her access to work, yet precisely because of her *French* habitus, she is 'shocked' to witness Black Londoners self-identifying as British. Migrating to London, therefore, and experiencing an alternative gaze – both as object and subject – has prompted a subversion of her originary habitus, shaking her into a consciousness of her own (mis)perceptions regarding race, identity and belonging.

Returnee, Moses, reiterates this comparative consciousness of social rejection in France, linked directly to phenotype:

I was born in France, so I've got that mix of two cultures: when I say I'm French, there's a whole lot of African on the inside … I feel at home here [in France], but I get the feeling people from ethnic minorities feel more at home in England than we do in France. I get the feeling they're really 'at home, at home', like, there's no doubt. Whereas in France, sometimes you realise people want to make us understand it isn't our home. When I was in London, I knew I wasn't at home, but people didn't make me feel it, actually, and that was good … In France, there's this constant preoccupation with origins and Colour.

In what Mulholland and Ryan pertinently refer to as a comparative epistemology of place (2017), Moses' testimony illustrates 'how non-white descendants of immigrants … are only provisional guests in French society' (Beaman, 2018: 12). The symbolic injury caused by such precarious positioning in his country of birth is emphasised by its contrast with the full belonging, irrespective of ethnicity, experienced in London. Moses later determines a correlation between the permanent othering experienced in French society and preclusion from employment, confirming the meritocratic pull of London (Mulholland and Ryan, 2015), but providing clearer insights into the racialised undertones of such decision-making, absent from Mulholland and Ryan's analysis:

> In England, when you turn on the TV … you can see Pakistanis, Indians and Black people, who are journalists, presenters or have high positions in government or the police. It's not like that in France yet. I know I can switch on the TV in France and won't see many journalists from minority ethnic backgrounds, even in adverts, which are supposed to represent us.

In London, the public presence of visible minorities in multiple professional contexts is taken as a sign of inclusiveness both within and beyond the labour market by Moses. Charles seconds this point, claiming that in the UK, 'you just have to turn on your TV … it's a real eye-opener to see how embedded and visible diversity is. Or even in public services and banks, diversity jumps out at you.' In both accounts, widespread minority ethnic representation contrasts the prejudiced subjectivities embodied in France's structures, showing how 'power is asserted and exercised … as an unnoticed violence' (Bourdieu *et al.*, 1993: 255–6).

While Paulette and Moses speak of the racial prejudice experienced in France from the perspective of the microaggression sufferer, it is significant that Charles and Miranda, a 28-year-old doctoral student from a village in North-East France, also bear witness to 'this "whitriarchal system"' (Larcher, 2018: 75) despite their biological whiteness. Miranda notes that 'in England, … there's no rejection by society [… where] people are put in housing estates and then left there … In France, it's so blatant, there's real division, and a lot of fighting between the two.' For Miranda, the schism proved so reprehensible that it was her single most powerful mobility trigger: 'that problem of racism, of fighting between people – between immigrant generations and "French French" people – I couldn't stand it any longer … it creates an incredible amount of tension, whereas here, you don't really see that tension'.

Compounding the sense of socio-professional alienation, therefore, is the physical marginalisation of low-income families to poorly connected peripheral *banlieues* (Bourdieu, 1996). Cut off from mainstream society, both concretely and metaphorically, 'these areas are routinely castigated as lawless zones inhabited by migrants (and their descendants)' (Wolfreys, 2018: 4), and the antagonistic isolation epitomises France's 'morbid resentment at the loss of empire' (2018: 41). This, coupled with ethnic-minority under-representation in the intangible space of television, save to reinforce stereotypical myths created by sensationalist press and propaganda (Bourdieu *et al.*, 1993; Fassin, 2018), constitutes a pervasive form of symbolic violence: the corollary of embodied mental structures of division (Bourdieu, 1996), tangibly perceived by the victims of such everyday racism (Moses: 'people want to make us understand we're not at home'). Moreover, by under-recruiting minorities to public office, the French state, as the ultimate wielder of legitimised power, extends the collective *social* rejection of the said groups to the domain of ex officio authority, which in turn implies institutional racialised symbolic violence.[9]

This quotidian discrimination contributed to several other interviewees' settlement in London; for example, 37-year-old Sarah, frustrated by the racism routinely directed at her Chilean husband in France, where the authorities treated him like 'cattle' and an 'illegal immigrant', or Sadia, demoralised by the everyday racism against her friends of Colour, systematically stopped and searched in Paris. Charles was equally damning, declaring France to be a 'Snow White country', where 'young people have learned to live with racism wherever they go'. He defines London as a space where minorities 'succeed more easily, doors open more easily, and there's less prejudice against them ... In France their confidence is crushed and by going abroad they rediscover their self-confidence and their identity.' London is thus a place where the self can be reimagined and reworked (Lawler, 2008), where migration serves as habitus sabotage (Bourdieu and Passeron, 1964), and where Frenchness can be expressed and experienced in Black and Brown terms. In this sense, mobility is, as Murphy-Lejeune underlines, a two-way journey, a chance to escape the French space and 'an opportunity for travelling inside ... a *rendez-vous* with self' (Murphy-Lejeune, 2002: 96). Paulette's mobility therefore enables the discovery of a Black Frenchness disentangled from the African identity thrust upon her in France: 'I'm not Black African; I don't know Africa', as well as enabling professional mobility:

> Here, truly, from a knowledge point of view, if you know, you can climb. The progress I've made in this company, in this country, in terms of salary, status, work ... I don't think I'd ever have been able to get that in a whole lifetime in France ... They didn't even want to give me a job as a PA.

The unprejudiced gaze of her employer contrasts the symbolic violence systematically encountered in the French professional field, where, as Moses concurs, 'it's more about how old you are, your gender, that sort of thing, sometimes even where you're from. Despite the timid tone of Moses' words ('sometimes even'), the sense of regained self-worth comes through in his narrative. Likewise, familiar with employment rejection in France, ostensibly on account of her ethnicity, Paulette is empowered by being entrusted a 'position with a lot of responsibility' in London, managing a team of employees. Such trust illustrates the mutual respect perceived between employer and employee, at variance with the discriminatory infantilisation encountered by a number of interviewees in the French professional field. Arthur's migratory elevation, emancipation even, is equally striking. As a French migrant of Colour from Reunion Island, he is unequivocal in his condemnation of the working environment encountered during his initial migration to Paris: 'It was hard for me. I had problems with racism: at work people treated you as if you were a slave ... I did everything I could to please them, but they took advantage of it; some people have no respect.' The figurative violence of Arthur's words is meaningful, and undoubtedly a reflection of the repeated microaggressions suffered. However, it is only through comparison with his current managerial status in London, that such wounds are reopened and the imbalanced power dynamics of the French professional space revived.

Indeed, this inequality was a recurring observation, with many participants, regardless of ethnicity, referring to the 'rigid, hierarchical and structured' (Marie) configuration of the French workplace, in opposition to the equality experienced in the London equivalent, considered to be devoid of such stratification and supported by Tzeng's research (2012: 124). Significantly, the 'more open ... more transparent' (Chantal) and more 'equitable' (François) subjective parameters of the diasporic working space are seen to translate into the objectivated working environment, being initially embodied 'as a mental structure' and 'reconverted into physical structures' (Bourdieu, 1996: 16). Paulette substantiates this materialisation in reference to the layout of her open-plan London office:

> If you don't know who the boss is here, and you walk in, you wouldn't be able to tell. In France, the managing director has a separate office with a secretary, who herself has a separate office. It's very different. In fact, our offices in France are like that: it's the same company, but the managing director has his own separate office.

Here, in 'a sort of spontaneous metaphor' (Bourdieu, 1996: 13), the rigid, hierarchical mental structures to which Marie alludes are converted into stratified material spaces in France, functioning as a socio-semiotic marker of the CEO's supremacy. Contrasting this model is the layout of the London branch of the *same* company, where all desks (CEO included) are positioned within the same open space, the few physical divisions taking the form of transparent partitions (behind one of which Paulette and I are talking). This layout therefore objectifies the interviewees' words, and serves, as seen in King *et al.*'s (2014) study, as a compelling settlement factor. The French office space is experienced as the material incarnation of the discrepancy between France's egalitarian ideals and the inequity of its practices. In contrast, the London workspace suggests a transformation of originary (corporate) field and (individual) habituses to a more egalitarian framework.

By analysing my empirical data through the prism of workplace symbolic violence, I have drawn attention to the powerful, yet often implicit, forms of professional discrimination that has motivated several of my research participants' mobility. Whether in terms of the institutionalised symbolic capital which renders precise qualifications a prerequisite for even the most menial of jobs and the seal of a *grande école* the passport to the most lucrative; the social capital that is inherited from those fortunate enough to have been born into influential circles; the insidious racism that prevents France's first, second and third generation ethnic-minority migrants from attaining positions which tally with their abilities; or the social hierarchies that exist in the mentalities and materialities of the French workplace, the microaggressions I have described here have all contributed to migration and/or settlement choices. In the final section of this chapter, I explore how microaggressions in the broader social space have also fed into the decision-making, and how such discriminatory attitudes and practices are able to flourish in France.

Everyday microaggressions: rejecting universalism, sexism and homophobia in the French social space

Extending beyond the field of education and employment, this section considers insidious migration push factors in France's broader social field, focusing on the invisibilisation of cultural differences and on gendered symbolic violence, in both misogynistic and homophobic forms. Developing the transnational approach prescribed by Kelly and Lusis (2005: 832), whereby migrants' current lived experience should be apprehended in relation to their trajectories from the originary social space, I unearth additional sub-surface motivations for leaving the 'homeland'.

'You can't force integration'

In France, as shown, Paulette's skin colour is deemed highly visible in the collective consciousness, yet rendered invisible in official discourse, leading to formalised disenfranchisement: 'the strategy to invisibilise minorities, on which [France's] universalist political equation is based, does not ensure them protection and access to equality, as promised, but instead disarms them in the face of ethnic and racial hierarchies hidden behind formal equality' (Simon, 2006: 162). Owing to legislation preventing French authorities from discriminating between its citizens in ethnic, racial or religious terms, discrimination is thus allowed to prosper 'legitimately'.[10] This cultural and administrative 'erasure' (Puwar, 2004: 117) provokes resentment on the part of those affected, fuelling social unease and, in turn, migration. Bourdieu and Fassin note the phenomenon among France's LGBT communities, conceptualising state 'invisibilisation' as a form of oppression (Bourdieu, 1998: 162) and normalisation as cause for disgust (Fassin, 2015: 86), but the same stigmatisation applies to France's ethnic and religious minorities, be they the thousands of French Jews fleeing France in the mid-2010s, many of whom settled in London (Malka and Malka, 2016), or its disenfranchised minority youth, as Charles explains:

> Young people from immigrant backgrounds aren't naïve [about] racism; what shocks them deeply is the inertia of the French authorities. We've had an earful of rhetoric about Republican qualities, but in general the tolerance of intolerance is huge in France.

The French authorities' failure to acknowledge racism is thus in itself deemed racist, experienced by the victims of such institutional 'inertia' as an unequivocal act of symbolic violence. Exclusion from official statistics denies France's minorities a social presence, just as the non-recording of hate crime (in)validates the offence. More broadly, it is a convenient mechanism for the state to negate the social damage caused by its colonial past, legitimating 'the national amnesia of French empire' (Puwar, 2009: 372). People of Colour are therefore lawfully effaced from national debate: 'in France, we're all equals ... In the name of universality, we crush people whose roots aren't French' (Roudaut, 2009: 70, citing Odile, originally from the French Caribbean).

Camouflaging discrimination behind egalitarian moralities is not a new phenomenon, however, as the state's relative success at eradicating regional identities and languages testifies (Roudaut, 2009: 70). Nor is it the preserve of the French body politic, having infiltrated the social space: 'deep in their hearts, I think people would quite like them to go back to where they came from. They feel like they're raking up all their jobs; they don't really get it' (Marie). Such attitudes have caused Paulette, on the receiving end of the symbolic violence, to conclude that she will 'never go back to France, it's over ... it's not getting any better, it's not a life I want for my children'. Proud of her 'difference, just the fact that [we're] different' and enlightened by her French education, she realises the incompatibility of her situation and that 'asserting one's difference is almost a betrayal of the, clearly very exclusive, Republic' (Roudaut, 2009: 70–1). Permanent disembedding from the environment where assimilationism is standardised (Koser, 2007) is thus par for the course, for '[w]hen the mother country rejects its children, the least stable will look for replacement parents' (Diallo, 2015). In almost a reverse enactment of the imperial subjectivities of whiteness recounted by Fechter (2005), Leonard (2008) and Walsh (2018), where the expatriate population is afforded privileged status within the diasporic space as a postcolonial legacy, here, it is the postcolonial tensions of the originary space that drive migration. Dejected minorities (and their empathetic counterparts) find themselves revalued and free to assert their Black and Brown identities in the 'more tolerant', to use Séverine's terminology, London context.

France's quest for equality is effectively refusing its citizens the right to difference. However, as Chantal, a 48-year-old mother of two, declares: 'integration by force doesn't work'. The founding principles of *laïcité*, namely, to award *all* religions equal status (French Constitution, 1958, Article 1), have over time metamorphosed from tenets of tolerance to an ideology of eradication, of blanket conformity at the expense of diversity. This refusal to embrace, or even 'tolerate', difference is isolating entire sections of French society, be they communities of faith, ethnicity, class or other dissenters from the norm (Gauthier and Jobard, 2018), as confirmed by the rise of the disenfranchised *gilets jaunes* in 2018. 'France's effort to transform non-French [or non-white?] people into citizens is hopeless', according to Séverine, and it is the vanity of such an enterprise, against the comparative indifference of superdiverse London, that motivates much French mobility.

'In Paris, you have to stick to the template'

Valentine argues that '[b]odies are marked by social norms and expectations which shape what we think they can and cannot do' (2001: 49). Accordingly, 'lookism' has attracted increasing cross-disciplinary attention, from law and education to psychology (see DeCastro-Ambrosetti and Cho, 2011; Warhurst *et al.*, 2012; Cavico *et al.*, 2013). Added to this is a cultural dimension, which, in France, has conditioned attitudes and shaped habituses, according to the dominant egalitarian rhetoric. Incorporated materialisations of difference are consequently reprobated in the social space: 'as soon as you distance yourself a bit from the standard look, everyone stares at you' (Focus Group Two comment). Miranda, adorned with multiple tattoos and piercings confirms the sentiment: 'when I go out in Paris, if my legs aren't covered, people are like "oh my God, she's different". When I go back home, people hurl abuse at me in the street. But no one bothers me here.' Such intolerance of difference constituted a key migration trigger for Miranda: 'I was really suffocating in that very judgemental, very narrow-minded village; I really needed to go somewhere nobody knew me'.

In his autobiographical London chronicles, de Roquemaurel underlines the same 'comfortable anonymity' (Favell, 2008a: 37) that migration provides, allowing him to leave behind the 'mental, familial and social structures' (de Roquemaurel, 2014: 164) and enjoy the 'freedom to evolve in a completely anonymous environment, where nothing [he] might have represented in France has the least significance' (2014: 164). Conradson and Latham observe similar postures, with 'the diversity of London [... imparting] a sense of freedom by virtue of a diminished sense of personal visibility (Conradson and Latham, 2007: 241). However, rather than 'a double-edged state' (2007: 248), with simultaneous liberation and disembedding from the familiar networks of the originary space produced among Conradson and Latham's (2005b) participants, my respondents were unanimous in their foregrounding of the emancipatory dimension. This, as Sadia's sartorial testimony shows, is perhaps a corollary of the degree of conformism demanded in the French social space, together with its misogynistic undercurrents:

> There's an aggressive side. Actually, I could never wear a skirt. I put a skirt on about twice, skirt plus high-heels, and it was horrendous. Everyone stares at you. It wasn't a mini-skirt, I'd wear it here no problem. And I know my sister's never dressed 'like a girl' in her entire lifetime.

Sadia demonstrates how non-verbal microaggressions in Paris, especially but not exclusively against women, pressurise them into conforming to the emasculating 'jeans & T-shirt' standard (Huc-Hepher and Drake, 2013: 415).[11] Significantly, this finding concurs with Mulholland and Ryan's study (2017), which itself echoes the search for embodied empowerment among East Asian women migrants (Wang, 2013a). Mulholland and Ryan specifically emphasise the 'freedom from the normative judgement of others' (Mulholland and Ryan, 2017: 143) experienced by their highly skilled London-French respondents and how 'women's presence in the public sphere was seen to be governed by a set of evaluative criteria concerned with how women 'look', [whereas] London was defined as a place where a woman could enjoy autonomy' (2017: 143). However, what does not emerge in Mulholland and Ryan's analysis is how such lookism is fundamentally entwined with everyday sexism in the French social space and how profoundly it can be experienced as an articulation of symbolic violence.

'I experienced the aggression, the sexual aggression'

While France statistically outperforms the UK with regard to the gender pay gap, with a male advantage of 11.6 per cent against 17.9 per cent in the UK (Chamberlain *et al.*, 2019), and its childcare provision, these figures hide the everyday sexism that women respondents recounted and some male participants embodied. The 2011 Dominique Strauss-Khan (DSK) case or 2017 *#BalanceTonPorc* (snitch on your hog) movement (France's #MeToo, launched by Sandra Muller) are high-profile examples of the phenomenon, but the nation's response to such cases is more illuminating.

When several hundred sexual harassment complaints were brought against DSK by Air France clients and staff, internally mitigated by imposing male-only first-class cabin crew on DSK flights, neither the airline nor its union endorsed the claims. When a formal charge of aggravated pimping was brought against him and several other leading figures in France, including powerful entrepreneurs and a police chief, the jury's verdict was acquittal. After silence-breaker Sandra Muller was elected a 2017 Person of the Year in US *Time* magazine, in France she was accused of slander by her alleged aggressor, Eric Brion (represented by a *woman* lawyer). While the *#BalanceTonPorc* movement generated almost a million responses from sexual harassment victims in its first year, it also resulted in widespread opposition from prominent French women. One hundred of these, including Catherine Deneuve, published an open letter in *Le Monde* condemning the movement and defending men's rights. This non-exhaustive list exposes the insidious gendered symbolic violence prevalent in France, where, as Bruno explains, 'that type of sexism is normal', and where there is a universal code of silence (Le Collectif 'Levons l'omerta', 2016), which, until the introduction of the 2018 Schiappa law against sexual harassment in the street and on public transport, had allowed such practices to prosper with impunity.

Confirming the omnipresence of this gendered symbolic violence are the remarks of a US study-abroad student of East Asian heritage, whom I encountered during my fieldwork: 'I didn't go out much in Paris because it was too anxiety-inducive … The men come up to you all the time, greet you in a soft voice, expecting a reaction, or blatantly grope you in the street.' From an intersectional perspective (Crenshaw, 1989), it is significant that she compared this everyday sexism with the everyday racism discovered while studying in the city: 'Paris is quite racist. People would "ni-hao" me all the time. Strangers, they'd just come up to me and say "ni hao".' Conversely, she reported feeling considerably more at ease in London. Her testimony seconds Sadia's recollection of male aggression experienced in Paris. The distinct sartorial/moral standards she professed French women are societally expected to maintain are themselves the incarnation of gendered discrimination brought about by 'l'œil masculin' (Bourdieu, 1998: 136). As Moses unwittingly exemplifies: 'the way I saw some women dress at night [in London], freely, completely undressed; I mean I know they'd be a bit more careful in Paris'. Rather than recognising these dress choices as a materialisation of women's rights, Moses denigrates the reckless nakedness they feel at liberty to reveal, and the very freedom enabling such empowerment. The act of gendered symbolic violence is therefore threefold: a promiscuity-culpability-obliviousness triad. An analogous embodiment of the 'domination masculine' reducing women to 'objets symboliques' (Bourdieu, 1998: 94) was expressed by a Focus Group Two white, male participant. Apparently unaware of the offensiveness of his words, he stated that 'women stay in their place in England. Whereas in France ... they put on a burqa to make people notice them or go out to work just to annoy their husbands'. The intersectional tone of his diatribe and unsuspecting manner, together with the unexpected nature of the intervention, all compounded the violence of his words.

Such normalised misogynism was evoked more explicitly by Sadia later in our conversation. Our coffee was by now cold, but her increasingly heated narrative bore witness to the continued rawness of her wounds:

> I experienced the aggression, the sexual aggression, like from men, like, when I was a teenager actually; they'd look at me, accost me, speak to me, as if ... So, like it traumatised me a bit, and now I see men a bit like ... There's a real 'humph' to it.[12]

The repetitive commonplaceness of these misogynistic acts is conveyed by Sadia's use of the imperfect tense (in French), and the trauma suffered is evidenced through her lexical *lacunae*: the sense of injury is so intense that she struggles to reanimate it through verbal articulation. Suspension points and lexical 'fillers' ('like', 'actually') therefore litter her account. It is this *sexisme ordinaire* (de Beauvoir, 1979) that prevents Sadia from dressing as she desires when in France, and which is still considered by my research participants to pervade the French social space, consequently functioning as a compelling factor in their migration and/or settlement decision-making.

The pressure to conform to an objectified, gendered norm was referenced repeatedly during my field research, regarding the 'collective expectations' of both slimness and sartorial 'sophistication' (Bourdieu, 1998: 88), considered significantly stricter than in London. In their attempt to meet the 'inviting, attractive, available *objects*' standard (1998: 94; original emphasis), French women remain in a permanent state of 'bodily insecurity' (1998: 94). Paulette is enlightening in this regard: 'when I was a student here, I ate at the canteen and actually put on 10 kilos'. However, was the weight-gain due to poor diet or to a relaxing of her internalised aesthetic standards, now less constrained to conform to the myth that '*French Women Don't Get Fat*' (Guiliano, 2007)? Could her decision to resist self-deprivation and shun the thin archetype be apprehended as an act of migratory empowerment, a liberating defiance of the toxic self-objectification noted by Bourdieu (1998: 136)? While these hypotheses are possible, it is significant that, during our discussion, Paulette self-identifies as French only in relation to her sartorially objectivated image: 'Us French – and now I'm saying "we" – we know how to dress, how to combine colours … They find it a bit more difficult here. I wouldn't have taken on an English dress sense. No way.' For Paulette, therefore, it is her aesthetic sensitivity that characterises her Frenchness and distinguishes her – favourably in her eyes – from English women in the migratory field (Benson, 2011).

There is consequently a tension between freedom, on the one hand, and internalised conformism on the other, a point observed by Mulholland and Ryan: 'whilst extolling the virtue of … liberation from the gendered regimes of control associated with women's public presentations of self in Paris, our female participants commonly took significant pride in, and attached importance to, what they deemed to be their own, nationally-characteristic, good taste in clothes' (2017: 144). In some ways, this diasporic tension reinvents the tension between the 'galanterie' supposedly intrinsic to French society (Poirier, 2006: 80) and proclaimed by one faction of French feminists (Ozouf, 1995; Théry, 2011), which the 2018 Deneuve open-letter defends, and Agnès Poirier considers to constitute France's femininity (Poirier, 2006: 80). Paradoxically, such 'feminism' recalls and perpetuates the 'considerate, submissive, discreet, restrained, erased even' femininity described by Bourdieu as a manifestation of 'masculine domination' (1998: 94). However, the romantically versed 'French touch' praised by Poirier and Ozouf and framed as 'séduction féministe' by some (Fassin, 2012), is often experienced as retrograde and oppressive by women who have moved to London and observed a different form of feminism. Rather than perceive the diasporic social space as masculine, virile, cruel and aggressive (Poirier, 2006), French women experience it as liberated and liberating. Only through the retrospective prism of their migratory positioning do they become aware of the 'countless, often subliminal, injuries inflicted by the male order' (Bourdieu, 1998: 128) and, as symbolic violence dictates, tacitly buttressed by women. Eric Brion's lawyer, Agnès Poirier and the one hundred signatories of the anti-#*BalanceTonPorc* open letter are but several examples of a societally embedded phenomenon. As Fassin explained in the wake of the DSK case, 'we really have to acknowledge the permanency of a certain sexism *à la française* that has had free rein' (Fassin, 2012: 48).

'We can hold hands without fear of being insulted'

In addition to acknowledging everyday sexism and normalised misogynistic microaggressions as tacit migration drivers, here I challenge the typical 'heterosexism of diaspora research' (Dhoest, 2018: 35) and early twenty-first-century gender studies (Fassin, 2015), and bring homosexuality into the gender/migration debate. Understanding contemporary mobility requires an understanding of the intersectional logics of the migrant experience (Salcedo Robledo, 2019). Thus, from a focus on race and gender, I now address sexuality, as experienced by one interviewee, who evokes the singular role played by homophobic mentalities in his mobility.

The longer Robert and I speak, the more he shares closely guarded experiences with me. Hindsight allows memories of small-minded attitudes towards homosexuality to resurface: 'I wanted to leave; I'd fallen out with my parents about my sexuality … It's a lot more closed in France, still. People too. I feel like people in England don't really care.' His migration acted as a protective barrier against the non-acceptance of his sexuality, a form of rejection also experienced at university: 'I had friends who turned their back on me when they found out I was gay. But that's never happened here. I don't feel that burden.' The homophobic symbolic violence permeated Robert's professional life also: 'it was heavy-going. I had to hide it in certain spheres; I was uncomfortable saying it. But I've never felt uncomfortable saying it here.' According to Bourdieu (1998) and Chauvin (2005), Robert's onerous experience of his sexuality in France stems from the shame engendered through his incorporation of the negative forces surrounding him. Caught between a fear of revealing his sexuality and a need to assert it, Robert's mobility is thus more than 'ideological' migration (Chiswick, 2008: 64), it is an escape, if not asylum per se, as Fassin's reference to 'sexual exile' implies (Salcedo Robledo, 2019: 174). Indeed, London, like Amsterdam for Favell's gay participant, constitutes a space of protection 'from the intolerant, the xenophobic, the small-minded. From persecution. From ingrained tradition, hierarchy privilege, thoughtless social reproduction. From other people's norms. From where you've come from' (Favell, 2008a: 5). Migration, then, granted Robert the right to *'invisible visibility'* (Bourdieu, 1998: 165; original emphasis) denied in France, where his identity was reduced to nothing more than his queerness. Like for Paulette in racial terms, and for Dhoest's (2018) gay participants, mobility is a liberation allowing for the affirmation of a new subjectivity.

Reflecting the extent of symbolic injury suffered in the French social space, the prospect of return migration remains slim for Robert, just as it was rejected by Paulette, both preferring 'express visits' to borrow Paulette's phrasing. Having 'move[d] increasingly further away from their old self, their family, and their old peer group … the "old" has become foreign and dislocating, while the "new" is now familiar and reassuring' (Lehmann, 2013: 9). Being perceived as an outsider in his native country, in a paradoxical inversion of the traditional model, Robert's return visits serve both as a painful reminder and a deterrent:

> [In London] we can hold hands without fear of being insulted or even feeling threatened. But last weekend we went to France, and at the bank there was a moment's silence when we announced we were a couple. And on the Saturday evening at a pizzeria, the waiter blatantly asked: 'but are you a couple?' That's the first time anyone's ever asked us directly. In London, people understand we're a couple, in a subtle way. But there's always this silence and need for justification there. People always ask 'so how's it going for you as a couple?', even though it's very personal and very private. That's something which bothers me in that French town.

Instead of his migrant status creating a positionality of otherness (Sayad, 1999) in London, it is Robert's sexuality that marginalises him in France. It is significant that during his fifteen years in London, only once has he fallen victim to a remark related to his sexuality; meanwhile in France, it is a regular occurrence, penetrating the family habitat itself. This implicit heteronormative othering from within the confines of the domestic space is identified by Valentine: 'Although home is supposed to be a medium for the expression of individual identity, a site of creativity or a symbol of the self, in practice this can mean that family homes express a hetero-sexual identity … while gay identities of individual household members are submerged or concealed. Because of this, many sexual dissidents can feel "out of place" and that they do not belong "at home"' (Valentine, 2001: 84).

This sense of unease, particularly in its extension to the wider social field, was the primary, yet underlying, cause of Robert's mobility. Emanating from a social space where conforming to the dominant model is a prereq-uisite for integration, and where, in Robert's words, the 'redneck' repre-sents the 'contemporary hero' of 'life revolved around family meals and Sunday-best', Robert's sexuality has affectively, effectively and irrevocably distanced him from the 'homeland'. In stark contrast to both his provin-cial and cosmopolitan French experiences (Mulholland and Ryan, 2017), London provides a setting in which Robert can 'fit in', not to a distinct gay community as such (Dhoest, 2018) but, all the more legitimately, to the established, heterosexual community (Bourdieu, 1998). Moreover, living in a predominantly 'straight street' in London (Valentine, 2001: 221), where he is now on Christmas-card terms with his Catholic neighbours, the invisibility Robert desired premigration is achieved through the very commonplaceness of his visibility (Fassin, 2015).

Conclusion

By examining symbolic violence in France's educational and professional fields, as well as in the broader social space, and focusing on affective forces as opposed to neo-classical structuralist or functionalist dimensions of migration (Wang, 2013a), in this chapter I have revealed often unarticulated, and hence overlooked, mobility triggers. Whether regarding the inequitable 'equality' of the classroom, the rigid hierarchical stratification of the workplace, the social capital drawn on in the pivotal space between the two, or the racialised and gendered symbolic violence permeating the social field, their role as insidious migration drivers was unequivocal.

London, as a diverse, multicultural, 'denationalised' (Block, 2006: 45) global city (Beaverstock, 2002, 2005) is often conceptualised as a magnet for those seeking opportunity and openness (Huc-Hepher and Drake, 2013), and, as such, studies focus on the appeal/advantages of London and migrant relationships within the capital (Ryan and Mulholland, 2013, 2014a, 2014b). However, they rarely scrutinise the social factors influencing mobility in the originary field. Non-economic, non-lifestyle factors in the premigration space are commonly underplayed if not altogether ignored, particularly in the case of intra-EU migration, the agents of which are referred to in positive, somewhat whimsical terms, as free movers (Braun and Arsene, 2009) and Eurostars (Favell, 2008a), which underplays the seriousness of their motivations. By setting the research participants' current situation within the comparative context of the premigration field, I have demonstrated *why* my interviewees and other French migrants conceive of London in these optimistic, open-minded, cosmopolitan terms. It is precisely the *contrast* that London constitutes in relation to the originary social space, even compared to the French capital (Mulholland and Ryan, 2017), that increases its appeal. Therefore, if the field of origin is not examined as an integral component of the migratory process and experience, any assessment of motivations or search for reasons remains wanting.

Through my exploration of the deep-seated social, political and cultural factors underpinning participants' mobility, important differences perceived between France and the UK have emerged as fundamental to the mobility process. Instead of envisaging both nations as relatively alike in broad socio-economic, demographic and cultural terms, as is often the case in macro-level migration research, which brushes over the significant meso- and micro-level triggers explored here (Van Hear *et al.*, 2018), I have provided the cultural insights that the study of migration in a diasporic vacuum overlooks. My nuanced understanding of the negative symbolic forces identified in France, considered less pervasive in pre-2016 London, constitutes an essential component of the sociocultural complex that is migration. In acknowledging the specificities of 'female immigration' (Salcedo Robledo, 2019: 174), as well as contributing to the developing conversation on 'sexual migrations' (2019: 174), I have demonstrated the inherently intersectional nature of migration, whose affective, incorporated dimensions cannot be disentangled from the overlapping (national) politics of migration, race and gender. Questioning the implicit push factors in France has also provided a necessary backdrop for the subsequent chapters of this monograph.

Notes

1 The inconsistency between collective imaginings and experiential knowledge of the systems is borne out by statistical data: in 2015, the UK outperformed France in science (15th position, compared to 27th respectively) and reading (20th against 21st) (OECD PISA rankings).

2 Neuroimaging has shown that the areas of the brain activated by symbolic violence, in this case social rejection, are identical to those affected by physical pain (Kross *et al.*, 2011).

3 Becoming a teacher is highly competitive in France's state-funded system. Most fail at least twice and, indeed, may never make the grade (see Block, 2006). Applicants compete in a national *concours* for the CAPES (le Certificat d'Aptitude au Professorat de l'Enseignement du Second degré), to fill a limited number of positions each year, guaranteeing lifelong employment.

4 British legislation acknowledges 'intimidating, hostile, degrading, humiliating or offensive' behaviour as harassment (*Equality Act*, 2010), but being based on age, disability, gender, race, religion, belief, sex or sexual orientation, it excludes class, socio-economic background and more nuanced manifestations of habitus.

5 French law is more equitable in this respect, but not applicable to an educational, teacher–student context because harassment falls either under employment or 'school harassment' in its inter-student form. The wording is, however, geared towards *emotional effects* as opposed to personal or social equality criteria, as in the UK, and resonates with Bourdieu's terminology: 'Psychological harassment is a form of insidious violence' (Service Public, no date).

6 In a survey conducted in 2010 (among 4,156 respondents), 41 per cent associated France above any other country with the word *piston*, against 3 per cent for England (*Le Monde*, 2010). 88 per cent thought high-placed social connections took precedence over talent when seeking work in France, and, complicit in the cycle of symbolic violence, 75 per cent admitted they would accept preferential

treatment through social ties if the opportunity arose, despite 40 per cent considering it unfair (*L'Express*, 2010).

7 According to Decree no. 2014–610 of 13 June 2014, the top 10 per cent of *baccalauréat* students in every lycée in France will be offered *classes préparatoires* places (two-year courses to prepare students for the *grandes écoles concours*). However, given the twofold written and oral test, it remains to be seen whether these positive changes will prevent discrimination at the subsequent *concours* stage.

8 'On' is translated here as 'you' to prevent the unintended social connotations of 'one' in English.

9 Although ethnic-minority representation in French advertising and media slowly increased in the 2010s, it came alongside state-led articulations of Islamophobia, such as the 2010 burqa ban or the 2016 burkini ban.

10 French law forbids the collection or processing of 'personal data which, directly or indirectly, reveals ethnic or racial origins ... or religious opinions' (*French Data Protection Act*, 1978: Article 8).

11 Brice, a 34-year-old business/IT consultant, and other male participants also reported being 'more at ease here now than in France, [because] you can wear anything whatsoever and no-one will notice'.

12 It is significant that *agression sexuelle* is ambivalent in French, meaning both sexual aggression and assault. This ambivalence increases the partiality of the translation, but also attests to a lack of differentiation in the collective consciousness, which belittles the significance of the 'assault'.

2

Looking in:
windows onto intimate London habitats
and homemaking across cultures

Introduction

[D]espite movement to a new field, there are ultimately limits to the possibilities of reinventing and transforming habitus. (Oliver and O'Reilly, 2010: 25)

Metaphorically defined as a 'virtual backpack' (Peters, 2014: 108) or soup
(O'Reilly, 2014), habitus is potentially mutable, yet engrained and 'durable'
(Bourdieu, 1980a: 88). In this chapter, I move away from the migration
motivations of the remembered originary field and focus on habitus in the
diasporic context. Having mapped out the physical places and spaces occupied by the London French in the Introduction, I return here to the material lifeworlds of my respondents and explore individualised processes of
emplacement (Ryan and Mulholland, 2015; Ryan, 2018; Wessendorf and
Phillimore, 2018) and homemaking (Walsh, 2006; Levin, 2016) in London.
Subdividing Bourdieu's original habitus concept into a triad composed
of habitat, habituation and habits, the following three chapters, broadly
speaking, examine participants' material homes, attitudinal change and
evolving practices respectively. In this chapter, I therefore delve into the
intimate interiors of my London-French participants. Like Walsh, I reject
the limited conception of 'intimate' as '*either* the negotiation of transnational family life ... or the negotiation of sexualities and romance' (Walsh,
2018: 146; original emphasis). Rather, I shift the emphasis away from the
directly interpersonal and apprehend intimacy in the *intimated* form suggested by Hage (1997), reading into the affective *intimations* of migrants'
material habitats.

Bourdieu distinguishes between primary habitus (family upbringing/
childhood) and secondary habitus (formal education/towards adulthood)
to acknowledge its potential for change despite its typically *reproductive*
nature. However, this binary distinction is somewhat over-simplistic, for
habitus is more plastic in practice, possessing both 'a generative capacity'
and the possibility to 'be *changed by history*, that is by new experiences'

(Bourdieu, 2005: 46, 45; original emphasis). This potential for change is particularly pertinent in the context of migration, where it is the rule rather than the exception to develop what could be called a 'tertiary' habitus, to extend Bourdieu's construct, conceptualised elsewhere as a 'third times-pace' (Sprio, 2013: 61, citing Lavie and Swedenburg, 1996), an 'ethnicised habitus' (Noble, 2013: 351), a 'diasporic habitus' (Parker, 2000: 75), a 'transnational habitus' (Kelly and Lusis, 2006), or, more figuratively, a 'patchworked existence' (Mata Codesal, 2008: 15), all of which attempt to encapsulate the complexity of migrant subjectivities.

Like a backpack whose contents evolve over the course of its owner's travels but whose basic form remains unchanged, or a soup, the ingredients of which may be enriched as it matures while the underlying stock is a constant, the habitus of a migrant is at once fundamentally rooted in its sociocultural origins and open to transformation. While there may be 'limits' (Oliver and O'Reilly, 2010: 25), the scope for habitus to evolve is significantly greater for migrants than 'stayers' (Favell, 2008a: ix; Braun and Arsene, 2009), given their exposure to new ways of experiencing the world in new fields and communities of people and practice (Block, 2006).

In this chapter, using on-land oral and observational evidence, I explore how participants' habitus of origin is both transposed to the postmigration setting (Bourdieu, 1980a: 88) and transformed therein (Thatcher and Halvorsrud, 2016), and whether there are any common threads which weave together to form a unified 'London-French habitus'. Although in any discussion of habitus it is necessary to acknowledge Bourdieu's twinned concept of field, for the 'habitus of concrete social practices does not exist in a vacuum of social relations' (Friedmann, 2005: 315–16), it is not my intention in the following three chapters to devote detailed attention to London-French field(s) dynamics. This is partly due to the field-level forces examined in Chapter 1 and readdressed in Chapter 5, and partly to my ethnographic approach, stemming from an arguably more habitus-centric disciplinary tradition, concerned with micro-level (Favell, 2008b) (material) culture and kinship (Miller, 2005: 15), as opposed to meso- or macro-level societal structures. It is nevertheless important to recognise London-French habitus as being set within, and contingent on, not only the field (external habitat) of the migration setting, conceivable as an overarching 'migratory' or 'diasporic' field (as in Oliver and O'Reilly's usage), but also between multiple subfields within which daily practices (or habits) are negotiated, such as the fields of work, leisure, accommodation, schooling, and so on. To operate effectively in these manifold fields, migrants must learn the (usually unarticulated) rules of the city (Noble, 2013; Thatcher and Halvorsrud, 2016), which are, to varying degrees of subtlety, different from those to which they are accustomed (habituated).

The following discussion of habitus should, therefore, be understood as inextricably linked to the diasporic field, for field and habitus are mutually constructive (Bourdieu and Wacquant, 1992), despite the confines of this book not accommodating a detailed mapping of the broader social structures involved. Although the crude deconstruction of habitus into a triad of habitat, habituation and habits could be seen as reductive, denying the concept its singular position at the interface of subjectivity and objectivity, and rendering it 'a mere principle of repetition', rather than 'a dynamic system of dispositions that interact with one another' (Bourdieu, 2005: 46), my intention is that the triad be envisaged as an inherently interconnected construct: if one element were removed, the triangle would collapse. Similarly, like the individual within the social field who cannot but experience it through a subjective interaction, this triad is an 'attempt to transcend subjects and objects' (Miller, 2005: 11) and explore the extent to which 'home and its inhabitants transform each other' (Miller, 2001: 2). In a reiteration of the self-consciously 'simplistic, artificial, and elusive' distinction made by Levin 'between the two sides of the home/house – its tangible and intangible characters' (Levin, 2016: 45), the habitat-habituation-habit triad allows me to unpack the overlapping subjectivities and objectivities of habitus for the sake of analytical ease and clarity.

Since home is often defined as 'a medium for the expression of individual identity, a site of creativity or a symbol of the self' (Valentine, 2001: 84), or, as Miller posits, a blank canvas for its inhabitants, the artists (Miller, 2010: 85), and since homes offer material insights into migrants' 'aspirations' (Benson, 2011: 117), 'sense of possibility' (Hage, 1997: 102–3) and 'assimilation' (Lozanovska, 2008: 1; Miller, 2010: 98), they concretise the habitus dynamics between the internalisation of external structures and subsequent re-externalisation thereof (Bourdieu, 1972). In this chapter, I argue that the ambivalent subject–object habitus dialectic has much in keeping with the meaning of 'home' itself in the English language. Rather than distinguishing between home and house as Levin does (2016), I argue that both the materiality of 'house' and affectivity of 'home' are encompassed in the single term: home. Similarly, by studying migrants' belongings within the home, we learn as much about their sense of belonging as their sense of longing (Levin, 2016: 24–5). Household artefacts can thus be seen as a materialisation of diasporic selfhood (Dudley, 2011), capturing the spatial (here/there), temporal (then/now), incorporated (inner/outer), and scalar (glocal (Robertson, 1995)) dynamics of (be)longing (Divita, 2018). I therefore look closely at the intimate physical spaces inhabited by participants and the ways in which they reconstruct a 'French' home, transferring material elements of the originary culture to the London space to recreate a sense of the familiar, a sense of belonging, and how they make use of

French broadcasting channels to mediate their migratory positioning. In so doing, I build on research by numerous scholars, who have approached migrant materialities and everyday placemaking practices from a variety of disciplinary perspectives, including Hage (1997), Law (2001), Petridou (2001), Sutton (2001), Ali-Ali and Koser (2002), Tolia-Kelly (2004), Blunt and Dowling (2006), Basu and Coleman (2008), Hardwick (2008), Lozanovzka (2008), Mata-Codesal (2008), Miller (2001, 2010), Benson (2011), Dudley (2011), Ho and Hatfield (2011), Levin (2016), Wang (2016) and Walsh (2006, 2018). Like Hardwick, the particular focus of my analysis of individual material habitats will be the ways in which they are 'spatially interwoven' (2008: 170) with the originary habitat, that is, concretised recollections of the homeland. In addition, and despite respondents' overwhelming assertions that they are not members of a London-French community, I demonstrate how common patterns of transposed originary 'fractal habitus' (Rowsell, 2011: 333) unite them in a collective whole, with a distinct London-French identity.

Constructing home, constructing community?

The concept of home in English, like the German *Heimat*, Welsh *hiraeth* or Portuguese *saudade*, is highly personal, place-/space-specific and conceptually elastic (Neto, 2019). There is no equivalent in French, which restricts the concept to either the subjective, personal *chez moi* dimension or the objectivated, material *à la maison* interpretation. In English, however, like the concept of habitus, home is intrinsically multidimensional (Longhurst *et al.*, 2009; King *et al.*, 2014; Levin, 2016). Crossing spatialities and temporalities, home is a 'site in which we live. But, more than this, home is an idea and an imaginary that is imbued with feelings' (Blunt and Dowling, 2006: 2). Consequently, home can be one's main family abode, the country where one is living, or the country from which one originates. Ultimately, 'home is where' and 'home is when one belongs' (Mata Codesal, 2008: 4), although in some cases, it can be associated with feelings of alienation (Valentine, 2001) or violence (Blunt and Varley, 2004).

Like habitus, home is subject and object, a reciprocally constructive dynamic within the individual and outside; it is a physical place or 'residence' (Blunt, 2005: 506), but also a 'dwelling' composed of people, feelings and 'lived experiences' (Blunt, 2005: 509). The idiom, 'home is where the heart is', conjures the affective familiarity which is felt when 'at home', whether that is a country, a land, a *terroir* or a bedroom. The expressions 'to feel at home' or 'make oneself at home' imply a space where one feels relaxed, at ease, somewhere one belongs and can relinquish external, societal guards and slacken politeness codes. Like habitus, therefore, home is where there is an implicit understanding and a common (family and cultural) heritage, which, as Bonnerjee *et al.* contend (2012), means that it can be understood as a space for common understanding and practices to extend from the private, personal level to that of the public sphere of the community as a whole.

Community is also one of the four core feelings associated with home by Hage, the others being security, familiarity and, as mentioned, a sense of possibility (Hage, 1997). The shared experience of home leads to the transfer of tacit knowledge and complicit communication, which, like habitus, allows communities of practice (Wenger, 1998, 2004) and communities of thought to evolve, implicitly and pre-reflexively. I therefore argue that objectivated diasporic commonalities could be seen to represent cohesive subjectivities and, as such, a sense of community belonging that transcends the dichotomy of belonging either to a national conception of the homeland or the diasporic space. This shared sense of self could also be apprehended as a tacit mechanism to overcome the 'longing that is both a motive and consequence of belonging and that which resists it' (Ilcan, 2002: 2–3, cited in Levin, 2016: 24–5).

Beginning with Bruno's physical habitat, it becomes immediately clear that aspects of the primary and secondary habitus have been transposed to his personal, tertiary, diasporic space. Since his arrival in 1991, aged 19, he has resided in several London locations, from Maida Vale to Pimlico, then moving south of the river to Peckham and Dulwich. He has now settled in West Norwood, where a French-run café named Cul de Sac opened in 2013 and the French language can often be heard in surrounding streets. The habitat of Bruno's home is telling as regards his migrant habitus. In the same way that the habitats of the British in the Lot revealed hordes of 'Marmite, tea bags, mango chutney, baked beans, salt and vinegar crisps, McVitie's chocolate biscuits, and Angel Delight instant dessert' (Benson, 2011: 142) or that Kerenni refugees consume specific foods in order to feel at home (Dudley, 2011), so Bruno's house bears the material mark of trips to French supermarkets and visits to relatives 'back home'. His cellar (Figure 5) is filled with €2 bottles of rustically labelled Clairet, fine Bordeaux Graves, and a few bottles of Ricard and Rivesaltes, which lie in waiting alongside less copious reserves of Teisseire menthe and grenadine cordials, tins of d'Aucy petits pois, La Belle Chaurienne cassoulet and saucisses de Toulouse aux lentilles, jars of raw-egg Bénédicta and Lesieur mayonnaise, home-made pâté, rillettes, foie gras, confits de canard and confiture de reine-claude (greengage jam). Voluptuous bulbs of plaited white garlic hang from the rafters and a small recipient labelled *piment d'Espelette* stands on the shelf next to the Peugeot pepper mill, both overlooking a bowl

Figure 5 Supplies of menthe cordial and pâté in Bruno's south London cellar

(made of olive wood from Nice – a family gift) filled with hazelnuts from his brother's Pessac tree.

It is significant that the material elements of Bruno's habitat he has transposed from the 'homeland' are those imbued with affective meanings, closely connected to memories of particular people: family, close friends and places: familiar, personal territories. This resonates with the practices of many other migrant communities, such as the Italians in Britain, where 'olives recently picked from a family member's tree served as a memory of that person as well as being something to be consumed' (Sprio, 2013: 162). Thus, through a process of mobilising elements from one material space, Bruno reconstructs a familiar/al environment in another, which corroborates Miller's assertion that food 'helps people to constitute a "home from home" at a time when people are increasingly having to live with a more portable concept of their home' (Miller, 2001: 9). However, this reconstitution of home is not limited to edible items in Bruno's habitat. Lidless, upturned wine crates bearing the names of Sauternes, Médoc and Côte de Blaye have been reconfigured into original, unmistakably culture-specific shelving for French DVDs, from *nouvelle vague* classics to childhood *Bronzés* comedies, providing further insight into Bruno's provenance,

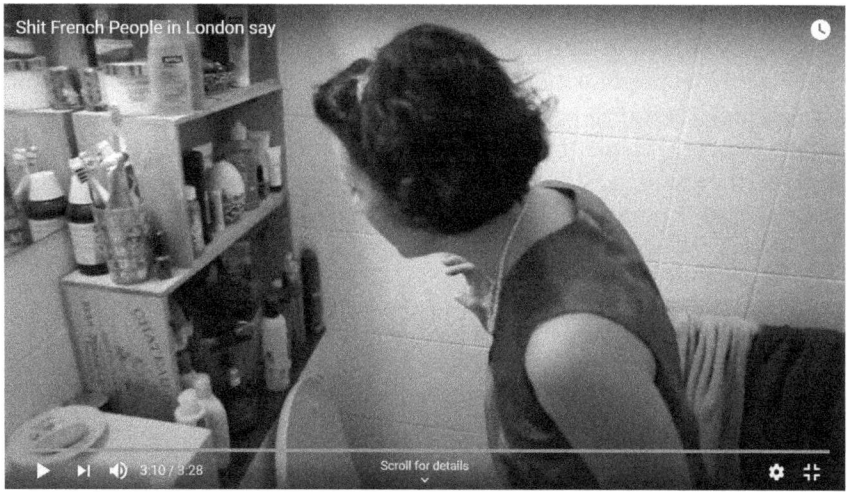

Figure 6 Still from amateur film *Shit French People in London Say*

as well as the wine they once housed. His bathroom is equipped with year-long supplies of organic, paraben-free toiletries and Petit Marseillais soap, and a medicine cabinet stocked with Doliprane and Aspégic analgesics.

Another French Londoner's intimate habitat, preserved on film in a sharp satire of French quotidian life in the capital, is illustrated in Figure 6. The short film transcends the comedic, however, demonstrating the demographic myths discussed in the Introduction to this book and the distinction (Bourdieu, 1979a) between French residents in 'South Ken' and 'New Cross' (significantly in the borough of Lewisham), embodied through a transposition of the originary habitus by the 'actors'. The film also serves to 'emphasise the disruptions to the sensorial and social worlds of the migrant, [and] to illustrate a mismatch between habitus and field' (Noble, 2013: 349). For example, in addition to featuring the illicit sale of products collectively deemed lacking in the migratory field, such as grenadine cordial and 'fraises Tagada' confectionery, characters appear standing on the *left-hand side* of an underground escalator, much to the displeasure of local residents, having broken the unsaid rule. Of singular pertinence to Bruno's material 'lifeworld' (Friedmann, 2005: 330), however, is that the frame shows his is not unique. Instead, the objects suggest the existence of a 'typical' London-French habitat and the practical emergence of a community identity, underscored by the film's parodic caricaturing of community characteristics.

The bathroom products and makeshift wine-crate shelving observed in Bruno's habitat and other homes visited during my fieldwork also feature in this frame. Bruno's objectified habitat is thus recalibrated within a broader, culturally defined interpersonal context that weaves an imperceptible web among disparate 'members' of the London-French community, thus reinforcing their expression of national identity (Tolia-Kelly, 2003). Supporting this argument are the – equally semiotically loaded – domestic materialities alluded to by Miranda. Despite having migrated to London from the Aube region 10 years ago, she recounts running 'desperately low on Ricoré', a coffee-based product unavailable in most London foodstores, and how in her Brick Lane (East London) flat:

> there are clues [that I'm French]: things to make *madeleine* and *cannelé* cakes, the pressure cooker, my French ice-cream maker; yeah, I've actually got quite a lot of French stuff, my kettle's French, the blenders ... And I've got loads of French beauty products: little soaps, surgical spirit, because you can't find it here, yes, mainly beauty products.

Her account underlines the commonality between the participants' habitats and their shared articulation of cultural positioning in the diasporic field, which supports the notion of a defined sense of a London-French habitat and habitus. For, as Leach asserts, '[a]s individuals identify with an environment, so their identity comes to be constituted through that environment. This relates not only to individual identity, but also to group identities' (Leach, 2005: 308). The French elements of Miranda's flat implicitly connect it to Bruno's house and others', thereby providing insight into their shared homemaking practices and group belonging (Levin, 2016). Through the mutual idiosyncratic interior 'design' choices that Lozanovska terms the 'mild aesthetics' (2008: 1) of the migrant home and the everyday objects of their intimate habitats, such as the wine crates or the madeleine and cannelé moulds (which also furnish Bruno's kitchen, together with a French pressure cooker and blender), the 'community' simultaneously, yet subtly (Pink, 2004), asserts its identity. Furthermore, the banal components of their objectified diasporic habitus serve to distinguish the migrants from their middle-class, Francophile, English neighbours. For although they also carry the material 'memories of well-spent holidays' back to Britain 'to recreate the holiday experience and fantasy' (Sprio, 2013: 154) in the form of French wine, crockery and so on, they are less likely to bring back French analgesics and pressure cookers – practical items which bind my London-French participants and silently speak of their shared homemaking practices.

Moreover, like Bruno, the features of Miranda's material habitat she considers markedly French are objects housed in the kitchen and bathroom: those which ultimately lead to incorporation. The traditional notion of 'immigrant incorporation' (Schmitter Heisler, 2008: 86), whereby the 'receiving' society incorporates its migrant communities, is therefore inverted, as here, elements of the 'sending' society are incorporated in individual migrant homes and bodies (Smith, 2005). The objects Miranda lists are also telling in their extension beyond the food itself to the *process* of preparing it. They point to the ritualistic potency of food preparation within the migrant home (Sutton, 2001; Dudley, 2011) and its symbolic function as a marker of distinctiveness within the wider social space (Bourdieu, 1979a). Petridou (2001) highlights it in her description of the pleasure taken by Greek students in London when collectively preparing food for each other and their English counterparts who 'don't cook. They prepare sandwiches' (Petridou, 2001: 94). The students assert their Greekness by rejecting the ready-meals, frozen foods and tinned vegetables that fill the shelves of local London supermarkets. By favouring process over efficient – yet tasteless – end-products, they actively distinguish themselves from the 'host' population, just as Miranda and Bruno affirm their Frenchness through the French foods they store, prepare and re-experience in the diasporic habitat. In a reversal of Benson's respondents' quest for authentic local living (2011), therefore, my participants and other EU migrants in London set their habitats apart from the local surroundings through the material performance of their nationally framed culinary authenticity, played out as status hierarchies of taste (Levin, 2016; Murphy, 2018).

In addition to the kitchen and bathroom products Miranda and Bruno ritualistically stock, Bruno's hallway contains two vintage French racing bikes (Figure 7), which he rides to his gastronomic workplace in central London: 'Two years ago, I would've said public transport annoyed me most here, but now I use a bike every day to go to work, so that's progress, or rather, it doesn't annoy me any more … Public transport here's packed full of people, it's expensive, it's often late and it's dirty.' We see, then, how the 'networks that supported a diverse range of opportunities were also at times a source of frustration', as Conradson and Latham contend (2007: 243).

Bruno's bicycles are therefore the material manifestation of a release from the pressure that the global city's congested arteries bring, 'the flip-side of London's "buzz"' (2007: 244). But beyond their practical advantages of reliability and cost-effectiveness, the Condor and Motobécane are incarnations of deeper meanings related to distinctive '[p]ractices of cleanliness' (Petridou, 2001: 96) and freedom. They revive memories of youthful independence experienced in the premigration habitat, while simultaneously compensating for the claustrophobia experienced in the London space that Bruno describes: 'From time to time I feel a bit hemmed in here because … it's hard to get outside London to go and see something different, because it takes so long to get out that you think twice before doing anything outside town. And the sensation's increased by the fact we're on an island.' His testimony invokes the agentive power of the city, not as a magnet to entice prospective migrants, as evidenced by Scott (2006) and

Figure 7 A Motobécane bicycle in Bruno's hall

Mulholland and Ryan (2017), but as an oppressive force to prevent them
from leaving. He bears witness to the internalised tension brought about
by the city's hold over him and his 'struggl[e] to reconcile [his] indigenous
culture (habitus) with those objectified [urban] cultures' of the migratory
field (Robbins, 2005: 21). The spatio-temporal relocation of bicycles from
Bruno's primary habitat consequently mitigate the disquieting mismatch
between remembered and current cultures. They 'construct a material
bridge' between the divide (Levin, 2016: 205) and provide an intimation
(Hage, 1997) of Bruno's settlement tactics.

An alternative strategy that Bruno adopts, to counter the oppression
generated by the sheer volume of London's eight million inhabitants, in
contrast to the million-strong population of his 'hometown' (Bordeaux), is
found to the exterior of his London home. From the south-facing wall of the
Victorian, semi-detached, London-brick house protrudes the arm of a satellite dish, carefully positioned to receive French television signals and symbolically pointing in the direction of the *terre patrie*, acting as a constant

reminder of his premigration home and devoid of the (English) class significations to which Fox alludes (2014).[1] The parabola holds implicit meanings nonetheless, which, like Bruno's bicycles, transcend functionality. In this transnational domestic space, objects superficially of transportational and communicational value are instead the materialisation of memories of a culture left behind (Tolia-Kelly, 2004) and highly charged with personal and environmental (Blunt and Dowling, 2006) mythologised meanings. Integral to the materiality of the bike is, for Bruno, the intangible practice of annually watching the Tour de France, live via the satellite dish. This reconnects him not only with the French landscapes of his youth, but with dormant memories of a previous existence: picnicking with his late paternal Basque grandfather on the verges of Pyrenean lanes, or repairing a *vélo de course* with his late maternal Italian grandfather. The satellite dish allows him to inhabit an in-betweenness, suspended spatio-temporally between the here of his present and the there of his past, 'haunted by pleasures past, present and future' (Pile, 2005: 236). Levin refers to this as a 'hybrid existence' (2016: 186), where pre- and postmigration cultures are merged and where 'the house lets migrants express these hidden parts of their habitus' (2016: 184). However, it is an in-betweenness that extends beyond Bordeaux/London cultures, involving simultaneous dialectics of objectified presence and subjectivised past, 'a double hauntedness … material and spectral … present and absent' (Pile, 2005: 248), because '[o]ne's past is forever apparent in its ghostly presence' (Sprio, 2013: 225).

The materiality constitutive of Bruno's fractal habitus is therefore 'stuff' (Miller, 2010) which wordlessly whispers tales of return journeys to family in the Pyrenees, of the 'annual ritual (unload and reload)' (King and Christou, 2008: 15) to replenish supplies of home-slaughtered and -prepared *cochon*. A muted recounting of Bruno's past visits to French supermarkets, to stock up on the cornichons, moutarde de Dijon and biscottes, unfolds through the presence of these objects in his London habitat. They narrate his heavy-hearted northward drive, at the end of the summer, unsure whether his dolefulness is due to the renewed upheaval from the 'home' habitat, where he was at ease in his native culture, or whether the melancholy is the same as that experienced by other holiday-makers once the sojourn and the season near their inevitable end. As King and Christou (2008: 18) emphasise,

> when return visits take place, they occur at a time of year (summer) and to places (villages, the seaside, islands) which are redolent of a holiday atmosphere where life is lived outdoors and at a leisurely pace. For the returning family on holiday, the homeland is indeed a 'big playground' where life is to be enjoyed away from work, and money spent not earned.

In these terms, the ritual pilgrimage to the 'homeland' and replenishment of vital supplies place the migrant in the position of both outsider and insider: 'roots tourist' (Wessendorf, 2007; King and Christou, 2008: 10) and local inhabitant, experiencing the remembered and since mythologised 'home' through an exoticising lens. Thus, the culinary products tightly packed into Bruno's car on the northbound route will serve to keep the myth alive on his return to the diasporic habitat. They will build 'little pockets of resemblance', which remind him 'of a certain feeling, a certain image, or a certain experience ... in relation to ... former houses or pasts' (Levin, 2016: 183). Ultimately, they will be ingested by Bruno, serving as a literal embodiment of his Frenchness, the primordial part which is most deeply embedded in his subconscious being. By bringing back these edible goods from his homeland, he is paving the way for a sustained carnal connection with his habitat of origin, one that can be hoarded, admired (re)visited, anticipated, then physically consumed and digested, during which an intense, sensuous proximity to the tastes, smells, sounds and preparers of the food and drinks of Bruno's primary habitus are vividly, if not entirely consciously, recollected and given form (Pink, 2004; Longhurst *et al.*, 2009).

Miller defines the intense physicality of eating and drinking elements of one's originary habitus in almost alchemistic terms, with 'food, cooking and eating, [turning] the superficial quality of taste into something that is sufficiently profound and rooted that it can appear as a more solid version of home than the mere house or flat in which [migrants] reside' (Miller, 2001: 9). Thus, their inclusion in Bruno's home, as objects and consumables, serves to construct a habitat that incorporates material elements of his premigration habitus, spanning the spatio-temporal gap (Law, 2001) alluded to and creating a transnational, or more accurately a translocal (Smith, 2001; White, 2011), space that encapsulates the 'habitus-turned-habitat' (Friedmann, 2005: 328) that Bourdieu described in his ethnographic study of the Kabyle house (1980a).

Reinforcing the sense of a collective rite, many of the London-French narratives recorded during my fieldwork include allusions to foodstuffs 'religiously' transported from the habitat of origin to that of adoption, retracing the same migratory pathways as the individuals themselves.[2] In Gabaccia's study of the 'yo-yo migration' (Brettell, 2008: 117, citing Margolis, 1995) routes of tomatoes, pasta and pizza, she illustrates how '[p]eople crossing borders carry along the tastes and sometimes also the seeds, recipes and ingredients of their homes' (Gabaccia, 2006: 1). Benson (2011), however, underscores the paradox of British migrants seeking authentic French living, yet stocking up on well-loved British foodstuffs. Sarah, originally from Lyon, who has been in London for ten years and currently lives in Greenwich, is another case in point. She describes the sorts of comestibles taken from home to home in the following terms: 'I don't use any French on-line shops at all to buy goods. We like to bring wine back with us; I bring back black pudding, pastry-cased pâté, Poulain chocolate when I go, but otherwise I do without.' It is pertinent here that Sarah would rather 'do without', than buy French food and beverages from a specialist London-based retailer. Given her comfortable socio-economic background (Head of Investment Risk in a city firm), this is unlikely to be because of the exaggerated pricing practised in such delicatessens.[3] Rather, in keeping with the other migrants studied, it is an articulation of her pre-reflexive desire to relocate and physically absorb material elements from *her* habitus of origin, part of the visceral pleasure being in the mental connections she, like the other migrants, makes between the act of consumption, displacement and ultimately home (Longhurst *et al.*, 2009).

The food and drink take Sarah on an affective spacio-temporal journey through her memory that mirrors that of the pathway of the foodstuff itself. It is this quest for authenticity, but in relation to the *originary home*, rather than the migratory space, as in the case of Benson's respondents (2011), that King and Christou underline. They argue that if the goods were not 'products of the "Greek soil"' (2008: 1), the lack of authenticity would undermine their value in the eyes of the migrants. Similarly, White recognises the capacity of a 'powerful translocal tie … to make [migrants] feel at home abroad' (2011: 13). Materialised translocal connections are thus intrinsic to my participants' homemaking practices and emplacement strategies within the migration context. The vivid reimagining achieved through the *boudin* brought back by Sarah from her 'hometown' would not be deliverable through a frenchclick.co.uk order, for however genuine the produce, it would lack the authenticity and affective potency of a shared migratory trajectory. This explains why Gabaccia's Italian-American migrants sometimes carried seeds with them, preferring to grow their own 'reproduction' of home than buy a local replica, hence maintaining a more authentic, agentive connection. Levin and Sprio support this contention, describing how Italian migrants in Melbourne and London respectively were keen 'to grow their own food on their own plots of land' (Sprio, 2013: 160), which allowed them 'to promote the feeling of familiarity through the performance of their "Italian" practices' (Levin, 2016: 57). Food, together with the sourcing, production and preparation surrounding it, therefore plays an active role in belonging and illustrates 'how the textures of intimacy in a particular place … shape both how and where people feel at home' (Walsh, 2018: 153).

Although my participants' unanimous rejection of London-French online grocery sites, such as frenchclick.co.uk and chanteroy-online.co.uk, can be understood within the framework of non-authenticity, it also offers important insights into their processes of belonging. It is paradoxical that the very items they cite as being (re)collected from their 'hometown', even those they assume to be the most obscure, such as K2R laundry stain remover, peppercorns, gherkins, mayonnaise, Poulain chocolate and French toiletry brands (e.g. soap-free Cadum and vanilla-scented Le Petit Marseillais shower gels) are *all* stocked by the London-French retailers. This suggests the reincarnations of 'home' my participants perceive to be individual choices, personal to their private habitat alone, are in fact repeated repertoires of belonging, representative of a wider community identity (Bonnerjee *et al.*, 2012). Such unintentional collective performativity of Frenchness, in spite of localised expressions to the contrary, not only confirms White's assertion that transnationalism and translocalism can coexist (2011), but that habitus is an effective lens through which to apprehend homemaking across cultures. By analysing my participants' intimate material habitats, 'a unified lifestyle, that is, a unified set of choices [... and] goods' has become apparent (Bourdieu, 1994: 23). However, it constitutes an inversion of the authenticity model proposed by Benson (2011), since it is my participants' premigration culture, their Frenchness that they reassert through the habitat as a form of distinction, but also – unwittingly – as a material community-building mechanism, their personal artefacts revealing collective attitudes and practices that belie individuated strategies of transnational belonging.

Negotiating shifting identities and the myth of return

When I talk to Suzanne, an elegant octogenarian, born in Lyon but raised predominantly in Dijon, who settled in London during the same period as the Italian diaspora referred to by Sprio, she reports regularly bringing back Bourgogne wine after long August holidays in France. In her chic, sumptuously furnished flat in Holland Park (W11), the many objects and textiles contained within the small space, being 'a material statement of who we are, where we have been' (Hecht, 2001: 123), speak of journeys to 'exotic' climes, possibly North Africa, Asia and beyond. The coffee cup with which I have been attentively provided is of compact, espresso size, its contents intensely black – not the milky English mug one might expect in another non-migrant London habitat – and reflects her immutable taste for the flavours, odours and crockery of the primary habitus, together with her long-standing reluctance to adopt those of the 'host' culture.

As she sips at her freshly filtered coffee, she recalls her first visit to London some 63 years previously: 'The first time I came to London, I went via the station ... I remember going into a Lyon's Tea Shop and I said to myself "there are so many different teas here". But I don't like tea; I've never liked it, and I still don't.' Despite spending most of her adult life in London, her unwillingness, or incapacity, to adapt her tastes maintains a phenomenological relationship with the primary/secondary habitus, which in turn reaffirms her French identity. Again, this statement bears a striking resemblance to an Italian migrant in London: 'In Italy they assumed I loved tea! I hate the stuff ... we grew up on espresso coffee just like them' (Sprio, 2013: 105). Both accounts demonstrate that an identification with coffee, and a proactive rejection of the customary hot beverage of the migratory field, are the realisation of a resistance to habitus transformation and an assertion of cultural positioning within the social field; for, as Sprio astutely points out, the line between integration and loss is a fine one (2013: 165). Suzanne's imperviousness to habitus transformation, as materialised through the coffee, is therefore a form of challenging the habitus (Friedmann, 2005), but not through a collective enterprise as Friedmann posits, rather through a fear of loss of cultural grounding. The proposition made by Waterson (2005: 339) that in contemporary society individuals 'are likely to become ever more self-conscious about what elements of the habitual repertoire they choose to maintain or to reject' is consequently a compelling one. It also supports the reconciled habitus model proposed by Ingram and Abraham (2016), whereby migrants internalise external elements of both the originary and the diasporic field, but have a reflexive hold over such choices.

Suzanne's choice of black coffee, over the tea-drinking norms of the adopted field, is therefore a loaded one. In their study of migrant women in New Zealand, Longhurst *et al.* (2009) observe the interconnectedness of identity, homemaking and taste. They posit that '[c]ultural difference is an embodied encounter and creating a domestic space where the body feels "at home" can help resituate and reconstitute the diasporic subject' (2009: 340). Moreover, in Suzanne's case, the power of the 'petit café' to engender a sense of comfortableness in her skin as a *Française de souche* is more crucial than for most, owing to her singular wartime trajectory. It is not merely a way of feeling at home, but the selection process itself (Marcoux, 2001) is an agentive affirmation of an aspect of her identity that once served as her salvation.

Aged 12 in 1944, Suzanne's Jewish heritage meant she spent the duration of the Second World War in hiding in Chambon-sur-Lignon, where her life depended, quite literally, on her embodiment of Frenchness. Baptised a protestant under a new 'French' (Huguenot) surname and educated by English exiles, every evening, she would brush shoulders with the British soldiers parachuted in to help with the resistance effort and attend 'a protestant service – we'd already been "protestantised" – and we sang. It was very optimistic; we'd sing *All Things Bright and Beautiful*.' At that formative time, therefore, she was at once extinguishing and igniting multiple identities: stifling any external displays of her innate Jewishness, in favour of her Frenchness and in addition to her borrowed Huguenot identity. All the while, she was immersing herself in a refreshing and romanticised new-found Englishness: 'We used to look at the [English] names of flowers in the fields.' Suzanne's reluctance to relinquish elements of the material habitat of her primary/secondary French habitus therefore comes as little surprise. Having made the bold decision to make London her permanent home, at the cost of a long and happy marriage, foregrounding Frenchness anchors her in otherwise shifting identities.[4] The reaffirmation of her national identity through the cup of coffee is hence a mechanism for bringing stability to an unsettled past and situatedness to an ambiguous diasporic existence. Our long and lively conversation concludes with a bowl of apricots and pistachio ice-cream, which I have no choice but to accept.

From a contrasting background, 32-year-old Sadia, of Franco-Algerian parentage, also elicits victuals and the role they play in her diasporic habitat. She speaks of her longing for French foods, lamenting the pitiful inadequacy of the fruit and vegetables on offer in London, which are as 'tasteless' and 'plastic' as those evoked by the Greek students in Petridou's study (2001: 95, 97). In France, Sadia explains, 'the garlic cloves are enormous; they're tiny here, mini. Really, the tomatoes are always green here, the fruits are always green, and the pears are never ripe. And then there's the choice – I mean the lack of choice.' She is mentally transported back to the generously stocked aisles in the supermarkets of her primary habitat, seeing the vast range of dairy products on offer (a point reiterated in the amateur film; Meard Street Productions, 2012), reliving the taste(s) and expectations. Another aspect of her originary habitat that she misses is the marketplace, not only the foodstuff available, but the entire weekly ritual, for 'migrancy is rather tasteless and odourless' (Miller, 2001: 14): 'I miss the market too, like, the basket, the market, the smells, the flavours, everything that goes with it … In fact, it's more than the food itself, it's the whole art of living.'

It is worth remembering that the French Ministry of Culture and Communication, in its application for Intangible Cultural Heritage status, 'insisted that "fresh" products from "local markets" were the "preferred" ingredients of French cuisine and carried "high cultural value"' (UNESCO, 5–6, cited in Murphy, 2018: 147), while a representative from another ministry asserted that 'France's "art de vivre" was inextricably tied to its "gastronomy" … described as a "cocktail of savors, of regions, of flavors, and of good products"' (2018: 146). The visual spectacle and olfactorily rich experience of the French marketplace not only form 'body memories' (Warin and Dennis, 2005: 165) for Sadia, being *mentally* reconfigured in the postmigration habitus with corporeal vividness, but they form part of a mythologised French identity constructed around culinary distinctiveness (Kelly, 2016). As such, they cannot be credibly re-performed in the diasporic field. Sadia has, in vain, tried to recreate this physical dimension of her primary habitus by visiting Croydon market, but, living several miles away, the undertaking feels awkward, painstaking and artificial, never equalling the entire phenomenological experience in France.

Again, inauthenticity emerges as a powerful obstacle to embedding in the diasporic context and it does so through spontaneous comparison with the remembered French experience of authentic living, alluded to repeatedly in its premigration imagined form by Benson (2011) and Korpela (2010, 2014). In this sense, then, the moral geographies referred to by Mulholland and Ryan (2017) are borne out – but in reverse – with France constituting the archetype of culinary quality and authenticity. However, as the authors assert, such juxtaposing 'may actively draw on a grounded comparative epistemology of place through employing their own partially "pre-scripted" and nationally-framed constructs of other places' (2017: 143). This raises questions over the objective differences in each location and the imaginaries constructed through common clichés in 'home' and 'host' contexts, resisted by other participants. For example, the experiences of Sarah and Brice both counter Sadia's 'pre-scripted' reservations.

They report that they depend on their local London markets to complete their tertiary habitat and, for Brice, the way of life the Hackney and Tower Hamlets (East London) habitat permits was key in his choice of long-term London neighbourhood: 'where I live there's a canal, a little park nearby, the organic market, the flower market not far away, some small galleries … There are little pockets of almost village life, right in the middle of town. I really like it.' In a reverse-configuration of his originary Carcassonne habitat – where the small city is set within an idyllic, rural landscape of hills rolling down to the Mediterranean Sea – in London, Brice has chosen a purportedly bucolic, village-like district set within the sprawling, urban cityscape. Aware of its reputation as a disadvantaged, dangerous area, yet providing evidence to the contrary, he appears deeply attached to this once gritty, 'abominable quarter' (Tristan, [1840] 2008: 58), spontaneously returning to it with affection at several points in our two-hour conversation. He describes the positive legacy of other migrant communities on the local habitat (Parker, 2000; Bonnerjee *et al.*, 2012), conceivable as a patchwork of 'affinity environments' (Friedmann, 2005: 325), and the gradual gentrification of the area, which Brice now feels part of. His participation in local community building gives him a sense of ownership and belonging: 'having seen this change, having been part of it, makes it "home" even more'. Many of his friends and family from France, and Carcassonne specifically, have also chosen to make this neighbourhood home and together are building a

London-French community within the broader sociocultural patchwork, having 'recreated a little home right here'. Brice goes so far as to refer to this Bohemian East London district as 'the place with the second highest number of French people – but it's a different population, a lot younger, a lot more students, artists, etcetera'.

The sense of a French community there is supported by Miranda, who has lived in E1 for several years, and asserts that 'the posh French are in South Kensington and the hip French are more towards Brick Lane'. Both evaluations serve as evidence to disprove the reductionist Black–white ethnic binary proposed by von Ahn *et al.* (2010), insomuch as my informants' East/West London preferences are ideological, political and/or age-related. More importantly, however, Brice's reconstitution of a French 'home' in a habitat he claims meets all his needs is indicative of a mismatch between his conscious embracing of its multicultural quasi rurality and an underlying need to re-establish interpersonal ties with other French Londoners and re-engage with the French facet of his identity. As an implicit constituent of embedding, Brice demonstrates a yearning to reinvent the originary habitus in the diasporic space, in a way that crystallises the 'longing that lingers with and within belonging' (Ilcan, 2002: 2–3, cited in Levin, 2016: 24). There is hence a tension between Brice's words and his practices, as noted among East European migrants in the UK (Fox *et al.*, 2015), and British expats in France (Benson, 2011) and Spain (Oliver and O'Reilly, 2010). It is an unwitting disconnect whose significance is increased with hindsight. That is, while Sadia's dissatisfaction with marketplace and food culture in London mirrored her desire to return to France (Marseille) by the mid-2010s, Brice's idealisation of his local area reflected his pre-2016 plans to remain in London, to the extent of considering an application for British citizenship. However, by 2019, and in a post-EU-membership referendum context, Sadia remains in London and Brice has seriously considered returning to France (Toulouse). In a practical reversal of their intentions, therefore, 'the myth of return' is endorsed by Sadia (Leavey *et al.*, 2004: 765), whereas Brice performs what could be apprehended as a 'myth of settlement'. In so doing, instead of embodying the 'lifestyle reasoning' proposed by Benson and O'Reilly (2016: 31), their practices characterise the 'undeliberate determinacy' posited by McGhee *et al.* (2017: 2, 109).

The myth of settlement is nevertheless atypical, since Brice's reflexive extolling of the quality and diversity of the fresh produce available in his local market is unique among my respondents. The others purchase supplies of French comestibles when they are in France to fill a void – culinary and affective – on their return. This reconstruction of the originary home through the edible produce results in a double presence, rather than a 'double absence' (Abdelmayek Sayad, 1999), alongside an awareness of physical fixedness in the diasporic space (Mata Codesal, 2008). In this sense, food, like the myth of return, serves as a 'pragmatic solution to being part of two contexts, two countries, two sets of values' (Al-Rasheed, 1994, cited in Leavey *et al.*, 2004: 765). Brice is perhaps more successful – superficially at least – in negotiating this transnational habitat and consequent hybrid identity than the majority of my research participants because, unlike them, his entire tertiary education took place in the UK. His secondary habitus was thus partly moulded by the cultural influences of the migration context, making him more adapted to the local field.

Although other participants also came to London at a young age, such as Miranda at 18, Bruno at 19 or Sadia at 20, not having experienced the British education system early in their adulthood meant that their primary and secondary habitus were established in France, and subsequent developments could be deemed the making of a tertiary, migratory habitus. This formative difference would explain the discrepancy between Brice's purported contentedness with his local habitat and other participants' overt desire to transport fractal elements from their premigration habitat to the diasporic field after each holiday, in keeping with the Greek and Italian communities studied elsewhere (Petridou, 2001; King and Christou, 2008; Sprio, 2013). The process of objectivated migration is thus a mechanism for the transposition and retention of that which is arguably the most essential aspect of their primary habitus, namely food. Sarah confirms the centrality of food in the construction and perception of her selfhood, as follows: 'my French identity is my language, the link to food, and nothing much else'. Such a comment corroborates Brillat-Savarin's dictum, 'Tell me what you eat and I will tell you what you are' (1848), but more intriguing is Sarah's emphasis on the *link* to food rather than the substance in isolation. This resonates with Petridou's observation (2001: 98) of Greek migrant identity distinguishing itself from local identities through their concern with food as *process*, as opposed to *produce*, and is therefore a habit feature of habitus to which I shall return in Chapter 4.

Although food has emerged as a key material factor in the diasporic habitat of my informants, as a means of asserting a distinct, authentic French identity, of resisting habitus transformation and of negotiating (be)longing in the diasporic context, it is worth mentioning that other fractal habitus artefacts were also observed and cited. Robert – unusual in his scientific detachment – estimates that 'there's about twenty per cent of French life at home, and the rest is English. But there's still that French presence.' In addition to food and wine, he mentions the contribution of books, magazines and music to the London-French habitat. Brigitte, a 35-year-old molecular neuroscientist living in Bethnal Green (herself a member of the East-London French community to which Brice alluded), instead favours clothes as the material expression of her Frenchness within the intimate space of her London flat. 'I'm really into clothes', she explains. 'When I go back to France, I've got my two or three little shops there. That's something I'd miss if I were never to return to France.' She recounts visiting the store websites when in London, choosing her preferred designs online, in order to make swift and efficient purchases when visiting her hometown. This self-confessed penchant for clothes, as material emblems of Brigitte's Frenchness, does not, however, translate into pleasure garnered from the act of shopping in the migration context. London's high-street fashion chains, in her opinion all selling the same identity-less apparel, leave her uninspired and unwilling to play the commercialised fashion game considered to dominate the diasporic field (Bellion, 2005; Tristan, [1840] 2008).

Thus, in keeping with the Filipino migrants of Kelly and Lusis's study, whose economic capital earned in Toronto had a physical impact on the environment of their originary habitat in Tagbilaran (2006), by refusing to purchase her clothes in the diasporic habitat/field, and instead investing her economic capital in the retail field of her originary habitat, Brigitte makes a micro-contribution to the local premigration economy (Brettell, 2008: 123). More importantly, this superficially inconsequential aesthetic decision (Miller, 2005) is a pragmatic manifestation of transnationalism and the myth of return (Brigitte: 'if I were never to return to France') that 'provides the individual with both a strategy for maintaining identity and affirming belonging in a community which stretches from homeland to new land' (Leavey *et al.*, 2004: 777). In Brigitte's case, the material transnational act is further accentuated by the inherently placeless digitality of its underpinning. From the comfort of her London chair, the sartorial elements she desires in her originary habitat are selected in a 'virtual' reality, caught between her *physical* London location, her *remembered* hometown and her *imagined* future inhabiting of the clothes, itself a form of embodiment of her primary/secondary habitus akin to that engendered through the consumption of the edible objects ritualistically (re)collected by other participants (Conlon, 2011; Dudley, 2011). Each in its own way is a form of physical self-appropriation of the individual's fractal habitus, one alimental, the other textile, both relating to taste and a revival, or reaffirmation, of their fundamental identity, for as Miller reminds, clothes are 'the fabric of identity' (2005: 10).

Placemaking and belonging: defining the in-between space

Although the notion of transnationalism has been a firm feature of migration literature since the early 1990s with Appadurai (1990) and Glick-Schiller *et al.* (1992) marking its inception, and many others adopting, redefining and challenging the construct since (see Vertovec, 2001; Smith, 2001, 2005; Kivisto, 2003; Portes, 2003; Gieles, 2009; White, 2011), my empirical findings, as touched on earlier, suggest that it is an ill-fitting term in relation to the London-French experience. Not only does London distinguish itself from the rest of England in the minds of migrants, as I argued in the Introduction to this monograph, but so too do their subjectivated habitats in relation to France as a nation state. The objects my participants choose to bring to their London habitats, and hence endow with additional 'value' (Marcoux, 2001: 84), tend not to be *French* commodities per se, but those closely connected to, and often emanating from, a geographically pinpointed locale in the primary habitat. This 'place perspective' (Gieles, 2009: 271) has implications regarding migrant/community identity construction, belonging and citizenship, and its cross-diasporic resonance only adds to its impact.

In an auto-ethnographic parenthesis, Spanish migrant, Mata Codesal, describes how she learned 'to value more than ever those small precious pots with [her] grandma's preserves that transport [her] to the long lazy mid-summer dinners in Castile' (2008: 5, footnote 10). She also underlines the flavoursome situatedness of her Ecuadorian respondents' points of reference, whether the specific characteristics of seafood in Quito or flour in Guayaquil (2008). Similarly, Petridou (2001) emphasises the highly localised rural and domestic significance of her Greek respondents' migrant foodstuffs, specifying strong cheese from a particular mountain range, olive oil from a local farm, and the popularity of homemade dishes. This echoes King and Christou's depiction of Greek migrants in Germany 'transferring ... what was "genuine" from Greece (food, wine, oil, products of the "Greek soil")' (King and Christou, 2008: 15), thus underscoring the connection to the local land despite the national framework of the study.

Kneafsey and Cox make an analogous evaluation in respect of Irish immigrants in Coventry, who remark favourably upon the authenticity and freshness of homemade or homegrown ingredients (2002: 11). King *et al.* foreground the notion of *Heimat*, 'denoted [as] the area or region in Germany where [the migrants] had grown up, a space or place that was replete with memories' (King *et al.*, 2014: 13), as well as 'the provincial mentality whereby [Italians] are strongly linked to their city, province or region' (2014: 22). Equally, Anne White highlights the 'often local rather than ethnic or national' (2011: 25) dimensions of the Polish migrant experience, travelling between small cities or towns in western England and villages in Poland, which mirrors the practices of Italians in Switzerland (Wessendorf, 2007) and Buckinghamshire (Sprio, 2013). This valuing of a particular regional, rural or urban place and identity favours earthy, grassroots belongings, in all their messy materiality, over artificial homogenising and top–down, national constructs. Mata Codesal (2001) illustrates the potential for harm caused by such essentialising (postcolonial) practices in her reference to the Spanish 'host' population's use of the term 'Latino'. Not only does the term fail to recognise culturo-linguistic specificities, flattening diverse subjectivities into an unrelatable whole, but it means 'scholars (and policymakers, journalists, survey researchers etc.) must think carefully about what labels and categories they are using in relation to migrants [... because] employing labels in policy has consequences for how those labelled are treated and governed' (Benson and O'Reilly, 2016: 25).

Returning to the migrants under scrutiny here, we find various participants expressing their localised affiliations in explicit terms: Suzanne from Dijon brings back wine from Bourgogne, the grapes for which have swollen and ripened on the hilltops close to her childhood home. Bruno from Eysines on the outskirts of Bordeaux hoards wine bottled in Eysines and preserves hand-crafted by his uncle in his mountain village near Pau. Sarah carries charcuterie from Lyon, the self-proclaimed Capital of French gastronomy (particularly *saucisson*), whereas Brigitte seeks out, and dresses in, attire sold in local shops in her hometown of Angers. Playing out repertoires of localised emplacement and belonging analogous to the aforementioned migrant groups, my participants attach increased meaning, authenticity and worth – good taste even – to objects from the originary habitat closest to the domestic space itself. This supports Cohen and Sirkeci's contention that the premigration household is key in the mobility process (2011), which simultaneously recognises the centrality of the affective. More than a form of regionalism, this attachment implicitly acknowledges that 'things take on their value from their association to events that are constitutive of the person or of the family's history ... "loved" objects do not come alive in a person ... but it is the person who lives in them' (Marcoux, 2001: 72). Thus, the more proximate the migrants' transported artefacts are to the individuals who populated their lifeworld and to shared experiences that took place in that world, the more they are infused with emotive meaning.

Consequently, the selection and localisation demonstrated by participants is, as Sadia astutely assesses, more a question of transposing '*terroir* produce, grown in local soil' than national products per se. This makes the argument for the transposition of fractal habitus yet more compelling: habitus relates not to abstract external constructs such as nationhood and class, but to intimate subject–object dynamics, at the interface of the individual and the place they inhabit in the physical environment, giving material form to abstract notions through practice and physical interaction with(in) that space. There is thus a dynamic relationship between localised place and identity, with 'individualistic practices constructing the identity of the micro-region' (Demossier, 2001: 7) and vice versa. It is for this reason that the physical, consumable elements of the primary habitat, such as the culinary, sartorial, literary and filmic, are transposed from the specific hometowns, villages and houses of the respondents to their London habitats, in an attempt to recreate a sense of closeness to that intimate habitat from which they are irrevocably distanced as long as they assume a diasporic existence.

The reconfiguration of the spatial positioning of the French (and other) migrant subjects, through their relationship towards objects transferred from a place-specific premigration habitat is important, not least because it suggests the need for a simultaneous reconfiguration of 'transnationalism' itself. While the construct lends itself well to the multidimensional in-betweenness of the migrant experience and home, what Levin refers to as their 'mobile habitat' (2016: 28), the term has been contested almost for as long as it has existed. The 'trans' element of the term adequately encapsulates the dialectic spatiality of migration, but the 'national' places it in a top-down administrative framework which is out of kilter with migrants' everyday lived experience. Appadurai (1995, 1996), Soysal (1994), Smith (2001, 2005) and Sassen (2002, 2006) have contributed positively to the debate on the inapplicability of national frameworks in an increasingly globalised and mobile world, with Soysal arguing that 'the logic of personhood supersedes the logic of national citizenship' (1994: 64) and Sassen proposing denationalized (bottom-up) and postnational (top-down) citizenship. Around the same time, Bourdieu also acknowledged the role of contemporary migration in recalibrating the idea of nationhood: 'being surplus to requirement everywhere, [the migrant] gives rise to a radical review of how to conceptualise legitimately the idea of citizenship and the relationship between the citizen and the State, the Nation and nationality' (Bourdieu, 1999: 13).

A decade later, Favell (2008b) was more explicit still, accusing the academy of falling into the trap of a seemingly scholarly habitus, whereby '[c]onventional views of governance, sovereignty, and control entirely reproduce the taken-for-granted convention of state power' (Favell, 2008b: 272). He claims it to be 'so effective that scholars of migration rarely question who are migrants or not' (2008b: 273) and 'no-one examines whether migration is in fact something only defined and derived from the state's need to classify and carve up spatial mobility in a certain way, [ignoring] that it could be defined another way' (2008b: 270). Since then, however, there has been a pushback. Retrieving the concept of the 'translocal' referred to by Appadurai (1990), but setting it within a simultaneously transnational context, 'translocality' is deployed by Gieles (2009) to reposition the migrant in a localised in-between place that straddles corporeal (diasporic) situatedness and imagined, affective and remembered (premigration) sites. Likewise, the 'powerful translocal tie' extended between small-scale pre- and postmigration places of residence and its homemaking potential are explored by White (2011: 14), who, quoting Flusty (2004: 8), asserts 'that ties across national borders are "the product of specific persons in specific locales"', which echoes Walsh's emphasis on 'intimate subjectivities across and through dialectics of mobility and settlement' (Walsh, 2018: 146). By developing the 'lifestyle migration' construct, Benson, Oliver and O'Reilly also challenge dominant typological, nationalistic and place-specific paradigms. Their foregrounding of 'the identity-making projects that are embedded in these migrations' (Benson, Oliver and O'Reilly, 2016: 23) reminds scholars that '[l]ifestyle migration … is a way of thinking about some forms of migration and not an attempt to homogenise discrete categories. It is a lens rather than a box' (2016: 25).

When contemplating my ethnographic findings through a lifestyle lens, the increased appropriateness of translocalism – 'transhomeism' even – in the lived experience of contemporary migrants is confirmed. Homing in on the domestic and *grounded* localism affords a better understanding of the spatial tensions and affective implications of migrant be-longing, as evidenced by multiple studies. The notion of *paesani* referred to repeatedly by Sprio (2013) recalls the *terroir* noted by my participants, who – significantly – were not from rural backgrounds. Parkhurst Ferguson (2004) defines *terroir* as 'this fidelity to the land, this rootedness' and links it to (regional and local) authenticity (2004: 23). Although Demossier (2011) casts doubt over the uniformity of this type of definition, drawing attention to the concept's pliability, and Murphy (2018: 146) challenges the sincerity of 'the branding of French cultural identity' through *terroir*, it nevertheless captures the centrality of the home-*land* in and across migrant experiences of identity construction and placemaking. One Greek migrant explains how '[f]eeling Greek is to feel emotionally and physically connected to the land … immediately united with the land, at one with the soil … As it ran though my fingers I felt it run through my veins' (King and Christou, 2008: 2). *Paesani* also bridges the gap between the physical locus and the people who inhabit it, being variously defined by Sprio as 'regional-based' (2013: 41), as 'somebody from the same town as you but … also … close family or friends' (2013: 14, footnote 39), as 'a member of the Italian community in Britain who comes from the same region in Italy' (2013: 113, footnote 25) or a 'person from the same *paese* (town)' (2013: 173, footnote 3).

The fluidity of the term and its ability to encompass the local in both the originary and diasporic habitats; its propensity to be both town and/or region; and equally to signify the people who represent these real, conceptual and overlapping spaces and relationships, detached from the artificial, top-down notion of the nation state, renders it a compelling alternative to transnationalism and translocalism, which covers the multifaceted aspects of placemaking and belonging emerging from my migrant narratives. Alternative iterations are also possible, such as *Heimat*, discussed by Moores and Metykova (2010) and King *et al.* (2014), who describe it as 'less to do with actual visits or regular connections, and related more to feelings of nostalgia – an imaginary space of the past' (2014: 13), which aligns it with the Welsh term 'hiraeth', evoking, in a single term, homesickness and a physical yearning for absent, and even mythologised, people and places. This emulates the 'culturally embedded concept of *saudade* – nostalgia for the homeland ... "that defines Portuguese identity in the context of multiple layers of space and (past) time"' (Brettell, 2008: 117, quoting Feldman-Bianco, 1992: 145; Neto, 2019). However, when used in an English-language context, all these terms are self-defeatingly *national* in character. Hoerder's concept of transregionalism (2013) circumvents many of the complications of transnationalism and effectively imparts the notion of bi-local belonging, but is overly place-specific (Benson and O'Reilly, 2016), lacking the subjective and affective nuances of the other terms. An alternative could be to coin a word from Latin, in an intertextual nod to Bourdieu's concept of habitus, for example, 'transdomism' (from Latin 'domus' – home). Or a term from classical Greek could be borrowed, such as 'atopical', stemming from the notion of the migrant as a 'placeless *atopos*', recalled by Bourdieu (1999: 13; original emphasis), or perhaps more convincingly 'polytopical' in view of the multidimensionality of home (Levin, 2016). Both 'transdomism' and 'polytopicalism' would be more congruent terms than 'transnationalism', with the added benefit of disembedding the notion from a *national* English (or US), Portuguese, French, German or (modern) Italian context, all the while evoking the elasticity of the concept and the inhabited space.

This elasticity, or more specifically the in-betweenness of the diasporic experience, spanning the micro-spaces of the homeland and adopted home, as well as on-land and on-line habitats – inadequately represented by the concept of transnationalism – leads to the next section of this chapter, namely habitus as it is lived through different media.

Mediating home

Emulating the blurry space between inner and outer experience intrinsic to 'transnationalism' and habitus, some London-French migrants bridge the physical gap between the diasporic habitat and that of origin by constructing a 'virtual' home (Barac and McFadyen, 2007: 110). Building on the seminal idea of the 'soundscape' proposed by Schafer ([1977] 1994) and the intersecting 'mediascapes', 'technoscapes' and 'ethnoscapes' evoked by Appadurai (1990: 296), in this section I explore my participants' media use spatially, regarding it as another textural (Tacchi, 1998) layer in their London-French habitat. Like Pink and Mackley (2013), I am interested in the ways in which media are used materially, as part of the placemaking praxis that contributes to making a house a home, considering 'how, as people move through the home as a place, [they] encounter other persons and things, [and] become co-implicated with them as their trajectories become entangled (Pink and Mackley, 2013: 683). However, my approach departs from Pink and Mackley's in its interpretation of such entanglement not as physical interactions in their literal form, but as affective connections and spatialities which both transcend the material diasporic habitat and construct it. That is, I recognise that they 'are not objectively given relations ... but ... deeply perspectival ... inflected very much by the historical, linguistic and political situatedness' (Appadurai, 1990: 296) of the migrants, not to mention their dialectical geographical positioning.

Supporting the observations of Gieles (2009), together with Duchêne-Lacroix and Koukoutsaki-Monnier (2016), I therefore contend that in a diasporic context, the (French) language and cultural reference points are necessary components of the mediated transnational and/or translocal domestic ethnoscape. This is confirmed by the authors in relation to French migrants' media use and the insights it provides into 'their (supra)national belongings' (2016: 136). They posit that 'the French population in Berlin ... have strongly internalised French culture [because] they watch French television or listen to French radio rather often (2016: 140). Gieles goes further, illustrating precisely how material and mediated 'stuff' (Miller, 2010: 1) quotidianly converges to create a transnational/translocal space within the home: 'Photographs on the wall of [the Dutch migrants'] living room show some relatives. Every day, [they] watch the Dutch news on the television and they watch the German news once a week ... [They] frequently surf the internet to visit the websites of the [local German] secondary school and hospital at which they are employed ... and to email and chat to friends and relatives in the Netherlands' (Gieles, 2009: 279). This mediated collage of languages, cultures and spaces means that while I concur with Pink and Mackley's 'non-media-centric and non-representational' approach (Pink and Mackley, 2013: 677), I apply it less narrowly. Language and content matter, particularly to migrants. They are component parts of the cultural materiality that constitutes not only the domestic habitat, but themselves. As Miller asserts, drawing on Bourdieusian habitus theory, 'objects make people' (Miller, 2010: 53); the content, the substance of the media used by my participants cannot, therefore, be entirely extricated from the media themselves, even if not my chief focus.

Since the media use of migrants is an under-researched dimension of the diasporic experience (Jansson, 2016), this section is essential. Benson's lifestyle-migration perspective shows that British couples in the Lot were 'pleased that they were still able to pick up British television … through their satellite dish' (Benson, 2011: 109). Similarly, I observed several other participants, like Bruno, succumbing to the lure of Fransat advertising by attaching satellite dishes to the walls of their diasporic homes. Being what Dhoest describes as 'connected migrants' (2018: 32), they reported regularly tapping into French media. Whether through satellite television, the internet or long-wave radio – or a combination of platforms – the linguistically and culturally situated content 'saturated' (Pink and Mackley, 2013: 677) their physical surroundings with the sounds, images, music and reference points of their premigration habitat. While most rejected the construal of such media saturation as an agentive step to create a French 'oasis' within the diasporic setting, the result could nonetheless be likened to one. Indeed, the existence of London-French companies specialising in parabolic installations bears witness to the demand (for example, www.french-tv.co.uk and www.prosatlondon.co.uk) and to the desire to let real-time French broadcasting habitually infiltrate their 'London' sitting rooms. Watching French television is not only a means of cultivating a technologically mediated, language-specific ethnoscape, but also of bridging temporo-spatial borders and re-engaging with the cultural here-and-now of the homeland.

Such immersion often comes as a welcome release after the efforts of speaking and thinking in a foreign language all day in the local socio-professional field, which is evidently at odds with the communicational spontaneity inferred by the notion of being/feeling 'at home'.[5] Participants' envelopment in the comforting familiarity of the mother-tongue mediascape demonstrates 'how media are implicated in the making of home and in making it "feel right"' (Pink and Mackley, 2013: 679). It enables pre-reflexive identification with tacit references to the rich and finely woven tapestry that constitutes the migrants' shared cultural heritage: home on a large scale. As they watch the images flicker before them and effortlessly decode the language, the migrants are also reminded that, being live transmissions, others in the originary habitat may be watching the same broadcast, at the same time, sharing in the same experience and therefore phenomenologically, if not geographically, proximate to and present in the migratory habitat.

Appadurai perceptively recognises that the 'invented homelands, which constitute the mediascapes of deterritorialized groups' (1990: 302) have a tendency, through 'image-centred, narrative-based accounts of strips of reality' to provide 'those who experience them' with 'a series of elements … out of which scripts can be formed of imagined lives, their own as well as those of others living in other places' (1990: 299). Thus, satellite television contributes to diasporic emplacement on several levels. It imbues participants' intimate habitats with 'continuity of personal identity, a sense of national belonging, and a connection between past, present and future homes' (Levin, 2016: 44). Nevertheless, as Sprio convincingly argues, televised broadcasts from the originary habitat/habitus can have the opposite effect, serving 'to alienate' viewers (2013: 167) whose habitus has imperceptibly evolved. Their mediated experience of the homeland is not so much invented (Appadurai, 1990) as it is remembered, and therefore increasingly distant and hazy. Reference points familiar to French stayers become cryptic for the migrants, who find themselves caught in a space–time vacuum and, as such, culturally excluded from the place they once called home.

Television is not always the medium of choice, however. Owning only a small, outmoded set, it plays but a minor role in Brigitte's East End home. She stays abreast of French current affairs through quotidian reading of French news websites on her smartphone or laptop, and keeps links with her premigration habitat intimately alive through regular submergence in the longwaves of French radio:

> I listen to the radio a lot … it's pathetic, I do everything in French: I read in French, I listen to French radio, I have everything on the internet or as podcasts now, so I don't miss it at all. I listen to Europe 1, I like Europe 1 mainly because I'm used to it … It's true that you wake up or go to sleep with them … and, actually, for years and years I'd always heard presenters like Laurent Ruquier in the afternoons at home, like forever, so that's why I listen to Europe 1. I think I actually listened to it less in France than I do here.

Unlike the conscious information-seeking exercise of consulting news websites, tuning into the familiar voices heard growing up is not an intellectual undertaking for Brigitte. It is an emotional, almost instinctive act to bring her tertiary habitat closer to that comfortable and comforting space of her childhood. The distinction she makes between *hearing* the presenters in the premigration habitat and *listening* to them in London is edifying within Schafer's theoretical framework, where it is possible to apprehend 'a radio programme as a soundscape' ([1977] 1994: 7). It suggests that Europe 1 broadcasts function as a keynote sound in her postmigration domestic soundscape, since '[k]eynote sounds do not have to be listened to consciously; they are overheard but cannot be overlooked, for keynote sounds become listening habits in spite of themselves' (Schafer, 1994: 11).

That Brigitte has unwittingly integrated this listening habit into her morning and night-time routine and thus rendered it a fundamental, tone-setting part of her diasporic habitat is not without significance. Pink and Mackley contend that 'bedtime routines … involve patterns of switching on and off that signify a transition, making the home feel right at night' (2013: 684) and that having an 'audio presence while going to sleep, and effectively becoming oblivious to it, in itself draws our analytical attention away from content and towards the routine dimension of the presence of these media' (Pink and Mackley, 2013: 685). In Brigitte's case, these moments, bookending slumber, emerge as times of heightened vulnerability, when the longing in belonging dominates and when the need for primal proximity is accentuated. As a result, the reassuring sounds of Europe 1 are accessed with greater frequency than in the premigration setting and become a habituated facet of her domestic soundscape. As Schafer points out, '[t]here are no earlids. When we go to sleep, our perception of sound is the last door to close and it is also the first to open when we awaken' ([1977] 1994: 11). Thus, like the Filipina mother who reported telephoning her children every morning and evening in Madianou and Miller's study (2011), Brigitte creates a mediated soundscape to fill the routine emptiness of the migratory space. The familiar voices emanating from the French radio broadcasts bring family closer, for 'hearing is a way of touching at a distance' (Schafer, [1977] 1994: 11) and, as such, an audible presence serves to vivify her diasporic habitat, the familiar and familial overlapping.

Although the habituated dimension of Brigitte's radio usage prevailed over content – bar language – in the example, several other participants placed an explicit emphasis on the subject matter, evoking a desire to reignite the humour of the originary habitat. Given the culture-specificity of humour as a communicative and representational form, and its reliance on unarticulated common knowledge (Westcott and Vazquez Maggio, 2016a – a theme to which I return in Chapter 3), this perhaps comes as little surprise. Bruno's regular tuning into the comedy and popular-French-music web-radio, *Rires et chansons*, when relaxing in his London home or via his smartphone on his daily Mayfair commute immediately plunges him into a familiar habitat, an intangible yet all-encompassing component of the primary/secondary habitus extracted to furnish the migration context, placing him in a space that bestrides the habitat of pre- and postmigration cultures. In his own words, 'I like listening to French radio in the background ... And then there are the childhood habits of listening to French radio.' The medium here again creates a soundscape on which the lived experience of the migrant is superimposed and, echoing Brigitte's words, crucially places Bruno in the well-acquainted, intimate territory of childhood. Despite foregrounding content initially, Bruno subsequently refocuses on the habitual, on the 'background' presence. The French comedic radio therefore adds an extra layer of texture to Bruno's habitat (Tacchi, 1998; Walsh, 2018), giving an 'affective rhythm' (Tacchi, 2009: 171) to his daily routine and implicitly re-connecting him with his premigration life. We see here, then, how the domestic soundscape feeds into the broader ethnoscape (Appadurai, 1990), and how technology and media converge to reinforce emplacement within the diasporic space. That is, Bruno's 'earwitness' (Schafer, [1977] 1994: 9) account testifies to the power of culture-specific radio 'to ignite intimacy ... and turn locality into a staging ground for identity ... spread over vast and irregular spaces, [where,] as groups move, [... they] stay linked to one another through sophisticated media capabilities' (Appadurai, 1990: 306).

The placemaking potential of radio is also identifiable in Robert's narrative. He expresses a regretful pleasure engendered through listening to French Radio London that transports him through time and space: 'It's really like "French radio for French people living abroad" ... Maybe it's the references to French classics we might listen to at home ... It's nostalgia for France rather than what's going on currently.'[6] In his selection of French Radio London, Robert bypasses the risk of alienation from contemporary French culture through the (overly) real-time television broadcasts highlighted by Sprio (2013), and instead takes comfort from the familiar and intentionally nostalgic song choices of the diasporic radio station. Perpetually locked into a fondly reimagined past, it is a remembered common history that unites the listeners of the community radio. In this sense, French Radio London functions in a multi-scalar capacity (Mulholland and Ryan, 2015): on a personal level, it constitutes auditory 'comfort food' (Mata Codesal, 2008: 13), reminiscent of the *cassoulet* which Robert describes in such terms. On a wider, diasporic scale it is a 'soundmark' (from landmark), representing 'the acoustic life of the community' and one 'which is unique [... and] specially regarded or noticed by people in that community' (Schafer, [1977] 1994). Unlike Brigitte and Bruno, therefore, whose radios function in their homes at a pre-reflexive level to reconnect them with the primary habitat in real time, Robert's listening practices are self-aware and content-focused. He acknowledges French Radio London as a 'soundmark', tuning in with consciousness of it being an indulgent, nostalgic substitute for the authenticity of national broadcasting.

The possibilities presented by online mobile communication devices, in addition to the media discussed here, not only make the distinction between the physical and virtual blurrier than ever, but they erase the boundaries between habitats of origin and destination to an unprecedented extent. For, as Daniel Miller found during his research, many migrants now connect to the 'homeland', through SNS and SMS, with increasing frequency and in increasingly incongruous physical settings (Miller, 2012). This recalls the incongruity of Bruno on his daily cycle to work, physically situated in London's urban infrastructure, yet simultaneously sealed off from it through his immersion in a French soundscape materialised through the digitised radio of his smartphone. Similarly, another London-French migrant, recorded in a French documentary on the community (to coincide with the London 2012 Olympics), was filmed connecting to her family and friends via her smartphone, wherever she found herself in the London habitat, at least ten times a day. In keeping with the migrants examined by Dhoest (2018), therefore, digital media contribute to belonging in a way that transcends the material, whether in terms of community, transnational or translocal embedding. In this ambiguous existential context, the physical act of displacement is arguably diminished through media (Madianou and Miller, 2011), but this mediation leaves the migrants with a more ambivalent habitus than ever before, physically inhabiting a foreign land yet constructing a 'virtual' habitat to create a tangible sense of home in the uprooted setting.

Conclusion

This chapter has provided a window onto the intimate lifeworlds of my participants, allowing a better understanding of the diasporic habitats they have (re)constructed within the broader social space and the role of such materialities within the settlement project. Although rarely identifying with the so-called French community (Huc-Hepher and Drake, 2013) and generally resisting the reductionist label considered to negate their '[i]ntra-group differentiations' (Erel, 2010: 649), my participants revealed considerable commonality through their habitats. Rather than creating an entirely French oasis, fractal and mediated elements of Frenchness were replicated from one abode to the next, thereby creating a material sense of community that participants' narratives rejected. In a ritualistic annual pilgrimage from the homeland to the adopted home, informants played out a shared practice of transporting micro-culturally meaningful products from the region or household that was once part of their primary habitus and in which they continued to be rooted. This highlighted the material cultural dynamics at play, with long-term London residents regularly re-inhabiting the French spaces they had seemingly left behind, and French objects and comestibles in turn transposed to the English habitat. It also confirmed the multidimensionality of 'home' and limitations of the 'transnational' as a conceptual construct.

The repeated evidence of French habitus-turned-habitat supported Bourdieu's contention that objectivated homes are more socially telling than subjective discourses alone (1972) and Benson's assertion that ambivalence is a more fitting description of migrants' positioning than the often-cited 'liminality' (2011: 21). For here, the migrants' private interiors spoke of simultaneous belonging to diasporic and originary fields, evidencing little desire for assimilation (Miller, 2010) or authentic local integration (Benson, 2011). On the contrary, in another inversion of the experiences and aspirations of Benson's British migrants in France, the contents of respondents' homes recounted stories of belonging fundamentally, corporeally and affectively to a localised premigration place. Food and culinary objects took on singular importance, being inextricably intertwined with French identity; not items associated with the nation as a whole, however, nor those contributing to 'integration into the local community' (Benson, 2011: 45), but artefacts, tastes and smells redolent of a particular French region, town, city, village or house(hold). In this way, not only did the migrants set themselves apart in the wider social space, reproducing an inherently more authentic, more flavoursome and distinctive gustative habitat, but by holding on to the originary culture, they resisted habitus transformation. The identities projected onto their material homes therefore testified to incomplete or ongoing transformation (Benson, 2011; Benson and O'Reilly, 2016; Pink and Mackley, 2013). Substantiating Oliver and O'Reilly's contention, the chapter showed that there are indeed 'limits to the possibilities of reinventing and transforming habitus' (Oliver and O'Reilly, 2010: 25), and this incompleteness resulted in a semi-agentive, hybrid habitat.

Through my deconstruction of habitus into three component parts and my focus on habitat as an objective, externalised disposition, the subjective positioning of my participants gradually emerged. Their homes evidenced a primal attachment to the micro- and meso-levels of the originary habitat (Hoerder, 2013) and a clear sense of belonging to a translocal or 'transdomal' space. The types of objects, be they jams, madeleine moulds, skirts or scents, demonstrated a desire for reliving carnal experiences sensorially associated with the localised premigration home. Moreover, participants' re-enactment of the mediated French habitat through the familiar audio(visual) waves regularly rippling through their London homes, intangibly, yet contributing to the cultural materiality of the particular 'scape', further complicated processes of emplacement, identity formation and belonging. On-land/on-line, present/absent, here/there, substantive/affective dichotomies (Walsh, 2018) were seen to become increasingly ambiguous, giving rise to new, dynamic forms of lived experience, intensified through twenty-first-century mediated technologies.

This casts doubt over where, in effect, the migrants are living, which brings us back to the definition of 'home' itself and the sense of habituation that inevitably arises after prolonged exposure to a borrowed culture, a theme I explore in the following chapter.

Notes

1 While Kate Fox's work targets a lay audience, her methodologies and insightful observations are academically valid, as are her anthropological credentials.
2 Consumption (bread and wine), embodiment ('this is my body' and 'this is my blood') and memory ('do this in remembrance of me') are key to the practice of the Christian faith, which underlines the elemental significance of the connection between incorporation and memory.
3 The target consumers are doubtless members of the South Kensington elite or the middle-class English Francophiles mentioned. Indeed, the 2011 introduction of Carrefour's high-end grocery range, *Reflets de France*, by UK online retailer Ocado, with its distinctly 'upmarket image' (*Guardian*, 2015), is testimony to middle-class British buyers' keenness to recreate the fantasy of holidays past (Sprio, 2013), and pay a premium for it.
4 In the early 2010s, Suzanne divorced her husband after decades of contented matrimony, because he wished to retire to his native Ireland. But for Suzanne, London was home and she was unwilling to leave it behind.
5 Illustrating this point was Brigitte's realisation, during our conversation, that it was perhaps the effort of communicating in a foreign language on a day-to-day basis with her ex-partners that had been the underlying cause of their subsequent separation.
6 French Radio London was launched in late 2011 to target a London-French audience, but an internal survey conducted the following year suggested an equally active English Francophile audience (again, perhaps attempting to recreate the fantasy of holidays past). Robert was the only participant to mention ever listening to the station, the others deeming it lacking in 'homeland' authenticity.

3

The imperceptible force of habituation: moving beyond agency

Introduction

Having considered the objectified habitats of my London-French participants, I now address the habituation component of the habitus triad. It is worth noting that all three elements have been explicitly alluded to in reference to Bourdieusian habitus, if never – to my knowledge – combined under a triadic analytical framework. Maton (2012) deconstructs habitus into a model with two etymologically related dimensions: habitat and habit, whereas Jenkins contends that the 'power of the habitus derives from the thoughtlessness of habit and habituation, rather than consciously learned rules and principles' (Jenkins, 2002: 76). By examining all three elements, I acknowledge the full scope of habitus; and by turning my attention to habituation at this point, that is, in-between the habitat and habit chapters, I underline the interconnectedness of all three components and the centrality of unconscious thought to both our intimate lifeworlds and our everyday practices. There is clearly overlap between habitats, habits and habituation, as observed in the non-content-centric mediated routines of the last chapter. However, bringing each into relief discretely allows for greater analytical depth than a single habitus approach.

As an internalised embodiment of external influences, habituation enables a reorientation towards the subjective dimension of habitus, conceived of as 'history made nature' and 'negated as such because it takes place as second nature' (Bourdieu, [1972] 2000: 263). Accordingly, habituation alludes to individuals' fundamental 'fish in water' (Bourdieu and Wacquant, 1992: 103) state of mind, which renders the world 'taken for granted' (1992: 103). Daniel Miller writes that 'an individual grows up assuming the norms that we call culture', adding that the habituated particularities of our external environment 'unconsciously direct our footsteps, and are the landscapes of our imagination … Bourdieu called the underlying unconscious order our habitus' (2010: 53). In this chapter, I propose that this unconscious facet of habitus can be apprehended as habituation and, by examining it, I reveal how the perspectives and attitudes of my participants have evolved, imperceptibly, as a result of sustained immersion in the London environment. I ask what effect habituation had on their initial mobility and how it continues to influence their emplacement and identity, as well as exploring the potentially disruptive effects of migration on the unconscious order itself.

Beginning at the premigration stage of the mobility continuum (Kelly and Lusis, 2006), I first consider how my participants rationalise their migration project in pragmatic, capital-based terms, but how underlying individuated habitus forces, such as exposure to other cultures during their formative years, can play a major role, planting the expatriation 'seed' (Findlay and Li, 1997: 38; Wang, 2013a) beyond their conscious decision-making (Benson and O'Reilly, 2009; Conway and Leonard, 2014; Ryan, 2018). I contend that such encounters, conceivable as inconspicuous 'contact zones' (Pratt, 1991; Higgins, 2019), tacitly habituate participants to the idea of living abroad and subtly foster openness to new experiences in distant lands (Murphy-Lejeune, 2010). My focus is therefore on the 'internal or ascribed characteristics' of migration (Van Hear *et al.*, 2018: 930) and the role of habitus-level '[l]andscapes of belonging' (Conway and Leonard, 2014: 128). The approach adds an extra layer of depth to the 'external structural elements shaping the decision' to migrate (Van Hear *et al.*, 2018: 930) that I explored in Chapter 1 and as such corresponds to a 'push–pull plus' framework (2018: 927).

Returning to the diasporic field, I examine how a habituated sensation of security, conceptualised as the 'securiscape' and often resulting from normative comparison with France (Mulholland and Ryan, 2017; Higgins, 2019), is integral to feeling 'at home' (Hage, 1997; Levin, 2016), and paves the way for spontaneous belonging and settlement (Leavey *et al.*, 2004; Ryan, 2018). Subsequently, by considering aspects of participants' embodied dispositions which have evolved during their London sojourn, I argue that these internalised changes tend to manifest when the migrants are reconfronted with the originary habitat, where they increasingly feel like 'fish out of water', and hence undergo a reverse 'hysteresis effect' (Bourdieu, [1972] 2000; Huc-Hepher, 2018). I also examine participants' silent habituation to, and incorporation of, fundamental values dominant in the external diasporic field, in an effort to understand how they leave an indelible mark on the subjective habitus. Referred to as 'transculturation' by Pratt (1991: 36) and 'adaptation' by Murphy-Lejeune (2002: 205), I explore how this transformative process creeps up on migrants, undermining their agency and foregrounding that of the external field. Finally, by examining the role of humour in the postmigration space, I reveal that habituation can play a simultaneously divisive and cohesive role. It excludes participants from culturally cryptic insider interactions (Westcott and Vazquez

Maggio, 2016) and unites them through a common appreciation of shared reference points inherited from the originary field (Walsh, 2018). This in turn suggests that habituation is implicitly instrumental in the formation of diasporic friendship networks and hence the community-making process.

Rationalising migration vs habituated settlement: 'It's good to have London on your CV'

Notwithstanding the underlying social currents pushing some participants away from the originary field in search of 'perceived openness' (Murphy-Lejeune, 2002: 108) and reduced levels of symbolic violence (discussed in Chapter 1), many were quick to supply pragmatic pull factors dictating their mobility decision. However, in keeping with criticisms of the structuralist push–pull model, I posit that subtle, individuated – innate and/ or cultivated – and open-ended forces are also at play. Murphy-Lejeune (2002), Carlson (2011), Benson and O'Reilly (2009, 2016) all draw on Bourdieusian theories to demonstrate how some individuals are predisposed to migration. This complements Chiswick's self-selection paradigm (2008) and demonstrates how habitus factors serve to undermine rationalist discourses.

In her conception of 'mobility capital', Murphy-Lejeune (2002: 51) establishes four features implicitly influencing migration: family history, experience of (foreign) travel/language, experience of adaptation, and personality. Quoting Baudelaire, she contends that 'l'invitation au voyage' (2002: 52) or – more prosaically – the 'travel bug' (2002: 56) 'precedes the actual experience in the imagination of the future wanderer' (2002: 52). Similarly, Carlson conceives of mobility as a habitus (2011), a taken-for-granted eventuality borne of exposure to foreign climes when young or to habitual familial narratives. Benson and O'Reilly also underline habitus, particularly its non-seeing, habituated dimensions. They postulate that individuals have grown so accustomed to the choice saturating contemporary society that deciding to migrate is both an articulation of such agency and a submission to it: 'lifestyle migration occurs as the result of the reflexive assessment of opportunities ... but these opportunities ... emerge from the habitus of the individual, and are thus constrained' (Benson and O'Reilly, 2009: 620). In this light, rather than ensuing from a Cartesian 'decision-making calculus' alone (King *et al.*, 2014: 10), the migratory 'act' is underpinned by one's childhood trajectory, by 'encounters with difference' (Higgins, 2019: 21) and a habituated openness of mind inherited in the originary habitus. This irrefutably concords with the pre-mobility experiences of several of Block's research participants (2006) and my own.

The results of my pilot survey revealed that the average time respondents had reflexively anticipated residing in London was one and a half years, while the actual average was twelve years, with future settlement intentions ranging from five years to 'my whole life'. This ambivalence regarding prospective and retrospective lengths of stay is a common feature of intra-EU mobility, such that the 'discrepancy between planned and actual return has become a truism in migration research' (McGhee *et al.*, 2017: 2,110). Indeed, the London-based German, Italian and Latvian migrants studied by King *et al.* (2014) bear witness to the phenomenon, as do their Irish counterparts, most of whom 'had originally considered migration as temporary, intending to return at some unspecified time' (Leavey *et al.*, 2004: 774). Many of Favell's 'Eurostars' also 'saw the move as a short-term "shot in the dark", rather than a long-term investment' (Favell, 2008a: 66).

The equally blurry intentions of Dubucs *et al.*'s Paris-based Italians are insinuated in their study ('for those who decide to stay', 2017: 558), but are central to Snel *et al.*'s (2015) analysis of Polish, Romanian and Bulgarian migrants in the Netherlands, and to research by Drinkwater *et al.* (2015), McGhee *et al.* (2017) and Ryan (2015, 2018) on UK-based Polish migrants. Ryan's findings correspond to mine with notable proximity: 'most people spoke about coming for a year … Nevertheless, [… they] had gradually, sometimes unconsciously, extended their stay over time' (2018: 233). Rather than the 'intentional unpredictability' posited by Eade *et al.* (2007) or the 'deliberate indeterminacy' of Moriarty *et al.* (2010), my 'habituation' construct tends towards the unconsciousness of the process highlighted by Ryan, thus echoing the 'habitus of "indeterminacy"' postulated by McGhee *et al.* (2010: 2,110). This habitus of indeterminacy emerged repeatedly in interviews through a 'narrative silence' (King *et al.*, 2014: 34), participants unwilling to commit to any long-term aspirations of either stability or mobility. Those who did, were undecided whether their futures would be in London, where it is for octogenarian Suzanne; in France, 'vaguement' the intention of Sadia and Bruno; or an alternative (anglophone) migratory destination, for which Paulette, Moses and Brigitte expressed a latent desire.

The indeterminacy about participants' future trajectories acts as an extension to that regarding their premigration projections (Fechter and Walsh, 2010: 1,207). Charles typifies the initial experience of many with his account: 'I didn't have any precise plans about the date of my return, but I didn't expect to stay long. I vaguely imagined, very vaguely, that after two or three years, my English would be perfect and I'd have gained a new experience, and then I'd go back to the homeland.' His testimony is meaningful on multiple levels: first, in its reflexive underlining of his former lack of reflexivity and the inherent nebulousness of the migration 'project'; second, in its focus on aspirational imaginings, which tallies with the lifestyle migration model proposed by Benson and O'Reilly (2016); third, in its perpetuation of the myth of return, which Leavey *et al.* (2004) argue is a mechanism for maintaining originary identity and ties; fourth, in its rationalisation of migration in capital-gains terms, that is, in the projected acquisition of 'linguistic capital' (Bourdieu, [1982] 2001; Heller, 2006: 15) and a life-affirming 'experience' to 'cultivate new forms of selfhood' (Conradson and Latham, 2007: 238); and fifth, in its testament to the ongoing nature of migration (Benson, 2011; Benson and O'Reilly, 2016; Van Hear, 2018), where embedding plays out as a process rather than a deterministic product (Ryan and Mulholland, 2015).

Given that Charles had already been in London for eleven years when he made that comment, the disconnect between his 'vague' premigration intentions and settlement practices is confirmed, which reflects the rhetoric/ evidence discrepancy observed by Oliver and O'Reilly (2010), Benson (2011) and Conway and Leonard (2014). Moreover, his children's enrolment in British schools suggests his embedding will continue to solidify, reinforced through quietly commanding filial relationships (Ryan and Mulholland, 2014b; 2015; Ryan, 2018). This reveals yet another mismatch between the articulated prospect of return 'to the homeland' and the performativity of socially and affectively mobilised embedding. Through this single testimony, then, we get an idea of the inherent complexity and paradoxes of the (lifestyle) migration experience.

Despite these complexities and the tacit influence of habituation, London's pull is at times rationalised by participants in well-rehearsed meritocratic and opportunistic terms, resonating with the reasoning advanced by Ryan and Mulholland's informants (2013, 2014a). London's generous salaries, upward mobility, investment opportunities and free-market ideals are cited. For most, however, career prospects are discovered *after* experiencing the London workplace first-hand (as discussed in Chapter 1). The principal lure voiced by my participants is the cultural capital represented by possessing fluent English (Bellion, 2005; Ledain, 2010; Huc-Hepher and Drake, 2013; King *et al.*, 2014), itself convertible into economic capital if and when the myth of return is realised. Arthur, the 34-year-old Reunionese food and beverage manager, sums up the thinking: 'It's good to have London on your CV; that was my plan.'

Mirroring the narratives of young Germans, for whom the 'economic rationale for migration is largely missing [and] improving their English' takes precedence (King *et al.*, 2014: 10), a London sojourn is deemed the ideal mechanism to acquire both the linguistic and experiential assets required for a distinctive advantage in France. In this light, the rite of passage, popularly termed *les années Londres* in the London-French press (Huc-Hepher and Drake, 2013), speaks to 'the experiential attractions that these individuals associate with London [... and how] these experiences might ... be construed as "becoming cosmopolitan"' (Conradson and Latham, 2007: 233). Through the practical advantages offered by London's proximity (Leavey *et al.*, 2004; King *et al.*, 2014) and flexible labour market (Ryan and Mulholland, 2011), coupled with the symbolic capital of embodied cosmopolitanism, including the acquisition of English as a global language, my participants are able to reflexively and retrospectively strategise their mobility. Furthermore, their reasoning is validated by objective data circulating in the press, according to which France's unemployment rate is almost double that of the UK's (10.3 per cent against 5.5 per cent in December 2014; Statistiques Mondiales, 2015). Perceiving London as a city of short-term professional gain is therefore not without foundation, even if it means accepting that long-term career prospects 'take a back seat' (King *et al.*, 2014: 10) and that the economic argument oversimplifies the multifarious and evolving forces influencing mobility.

Moses' experience as a Black return migrant, whose *années Londres* amounted to a two-year stay, is a good – but rare – illustration of the above rationalisation strategy in action. His difficulty in finding employment in France, despite an International Business masters' degree, was the initial push. He came to England with the clear objective of 'developing the language' in order to secure a foothold in his chosen career on his return. He describes, in our telephone interview, how surprised he was to have been able to find work on his first day in the capital, and how, in his own enthused words, he had 'opened a bank account, found work and found a flat in under a week – it's quite amazing really'. In diametric opposition to the bureaucracy and staidness of France, where, as Marie explains, 'it's not easy to change job', London's propensity for spontaneity, flexibility, dynamism, lack of administrative hurdles and ultimately opportunities is what pulled Moses. Adhering to his plan, he returned to France once he had acquired the linguistic capital sought and has since been rewarded with employment commensurate with his qualifications: 'I know what I did was worthwhile, and I can see the difference between the people who've been abroad and the ones who've stayed in France. I'm really pleased I did it.'

Moses' temporal investment in a relatively short sojourn in London, occupying that hybrid 'grey zone' (Schubert-McArthur, 2009, cited by King *et al.*, 2014: 12) between tourism and migration, paid lucrative dividends on the job market in France. However, his trajectory was the exception among my participants, for whom *les-années-Londres* rite of passage has tended to, imperceptibly and progressively, metamorphose into an indefinite timespan, habituation having set in (Ryan and Mulholland, 2015; Benson and O'Reilly, 2016). As well as glossing over the 'seed of migration' (Findlay and Li, 1997: 38–9) sown in the individual habitus, the positive spin and agency deployed by Moses negates the underlying 'push–pull plus' drivers (Van Hear, 2018: 927) associated with discriminatory attitudes in France (see Chapter 1). It is precisely such habituated, habitus-instilled influences, that I explore in the following section.

'I was drawn to English very early on'

As Benson and O'Reilly assert, 'habitus provides us with a middle ground to think beyond the structure agency dichotomy' (2009: 617) readable into Moses' testimony. In so doing, it allows space for brushes with the Other during migrants' formative years to be factored into the mobility complex. These 'affective atmospheres ... are ... the result of the interplay between human and non-human bodies' (de Backer, 2019: 3), which de Backer refers to in social, technological, legal, historical and, crucially, urban frameworks. I would argue, however, that in contemporary society, such 'contact zones' (Pratt, 1991; Higgins, 2019) can also be experienced in less literal, more fluid terms (Appadurai, 1990), and less confrontationally than in Pratt's original conception. The 'everyday cosmopolitanism' construct is no longer restricted to multicultural cities, but realised through contact with media, literature (Wang, 2013a), travel and family histories (Murphy-Lejeune, 2002). In other words, Appadurai's ethnoscapes, mediascapes, technoscapes and ideoscapes (1990) have become so prevalent that they forge the individual habitus. They normalise multicultural encounters – however intangible – and prepare the ground for international mobility. Significantly, these seed-planting encounters emerge from participants' narratives more regularly than anticipated, constituting a pattern that undermines the agentive account provided by Moses. For example, in passing, Séverine mentions attending a German school in Paris; Bruno – of Italian-Basque-Breton heritage – describes travelling across the USA with his parents at the age of four; Brigitte alludes to growing up in Africa and Chantal also comments on living abroad as a child. In Chapter 2, we discovered that Suzanne had forged friendships with English *résistants* during the Second World War and later spent a month at an English school on a language exchange. Antoine discloses that his biological parents were Greek and Italian migrants, and that he had undergone an initial migration to an unfamiliar family when they relinquished him to adoption. Paulette and Moses recount their parents' respective Beninese and Senegalese heritage as a boundary against belonging in France, and Sadia's paternal Algerian bloodline also brings tensions. Yet all these 'encounters between cultural worlds' (Higgins, 2019: 102) and remembered (hi)stories contribute to a trove of formative 'family legends' (Carlson, 2011: 6), moulding the premigration habitus in the process.

I therefore argue that this exposure to other peoples and places, if only in the imaginations of the prospective migrants, acts as a subliminal migration trigger, producing habituation to the idea of mobility and stimulating desire to experience otherness for themselves. Moreover, participants' brushes with strangeness and difference squarely map onto the 'mobility capital' construct established by Murphy-Lejeune (2002). With Bruno, Moses, Paulette and Sadia, we observe the influence of family history 'in the shape of direct blood lineage ... [and] in the shape of migration' (Murphy-Lejeune, 2002: 52–3). We see it 'in the form of plurilingualism or pluricul-turalism, [which] is their natural habitat' (2002: 53) but also the institutional habitat of Suzanne and Séverine. Mobility abroad leaves a lasting impression on Brigitte, Chantal and Bruno, whereas Antoine's mobility away from the original family unit embodies 'adaptation as an initiation' (2002: 63), causing him to be 'confronted with an unknown world ... which confers on [him] the status of temporary stranger' (2002: 64). The only aspect that has not been evinced explicitly here, then, is 'the travelling personality' (Murphy-Lejeune, 2002: 70; Favell, 2008a). Defined by Murphy-Lejeune as one which is predisposed to 'openness to others, whether ... intellectual ... affective ... or social and relational' (Murphy-Lejeune, 2002), it is nevertheless a facet to which I return and illustrate through Bruno's and Séverine's experience.

Their natural (intellectual) curiosity about, and (affective) attraction to, English culture and language are made manifest in Bruno and Séverine's youth, when encounters with the other are mediated through popular culture. Bruno defines his initial attraction to London in the following terms: 'I liked English music, pop etcetera, British culture, the image it represents in France, the "bobbies", the Union Jack flag and everything that goes with it: the cooler, in inverted commas, side than in France.' Through the images and sounds of the mediascape that contributed to Bruno's adolescent habitat – subtly stimulated by an earlier encounter with the anglophone culture of the USA aged four, which arguably contributed to his predisposition to openness – Bruno is not only habituated to the idea of otherness, but *attracted* to the difference. Over time, and fuelled by English-language pop videos and British branding, he incorporates an idealised image of London cool that at once objectively contradicts and subjectively resembles the rural idyll imagined by other lifestyle migrants. Irrespective of the cultural and structural differences in the destinations – the 'buzz' of the global metropolis (Mulholland and Ryan, 2017) vs the bucolic buzzing of bees in the Lot (Benson, 2011) – their mediated premigration imaginings plant the mobility seed in both cases.

The power of mediated culture to shape a mobility-inclined habitus is also evinced among the skilled, mainland-Chinese migrants investigated by Wang, whose idealised image of Hong Kong is engraved on their imaginations prior to mobility and feeds into their desire: 'Their limited and fragmented knowledge about Hong Kong mostly came from Hong Kong films, TV series and popular songs' (Wang, 2013a: 391). Instead, therefore, of asserting that 'current global flows occur ... *in and through the growing disjunctures between ethnoscapes, technoscapes ... mediascapes and ideoscapes*' (Appadurai. 1990: 301; original emphasis), I contend that, on the scale of the individual, it is not 'disjunctures' but positive encounters between the different 'scapes' and contact zones that facilitate 'openness to foreign realities' and encourage 'a taste for travelling' (Murhpy, 2002: 55, 56).

Embedded deep in the primary habitus and mediated through television, analogous mobility influences are described by Séverine. She recounts a pre-reflexive attraction to the culturally nuanced humour of English comedy acts, such as Benny Hill and Monty Python. 'I've always been fascinated by England', Séverine explains, 'beginning when I was a teenager through "cheap comedy" programmes; I soon became interested in English humour which I found endearing, so ... I was drawn to English very early on.' In a space-culture-language conflation, and a progression from curiosity to attraction, Séverine bears witness to the multidimensionality of habituation. The German language of her schooling and her fascination for English are testament to the diversified portfolio that mobility capital represents. Meanwhile, the culture-specific absurdity of these British comedies is at once strangely foreign and strangely familiar, giving her 'a taste for difference' (Favell, 2008a: 67). They contrast starkly with the television of the 1970s and 1980s in France and Italy (for both are strikingly alike), and offer an escape from the 'constant game shows disguised as family entertainment, that last on average three hours at a time ... pitched against the gritty reality that is the Italian [and French] news programme' (Sprio, 2013: 168). For Sprio's postmigration Italian participants this audiovisual diet functions, albeit ineffectively, as a transnational anchor. For Séverine, however, it is at the root of her mobility, habituating her to the cultural capital of the romanticised Other and implanting a yearning, a longing to belong in an imagined elsewhere.

The indistinctness of participants' premigration 'plans' and their everyday habituation to international mobility, as scrutinised in this section, therefore confirms Favell's tentative hypothesis that intra-EU migration goes 'beyond the rational' (Favell, 2008a: 69). My findings also corroborate Findlay and Li's contention that 'the meaning of an individual's migration decision is situated in his or her life history, rather than just in the moment when the decision is made ... underscoring the significance of historical linkages between the cultural-social milieu of a migrant and the formation over time of values [and personal characteristics] conducive to migration' (Findlay and Li, 1997: 38–9). Thus, to fully understand how migration arises on the level of the subject, it is necessary to move away from the rationalised rhetoric often proffered by migrants and to dig beneath the surface. The role of desire (Wang, 2013a) must be factored into the process, especially how such desire is primed in the premigration habitat. To do this, as I have demonstrated here, we must examine the seeds lodged in family histories and encounters with difference that implicitly predispose individuals to migrate, in short, the habitus as a biographical process (Carlson, 2011).

Securing home: 'Never have I, for a single moment, felt unsafe'

Hopkins *et al.* argue that security studies rarely consider 'young people's everyday landscapes of security and insecurity' (2019: 439), and yet they enable important understandings 'about contestation over identities and belonging … through to structural, symbolic and everyday violence' (Hopkins *et al.*, 2019: 440). Equally, I argue that such landscapes, or 'securiscapes', to draw on Schafer ([1977] 1994) and Appadurai (1990), are largely absent from (lifestyle) migration studies, particularly in the case of intra-EU migration and when apprehending security as a postmigration embedding factor, as opposed to insecurity as a premigration driver (Cohen and Sirkeci, 2011). Mulholland and Ryan (2017) make fleeting reference to the sense of security experienced by their high-skilled London-French migrants, but do not consider it in detail. Yet, since the feeling of security, that is, an unguarded comfortableness in one's external surroundings, is integral to feeling at home, it is a component of long-term settlement I am keen to address.

In the same way that my participants overwhelmingly reported feeling welcome in London, so they depict the city as a place relatively devoid of hostility or latent danger. Even among those interviewees whose primary/secondary habitus was forged in rural or provincial France, the megacity and its diverse and numerous inhabitants are not perceived as a threat: 'I feel totally safe in London, totally free' declares the – potentially vulnerable – slight, octogenarian, Suzanne. It is telling that her perception of security is intertwined with one of liberation, which may have its roots in her wartime past, when freedom and safety were simultaneously denied her. However, this security-liberty coupling is also found in the securiscapes of Mulholland and Ryan's participants, who report that they 'feel free … protected … really free … but secure' (2017: 143). Similarly, Favell's research participants apprehend the European destination city as a place that 'makes you feel free … as a *refuge*: from the provinces' (Favell,

2008a: 5; original emphasis). It is thus a dualism with further reaching significance than Suzanne's experience alone.

Beyond the symbolic freedom from violence evoked by Favell's participants and implied by the security-freedom dualism, my participants underline the physical safety felt in London in comparison to Paris. This again echoes the *relational* construction of a London securiscape evoked in Mulholland and Ryan's comparative epistemological framework (2017). It also underscores the affective potency of the city, because participants' feelings of safety are at odds with crime statistics. In 2015, London recorded 107 homicides, against 41 in Paris (Eurostat, 2015a), and more broadly, 4,338,295 crimes were recorded in England and Wales in 2009 (the latest comparative records available), against 3,521,256 in France (Eurostat, 2015b). Yet, as Charles, the 34-year-old, Crystal-Palace-based correspondent bears out, there is a feeling of security in London that defies statistical logic: 'not even in Brixton or Tooting, never have I, for a single moment, felt unsafe … I'd say I feel safer in London than Paris, I mean, in Greater London than Greater Paris.' The distinction he makes between Paris and Greater Paris is relevant, as my participants tend to perceive London as a city which can be explored fully, from its inner-city depths to its peri-urban breadths, without fear of misguidedly wandering into a 'no-go' area once its outskirts are reached. Contrastingly, Paris is apprehended as pleasant and safe at its heart, but few participants would comfortably venture into its conceptually and physically marginalised *banlieues* (Bourdieu *et al.*, 1993), for fear of attack or abuse. Séverine, who has lived in London for the last twenty-six years and currently calls Nunhead home, admits she has never once entered a Parisian *banlieue*, despite having lived in Paris all her pre-London life. While she is currently located in an area that shares a postcode with Peckham, notorious for its endemic crime in the public consciousness, Séverine feels in no way threatened there. In this instance, however, her local securiscape is partly supported by statistics, since in May 2015 Peckham was ranked fourteenth from last in London, with 108 crimes and a rate of 6.95 per 1,000 residens, against 379 crimes and a rate of 295.17 for first-place holders, Oxford Street, Regent Street and Bond Street (UK Crime Stats, 2015). Here, therefore, Séverine's habituated experiential knowledge of the neighbourhood resists public imaginings of the place, whereas her experiential ignorance of Paris's *banlieues* fires the myth.

These 'invisible boundaries' (Abutbul-Selinger, 2018) separating inner-Paris from its outskirts in the minds and practices of most participants are partially embraced and partially rejected by returnee, Moses: 'there's a huge difference between Paris and the suburbs. I actually live in the *banlieue* and I know it's not Paris, there's no comparison.' Although Moses feels entirely safe in all areas of Paris, as was the case in London, having lived in areas as disparate as Dartford, Leyton, Abbey Wood, Arsenal and elsewhere, he recognises the gendered subjectivity of his outlook: 'in Paris, I myself don't feel threatened at all … maybe women feel differently about it. I do get the impression that, for a woman, London would feel a bit safer than Paris.' External space is thus internalised as a subjective imagining (Duchêne Lacroix and Koukoutsaki-Monnier, 2016), acting as 'structuring structures' (Bourdieu, [1972] 2000: 256), where experiential knowledge of the place can lead to habituation and consequent 'ontological security' (Hopkins *et al.*, 2019: 440) for some, but where for others, fear of the unknown fuels the apprehension. Moreover, while ethnicised boundaries may be becoming more porous in Europe's cities, gendered divides persist: '[t]he parochial atmospheres produced by groups of men indeed order the social and physical space of the neighbourhood and the wider city region' (de Backer, 2019: 13), leading to 'young women avoiding certain places due to the atmosphere of social control exerted by men' (2019: 17). Perceived to be a space comparatively free from the invisible gendered and ethnicised boundaries of Paris, where such parochial atmospheres (evidenced through the microaggressions discussed in Chapter 1) are compounded by the city's urban-planning, London's 'affective atmospheres' (2019: 3) and intermingling contact zones therefore contribute to its 'everyday cosmopolitanism' (2019: 2) and, as such, to a habituated sensation of combined security and freedom.

Until now, I have analysed how my participants envisage their securiscapes along dichotomous London–Paris lines. However, '[e]veryday landscapes of security and insecurity … can be shaped by factors positioned nearby as well as those that are geographically distant and remote' (Hopkins *et al.*, 2019: 442). Miranda and Brigitte confirm this, and support Moses' suspicion that for women, London feels relatively safe. Although they live in its notorious East End, which in their opinion has an unduly 'bad reputation' (Brice), Miranda feels 'strangely … safe here', thanks to the constant presence of other people in the surrounding streets. In an articulation of the 'normative geographies' defined by Higgins (2019: 101), Miranda compares her London securiscape with the rural village of her primary habitus, where at night she feels afraid to walk alone: 'there's absolutely nobody on the streets, and I'm scared to go home'. Similarly, Brigitte contrasts two London poles: 'I feel a lot safer here [in Bethnal Green] … than, for example, when I go out in West London. Notting Hill's very pretty, but it's very residential, and when you go home, nothing's open.' Paulette confirms Brigitte's misgivings, having had first-hand experience of hostility in the West London area where she resides, but nonetheless perceiving London as an unthreatening space: 'I feel safe in London, even though I was assaulted here once, which is something that's never happened to me in France.'

Despite her negative experience, Paulette continues to see her adopted home in a paradoxically favourable light, which could be explained by the unconsciousness recounted (in English) by urban planner, Antoine: 'I feel safe in London. In Paris I wouldn't go in some places at certain times. In a way, in London you are more oblivious to it than in Paris.' This raises the question of whether my participants are seeing and experiencing the British capital through an unrealistically idealised prism (Farrer, 2010). In a continuation of the romanticised lens established in the premigration context, are they effectively blind to the city's vices as a result of not having been subjected to the habituated transmission of parental fears, taken for granted in the primary habitat/habitus?

Such an idealised construction of their London securiscape could be an unintentional mechanism to convince participants (and relatives or friends left behind) that the aspirations they had hoped to achieve through mobility have been realised, in other words, that 'the good life' (Oliver and O'Reilly, 2010: 5) has been found. Alternatively, it is possible that their propensity for optimism, utopianism even, is a disposition typical of those who have voluntarily opted to migrate, a characteristic intrinsic to Murphy-Lejeune's 'travelling personality' (2002: 70). Chiswick explains that 'economic migrants tend to be favourably *self-selected* ... tending, on average, to be more able, ambitious, aggressive, entrepreneurial, healthier, or otherwise have more favourable traits than similar individuals who choose to remain in their place of origin' (2008: 64). Although I do not position my participants within an economic typology, I do contend that their optimism falls within the category of other 'favourable traits' and is a disposition that might explain their exaggerated sense of security. In this way, Chiswick's observation both confirms the 'special kind of mentality' alluded to by Favell (2008a: 66) and situates the feeling of security within the 'mobility capital' framework developed by Murphy-Lejeune (2002: 51).

As we have seen in this section, the affective and subjective dimensions of the migrant securiscape have dominated. In a spontaneous normative juxtapositioning with spaces and places within and beyond London, participants have manifested ways in which their 'security landscapes are embodied, emotional, intimate and marked by age, gender, and racialised social and cultural relations' (Hopkins *et al.*, 2019: 440). Through the prism of security, therefore, I have demonstrated the powerful and circular interplay between feeling safe and feeling 'at home', both of which are contingent on habituation and conducive to long-term settlement. By asserting that they feel safe in their diasporic habitat, as opposed to the homeland or other parts of London, participants perform their embeddedness and attainment of an unseeing sense of belonging. In this way, the construction of imagined securiscapes is habituated settlement in practice.

The transformative creep of habituation: 'You could end up becoming a Londoner without realising'

The concluding chapter of Murphy-Lejeune's monograph on intra-EU student mobility is dedicated to 'adaptation' processes (2002: 205). While it presents some useful parallels to the transformations my participants undergo, I consider the term 'adaptation' to be overly agentive. Building on the premigration and postmigration aspects of habituation examined thus far, the focus here is on *pre-reflexive* transformation over time, on 'the agency of the world city' (Scott, 2006: 1,110) to change the migrants beyond their conscious control, rather than their ability to adapt to their surroundings (explored in Chapter 4). A key facet of habituation is the transfer of tacit knowledge (Polanyi, 1975), often through unvocalised, embodied learning (Streeck, Goodwin and LeBaron, 2011; Bezemer *et al.*, 2014). Unlike a calculated 'lesson', this implicit, corporeal teaching is absorbed in a taken-for-granted, incognisant and reproductive fashion (Jenkins, 2002). The transformative potential of this tacit 'learning', encapsulated in my habituation construct, is important, since it explicitly acknowledges the generative capacity of habitus (Maton, 2012). Cornejo Torres and Rosales Ubeda argue that the dispositions constituting one's habitus are 'inculcated in a lasting way ... by a pedagogical action' (Cornejo Torres and Rosales Ubeda; 2015: 1,249) within the context of external conditions. Despite the durability of individual characteristics, 'identity belonging is not "destiny"' per se (Duchêne Lacroix and Koukoutsaki-Monnier, 2016: 150); it arises through 'the accumulation of experiences and dispositions' (2016: 150), some of which 'are activated or inhibited, improved or diminished within certain conditions' (2016: 150–1).

Thus, it is the agency and effects of the diasporic conditions that I examine in this section, assessing how participants' internal subjectivities have been altered by their surroundings, looking particularly at the 'double historicity of mental structures' (Bourdieu and Wacquant, 1992: 113). That is, how habitus, as incorporated patterns of thinking and practice (1992: 113), is acquired twofold, in the inherited dispositions developed in the London social space over generations and in the present 'acquiring [of] "a history" over time' (Murphy-Lejeune, 2002: 209). In other words, this internalised double historicity corresponds to the characteristics that are associated with the London space as a result of its past peoples, practices and attitudes, and how these dispositions are incorporated by my participants as an embodied history (and potentially retransmitted). It is what I conceptualise as habituation to the local environment, to such an extent that London history-turned-social-structure becomes – indiscernibly – part of who the migrants are, or who they have become.

'That's how we live in London, why change when I go back?'

This form of habituation manifests itself in myriad material ways, for instance in the subtle changes to my participants' habitats and habits resulting from their long-term settlement in London, as evidenced in Chapter 2, where Robert alluded to the 80:20 ratio of Englishness to Frenchness in his home. Sarah reflects on a similar phenomenon, but addresses the transformative potential of settlement: 'To begin with I brought back quite a lot of personal artefacts [from France], and then over time they've gradually broken and been replaced; now I don't have many things that are truly French at home. It's the passage of time that brings about integration.' Her journey of dislocation, relocation and ultimate detachment from the originary habitat/habitus is materialised through the displacement and gradual *disintegration* of the objects, resulting in a passively contented sentiment of subjective *integration* in the London habitat. Her feeling of embeddedness is achieved not through design, but through an organic, unforeseen, and therefore more potent, process of regeneration over time: from disintegration to integration. However, my focus here is on participants' assimilation of local mentalities and dispositions embodied unwittingly through the transfer of tacit knowledge within the diasporic space.

As they discuss their migrant trajectories with me, many interviewees embark on a journey of self-discovery, being placed in the rare situation of having to objectify their subjective experience through the very act of articulating memories, feelings and intimate thoughts. By transposing them into the material form of spoken language, they are, in some cases for the first time, detaching themselves from their day-to-day existence and taking time to consider their positioning within the migratory field, both from the inside out and outside in, which again mirrors the subject–object dynamics of habitus. Birch and Miller (2000) confirm that 'the interviewee may experience the action of disclosure as a revelation, prompting a new understanding of past events' (2000: 190). Atkinson (2012: 123), on the other hand, places the meaning-making potential of the interview on the 'personally sacred' bond forged between researcher and interviewee, which 'creates a clear and strong sense of coming to know something new and valuable through the relationship created by the interview itself' (2012: 123). In my interviews, the reflexivity required by the interaction often triggers an awakening to participants' 'drift of character' (Elliott, 2008: 140) or, more deleteriously, 'corrosion of the self' (2008: 140). Their awakenings are not, however, necessarily experienced in the negative manner implied by 'corrosion' or 'risk of local infection' (Murphy-Lejeune, 2002: 220). For many, transformations such as increased resilience and confidence levels are noted.

Séverine is a case in point. During our conversation, she becomes aware of how London has not only remodelled her into a more liberal and insouciant individual, but equipped her with the personal attributes needed to progress in the socio-professionally more competitive diasporic field. Recalling the characteristics identified by Chiswick (2008), she declares: 'I've become less anxious, more tolerant ... maybe be more resourceful. I've developed a more entrepreneurial temperament.' Forty-two-year-old Laura, a singer-songwriter based in Clapham, describes her newfound self-confidence in the sartorial-transformation terms alluded to in Chapter 1 and shared by many of my London-French students. Beginning their undergraduate degrees embodying the archetypal image of (white) bourgeois France (long, flowing, natural hair, discreet attire, no obvious jewellery), I have observed many ending their studies with shaven heads or blue hair, piercings in a variety of body parts and clothes that would be perceived as entirely 'from the side of the Other' (Bourdieu, 1999: 13) in 'conservative' (King *et al.*, 2014: 20) France.[1] In Laura's account of her sartorial transformation, she expresses a rare awareness of the subtle codes that differentiate her French and UK audiences:

> when I'm here, I deliberately wear outfits I know will look a bit *français* ... I've got a dress I think looks quite French. I wear it here, but I wouldn't wear it in France. It's black with small white polka-dots, and at the bottom there are little frills. And in France, I'm more likely to wear jeans and a T-shirt, more everyday; a bit more dressed-up in England than in France ... more rock 'n' roll. If I'd never come to England, I think I'd be more uptight about loads of stuff, I'd never have dressed like that.

Going from the Paris Stock Exchange to a singing career in London, Laura's growing sartorial confidence is the material reflection of an overarching identity shift, representing her 'freedom to take risks ... freedom to decide which moral code [she] is going to live by; [and] freedom to present [her]self as a different sort of person, freedom to become a different person' (Conradson and Latham, 2007: 245). Thus, rather than being a solely reflexive decision to appeal to her respective audiences, Laura's sartorial transformation is an expression of the liberating force of the migratory field, an embodiment of the relationship between appearance and surrounding 'social norms and expectations' (Valentine, 2001: 29). However, the transformation is not complete; for the polka-dot dresses and 1970s' velvet suits from Clapham's 'shabby-chic' vintage/charity shops are rejected when Laura is in France. This substantiates Bourdieu's contention that '[d]ispositions are long-lasting: they tend to perpetuate, to reproduce them-selves, but they are not eternal' (Bourdieu, 2005: 46). Although Laura's dispositions are undergoing change, with her habitus 'being re-structured, transformed in its makeup by the pressure of objective structure' (2005: 46), such change is subject to the competing pressures of both the originary and diasporic fields. Laura's overtly feminised London attire is not, therefore, replicated in France.

As we saw in Chapter 1, '[t]he decision over what to wear incorporates the normative expectations of what is acceptable to wear' (Woodward, 2005: 25) and these expectations differ in France and London (Mulholland and Ryan, 2017). Having established in the last section that 'women … do not enjoy the same spatial liberty' (de Backer, 2019: 11) in Paris as in London, we begin to understand why Laura might deploy 'defence tactics when navigating that space (dressing appropriately)' (de Backer, 2019: 11). Her growing expressive confidence – garment- and performance-wise – is nevertheless *in the process* of constituting a habituated London aesthetic, and one she is now tentatively carrying back across the Channel in what could be conceived of as a non-economic, cultural remittance (Cohen and Sirkeci, 2011): 'as a result of living in England … there are things I wouldn't have done before, but now I say to myself that's how we live in London, why change when I go back [to France]? For instance, I wear blue nail varnish on stage!' If not a major transformation, the blue nail polish bears witness to Laura's increasing indifference to the judgemental gaze of her Parisian audi-ence (Mulholland and Ryan, 2017). Her migratory experience is progres-sively empowering her to embody the 'imperfection and eccentricity' (Deen and Katz, 2008) deemed to epitomise London and to subversively flout the sartorial codes of Paris, supposedly 'the epitome of perfection and elegance' (Deen and Katz, 2008). In this sense, when performing in France, through her growing rejection of the taken-for-granted sartorially understated (stereo)type, Laura is performing her habituation to, and embeddedness in, the London field. At the same time, she is potentially transforming mentali-ties in Paris. Her cautious Paris-based embodiment of the whimsical tastes permeating the London habitat is increasingly, therefore, 'not an expression of other people's "gaze", but rather an interiorized and more controlled replacement of those absent others' (Miller, 2001: 7) – in this case, Laura's physically absent, but subjectively present, *London* audience and identity.

This (re)gained confidence is a trait shared by many of my participants. It is doubtless a corollary of the confidence boost provided by the initial migration, the 'circularity' of which is bolstered by the continued naviga-tion of, and habituation to, the migratory field. It is also a feature of other studies, which underline the 'self-actualization' (Cohen and Sirkeci, 2011) and 'resubjectification' (Conradson and Latham, 2007: 234) potential of mobility, or the 'cultural capital (i.e. specific skills, qualifications, knowledge and dispositions)' acquired (Carlson, 2018: 468). Benson and O'Reilly refer to the 'liberatory potential, instilling into people the idea that they can do anything they want' (2009: 611), and Roudaut describes a young Guadeloupian migrant's experience of finding 'abroad what France made him lose: his self-confidence' (2009: 65). Laura's immersion in the London social field has equipped her with the self-worth needed to realise her singer-song-writing aspirations. Likewise, Miranda, officially a doctoral linguistics student, and Brice, a business consultant, have developed the confidence to perform their newfound 'Londonishness' (Engel, 2014: 496) in ways they would not have considered premigration: respectively pole-dancing and amateur dramatics. Both participants have become habituated to such pastimes through immersion in less conservative attitudes than France, perceived to be a society, like Italy, 'incapable of change and inimical to progressive life-courses for young people, who feel they have no control over their destiny' (King *et al.*, 2014: 22). Contrastingly, in the diasporic space, the agency of the city has exerted its power to habituate them to local mentalities, the empowering appropriation of which has enabled greater postmigration agency over their destiny, or at least their identity. In short, it has allowed them to take 'on fresh cultural freight from their new ambiance' (Cohen, 2014: 2) and express it through their liberating after-dark practices.

'You always learn to say "please, thank you, could you" here'

While not expressed as confidence per se, and not outwardly manifested in his clothes or practices, Charles undergoes what could be termed an 'ideological transformation':

> I feel like my perspective on certain things has really changed since I've been here; I don't see things in the same way anymore. I've really radically changed on a number of points … I decided to stop … following a sort of ideological catechism, and so now I prefer to be more pragmatic and judge things based on evidence rather than on what it's right or wrong to think. And I think that's something I've learnt here in Britain. I think by expatriating, you liberate yourself from some ideological shackles.

As with Laura, the act of migration is emancipatory, freeing Charles from the (left-wing) ideological dogma of the originary socio-professional field and French intelligentsia habitus set within it. He cannot, however, be deemed an ideological migrant (Chiswick, 2008), since his epistemological 'drift' is the habituated *product* of the migratory field (Thompson, 2010), rather than a mobility objective. Despite its liberating force, Charles's politico-phrenic transformation and agentive 'de-habituation' from the dominant premigration *Weltanschauung* is also indicative of increasing detachment from the homeland (Conway and Leonard, 2014), brought to bear yet more emphatically by Arthur.

Along the journey of our conversation (Atkinson, 2012), Arthur describes an attitudinal transformation conveyed through a softening of the 'harsher' Reunionese edges of his personality and the adoption of local politeness codes. In his words, 'you always learn to say "please, thank you, could you", here', such that both his personality and outlook have metamorphosed: 'I'm not the same person anymore; there are things, if I go back to Reunion, that I won't like: the way people speak, the way they react. For instance, my family say "you've really changed; you're calmer; you think more" – and that's the more positive side of having lived here. I think I'm a little bit English now.'

As a consequence of habituation to the perceived 'gentlemanly civility' of the migratory field, Arthur has unwittingly undergone a process of 'transculturation', adopting the politeness dispositions and expecting the same of those around him. Similarly, Mulholland and Ryan's French participants have a 'sense of London as a place marked by a virtuous form of public sociality [and ...] inheriting a tradition of rule-abiding public civility' (Mulholland and Ryan, 2017: 142). These accounts therefore bear witness to the 'double historicity' (Bourdieu and Wacquant, 1992: 113) of the habituation process, being embedded in the migrants' common self-appropriation of 'the complexities of local history' (Murphy-Lejeune, 2002: 224) and in the inherited traditions of the London social space, internalised as a '"life lesson"' (2002: 226). The power of the city to 'soften their personality' (2002: 226), in Arthur's case as in Séverine's and, more pragmatically, Charles's, effectively distinguishes them from those of the primary/secondary habitat and substantiates the tertiary habitus hypothesis posited in Chapter 2. Just as Bourdieu contended, the confrontation between Arthur's subjective dispositions and the differing objective structures of the diasporic field has resulted in a restructuring of his originary habitus (Bourdieu, 2005), which has rendered him 'out of sync' with the originary habitat.

In this sense, therefore, we note the emerging potential of habituation to alienate migrants from the people and places they once called home, in an operationalisation of what Bourdieu refers to as the 'hysteresis effect', but in reverse. Hysteresis arises when there is a discrepancy between a migrant's subjectivised habitus and the external field (Bourdieu, [1972] 2000). This unsettling lack of synchronicity is most often associated with the 'culture shock' (Walsh, 2012: 49, citing Oberg, 1960 and Pederson, 1995) triggered by confrontation with the migratory field (Thatcher and Halvorsrud, 2016). However, I argue that once postmigration habituation to local mentalities and practices has crept into individual subjectivities, there is greater likelihood of a 'reverse hysteresis effect' (Huc-Hepher, 2018), or what Murphy-Lejeune refers to as 're-entry shock' (2002: 225). Noble (2013) gives prominence to this surreptitious phenomenon in his ethnographic study of a Lebanese-Australian academic who awakens uncomfortably to his evolved habitus during a short visit to the 'homeland'. The cultural encounter gives rise to a profound sense of reverse 'habitus hysteresis' (Bourdieu, [1972] 2000: 278), the stare of 'the Other' (Fechter, 2005) bringing the migrant face to face with his embodied Australianness, of which he had been previously unaware. He demonstrates the pervasiveness of the diasporic field, affecting not only objectified dispositions, such as attire (shorts) and habits tacitly acquired (using a seatbelt, eating a sandwich while walking in public), but subjective characteristics (in keeping with Arthur), such as attitudes towards driving practices. More disconcertingly for the participant, this cultural confrontation brings a consciousness of his acquired ethnicity, that is, his tacitly embodied 'whiteness', recalling the experiences of Turkish returnees, dubbed the '*Alamanyali*, the "Germanlike"' (Brettell, 2008: 117, citing Mandel, 1989) and Portuguese '*franceses*' (Brettell, 2008: 117, citing Brettell, 1986). Encounters with the people and structures of the originary field often, therefore, instigate a rude awakening to hitherto habituated dispositional metamorphoses, for 'reality is relational' (Bourdieu, 1994: 17).

Although Arthur's and Charles's growing awareness of their civility/ ideology habitus mutations are less disorientating than those of Noble's informant, they are equally prevalent. Echoing Arthur, habituation to diasporic articulations of courtesy are referred to repeatedly by my research participants. Their examples range from the escalator etiquette mentioned in Chapter 2[2] and mythologised queuing at bus stops, to the 'agreeable experience' of car-drivers systematically giving way to pedestrians at zebra crossings (Cordier, 2005: 132) or to oncoming vehicles, as Laura explains:

> And as for driving ... the real joy is that people let each other pass: it's a pleasure to stop before the other car to let it go first. In France, both cars will stop nose-to-nose for sure, and the one who manages to get through will say 'got you!' That's what it's like in France, people wouldn't dream of letting someone else go first. The French have lost their enjoyment in being obliging, because they think they'll be seen as idiots if they are.

Laura's testimony is indicative of her culturally and moralistically situated gaze (Noble, 2013). My London-French participants (and Mulholland and Ryan's, 2017) are again not alone in this respect, since Fox's crossnational interviewees are equally 'impressed by our [English] courtesy' and it is 'among the most common responses in SIRC's international discussion groups and surveys' (Fox, 2014: 232–3). Previously oblivious to 'discourteous' practices in the homeland, only through habituation to a set of – idealised – structures in the diasporic field do the migrants become aware, and critical, of the mores of the originary social space. Nevertheless, these normative awakenings potentially have wider implications, for imperceptible 'values [are] internalised and embodied by individual actors, in processes of socialisation into a culture' (Waterson, 2005: 336). Playing out 'the partly pre-scripted perceptions and imaginings of their places of dwelling, and the affective/atmospheric qualities of those places' (Mulholland and Ryan, 2017: 149), such stereotypical value judgements therefore perpetuate the essentialisation of 'the English' as a distinctly law-abiding and courteous nation. This in turn carves out space along national lines, entrenching normative geographies (Higgins, 2019) and histories.

In this way, participants subtly contribute to processes of cultural and national division rather than transnationalising the EU horizontally, as one might expect (Carlson, 2018). By relying on the age-old tropes of English civility and humour (another common finding), they subliminally affirm the (self)fulfilment their mobility brings (Benson and O'Reilly, 2009) and are blinded to London's grittier reality. This therefore confirms that 'contact across differences does not necessarily lead to changing attitudes, just as daily cross-cultural courtesies do not automatically preclude the existence of prejudices and stereotypes' (de Backer, 2019: 3; citing Valentine, 2008). No matter how positive, participants' habituated stereotyping thus undermines the 'everyday cosmopolitanism' associated with London and other global cities (de Backer, 2019: 3), and instead foregrounds the historicity and reproductiveness of habitus (Bourdieu and Passeron, 1970). Indeed, a reflective anecdote provided by Suzanne illustrates the sub-surface workings of these 'cross-cultural courtesies' in London, which Fox positions within 'a predominantly "negative-politeness" culture – concerned mainly with the avoidance of imposition and intrusion – [and having] very little to do with friendliness or good nature' (2014: 271). She recounts:

> I'll always remember; I was walking up … Park Lane and as I passed a bus-stop, I saw an Indian chief with feathers all around his head that went right down to his feet. It was very, very remarkable, and I looked at all the people who were queuing up (because we always used to queue waiting for the bus, people would be one behind the other), and I looked at all those people, and not one of them, not a single person looked round to watch the Indian chief walk past. That's just to show you how you had to behave, it was every man for himself. That's why I was told it would take me two years to get used to it.

Rather than interpret this disregard as a form of politeness or openness to other cultures, the queuers' lack of (eye) contact communicating their respect for individual privacy (Fox, 2014), Suzanne perceives it to be hostile. Her reaction is important because it counters the extolling of London's laissez-faire, open-minded attitudes cited elsewhere in the literature (Conradson and Latham, 2007; King *et al.*, 2014), as well as shedding light on my own findings (for example, a Focus Group One participant spoke fondly of the complete lack of reaction to her mother's public pyjama-wearing in Newham). Suzanne's narrative thus challenges the assumption that habituation to London's 'overlapping transnational fields' (Carlson, 2018: 468) necessarily produces the everyday cosmopolitanism expressed by Robert: 'this British, even cosmopolitan, culture ... has opened my mind, not only to British culture, but to other cultures actually: Latino culture, Asian culture, which I never had any exposure to in Lille'. Instead, Suzanne confirms de Backer's contention 'that "civility towards diversity" ... is actually a sort of Simmelian indifference towards diversity [... not ...] an expression of openness' (de Backer, 2019: 3), or what Mulholland and Ryan term 'tolerant disinterestedness' (2017: 143). These affectively, culturally and morally charged migrant stories again give a sense of the multi-layered complexity of habituation, as well as its wider, societal implications.

'If there isn't someone from outside to give you feedback about your behaviour, you don't actually see it'

Further evidence of this is provided by entrepreneur-cum-author, Hamid Senni. Once a second-generation Moroccan migrant in France and now a first-generation French migrant in London, he bears witness to a realisation considerably less comfortable than Robert's. Tinged with shame, his account describes his spontaneous reaction to an encounter with a Sikh in his City office: 'I also remember this IBM expert with his turban on his head ... At first I mistook him for a cleaner: a completely French reflex which automatically places people from abroad at the bottom of the ladder' (Senni, 2007: 168). The wording chosen to relate the experience is telling: 'reflex' and 'automatically' illustrate the habituated, tacit workings of the French field having moulded Senni's profound habitus, of which habituation to postmigration mindsets now makes him aware. Whereas his lack of cultural sensitivity ('with his turban on his head') demonstrates the insidiousness of the originary field, the author remaining apparently unaware of the potentially offensive tone of his language.

In this way, Senni's testimony paradoxically (given his minority positioning) bears out Colquhoun's (2012: 38) assertion that the 'most difficult thing about majorities is not that they cannot see minorities, but that they cannot see themselves. There is no contrast, no dissonance, everything is white on white' (quoted by Higgins, 2019: 88). Irrespective of his inherited ethnicity and the discrimination to which he was subjected as a result (explored in Chapter 1), Senni has incorporated the discriminatory views of the premigration social space (Simon, 2006). In a reformulation of the process described by Noble (2003), Fechter (2005) and Leonard (2010a), mobility has brought his acquired 'whiteness' to light. 'Are French people white?' asks Beaman in her 2018 paper. Senni's experience would suggest they are, even when they are not, such is the power of field and habitus dynamics. For habitus is 'a product of history, that is of social experience and education' (Bourdieu, 2005: 45), and because the dispositions and 'habitus of a determinate person ... have something in common, a kind of [(white) French] affinity ... a systematicity' (Bourdieu, 2005: 44), it means they 'cannot be corrected completely, despite all one's efforts' (Bourdieu, 2005: 45). Senni's realisation that he does not have complete agency over his outlook, despite the symbolic violence suffered in France, despite his *intellectual* desire for racial equality and despite believing he had grown habituated to the multicultural indifference of the London social space, comes as a blow. Habituation for Senni is, therefore, partial, with social conditioning and (imperial) historicity (Fechter, 2005; Fechter and Walsh, 2010; Higgins, 2019) functioning as a barrier to transformation of the self (Conradson and Latham, 2007).

Senni's avowal provides insights into both the potency and the limits of habituation. These are stressed further by 52-year-old François, a surgeon from eastern France, whose disquieting awakening to his nascent Londonishness is, in keeping with Laura and Noble's informant, realised through local motoring practices:

> London's changed me ... It's warfare here [at the wheel], I'm really aggressive, five centimetres away from the bumper in front of me. And if there isn't someone from outside to give you feedback about your behaviour, you don't actually see it. You have to be very careful here ... because otherwise, you could end up becoming a Londoner without realising. I don't see any nastiness in Londoners, but I don't see any generosity either. And I'm sure it's not because they're like that: London changes you.

Here, the implicit agency of the city – 'London changes you', but 'you don't actually see it' – is central to François's understanding of the habituation process. Yet, the urban agency evoked does not equate to Mulholland and Ryan's conception of cities 'as agents seeking to attract highly skilled migrants' (2017: 138). Rather, we see the noetic and praxial effects of London in action, shaping François's habitus and committing him to 'a complex interaction during which an awareness of self and others undergoes a metamorphosis' (Murphy-Lejeune, 2002: 2016). This subjective transmutation, brought into relief by others, leads to an 'order of mirrorings ... between the self and the environment' (Leach, 2005: 307), where the aggression of the city is reflected in François's aggression. His reflexive consciousness of London's transformative power thus generates his active resistance to it ('you have to be very careful ... because otherwise'). In this way, his experience tallies with that of a British teacher in Hong Kong, who 'admits that he feels his identity is slowly being crafted for him, and, albeit somewhat remorsefully, he can feel his resistance to this slowly ebbing away' (Leonard, 2010: 1,259).

A charmingly courteous and wholeheartedly 'generous' individual, François has dedicated his professional life to helping others in his capacity as a consultant in an inner-city NHS hospital. He is generous enough to grant me over two hours of his limited time, despite several urgent interruptions for therapeutic advice from junior colleagues. Far from being 'aggressive', he appears calm, longanimous and able to decelerate to enjoy London's hidden 'islands of well-being', not least the tranquil surroundings of the Richmond houseboat he now calls home. The aggression he claims to embody is therefore as much a revelation to me as it is to François. More surprising, however, is the contrast it represents to Laura's rhapsodised account of London driving practices. Words such as 'joy', 'pleasure', 'enjoyment' and 'obliging' ornament her description, whereas 'warfare', 'aggressive', 'bumper' and 'nastiness' dominate François's. The diametric opposition between both semantic fields: dreamy pleasure vs physical hostility, not only reflects the divergence in their habituated experience of London motoring, but bears witness to the diversity of voices represented by participants (Walsh, 2018). Indeed, my findings correspond to the 'narrative polyphony' evoked by Murphy-Lejeune (2002: 49) and Leonard (2008; 2010b), and confirm the difficulty in attempting to shoehorn London-French mobility into one typology (or even six, as in Scott's lifestyle morphology of Paris Brits (2004, 2006)). Although commonalities emerge from my research, it is important to acknowledge the myriad lived encounters with the global city. For Laura, a trailing wife (Kofman, 2004), whose mobility was prompted by her husband's career, London feels like a permanent holiday, which recalls the 'tourist' metaphor used by one of Conradson and Latham's respondents (2007: 242) and the '[r]esidential tourism' associated with lifestyle migration by Benson and O'Reilly (2009: 611, citing Aledo Tur, 2005). For François, on the other hand, quotidian exposure to the raw, brutalism of an inner-city London hospital has a profound effect on his London experience:

When the young ones in my team do the morning ward rounds, it's not to find out *if* there have been any stabbings, but to find out how many. And each week, we don't wonder *if* there's been a shooting, it happens every week. If you go for a walk through the hospital corridors, in practically each wing there'll be two armed police keeping watch ... The media focus on teenagers, so if you're under 15, you show up in the media, and if you were carrying a gun and you shoot another 14-year-old – that, that will end up in the papers, but there are adults too, and it's every day, every day, every day ... I'm in the thick of it here; it's not the most violent area, but in terms of drugs, it's one of the most affected.

Recalling the way in which one of Leonard's informant's 'early identity was gradually displaced by the organisational one' provided by his employer, the Hong Kong Police (2010a: 1,255), the particularly violent professional field in which François operates has infiltrated his habitus, causing apprehension in the face of transmuting dispositions considered characteristic of the 'host' society. François's agentive resistance to this embodied habituation, 'through [a] process of awareness and pedagogic effort' (Bourdieu, 2005: 45), is therefore proportional to the anxieties generated by the specific field. Drawing on Bourdieu, Carlson (2018) conceptualises European society as a set of coexisting fields and contends that migrants, as 'actors within these fields ... have internalized the corresponding ways of thinking and acting and, in turn, have developed appropriate strategies' (Carlson, 2018: 474). Consequently, I posit that François's agentive resistance to the creep of Londonishness is a coping tactic to mitigate the day-to-day psychological pressure of his professional field. Importantly, his testimony also provides insights on a broader scale, illustrating not only the polyvocality of the London-French experience, but the agentive 'polyspatiality' of the global city itself, different fields creating different spaces and transforming habitus in different ways.

Bringing this section to a close and bearing witness to the overwhelming force of the postmigration field on habitus subjectivities, is the account of one of the few returnees interviewed. Catherine, now an English teacher in Bordeaux, lived in South Woodford and Acton for five years in the 1980s. However, the extent of her embedding in London over that relatively short period of time only becomes apparent to her on return to France:

It's a bit like what happens to people who suddenly become unemployed ... having to reintegrate into everyday life, in another country [France], having to find your bearings again and your old habits in another setting isn't easy ... I wasn't at home in France anymore; my home was in London. I think that's it: I hadn't realised that I wasn't at home in France anymore.

Catherine's recollections endorse Noble's observation that re-immersion in the homeland can instigate a realisation that returnees 'are not the person they were; but it is perhaps not so obvious that they have become a particular kind of difference' (Noble, 2013: 350). This reverse hysteresis, gradually and undetectably creeping up on participants, can leave them with a cleft habitus (Bourdieu, 2004; Thatcher and Halvorsrud, 2016), or 'painfully fragmented self' (Friedman, 2016: 110), resulting from the 'considerable disjuncture between their present circumstances and the world' they have left behind (Thatcher and Halvorsrud, 2016: 89). The 'painfulness' of the experience is not to be underplayed, as Catherine demonstrates, likening it to the sense of loss caused by sudden joblessness. Similar feelings are called to mind by Walsh, who juxtaposes her sense of belonging in Dubai with the 'disorientating ... sense of non-belonging' on her return to the UK (Walsh, 2018: 152). While Karen Till (2001: 46, cited in Walsh, 2018) describes the 'almost schizophrenic' feeling, 'torn between worlds, cultures, sets of social relations and selves'. Of theoretical significance, however, is how Catherine's words map directly onto my threefold habitus construct. Her spatial alienation in the French *habitat* is conveyed through finding her 'bearings again' in the 'setting'. She refers directly to re-adopting what have now become unfamiliar 'habits', while habituation is conjured through her not having 'realised' she was no longer at home in France.

Catherine's testimony therefore validates the habitus triad that has grown out of this ethnography. More importantly, it confirms migration's quiet capacity to re-sculpt habitus, in both its embodied and praxial forms, according to the structures of the diasporic field. Beyond her reflexive agency, Catherine, like the other participants examined in this section, has undergone profound 'identity slippage' (Mulholland and Ryan, 2011: 5). Yet, such transformation has emerged indiscernibly and over time, thereby supporting Block's argument that identity should be conceptualised as a process (2006: 29). This, in turn, brings us to Freud's notion of the 'dynamic unconscious' and the way it 'continually disrupts the things we take for granted and subverts the things we take to be true' (Frosh, 1997: 242, cited in Lawler, 2008: 79), such is the power of habituation.

Reaching the limits of habituation: 'I like English humour, when I get it'

In this final section, I examine the particular role of humour in participants' habituation to British and London culture. Given its subtle, culturally codified workings, it is an aspect of habituated belonging which can serve both to include and exclude (Westcott and Vazquez Maggio, 2016). It is also a key aspect of sociability and friendship, providing insights into migrants' unconscious everyday embedding. Walsh argues that friendships reflect the 'coproduction of intimacy' (2018: 30). Equally, I argue that, in order to function, humour demands reciprocity. When such mutual understanding is reached, intimacy is enhanced; when it is not, an inverse process of alienation is operated. It is worth mentioning that on no occasion did I raise the subject of humour with my participants. Rather, the theme arose organically and is thus testimony to the ontological importance of humour in the migrant experience. Moreover, since humour purportedly 'permeates every aspect of English life' (Fox, 2014: 78) and, as mentioned earlier, is considered a favourable 'national characteristic' by many participants – however naively and stereotypically – it is a component of diasporic embedding that, although often overlooked, demands closer attention.

Having lived in London for twenty-two years, Antoine is now equipped with the cultural wherewithal to grasp the subtleties of humour in both pre- and postmigration contexts: 'humour is different in both countries; self-deprecation is very, very English and it's very funny. It's a funny take, kind of like a double-take, being able to make fun of oneself.' Echoing Antoine's words, and Laura's on motoring, Charles's offer insights into the perceived differences in both countries: 'humour is always nasty in France, aggressive at the expense of other people … the English have a sense of self-deprecation that the French don't have at all. Generally speaking, the French like to mock other people, but not themselves.' These reflections are in part supported by Fox (2014), who observes that 'the humour of English self-deprecation, like that of the English understatement, is understated, often to the point of being almost imperceptible – and bordering on incomprehensible to those unfamiliar with English modesty rules' (Fox, 2014: 94–5). Fox's account is pertinent in its appreciation of the subtlety and cultural awareness involved in humorous interactions in the UK, a point experienced first-hand by North American ethnographer Katherine Smith. When conducting fieldwork in Greater Manchester, through lack of cultural familiarity, she was unable to distinguish between irony and earnestness: the 'comment seemed to me to be an attempt to have a barter, but I was not sure' (Smith, 2012: 39). Antoine's and Charles's understanding of local humour demonstrates their pre-reflexive habituation to its intricacies, which shorter-term sojourners have not yet acquired. In so doing, they display a level of local embeddedness and incorporation (externalised and internalised) tantamount perhaps to their length of London stay (twenty-two and eleven years respectively).

In contrast to Antoine and Charles, Sadia measures her underlying lack of affinity with non-French London friends in equally humour-centric terms: 'I haven't really made that many friends where we really click, like, really a hundred per cent the same sense of humour.' Sadia's spontaneous association between friendship and humour is telling, demonstrating an intuitive awareness of the distinct approaches to humour and its capacity to act as an invisible barrier to impulsive and implicit friendship. Recalling the 'invisible cultural normalcy' imposed by those whose humour belongs to a shared dominant group (Tyler, 2003: 401), through the inability to wittily 'click', not only is Sadia's pathway to friendship impeded, so is her route to settlement, given their mutuality (Ryan and Mulholland, 2014a, 2014b, 2015). The performativity of humour as a constituent of local belonging – or otherwise – is also supported by Smith, who contends that an inability to engage in a common sense of humour 'leaves individuals in a specific position that may remain liminal, if not "outside" of most group relationships' (Smith, 2012: 153). Sadia's experience is therefore an inversion of the humour-infused friendship and embedding processes noted by Walsh, where 'Janet and Emma were in fits of giggles telling [her] how they got to know each other' and how their 'quickly formed ... close friendship ... linked families' (Walsh, 2018: 102).

Here, we observe the snowballing effect of humour in action, going from shared laughter, to friendship, to family ties. It is important to note, however, that Walsh's anecdote concerns the spontaneous bonding of two British expats in Dubai, rather than a cross-cultural one. In this sense, it reflects Sadia's proactive search for French friends with whom to share habituated humoristic exchanges, even going so far as to place a classified advertisement in a London-French newspaper. Recalling Gill Valentine's paper, 'Desperately Seeking Susan: A geography of lesbian friendships' (1993), minus the sexual implications of such intimacy (Walsh, 2018), Sadia's desperate and deliberate quest for friendship is revealing on several levels. It is superficially indicative of her desire for French companionship, which signals a deeper need to tap into shared ways of performing humour intuitively, but is equally suggestive of her lack of habituation to English jocular practices and consequent detachment from the local social space. Notwithstanding more obvious expressions of emplacement in the post-migration field, such as Sadia's twelve-year residency, her marriage to an Englishman and raising of three, undeniably anglophone, children, her incapacity to 'click' into the local sense of humour, and hence friendship circles, is representative of a more profound sense of displacement.

Moreover, her experience resonates with that of other London-French migrants, such as Block's interviewees, the most Anglophile and ostensibly 'integrated' of whom 'professed to having few if any English friends' (2006: 132). Similarly, 'a strong pattern of mothers actively seeking out relationships with other French parents' is noted by Ryan and Mulholland (2014b: 264; 2015). Mirroring this, Scott (2006: 1,118) explains how '[o]ne of the main "gripes" of the young British professionals [in Paris] related to the impenetrability of French social networks'. Conradson and Latham observe similar affective practices among New Zealanders in London, who seek 'like-minded others with which [*sic*] to socialise' (Conradson and Latham, 2007:

246; 2005b). However, I depart from the latter assessment of such friendship networks constituting 'a localised social backdrop against which an otherwise relatively disembedded – and thus potentially disconnected – lifestyle could be practised and sustained' (2007: 246; 2005b), because these closed friendship circles, through their conduciveness to (in-)group belonging, serve to discourage embedding in the wider social space. Their 'ethno-cultural' friendship boundaries (Dhoest, 2018), forged through habituated humour affinities, result in 'normative geographies of who is "in" and "out of place"' (Higgins, 2019: 101) and therefore ultimately lead to cultural 'communities' living parallel lives (Valentine, 2008; de Backer, 2019).

A similar phenomenon is identifiable in Brigitte's and Laura's narratives, who intuitively correlate humoristic practices with internalised marginalisation in the migratory field. Their deficiency in the requisite culturo-linguistic dispositions to grasp postmigration humour leads to a lack of belonging and a consequent longing for light-hearted interactions with individuals possessing a similar primary/secondary habitus. In this sense, familiar French friendship networks create the collective belonging alluded to by Conradson and Latham (2007; 2005b), albeit a disembedded one as regards the wider context of London. Access to 'meaningful relations with (especially native) others in the city' (Mulholland and Ryan, 2017: 140) therefore depends more here on cultural capital than on the social capital (Bourdieu, 1986; 1979b; 1980b) proposed by Ryan and Mulholland (2014b). As such, the affective embedding operationalised through postmigration habituated humour practices is not so much about *who* you know, but *how* you know. Noble's Australian-Lebanese informant corroborates this: 'What used to make me feel *out of place* is when jokes are said and I wasn't able to catch the humour' (Noble, 2013: 349; my emphasis). The displacement, or lack of fit, caused by the ironically divisive role of humour (Westcott and Vazquez Maggio, 2016; Huc-Hepher, 2019) and its converse London-French unifying potential (Smith, 2012: 147) is precisely what Brigitte, a neuroscientist in a leading London university, describes:

> I like English humour, when I get it – because it took me a while. Now and then I realise I still haven't quite got it yet … Sometimes I just need to have a laugh during the day; that's when I'm so happy I've got my [French] friend up on the eighth floor. We send each other silly messages; we have the same points of reference … It like relaxes me. But sometimes there'll be a thing, a joke, that comes to you, and you'll try to explain it [to English people], and it will fall completely flat, and then you feel very, very alone in the world. I must say I miss that, being with people who have the same reference points.

While Brigitte appreciates English humour, like Sadia, she is not habituated to it. On the contrary, she is painfully aware of the intercultural shortcomings present in her amicable relationships with non-French friends. Her failed attempts at sharing a joke, due to the habitus discrepancy between the parties (Draitser, 1998), leave her feeling profoundly isolated. As Westcott and Vazquez Maggio assert, being unable 'to maintain face can lead to emotional consequences of embarrassment, shame, frustration, or alienation that threaten the individual's sense of ease' (2016: 507). Counterbalancing the sociocultural exclusion, however, is the habituated complicity provided by playful exchanges with a 'mother-tongue' colleague. Cardeña and Littlewood (2006) confirm the role of humour in *social* identity construction, but Cohen (2000) goes further, foregrounding the importance of the *national* dimension, proposing 'that perhaps the sense of a shared humour, or of common ability to appreciate the language and the imagery, is precisely what the sense of nationhood is about' (both cited in Smith, 2012: 138). In Laura's account below, the relevance of *language* in the humour-nationhood-identity complex is also underlined, as is its essential role in facilitating or impeding friendship and belonging (Westcott and Vazquez Maggio, 2016):

> Actually, the big problem when trying to make English friends is that I'm not bilingual. As soon as you try to make a joke, as soon as you enter into the realm of affinity, of nuance and so on, not mastering the language is difficult, so I seem to end up having conversations based on everyday matters, which is very boring. You can't get into the banter, or make a little aside or an innuendo ... After a while, that's what I've missed, it's also why it would be nice to go home.

The immutability of Laura's originary comedic dispositions places her irrevocably in the position of outsider within the migratory field. As Smith reminds us, 'jokes themselves are not necessarily external to the individual but part of the positioning and identifications of the individual in social contexts' (Smith, 2012: 158). Laura's light-hearted externalisation of her culturally and linguistically situated subjective habitus within the migratory social field create a twofold mismatch: first, between her French sensibilities and the differing comedic codes of London, and second, between her wit and the inadequacy of her English to express it. The effects of (un)habituated humour could, therefore, again be likened to hysteresis, contributing to a '[l]andscape of un/belonging' within the migratory space (Conway and Leonard, 2014: 128). Rather than being a positive force, for Brigitte and Laura, humour gives rise to an unsettling feeling of outsiderness, again triggering a sense of loss and longing (Hage, 1997; Levin, 2016), or 'hiraeth'. Testifying to the commonness of the (un)habituated humour phenomenon, Brigitte and Laura's accounts are lexically close. They both employ the verb 'manquer', meaning to miss, and to be missing/absent, and they both become aware that they miss the embeddedness and cultural belonging that the habituated humour of the originary habitat/habitus brings, perceiving the shared points of reference that are missing from their adopted 'home'. In turn, they gain a rare sense of their 'fish-out-of-water' state (Bourdieu and Wacquant, 1992; Conway and Leonard, 2014), to such an extent that Laura defines her lack of comedic finesse as the reason behind her desire to 'go home'. Could humour, therefore, paradoxically, be the ultimate cause of homesickness, a dormant homesickness of which the individuals are almost unaware, content in their 'residential tourist' (Benson and O'Reilly, 2009) positioning until reminded of its inherent liminality?

Conclusion

In this chapter, the notion of habituation – fundamental to Bourdieu's concept of habitus and distinguishing the construct from merely habits or habitat – has been assessed in four discrete, yet overlapping, frameworks. The first of these was the manner in which habituation to the idea of mobility was implicitly honed in the premigration habitat/habitus and, upon migration, translated into equally indistinct settlement 'plans'. The second considered the function of security in the settlement process and how the emergence of localised diasporic 'securiscapes' subtly contributed to a sense of embeddedness and feeling 'at home'. The third apprehended habituation as a form of embodiment, with participants bearing witness to their evolving outlooks, attitudes and expectations, having incorporated certain values and characteristics from the destination culture, and thus recognising 'that in some sense they had become, or were becoming, different people by virtue of spending time in Britain's capital' (Conradson and Latham, 2007: 250). Finally, habituation was approached from the perspective of humour, which emerged as a forceful reminder of the immutability of the originary habitus, whereby pre-reflexive, shared comedic codes were seen to strengthen ties between members of London's French community, all the while inhibiting full integration into, and of, the 'host' culture. This is perhaps the sentiment Sayad was attempting to capture through his reference to migrants' 'double absence' (1999). An initial absence was engendered through the lack of habituated understanding of comedic devices in interactions with non-French Londoners, the migrants feeling as though they had 'missed' something and were therefore 'missing out'. A simultaneous absence was triggered by the unanticipated sense of longing for the inherited habituation to the humour mechanisms of the originary habitat/habitus, with the migrants 'missing' the implicit connections of the homeland.

Through my focus on habituation, I have demonstrated how pre-reflexive processes are key determinants in (lifestyle) migrants' embedding and settlement practices. In its multifarious forms, a habituation lens has revealed the internalised, subjective dimensions of belonging; that is, belonging within London as a safe space and therefore feeling at home, but also belonging within the self, mobility facilitating the comfortable ownership of dispositions that participants had previously suppressed. In addition, through the prism of habituation, the limitations of belonging and resistance to change have emerged. We have seen that migration does not necessarily represent 'the break from their pasts that [participants] had previously envisaged' (Benson and O'Reilly, 2009: 618), which confirms both the historicity and permanency of habitus (Bourdieu and Wacquant, 1992; Bourdieu, 2005).

By focusing on the generally unnoticed dynamic relationship between habits and habitat, the indiscernible creep of habituation has come to the fore. Only upon reflection during our conversations did these gradual, but profound, changes to participants' inherited habitus, constituting defining components of their shared histories and heritage, become apparent. It is this unforeseen, undetectable nature of habituation that constitutes its potency and warranted its scrutiny here, providing insights into the affective subjectivities and underlying fluxes governing the migratory experience. The power of imperceptibility has thus been central to this chapter, allowing for an understanding of participants' constructions of identity and diasporic emplacement which might otherwise have gone unnoticed, and revealing the limits of their agency. My emphasis in Chapter 4, however, returns to the surface of participants' lifeworlds, examining their everyday externalised habits as an articulation of identity performance.

Notes

1 An amusing example of incorporated transformation came towards the end of one student's first year, when she arrived at an oral exam, almost unable to speak, owing to a tongue piercing performed the previous day.
2 Engel also proffers a light-hearted escalator anecdote: 'London, if not exactly welcoming, ignored you [migrants] benignly, was full of [your] own fellow countrymen, had a language that was far more accessible and pliable than any other, and made few demands – certainly no expectation of adaptation to the new surroundings – as long as you remembered to stand on the right of the escalators' (2014: 504).

4

Adopting the habits of the London field: French community rejection and projection

Introduction

Being performed at the intersection of pre-reflexive thought and externalised practices, habits can be conceptualised as occupying the dynamic space between the objective (habitat) and subjective (habituation) migratory experience of home. Indeed, dictionary definitions of the term emphasise this dynamic: a habit is 'something that you do often, and regularly, sometimes without knowing that you are doing it' (*Cambridge Dictionary*, 2021) and as 'an automatic reaction to a specific situation' (*English Oxford Dictionaries*, 2017). By observing habitus through the prism of habits, it is thus possible to gain a more nuanced understanding of home as played out through participants' actions within, and reactions to, the diasporic field. To draw a connection with the objectivised habitats observed in Chapter 2, I concentrate on habits fundamental to the daily lives and corporeal experiences of my research participants, related to eating, drinking and health. As Leonard asserts, '[c]ombining the subjective with a materialist turn allows a focus on the interplay of identity with nation, race, gender and class' (2010a: 1,249). It is precisely these broader readings that my examination of participants' habits will enable. I argue that by studying London-French habits, we gain insights into individuated and community belonging, diasporic emplacement, transnational cultural capital flows and premigration attachment and/or detachment.

Given that 'habit performance reflects the routine repetition of past acts ... cued by stable features of the environment' (Wood *et al.*, 2002: 1,281), I ask how prolonged immersion in the London environment, or habitat, affects participants' habits and how the performance of engrained, premigration habits ties them to their pasts and – non-agentively – with other London-French migrants. Since the 'tendency to perform habitual behaviors is implicit ... and ... may not be reflected in people's thoughts or reported intentions' (2002: 1,281), my emphasis on habits not only establishes a necessary link to the habituation habitus component discussed in Chapter 3, but it also interrogates the extent to which migrant habits remain 'automatically' embedded in a premigration setting/mode, despite field pressures. Given that habits trigger 'behavioral goals or intentions, which then can be implemented with minimal thought' (2002: 1,282), I also ask what hidden intentions and values participants' habits might be enacting and what they tell us about their diasporic positioning. By looking at the depth of my participants' experience, that is, its historicity within the postmigration space, and its breadth, namely how their culinary habits are crossing borders and impacting the French social space through technoscapes and transnational mediascapes, I show both the historic and spatial scope of habits. I argue, using drinking and healthcare habits as examples, that embedded practices can again serve as mechanisms for exclusion as much as emplacement and have far wider-reaching ideological implications than initially apparent, speaking of hidden hegemonies and gendered/sexualised discrimination.

Bourdieu rejected the substitution of habitus for habit(s) alone (Jourdain and Naulin, 2011; Maton, 2012) precisely because habit does not allow for the interplay between habitat and habits, and by foregrounding the repetitive it negates the reproductive, 'generative and organisational principles of practices' (Bourdieu, 1980a: 88). Nevertheless, habits must be recognised as an integral component of habitus and as crucial to ethnographic enquiry, for when unconsciously replicated from one participant to another, they are representative of the wider community. They display 'the unity of style that unites the practices and possessions of a single agent or class of agents' (Bourdieu, 1994: 23). Such unity, as argued in Chapter 2, develops a 'common-unity' of practice, even if most participants do not identify with the essentialising epithet of 'community' belonging. The analysis of habits is also crucial because it sheds light on 'that invisible reality you cannot show or put your finger on' (Bourdieu, 1994: 25), such as abstract 'community' and 'class' constructs, but also identity, cultural belonging and diasporic emplacement. In the same way that scrutinising habits gives physical shape – and ethnographic validity – to otherwise abstract notions, so studying the ordinary reveals the extraordinary and 'socially pertinent' (Bourdieu, 1994: 24). Both Noble (2013) and de Backer (2019) recognise the critical role of habits in everyday cosmopolitan diasporic living and the potential of habits' 'iterative character [... to] transform everyday practices into something more durable', which 'refers not only to social relations between acquaintances, but also to places, patterns and rituals' (de Backer, 2019: 15). In the section below, it is precisely these insights into the places, patterns and rituals of my participants that the familiarity of habits brings to bear.

Eating practices, rituals and London-French belonging:
'Every country in the world is represented culinarily in London'

Although I concede that habits are not a substitute for habitus (Bourdieu, 2005), because the latter exists 'across time as sets of dispositions that generate performances that coalesce into regular but evolving social practices' (Hillier and Rooksby, 2005: 406), they provide a window onto the taken-for-granted mores constitutive of community. Since habitus is reshaped by changing contexts and cultures, I seek to understand how participants' habits have evolved in the diasporic field, how they emulate their reinvented – 'within limits' (Bourdieu, 2005: 46) – habitus, which 'host' habits they have adopted and which they have agentively rejected. I am also interested in the 'insulating quality' of habit performance and its capacity to minimise 'the immediacy of emotional experience' (Wood *et al.*, 2002: 1,295). Habits might then be understood as mechanisms to reduce the emotional impact of dislocation from the familiar parameters of the premigration habitat.

Once again, it is the culinary that emerges as singularly important to my participants' everyday lived experience. As observed in Chapter 2, food is a physical element of the originary habitat that many choose, or feel a desire, even a compulsion, to transfer from their native land and reposition in the diasporic habitat. Specific brands and goods, such as Ricoré, Poulain chocolate, Teisseire menthe and grenadine, home-made preserves and so forth, have been cited as examples of comestible emplacement devices. However, this desire to own and physically absorb components of the habitat of origin in the diasporic context does not, by the same token, equate to a refusal on the part of my participants to espouse the eating habits of London. On the contrary, François and Sarah alone report maintaining a typically French diet. François quantifies his cooking habits in the following manner: '80 per cent French, 10 per cent Italian cuisine, because it's quick to make, and a good little 10 per cent of Indian cuisine; I learnt that here'. While Sarah, who cooks only French food, but whose Chilean husband adds his cultural background to the culinary habits of the household, is emphatic in her denigration of English eating practices, bemoaning English Londoners' failure to invite friends to dinner because: 'One: it's not in their culture, they're not in the habit of doing so; two: in my opinion they don't know how to cook as well as us; and three: it's of less interest to them, food is less important for them.'

Pertinently, Sarah conceptualises her personal views/experience in Bourdieusian habitus terms, distinguishing her own eating practices in relation to the perceived 'habits' and 'culture' of London society (Hillier and Rooksby, 2005). Only through comparisons within the diasporic field do her own practices emerge as superior, and hence voluntarily immutable.

Sarah's persistent use of 'they' and 'them' to refer to English members of the 'host' society and 'us' to refer to a collective French imaginary, serves to reinforce the ontological differentiation through implicit lexical means. Her culinary habits emerge as a 'sign of distinction' (Bourdieu, 1994: 25) and their maintenance symbolises a longing for the perceived authenticity of French lifestyle left behind (Benson, 2011). Sarah's testimony also confirms the benefit of conducting my interviews in French (bar one), as the unifying role of language permits candid responses about 'the English'. Indeed, she concludes that 'in general [the English] don't know how to cook; that's not an impression, it's a fact. I haven't seen any progress as far as cuisine is concerned in the last ten years here.' Reflecting on culinary habits has therefore enabled invisible, national divisions to solidify in Sarah's mind. Rather than functioning as an emplacement strategy, eating practices displace Sarah, hierarchising her positioning within the local social field. This again undermines the notion of global cities' inherent cosmopolitanising effect, as well as the 'self-conscious self-cosmopolitanisation' described by Conradson and Latham (2007: 247). Instead, Sarah's reliance on pre-established clichés recalls Mulholland and Ryan's observations (2017) and confirms Farrer's contention that '[u]rban settlers inevitably hide exclusion clauses in their claims to a re-territorialised cosmopolitan citizenship, with internal boundaries framed in stereotypes' (Farrer, 2010: 1,225).

Sarah's somewhat damning assertions are, nevertheless, not voiced by the remaining participants, who describe how their culinary practices and tastes have evolved following exposure to the multitude of ingredients, flavours and cultural traditions encountered in the London habitat. They comment favourably on London's gastronomic 'progress' since the turn of the century and on their new-found culinary audacity, understood as an expression of the cosmopolitanising effect of the city. Just as the English have fondly adopted Indian curry as a 'national' dish, so London's French residents have grown accustomed to incorporating Britain's colonial history from the contents of their plates. As Said penned (1994: 8), '[i]mperialism lingers where it has always been, in a kind of general cultural sphere as well as in specific ... social practices' (cited in Leonard, 2010a: 1,247). Through their culinary habits, therefore, my participants perform the 'double historicity' described by Bourdieu and Wacquant (1992), eating their way through both a British colonial past and a locally infused heritage. Séverine explains how 'every country in the world is represented culinarily in London. There are Ethiopian restaurants ... Living in London is a real culinary adventure; it's not homogenous.' She attributes the diversity and innovation found in the London restaurant scene both to the multiculturalism of the capital and to English chefs' chance to work from a clean slate, free from the burden of France's gastronomic heritage: 'the English will play around with flavours and colours, and will have less respect for traditional recipes. They allow themselves to venture into new, more original combinations.' Here, we sense 'the multiple temporalities' (Farrer, 2010: 1,225) of migration materialised through cookery practices, and how the past and future play out differently in contemporary pre- and postmigration contexts.

In Séverine's opinion, France's gastronomic tradition is a hindrance to creativity and change. That the 'Gastronomic Meal of the French' was formally inscribed as part of Humanity's Intangible Cultural Heritage by UNESCO in 2010 only serves to crystallise the tradition further and hence add to the burden of history. This is an important point, for it resonates with other criticisms of heritagisation (Wang, 2017) and of France's paradoxical failure to embrace its avant-garde past today, reminiscent of what Hanchao Lu (2002) refers to as 'nostalgia for the future' (cited in Farrer, 2010: 1,214). For example, Charles alludes to French imperviousness to self-deprecation as a hurdle to creativity in advertising, while Brigitte, Suzanne, Séverine and Antoine perceive Paris's historic architectural assets as obstacles to urban innovation. All have the normative effect of elevating London to a place of desire (Wang, 2013a; Mulholland and Ryan, 2017). In Séverine's words, 'London's in perpetual transformation, so you never get bored … people demolish and rebuild. Paris is a frozen city … I find Paris very beautiful, but Paris hasn't changed, Paris hasn't renewed itself.' The consequence of looking nostalgically backwards at a glorious past is a Paris that is 'folded in on itself', according to Suzanne, and a France that is struggling to look forward and welcome the future (Parisot, 2007). For young, enthusiastic, open-minded individuals, predisposed to migration (Murphy-Lejeune, 2002), France's nostalgia constitutes London's appeal (King *et al.*, 2014). Through eating habits alone, we thus observe the performance of morally charged epistemologies of place (Mulholland and Ryan, 2017).

When asked which London restaurants they prefer, a pluralistic range of responses are given: 'A Greek restaurant called Gini, where I ate an onion soup made by a Swedish woman that was the best I'd ever eaten, even in France' (Suzanne); or 'a Lebanese restaurant' (Suzanne); 'Sketch, in Conduit Street' (François); 'not necessarily French, we like Japanese food, we go to the Spanish restaurant nearby, it varies' (Chantal); 'on Friday I ate Vietnamese, on Saturday, it was a gastro-pub, but it seemed more French to me, and yesterday, Lebanese … I like everything, I like to keep it varied. Italian – I go all the time' (Brigitte); 'pub lunches, fish and chips … Indian, Asian, Lebanese restaurants … it's not particularly French' (Robert); 'Tokyo Diner restaurant in Soho' (Miranda); 'the local Indian' (Bruno); 'St John's, it's very English. It's a French joke that there's no good food in London, so I take [French visitors] there and they find there's something different' (Antoine); 'my favourite restaurant in London is an English restaurant ... St John's' (Brice). The variety of restaurants and national cuisines cited bears witness to participants' evolving eating habits and embodiment of London's everyday cosmopolitanism. Such habits also enable performativity of belonging. The agentive selection of English restaurants functions as a strategic emplacement method within the British context and the multicultural array of the others indicates conscious 'resubjectification' (Conradson and Latham, 2007: 234) as 'globalization's new cosmopolitans' (Leonard, 2010b: 509).

Online evidence substantiates this culinary and subjectified reinvention, with many London-French blogs dedicating considerable proportions of their 'diasberspace' to reconfigured cooking habits (demonstrated further in Chapter 6). The blog names alone are revealing: Food for Thoughts, Teatime in Wonderland, Travels Around My Kitchen, or Pauline à la Crème anglaise (all of which are archived in the LFSC). Surprisingly perhaps, the blogs tend not to promote French recipes to a potentially English audience, nor do they correspond to the Asian and Lebanese tastes favoured above, in an enactment of 'the lingering endurance of [French] imperialism' (Leonard, 2010a: 1,252). Rather, they celebrate traditional *English* dishes and a particular penchant for desserts. As Pauline (*à la Crème anglaise*) writes in her Welcome section, the 'blog is about my love affair with British food, and my adventures as a French expat tackling traditional British baking' (Pauline, no date). Like Brice's and Antoine's deliberate dining at the archetypally English St John's, Pauline's reference to 'tackling traditional British baking' is suggestive of her efforts to perform postmigration embedding through her culinary praxis, playing out her adopted national heritage through lemon-drizzle and custard making. It also recalls Petridou's emphasis on *process* (2001), which is of equal prominence in UNESCO's Intangible Cultural Heritage entry for the French gastronomic meal, where 'enjoying the process of choosing recipes, shopping for the best products [and] cooking together' (UNESCO, 2010) are cited as integral elements of 'the meal'.

Jacqueline, a 42-year-old French-Canadian who has lived in London for nineteen years is equally intent on performing her belonging through regular preparation of English desserts. During our interview, she singles out making 'sticky-toffee pudding' as a preferred adopted habit, which complements several blogs' visual representations of Victoria sponge, flapjacks, shortbread and scones. This embracing of local baking practices doubtless adds a sweetness to the migratory experience and contributes to 'the "stickiness" of global cities as places of settlement' (Farrer, 2010: 1,212). For, as Farrer asserts, 'narratives of emplacement are also simultaneously narratives of displacement, dislocation and even exclusion' (2010: 1,212). By adopting local baking and eating habits, the migrants are actively placing themselves within the London culinary tradition, becoming part of the historicity of the place. Furthermore, since 'emotions during habit performance are likely to emerge from the thoughts that intrude during action, including reflections of past and future experiences' (Wood *et al.*, 2002: 1,291), their culinary habits may help participants bridge transnational spatio-temporal divides by instigating thoughts and emotions connected with the remembered premigration space, as well as those linked to postmigration aspirations. In this sense, culinary habits can be understood as ways to perform 'belonging and longing [... engendering] feelings that may connect one with a people, a place, a home' (Levin, 2016: 25).

Adopting local culinary habits also has further-reaching implications, perceivable in the non-economic, cultural remittance terms posited by Cohen and Sirkeci (2011). The relatively recent cross-Channel migration of English (and North American) sweet classics to French dining tables, notably *le crumble*, *le cheesecake*, *les muffins* and *les brownies*, suggests the tide is turning as regards France's status as the global culinary super-power, and that our connected world is causing the French to internalise globalisation (Conradson and Latham, 2007), opening them to external cultures, tastes and eating habits. I argue that this shift has been prompted by the recipes, practices and changing tastes exported to France by migrants on return visits.

To test the influence of Anglo-American desserts on France's culinary and broader social fields, I conducted a Boolean Google.fr search, allowing the big data to speak for itself, as advocated by Kitchin (2014) and Mayer-Schönberger and Cukier (2013). Taking the aforementioned examples (and ensuring the language was set as French and the French definite article was used to minimise anglophone skew), '*le muffin*' generated almost half a million 'hits', '*le crumble*' and '*le cheesecake*' almost 200,000, and '*le brownie*' around 150,000. Associated predictive text was 'fait-il grossir' ('is it fattening') and 'comment faire le cheesecake' (how to make cheesecake), thus supporting the 'Heathrow injection' effect of the British diet (Conradson and Latham, 2007: 245) and the *practical* emphasis mentioned. The quantitative scale of this 'raw' data and the focus of many results on baking methods serve to triangulate my empirical findings on the growing adoption of 'Anglo-American' eating habits in the francophone world. In turn, they are corroborated by my observations in the offline environment, where cultural remittances in the form of cheesecake and crumble have become regular features on restaurant menus in France and those of 'English/Irish' pubs (Kelly, 2016). Moreover, the same desserts have become part of the French 'mediascape' (Appadurai, 1990), both appearing in the 2015 grand final of the popular television series, *Qui sera le prochain grand pâtissier?* (France's equivalent to *Bake Off: Crème de la Crème*). The episode entered over two million homes when aired by

France 2 (Boucher, 2015) and, instantaneously, cheesecake and crumble entered the collective imagination of the nation, disrupting established eating habits.

The success of English celebrity chefs, such as Jamie Oliver and Gordon Ramsay, both regular features on French television (with their respective *Naked Chef* and *Kitchen Nightmare* series, among others) has contributed to the mediascape, which, I contend, has been quietly underpinned by the transnational influence of UK- and US-based French migrants. Their '[impressions] understood literally as imprints or feelings left in one's mind' (Murphy-Lejeune, 2002: 74) have in turn left imprints in the minds of friends and family in France. Similarly, the mediated influence of Oliver and Ramsay has left its mark on the physical French habitat. Ramsay, described in *Slate* as 'practically French' (Michel, 2014) has opened restaurants in Paris and Bordeaux, while Oliver has published twenty-three recipe books with French publisher Hachette, some of which have a distinctly 'Anglo-American' theme. The titles demonstrate the impact of 'English' eating habits on practices in the French social field: *l'Amérique de Jamie* (2010); *So British* (2012); *Burgers, Barbecues et Salades* (2012); *Desserts* (2012); *Curry* (2013); and – pertinently – *Comfort Food* (2015).

Another prominent figure in the French mediatised culinary field is herself a UK migrant: Trish Deseine. A Northern Irish Parisian since the 1980s, she re-migrated to the south of France in 2014. Like Ramsay and Oliver, she has promoted 'authentic' British recipes across the Channel in regular (sweet) features in *French Elle* magazine, as well as in twelve award-winning French-language cookery books. Her bestselling *Je veux du chocolat* (2002) sold over 400,000 copies (Deseine, no date). Unlike Ramsay's and Oliver's translated (from English) publications, however, Deseine's are conceived for a French audience. Consequently, they may offer a less 'authentic' version of the dishes, but the cultural refashioning to her readership's expectations and desires could render the English eating habits more palatable for the French audience. In this sense, her publications could be considered a form of critical, transnational repurposing (Hester, 2018), whereby intercultural awareness developed in the diasporic context leads to a multidirectional, creative 'process of selective appropriation and recontextualization' (2018: 102).

Epitomising the cultural dynamics of the 'mediascape' (Appadurai, 1990) and the theory of transnationalism 'as a system of networks, institutions, and relationships that connects people in host and receiving countries, including those who are not migrants' (Schmitter Heisler, 2008: 96), Deseine has also broadcast several series for Irish television. These include *Trish's Paris Kitchen* and *Trish's Mediterranean Kitchen*, which transpose her diasporic culinary practices to the mediated premigration space in a reversal of the aforesaid model. Rather than being a one-way cultural remittance, therefore, these international exchanges constitute circular cultural capital flows. Through the publication of recipes, themselves an immaterial reconstitution of practices, the chefs modify field habits in both pre- and postmigration spaces. Materialised in paper or audio-visual form, as Parkhurst Ferguson affirms, their '[c]ooking turns the raw into the cooked, and [their] writing transforms the cooked into the cultural. By enunciating cultural practices, values, norms, culinary texts instil the consciousness that turns cuisine into a full-fledged cultural product' (2004: 22). All three celebrity chefs also represent a significant departure from their regionally embedded French predecessors, such as 'Maïté' (Marie-Thérèse Ordonez) from the Landes in southwest France, whose regional identity was embodied through her 'thick' accent (de Roquemaurel, 2014: 87), stereotypical pseudonym and the rustic dishes she popularised on national television throughout the 1980s and 1990s. Maïté was ranked among the twelve most popular television personalities of the 1990s (Iriarte, 2015), whereas Trish Deseine appeared in French Vogue's forty most popular women of the decade in 2012 (*Vogue Paris*, 2012). This gives an indication of the shift away from the domestic and regional, to a more open embracing of inter/transnational figures, foods and practices, underpinned by the European project and free movement of people across national borders. Crystallising Ordonez's decline in popularity in the French social field and the reorientation of the public imagination *away* from the regional, *towards* the Anglo-American, her Dax restaurant, Chez Maïté, was declared bankrupt in 2015 (Bosio, 2015).

'We always eat at the dining table, never in front of the TV'

Although the French interviewed for this study generally report having different tastes today than upon their arrival in London, representing what could be termed 'gustative acculturation', the habits that surround the ritual of eating tend to be more enduring. Brice explains that he appreciates taking time over his lunch and leaves his work premises in order to savour it – a habit typical in France, where it is commonplace to have a two-hour lunch break, even at school, with children habitually served four courses. However, in practice, Brice admits to often having time only for a sandwich. There is thus a tension between his desires, informed by the routines of his past, and his everyday lived experience, where diasporically induced habits lead to somewhat uncomfortable embedding. The discrepancy between Brice's discourse and the ontological fact of his practices recalls the disparity between the classlessness rhetoric of the British community in Spain and the class distinctions observed in the field (Oliver and O'Reilly, 2010).

Rather than being the sign of an underlying need to validate his migration through the reflexive assertion of idealistic postmigration imaginaries (Benson and O'Reilly, 2009, 2010), the tension in Brice's account is due to a simultaneous wish to maintain his originary performative identity and adapt to the local environment for operational effectiveness. As Murphy-Lejeune notes, superficially adopting 'cultural signs, habits and customs ... constitutes a fist level of adaptation [... or] accommodation to the physical milieu, climate, habitat, places' (2002: 207). In this sense, although Brice's narrative rehearses primary habitus practices, his habits are agentively adapted for the purpose of diasporic functionality, constituting a 'chameleon' tendency (2002: 208) whereby 'a foreigner may temporarily change to suit a particular community or environment without changing [their] own inherited traits' (2002: 208).

The tension between Brice's discourse and actions is not, however, replicated across all participants. Chantal, a stay-at-home mother, originally from Paris, describes her family's eating habits with a level of accuracy commensurate with her comfortableness in her French-inflected diasporic home. Among all my informants, Chantal, conforms most closely to the French 'community' stereotype. She lives in a large Georgian terraced house in affluent Kensington and is financially secure enough not to have to rely on her institutionalised cultural capital (Bourdieu, 1979b), namely her *grande école* qualifications. Her habitat and habits are decidedly of the French 'clam' typology, 'closed on itself' (Murphy-Lejeune, 2002: 205), and correspond to the practices of the originary space with clockwork precision. Her mealtimes are later than the British norm and she remarks that French 'children in English boarding schools find they eat too early'. Laura is also of the 'French clam' ilk and an unapologetic member of the French community that has developed around the Ecole de Wix Primary School (a Lycée Français feeder) in Clapham. She plays out the eating rituals of her premigration habitus with systematic fidelity. As we speak in an airy South Clapham café on a warm, late-spring afternoon, we are interrupted more than once by other French Londoners engaging in polite conversation with her (in French), while choosing French comestibles of their own to take back to their London abodes. Like Chantal, they doubtless emulate Laura's eating habits: 'we live in a completely French way: we eat mainly organic, we eat fruit and vegetables, we don't eat ready-meals, there are no sweets in the house, we drink water from a jug at the table. That's the kind of thing, stuff French people do. We always eat at the dining table, never in front of the TV.'

Her taken-for-granted reference to 'stuff French people do' is an indication of the ritualistic, community-building role of these habits. Indeed, in UNESCO's elevation of the French Gastronomic Meal to the intangible heritage of humanity, the notion of the *ritual* dominates. Rather than being 'about eating, it is a highly ritualised affair ... a social custom that ritualises the pleasure of being together' and is acted out in homes across France according to strict 'ceremonial' codes of practice (UNESCO, 2010). In fact, the quotidian quality and commonplaceness of such practices in the French social space – largely eclipsing class divisions – renders the 'gastronomic' label unrepresentative of the domestic lived experience, in which complex eating rituals are 'simply part of the taken-for-granted texture of daily existence' (Conradson and Latham, 2005a: 228) in pre- and postmigration contexts.

Significantly, Laura's words recall those of return migrant, Marie, who lived in Wandsworth some forty years previously and whose then husband appreciated the sociality of eating together as a family *à la française*: 'Back then they [the English] tended to eat on the sofa in front of the telly, and I'd always eat at the dining table because I'm a proper Frenchwoman. And my husband used to like it because it is sociable after all.' However, leading a diasporic 'existence is an inside outness' (Noble, 2013: 349) and establishes an English–French binary that overlooks the social complexities of the migratory space. Possessing a habitus not entirely congruous with the field, participants who apprehend English eating habits in such terms fail to appreciate the class distinctions present. To quote Bourdieu (1991), habitus 'forms specific preferences for a more or less adequate use of habitat' (cited in Friedmann, 2005: 331), resulting in a 'unity of behaviour' (Bourdieu, 2005: 44) between individuals within their habitat. Being in a position of 'inside outness', some participants' views of the 'host' society's use of habitat are irrevocably homogenising, which, in an inversion of the usual model where the 'host' essentialises the migrant (Schmitter Heisler, 2008), reduces subtle structures and practices to a uniform (stereo)typical model (Mulholland and Ryan, 2017). The cultural and historic foundations of participants' habitus therefore prevent them from detecting socio-economically nuanced distinctions of practice. Thus, Sadia's perception of the English eating at 'five o'clock ... off a tray in front of the telly' is not so much a national practice as a class-inflected one, with London's (upper-)middle-class eating habits emulating those of France. As Kron noted over a century ago, in London 'simple or poor families cannot afford a stylish (late) dinner of half-a-dozen courses. They have to content themselves with a plain (early) dinner of one or two courses' (Kron, 1907).

We again observe the fundamental 'double historicity' (Bourdieu and Wacquant, 1992) of local practices. Middle-class habits such as eating mid- to late-evening at the table, with the television switched off, perhaps having a starter or a salad course, drinking wine chosen to complement the food, and the food itself playing the role of discussion point have been acquired over generations in the London social field and are more related to class than culture (Kelly, 2016). Conversely, in France, a predominantly agricultural heritage has permeated the habituses of the masses, resulting in the valuing of local produce and enjoyment in the ritual of food preparation and eating as constituents of pre-reflexive, everyday practice.[1] In both spaces, we note the 'acquiring [of] a history over time' (Murphy-Lejeune, 2002: 209) and the realisation of history over different temporalities and spatialities (Farrer, 2010). That is, just as Anglo-American twenty-first-century baking habits are observed being exported to France and becoming part of the local habitat through technological and mediated networks, so French culinary habits have left their imprint on British bourgeois practices over centuries of cultural capital importation and France–London migration (Kelly, 2016). The historic function of French culinary practices as a symbol of distinction (Bourdieu, 1979a; 1986) in the London social space has therefore rendered them emblematic of a habitus of class, but one which eludes contemporary London migrants, so engrained are their nationally framed imaginaries. Furthermore, judging by the lack of 'genuine' friendships between the London French and 'native' Londoners that emerged from my interviews and survey (see Chapter 3), as well as Ryan and Mulholland's findings (2015), it is likely that they, like London-based Germans, Italians and Latvians, have 'very little contact with English people' (King *et al.*, 2014: 15). This is particularly true of those not in a relationship with a British partner, who are consequently socioculturally ill-equipped to pass judgement on domesticised 'host' habits and more likely to maintain stereotypical positions.

It is not, however, solely the content of meals, their timing and spatial performativity within the home that distinguish French eating habits from the perceived London norm. Their ritualistic formality extends further into materialised habits; for example, Bruno will drink wine only from a wine glass. For him, drinking wine from a tumbler removes a significant aspect of the ceremonial pleasure from the experience. In this sense, the object transcends its superficial functionality and incorporates an affective symbolism reminiscent of what Leach refers to as 'the process of identification which involves a twofold mechanism of grafting symbolic meaning onto an object and then reading oneself into that object, and seeing one's values reflected in it' (2005: 305). The vessel used is thus intrinsically connected to Bruno's experience of ingesting the liquid and the value he places on that process, itself imbibed with cultural meaning as an element of his fractal and ritualistic habitus of origin, as discussed in Chapter 2. In other words, his insistence on drinking from a wine glass is not a question of outward appearances or 'keeping up with the Joneses' (Miller, 2001: 6), as it may be within the borrowed French culture of bourgeois British circles. Rather, for Bruno and other members of the community I encountered, it is a matter of savouring the wine, of doing the substance justice, and thus constitutes another component of the 'gastronomic meal of France' and, in turn, Bruno's French identity. Equally compellingly, the habit is the product of years of practice inherited from his father and generations before him, that is, the makings of culture and a historically embedded sense of belonging.

'Attending to everyday practices' (Conradson and Latham, 2005a: 228), in this case the dining habits of the London French, has thus brought to bear the ways in which emplacement is fluid, representing a spatio-temporal 'in-between-ness' (2005a: 231). On one hand, the habits position participants in a present-day 'French' framework of praxis within the London field, and on the other, they operate over time, with 'the residual effect of past behavior [impacting] on future behavior' (Wood *et al.*, 2002: 1,281). This results in a distinctive form of embeddedness that, as far as the migrants' habitus allows them to appreciate, both separates them from the London social field and connects them to the collective community presence. In this way, as seen in Chapter 2 through their material habitat, French migrants are participating in a tacit 'common-unity' of practice; that is, a take on Wenger's 'communities of practice' (Wenger, 1998, 2004), whereby the action serves to bind the group implicitly and '[c]onnections are circum-scribed by the enterprise' (Cox, 2005: 532). As Cox posits, 'a community of practice is defined as a group that coheres through "mutual engagement" on an "indigenous" (or appropriated) enterprise, and creating a common repertoire' (2005: 531).

The retrospective lens used in Chapter 1 revealed a strong rejection of discriminatory social practices and mentalities associated with the premi-gration environment, partly because 'migrants' representations of the ills of their home society are often overstated' in a bid to validate present lifestyle choices (Benson and O'Reilly, 2009: 610). Yet, here, through the prism of practice, we observe the protection and projection of originary habits into diasporic futures through a common, historically situated praxial reper-toire. Although the 'French "community" is socially divided and lacking in solidarity', as indicated by one of Duchêne-Lacroix and Koukoutsaki-Monnier's respondents (2016: 146), a sense of collective identity is nevertheless performed through common habits transposed from the prem-igration space to the postmigration field. Focusing on the permanency of drinking practices in the following section, I demonstrate further how my participants' autochtonous habits are at variance with those perceived to dominate the London social space, placing them in a bitter-sweet position of dislocated emplacement (Farrer, 2010) and coincidental community.

Defying deep-seated drinking practices: 'London's a giant booze-up'

The contrast between English and French drinking habits, expressed in material form by the wine-glass example, acts as a leitmotif of my interviews. Though several participants refer to London's pub culture in fond terms, for instance Brigitte, who exclaims 'I love pubs, and what's more I'd miss them a lot if I went back to France', and Sarah, who finds 'going for a drink straight after work's a very London thing to do', many are critical of alcohol's role as 'an end in itself', to quote Antoine. In Conradson and Latham's study of London-based New Zealanders, 'going for drinks with colleagues from work' (2007: 243) is presented as a source of enjoyment, which resonates with Sarah's observation. Similarly, Mulholland and Ryan refer to London pub culture in predominantly positive terms, underlining its affective affordances and historic importance within contemporary urban playscapes (Mulholland and Ryan, 2017). Their 'participants were clear that the institution of the pub contributed a particular "atmosphere" to London's public sociality, drawing an important contrast with Paris' (2017: 146).

However, the authors acknowledge that the pub's role as a key emplacement mechanism in London can also have the reverse effect 'for those who don't drink, [... serving to] exclude, especially where the pub becomes a space in which business-related interaction takes place' (2017: 147). This ambivalent functioning of pub sociality is also noted by Scott, whose British migrants in Paris recognise alcohol's bonding potential, 'helping to forge transient networks relatively quickly and involving almost no broader or long-term commitment' (Scott, 2006: 1,118). But they place equal emphasis on 'the impenetrability of French social networks', and the disinclination of French colleagues 'to go for drinks after work was lamented' repeatedly (2006: 1,118). So entangled in affective practices in London and so critical to embedding and belonging (Mulholland and Ryan, 2017), drinking habits thus warrant closer attention.

Mulholland and Ryan (2017) make an original contribution to the discussion with their allusion to gender and the historicity of pub-drinking habits in London. I too argue that both these aspects are central to our understanding of the role of drinking practices in the London-French diasporic space. However, our findings are not entirely compatible. Whereas Mulholland and Ryan (2017: 147) draw attention to 'traditional' drinking habits' capacity to grant migrants a place in their local London (hi)story and hence a sense of situatedness and belonging, I contend that the 'excessive' alcohol consumption witnessed by participants in the London social space marginalises them in a manner which re-enacts local histories with stubborn accuracy. Indeed, the unruly, alcohol-induced behaviour of the English has been noted by both cultural 'insiders' and 'outsiders' for centuries, with examples ranging from The Pardoner's Tale in Chaucer's fourteenth-century *Canterbury Tales*; Shakespeare's Sir Toby Belch in *Twelfth Night* and Porter in *Macbeth*; together with references in Fielding ([1749] 1985), Fiévée (1802, cited in Carpenter, 2013), Tristan ([1840] 2008), and more recently Block (2006), Favell (2008a) and Fox (2014). An especially relevant comment is made in King *et al.*'s paper on graduate migrants in London, the German interviewee declaring: 'I don't know at all what English people do all day long, what they do in the evenings … apart from going to the pub and getting drunk' (King *et al.*, 2014: 15). The statement confirms my contention that migrants' culturally bounded habitus impedes a nuanced understanding of 'host' habits and encourages a reliance on pre-established tropes. For, as Murphy-Lejeune posits, '[i]n the stranger, individual traits are at first invisible. This is why strangers are not perceived as individuals, but as strangers of a certain type, not to be evaluated individually, but collectively' (2002: 25). While the 'host' population are no longer strangers per se, migrants' inherited cultural distance leaves them partially invisible and hence perceived in non-individuated, stereotypical terms. Moreover, the repetition of such collective imaginings over time serves to reinforce them.

This effect can be seen through a comparison of King *et al.*'s interviewee's critique (2014) with an analogous one made by Flora Tristan 180 years earlier, where the 'typical' Londoner is defined as being in haste to 'finish with his chores of the day, not to go home, where he would have nothing to say to his wife or children, but in order to go to his club, where … he will get drunk' (Tristan, [1840] 2008: 28). It also echoes the comments made by another visitor from mainland Europe over a century ago, Dr. R. Kron of Germany, whose 'textbook' for students of English (inspired by *Le Petit Parisien*), *The Little Londoner: A concise account of the life and ways of the English, with special reference to London*, describes pubs as overflowing with inebriates and the city as the most noticeably drunken metropolis in Europe (Kron, 1907). Similarly, eighteenth-century images by Hogarth add 'insider' historical credibility to the current stereotype, as aptly titled *Beer Street* and *Gin Lane* (Figure 8) are explicit in their depiction of the negative effects of alcohol 'as an end in itself' in the English social field, 'not an accidental by-product of the evening's entertainment, [but] the primary objective' (Fox, 2014: 382).

Hogarth's juxtaposition of the sociable practice of drinking beer at the 'pub' echoes Brigitte's account, as well as Mulholland and Ryan's (2017), and Conradson and Latham's (2007) findings. The jovial facial expressions and postures, ostensibly healthy, well-heeled appearances, and the dilapidated pawnshop of *Beer Street* starkly contrast the socially and physically

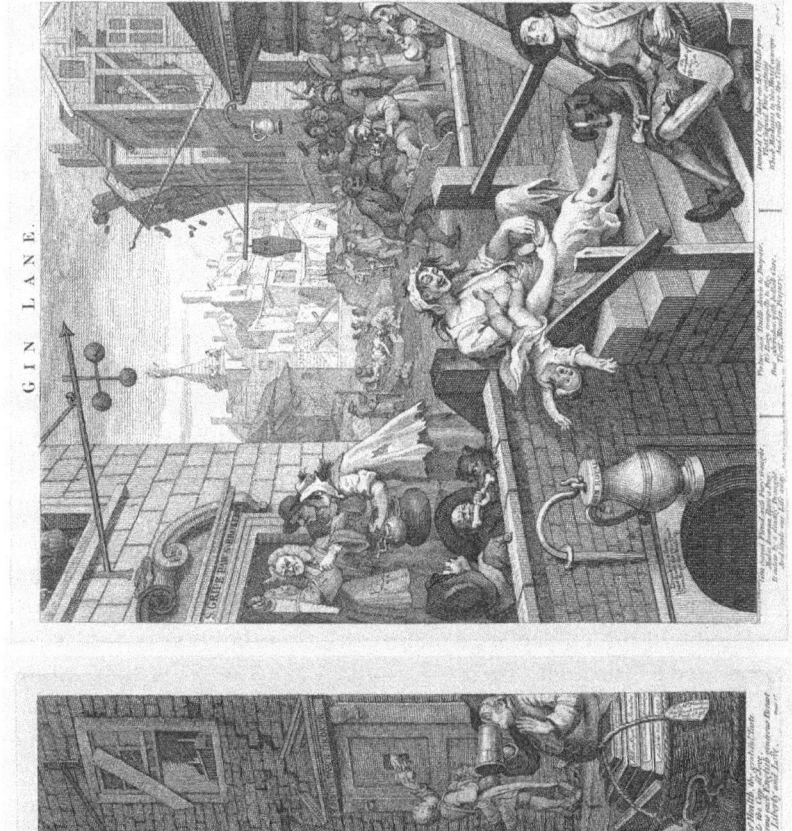

Figure 8 *Beer Street* (left) and *Gin Lane* (right)

detrimental effects of spirit abuse in *Gin Lane*, particularly among women. The socio-economic destitution of the gin drinkers is depicted through their skeletal, ulcerated bodies, ragged attire, background scavenging and patronage of the pawnbroker. The negligence of the woman carer, allowing her child to drop to the ground from a height, is testimony to the far-reaching effects of London's 'gin epidemic' from 1720 to 1751 (Abel, 2001: 401), itself connected to the present linguistically via the colloquial name for gin: 'mother's ruin'. The scourge of alcoholism, attributed in part to mass rural–metropolis migration and subsequent urban squalor, corresponds to Flora Tristan's description of the working classes of early Victorian London, who 'frequently go from insufficient nourishment to the excesses of drink; all these poor souls are scrawny, ricket-ridden and sickly, too; they have thin, sagging bodies, weak limbs, a pale complexion and dead eyes; one would think they all had consumption' ([1840] 2008: 58–9). Alcohol here, as in Hogarth's etching, is depicted as a disease, both physically and societally. Furthermore, it is one which spans time and social class: Tristan refers both to gentlemen ([1840] 2008: 28) and factory workers ([1840] 2008: 58), while Abel notes that in Georgian London 'drunkenness was "business as usual"' (Abel, 2001: 405) across society, if 'simply amusing' for 'the middle and upper classes' (Abel, 2001: 402). Characteristic of an 'epidemic', alcohol (ab)use in London is also seen to transcend gender distinctions, as Tristan demonstrates: 'Many women have recourse to the same methods. That which matters above all else is to forget *that one exists*' ([1840] 2008: 29; original emphasis). In all these portrayals of historic alcohol consumption in London, however stereotypical, it is, as Antoine noted, unequivocally 'an end in itself', a form of escape from the harsh experience of life in the capital, and – significantly – one resorted to by both sexes.

Attesting to the historicity (Bourdieu and Wacquant, 1992) and reproductive tendency of habitus (Bourdieu and Passeron, 1970), almost three centuries after Hogarth and Fielding's concerns, and two after Tristan's, returnee Moses remembers being shocked by the same pervasive phenomenon: 'It's all a bit too geared towards pure alcoholism, like to get really drunk ... It's a bit of a competition to see who can get the drunkest. It's completely excessive. I'd often see girls of ten or eleven drinking beer, and that shocked me quite a lot.' Moses is not only perturbed by the quantities of alcohol consumed and ages of those involved, but, like Tristan, by their gender. Laura is yet more explicit in this respect: 'English women drink a lot more than French women; they're capable of drinking until they're really drunk ... It's ugly.' The intersectional disparagement of English women descending into the vulgar drunken behaviour more often associated with men in the premigration habitat is culturally meaningful, indicating an acceptance, presumption even, of the underlying sexual inequality that has emerged from my interviews and Focus Groups (see Chapter 1; Huc-Hepher and Drake, 2013).

While both Moses and Laura are critical of alcohol intake in the diasporic field in quantifiable terms, what they find particularly offensive is its embodiment by women; a point reiterated in the parodic film, *Shit French People in London Say*, in which the (woman) protagonist exclaims: 'English women are such boozers!' ('Qu'est-ce qu'elles picolent les Anglaises!'; Meard Street Productions, 2012). These stereotypical remarks bear witness to the sociocultural conditioning of the premigration space, instigating a pre-reflexive expectation of distinct male and female behavioural codes (Bourdieu, 1998), found to be wanting in the drinking habits of the diasporic field. Further, Laura's allusion to intoxicated women being 'ugly' compounds the comment's intersectional force, extending it to the realm of the aesthetic. Akin to what Bourdieu terms 'aesthetic racism' (Bourdieu, 2005: 44; 1979a), the reproach demonstrates the gendered double standards prevalent in French society and transposed to the London space, where they evolve into a form of othering. The strangeness of English women's drinking practices and their incompatibility with those of the originary field/habitus sets the French migrants apart, placing them in a perceived position of moral superiority, underpinned by their habitus-based inability to apprehend the underlying freedoms to which such habits testify (Murphy-Lejeune, 2002).

This spontaneous gendering of London drinking habits nevertheless departs from the contentions of Mulholland and Ryan (2017), whose participants disparaged what they interpreted to be a greater gender divide in London pubs than in Paris bars, with groups of men and women seen socialising separately in pubs. I argue instead that rather than symbolising division, these gendered groupings are the result of increased freedom for women to engage in London's nightlife without the need for a chaperon. Indeed, Chantal notes such liberation during our conversation:

> what struck me here was how men and women don't necessarily go out together ... and when the English have their first child, the man babysits one day of the week, so the woman can go out with her friends. And the woman will do it for the man on another day. That never happens in France. We have girls' nights' out occasionally, but it's rare. We usually go out with our husband or boyfriend. I was really struck by that.

Chantal, who has lived in London since 1989, compared to Moses' and Laura's two- and five-year respective sojourns, has a degree of cultural insight that belies her originary habitus. Now as accustomed to London practices as those of France, she is able to read into the ostensible gender segregation in a manner that Moses and Laura cannot. She notes that 'girls would go to one pub and lads to another', but understands this division to come from the bottom up and to illustrate women's equality as opposed to their submission. Likewise, I posit that the excessive drinking habits Moses and Laura consider shocking and 'ugly', are in fact an articulation of gender equality, an enactment of women's emancipation and a gesture towards 'gender abolitionism' (Hester, 2018: 22). Curiously, Mulholland and Ryan's women participants confirm this comparative freedom (discussed in Chapter 1), with Paris deemed a place 'where a woman's presence in the public sphere was seen to be governed by a set of evaluative criteria concerned with how women "look", [whereas] London was defined as a place where a woman could enjoy autonomy' (Mulholland and Ryan, 2017: 143), yet they fail to associate liberal drinking practices and thus potentially looking 'ugly', with third-wave feminism. This oversight is doubtless due to the relative brevity of their migrancy, meaning for them, the 'host' continues to be the stranger, and the 'stranger becomes the sign of what is incomprehensible, impossible to assimilate, a sublimated expression of inequality' (Murphy-Lejeune, 2002: 27).

According to the French consulate in London, in 1992, 20,002 women were registered as residents, against 9,956 men. Ten years' later, that figure had risen to 37,475 and 22,610 respectively, rising to 39,826 against 24,216 in 2003 (Bellion, 2005: 8). Although the numbers are more balanced today, these considerable differences point to the emancipatory role of London mobility for French women (and other minorities) in the post-Maastricht era, with local drinking habits being merely a performance of these freedoms. That Moses perceives them through the prism of his male gaze and Laura from her 'trailing wife' perspective (Cooke, 2001; Stockdale, 2016) blinds them to the habits' liberating function, which in turn erects an invisible boundary between them and the 'host' society. These everyday drinking habits, therefore serve to dislocate as much as they do to embed (Conradson and Latham, 2005a; Farrer, 2010).

Gendered discourse aside, François, the NHS surgeon, injects additional validity to Moses', Laura's and other participants' impressions of the normalised alcohol abuse they perceive to constitute an intrinsic habit of the London social field, by substantiating them with scientific evidence:

> Statistics show that in France cirrhosis is decreasing in every region, at varying rates, but everywhere. This is the only country in Europe where it's increasing. And [this hospital] is the biggest liver transplant centre in Europe – that's why. This no-nonsense drinking culture is all very well, but … it's one pint, then two, then three, and it's half a litre each time, so that makes three litres of beer, and afterwards you have to go to bed. I mean London's a giant booze-up.

Despite recognising François's assertion that London symbolises dispro-portionate drinking habits, Brigitte is divided as to the drinking habits of the migration habitat and epitomises the emplacement–displacement dichotomy. She enjoys the conviviality of the pub scene (Conradson and Latham, 2007) and its function as a mechanism for cementing amicable ties (Scott, 2006) among otherwise distant colleagues (Mulholland and Ryan, 2017), but is wary of the trap into which she sees herself falling by adopting such local habits. Given the difficulties encountered making English friends in London (Huc-Hepher and Drake, 2013), the social capital represented by taking part in local drinking practices is not to be underestimated. As well as facilitating bonding, it allows participants to perform their belonging. Brigitte describes going to the pub on average three times per week because she values its 'fairly laid-back side' but has noticed 'drinking a lot more here than in France … You go to the pub here, and then it's one round, two rounds, three rounds … We all feel we drink a lot more here than in France … So, I'm being careful now, I drink coke or orange juice. It's just that I don't want to slip into a systematic pattern.'

However, by opting for non-alcoholic drinks, as Mulholland and Ryan postulate (2017), Brigitte risks distancing herself from the 'in-group', inad-vertently positioning herself on the outside of the 'parochial atmosphere' of the pub (de Backer, 2019). As de Backer explains, parochial atmospheres correspond to 'the feeling of having something in common without any necessary bonds of family or friendship … While they are characterised by belonging for the 'insider', the outsider may perceive them as a threat' (2009: 12). Thus, Brigitte's informed decision to refrain from drinking alcohol regularly after work brings with it the possibility of alienation.

Brigitte's allusion to purchasing 'rounds' is also important, since the practice is not commonplace all over Europe. While in France the habit exists, as the equivalent word 'tournée' illustrates, it is not a given, and in other parts of Europe, Sweden for example, the custom is for each individ-ual in a group to purchase their own drink. There is an alternative practice in France, whereby a group of friends combine their funds to purchase an entire bottle, of whisky for example, which they then mix with other soft drinks from collective jugs on the shared table. This is evidently equally as convivial as the English round-buying model, but perhaps advantageous in that individuals can measure and pace their drinking from the collective vessels (with the option of not alcoholising the mixer). In London, however, should one individual purchase a 'round' for six or more friends or col-leagues, this tends to result in six or more (alcoholic) drinks being con-sumed by each member of the party for fear of being deemed egotistical or exploitative if failing to play one's part in the drinking ritual. Fox attributes the round-buying ritual to the 'principle of gift-giving' (Fox, 2014: 375), or a gestural way of declaring one's friendship, that is, the 'Englishman's substitute for the expression of emotion' (2014: 372). As such, failing to return the compliment is considered impolite in the extreme. Consuming substantial quantities of alcohol has therefore evolved, over centuries, into what is now a matter of courtesy in the migration habitat, causing offence if the politeness codes of post-workplace socialising and drinking by the 'round' are flouted. By failing to comply with these subtle sociability codes, François and Brigitte again marginalise their position within the diasporic social space.

Favell (2008a: 170) refers to these work-related drinking customs as the 'liquid lunch' – recalling Fox's (2014: 372) round-buying 'liquid handshake' – and also remarks a reluctance on the part of European highly skilled migrants to adopt such normalised and 'intense' habits (2014: 372). Yet, for some, London's unrestrained drinking practices are an attraction, such as Arthur, for whom 'it was positive'. He nevertheless acknowledges that 'for other people it can be negative; some fall into drugs, alcohol, etc.' Indeed, Sadia's husband, whom she depicts as being 'haunted' by drugs, demonstrating the research interview's capacity to be a 'therapeutic encounter' (Birch and Miller, 2000: 191), is a case in point. As a result of their long-term struggle with drug and alcohol misuse, they have both felt compelled to relinquish alcohol consumption definitively. This has compromised Sadia's relationship with, and happiness within, the diasporic field, as in her opinion, 'everything that's fun to do in London is linked to that, to alcohol and drugs'. This again underlines the twofold functionality of London drinking habits in mobility and emplacement processes. On one hand, they appeal to the younger French, frustrated by the rigidity and gender inequality of the socialising practices of the originary field, like the Italian and German graduates participating in King *et al.*'s study, who seek 'adventure' and 'the "affective possibilities" of London as an exciting setting for the migrants' journey of self-discovery and maturation' (King *et al.*, 2014: 12, 10). On the other, they are found to be disagreeable to longer-term or more mature French residents, now fatigued by the continual excesses of London social life and aware of the risks posed to their long-term well-being. Sufficiently secure in their affective diasporic networks, they are arguably in a position to withstand the exclusion that can accompany non-participation in local drinking rituals and thus 'spoiling the party' (Favell, 2008a: 171). In fact, prolonged confrontation with the spirited socialising of the diasporic field ultimately encourages participants to reject their 'chameleon' emplacement tendencies and instead re-engage with their 'clam' side (Murphy-Lejeune, 2002), defiantly reasserting their Frenchness and perpetuating the more measured drinking practices of France (Benson, 2011), that is, with food and not as an end in itself.

It might seem that diasporic eating and drinking habits, together with food as a habitat component, have disproportionately dominated this book. However, the emphasis is attributable to the centrality of food, without any design on my part, in my conversations with, and observations of, participants. Mata Codesal confirms that this is not a unique phenomenon, stating that in 'a report about migrants' integration in the northern Spanish province of Cantabria, an astonishingly high number of migrants refer to food, even though they have not been asked about it' (Mata Codesal, 2008: 5). Similarly, Johnson and Rowlands assert that 'as an interview progresses, it often takes unexpected turns or digressions that follow the informant's interests or knowledge' (2012: 107). The significant weight I have afforded eating and drinking habits has therefore been largely determined by my participants themselves, as equal partners in the research enterprise. Moreover, being in search of ethnographic meanings pertaining to individual and community cultural identification and dynamics (Brettell, 2008), I have naturally foregrounded everyday '[f]ood sharing practices, cooking and eating … imbued with powerful meanings that are most of the time taken for granted' (Mata Codesal, 2008: 3). As Parkhurst Ferguson contends, '[i]ndividually and collectively, though in a very complicated way, we are indeed what we eat' (2004: 15). In order to discover who my London-French research participants *are*, therefore, I have needed to discover *what* (as well as how and when) they eat and drink (Bodomo and Ma, 2012). Lastly, the prominence is explicable in terms of my own belonging within a London-French family, set within a wider national French preoccupation with food, now formally recognised by UNESCO. Conversations with my French friends and family inevitably turn towards the culinary, irrespective of the point of departure; similarly, they have surreptitiously entered this ethnography. It is thus quite natural, and in keeping with the habitus of the London-French diaspora under scrutiny, that food and drink, as cultural objects and practices, should play a key role in the study. At this point, however, I turn my attention away from food and concentrate on a final ritualistic practice to which the participants have repeatedly drawn attention: therapeutic habits.

Towards a third-wave de-medicalised self: 'In France, we use too much medication, we're too worried about our health'

Compared to eating and drinking, healthcare practices are an under-researched area of migration studies, particularly within an ethnographic, lifestyle framework. While there have been numerous studies on 'medical tourism' from a range of disciplinary perspectives (e.g. law, health, tourism, human resources), less research has focused on the medicalised mobility and/or settlement of EU 'free movers'. Furthermore, in much of the literature, there is an emphasis on policy and the economic implications of medical and reproductive migration, but little understanding of the affective and ideological dimensions influencing 'healthcare migrants' (Horton and Cole, 2011; Inhorn, 2011). Moreh, McGhee and Vlachantoni's (2018) work on EU migrants' attitudes to UK healthcare and Horsfall's study on 'medical tourism' from the UK to Poland (2019) suggest a turn towards the medicalised intra-EU migrant; however, their findings tend to confirm preconceived ideas that contradict my own. In this section, therefore, I focus on participants' healthcare habits to discover what they tell us about feelings of displacement and emplacement in London, the extent to which they dispel common myths regarding healthcare in Britain and how they are an enactment of underlying ideological concerns. Horsfall calls for a more 'joined-up', 'more detailed understanding of how recent migrants access healthcare and how this varies between migrant communities and changes over time' (2019: 9). In this section, I aim to contribute to this overarching picture, providing insights into the London-French experience and performativity of healthcare.

In view of the negative tropes that dominate French media regarding the UK's purportedly substandard healthcare provision, such as *La Croix*'s headline, 'British health system in complete chaos' (de Bourbon, 2018) or *Le Monde*'s 'British sickened by their health system' (Albert, 2013), it is somewhat surprising that most of my participants have undergone a process of medical 'acculturation' in the migratory field. The existence of multiple French private healthcare centres in London (Medicare Français, La Maison Médicale, La Clinique Française, etc.) and charitable provisions (Le Dispensaire français), together with eight pages of classified London-French healthcare advertisements in the September 2019 edition of *Ici Londres* magazine, from allergology and cardiology to psychotherapy and urology, would suggest that a considerable proportion of the community prefers French medical services to the UK equivalent. Such preferences are also corroborated by the so-called NHS 'paracetamol service' (Horsfall, 2019: 11) evoked in London-French mother-and-toddler groups and social gatherings. Yet, most of the French Londoners taking part in my study report positive experiences of the NHS, even those who have been afflicted with serious ailments, such as stroke or cardiac arrest, or hospitalised for the life-changing event of childbirth.

There are, however, a few exceptions to this rule.[2] Charles, who has had no direct experience of the NHS, returns to France for medical and dental treatment. He is dubious of the NHS owing to preconceived ideas about the system being of 'third-world' standard (an outdated term that is nevertheless widely used in France and in *Shit French People in London Say*; Meard Street Productions, 2012). Charles thus corresponds to the 59 per cent of western Europeans who would rather have medical treatment in their home country than the UK (Moreh *et al.*, 2019), and for whom perceptions over the poor quality of the NHS 'were the main factor in pushing [them] away from healthcare treatment in the UK' (Moreh *et al.*, 2018: 4). Having had a negative experience in the NHS, Miranda has turned to private surgical treatment in London, and Séverine is semi-critical of the NHS, denouncing the anonymity of the doctor–patient relationship and GP appointment waiting times, also noted by Polish migrants in the UK (Horsfall, 2019). It is useful to consider that Charles has been a London resident for eleven years, Miranda for ten and Séverine for twenty-six. As Moreh *et al.* posit, '[m]igrants who are more integrated into British society are significantly more likely to prefer medical treatment in the UK, but not necessarily because of perceived higher quality standards' (2018: 1). The considerable length of Séverine's stay and consequent integration could, therefore, explain why she counterbalances her criticisms of the NHS with positive remarks:

> I have a GP in London, of course, but you're a bit of an anonymous number. If something happens to me in England, I won't go and see a doctor straight away, I'll ask friends, I'll use Chinese medicine, I do internet research by myself ... Maybe I have more confidence in that respect ... When I look at my sisters who haven't left France, I know that when they're ill with the flu, its antibiotics straight away. I've changed in that way, when I first came to live in London, I decided to abandon that culture, and I was healthier for it, taking less medication, not taking antibiotics, seeing fewer doctors and adopting a more preventive attitude.

Dissatisfaction with the faceless practice of visiting her doctor in London has the paradoxical effect of altering Séverine's habits for the better, resulting in what she deems to be improved well-being, more measured use of prescribed medicines and greater assertiveness in the self-management of her health. This last point is important, given that women's control over their personal health(care) is an expression of their feminist agency and freedom (Lazarus, 1994; Skowronsk, 2015; Hester, 2018). In the case of women migrants, it is also an articulation of diasporic empowerment (Wang, 2013a), 'releasing them from ties and enabling them to live lives more "true" to themselves' (Benson and O'Reilly, 2009: 610). Adopting 'host' healthcare habits thus gives Séverine increased ownership of her body in a way that recalls the *Our Bodies, Ourselves*, second-wave self-help feminism of the 1970s and distinguishes her positively from her non-moving siblings. In so doing, it grants her greater agency over the performativity of her migrant-London-woman identity and tends towards the xenofeminist activism advocated by Hester (2018). Séverine's rejection of the praxial normalisation of over-medicating in France and her adaptation to the therapeutic norms of the postmigration culture therefore reinforce her sense of embeddedness in the diasporic field and disembeddedness from the 'homeland' and its endemic inequalities.

Marie reiterates the sentiment that attitudes and habits pertaining to health are healthier in the diasporic field and that habitus shapes the habitat (Friedmann, 2005: 331, citing Bourdieu, 1991). She perceives such structures as The Royal London Hospital for Integrated Medicine (formerly the Royal London Homeopathic Hospital) and the reluctance to prescribe 'mainstream' medication as institutional acknowledgement of alternative medicines. This recognition of non-standard healthcare is – somewhat ironically – thought to be more progressive than the medico-technically advanced approaches driven in France:

> You're a lot more advanced in England than in France when it comes to alternative medicine, oh, yes, yes. I mean alternative medicine's really integrated in England, even in hospitals. Whereas here it's still seen as a bit wacky. I saw for myself, there are sophrology departments, hypnosis departments, departments for all those sorts of things, but I mean incorporated in the hospital. In France, we use too much medication, we're too worried about our health.

Like food, personal health is indeed a national preoccupation in France, one that is generally relieved by – highly marketised and hegemonised – medication. Should a patient leave a doctor's surgery without a threefold prescription, they may well feel short-changed, as if, having contributed generously to the semi-private system, and making additional payments upon each visit (with reimbursement postponed and often partial), medication is deserved in return for the financial outlay. In London, however, the NHS, 'free at the point of use' as a matter of principle (Moreh *et al.*, 2018: 4), is akin to a religion in the collective imagination, a point confirmed by its incongruous prominence during the opening ceremony of the London 2012 Olympic Games (Albert, 2013; Moreh *et al.*, 2019), as well as in media and political discourses (O'Grady, 2011). It is held in sacred esteem (Laplace *et al.*, 2002; de Bourbon, 2018) irrespective of political persuasion and is perhaps comparable, therefore, to the reverence that surrounds the state education system in France, similarly free at the point of delivery and similarly prized as a 'national treasure'. The parallel positioning of education in France and healthcare in the UK is confirmed by the 'factory' metaphor applied to Britain's health system by Séverine, but to France's education system by a participant in Focus Group Two. The ideology behind each of these nationally cherished public services takes precedence over the practical failings of both, as 'insider', François, occasionally reveals. Although highly praiseworthy of the generous NHS funding invested in his operating theatre, now fitted with all the latest equipment he requested, he is profoundly frustrated by the time and resources wasted on 'committees' and through poor planning. The NHS's worthy principles therefore progressively blind (a term Robert uses) long-term residents to operational shortcomings that more recent or more implicated migrants observe.

Even among my other participants, appreciation for the NHS is nurtured at the rate at which they become habituated to the migratory field and gradually assume local mentalities (Bourdieu, 2005). Integration dislodges engrained therapeutic practices and attitudes over time, which has wider political implications within the London space. For it means that 'contrary to political rhetoric emphasising the migratory pull effects of free healthcare in the UK, it is in fact those with higher levels of temporal ... cultural ... and civic ... integration' who use it (Moreh *et al.*, 2018: 4). The healthcare habits of Marie's daughter (herself a London-French migrant) demonstrate this processuality, as they develop according to her first-hand experiences of childbirth in the NHS. Habituated to France's 'high-tech, "mechanistic" philosophy' (Skowronsk, 2015: 27), whereby epidural and routine visits to a (usually male) gynaecologist are taken for granted, Marie's initial negativity has transformed into an appreciation for the de-medicalised approach encouraged in London:

> My daughter had her first child in hospital, and it went very, very badly ... She didn't like giving birth in hospital at all. So, she had the second one at home. In France, people find that completely preposterous [she laughs]. [It was] great, and she was delighted; it went really well. In France, medicine is technical and people are afraid for their health.

While the French system is perceived to be efficient, its over-medicalisation has led to the pathologisation of childbirth, expunging the humanity from the care. It is the comfortable, familiar and familial surroundings and 'non-medical' approach that Marie's daughter appreciated in her home birth. The midwives dedicated their attentions to her alone, which added value to the experience and re-humanised it. Moreover, the fairly routine habit of home births in the UK is based on a long history of feminist activism. It began with first-wave, early twentieth-century feminists' demands for analgesic care and the right to give birth in hospital. In the 1960s and 1970s, it translated into a rejection of such medicalised practices by second-wave feminists, who believed doctors had 'created a patriarchal devaluing of women's bodies by viewing them mechanistically' (Skowronsk, 2015: 27) and consequently called for a return to natural childbirth practices overseen by (mainly women) midwives. Today, third-wave feminists 'seek to reposition women's choice as the central issue' (2015: 28). They challenge the notion of pain inherent in the 'natural' of 'natural childbirth' and the notion of (women's) domesticity inherent in the 'home' of 'home birth'.

Once again, therefore, we see the 'double historicity' (Bourdieu and Wacquant, 1992) of the migrant experience. Marie's daughter's choice to give birth at home re-enacts the activism of her mother's generation of feminists in the UK, including such instrumental figures as Prunella Briance, who established the National Childbirth Trust in 1959 from her sitting room (NCT, no date). Simultaneously, Marie's daughter's experiences of childbirth play out contemporary third-wave xenofeminist history-making in their foregrounding of *choice* and 'reproductive sovereignty' (Hester, 2018: 88). Through her move from the technomaterialist hospital environment to the home birth, as well as from France to London, her experiences illustrate her agency, together with the emplacement/displacement potential of everyday habits (Farrer, 2010; Conradson and Latham, 2005a). Their local historicity embeds her within the diasporic context and culture, while distancing her from the 'homeland', where homebirth practices are often ridiculed, thus crystallising the myth of the NHS as an archaic, crumbling system. Marie illustrates this when referring to the reaction to her daughter's home birth: 'in France, people find the idea of it crazy'. In an auto-ethnographic turn, having given birth at home myself in London and repeatedly been met with incredulity in the French social space, I can vouch for the perceived backwardness of the practice. The discrepancy between pre- and postmigration childbirth practices and attitudes therefore gives rise to a process of othering generally associated with early mobility and immersion in the postmigration field (Thatcher and Halvorsrud, 2016). It hence recalls the 'reverse hysteresis' or '[r]e-entry shock' (Murphy-Lejeune, 2002: 225) discussed in Chapter 3, which itself can result in a 'destablized habitus' (Ingram and Abrahams, 2016).

In Moreh *et al.*'s 2018 briefing on EU migrants' attitudes towards healthcare, assumed NHS inferiority is seen to encourage return medical mobility, a phenomenon also noted by Horsfall (2019). Conversely, the majority of my participants feel more 'at home' in the British system. Although they do not dispute the quality of medical standards in France, they criticise the pathologisation of childbirth and over-medicalisation in general. The childbearing trajectory of Chantal differs from that of Marie's daughter, as Chantal gave birth to her first child in a London hospital and her second in Paris, but she nevertheless reaches the same conclusions: 'I didn't like the French system at all, actually. There were so many precautions there, it was as if I was ill, that something was necessarily going to go seriously wrong.' This pessimistic outlook and resulting overcautious medicalisation, was experienced as invasive and unsettling, depriving a fundamentally organic, primal process of its inherent naturalness and humanity. I accept that this emphasis on the natural is challenged today by third-wave feminists. They feel its idealisation reinforces the binaries xenofeminism aims to overcome (Hester, 2018), such as men being 'analytical, women intuitive', or that 'men tend towards technology, women towards nature, and 'men are empowered in the workplace, women at home' (Skowronsk, 2015: 27). I support the argument that 'natural childbirth' is considered 'as some sort of cultural initiation into the rightful world of women', so that 'those who do not conform to the "natural" ideal are disenfranchised as "unnatural" or even "bad" mothers' (2015: 27). Yet, having experienced the 'trauma attached to … medicalised birth' (Hester, 2018: 153, endnote 22), my participants are keen to underscore the comfort engendered through the more humanistic approach encountered in London.

Importantly, these critiques of the French health 'care' system are not made by women participants alone, since Robert, openly gay, is even harsher in his comments. His account suggests that the 'oppressive pathways of healthcare' (Hester, 2018: 85) encountered in France can be interpreted not only as articulations of 'medical sexism' (2018: 122, citing Ehrenreich and English, [1973] 2011), but potentially as medical homophobia. Such discrimination has – to retain former MP Nigel Lawson's analogy of the NHS being 'the closest thing that the English have to a religion' (Curtis, 2018) – thus 'converted' Robert to the British system:

> I have blind faith in the NHS. When I was in France, I had a very, very serious illness; I was treated quite properly, but the medical care there's pretty shameful, and actually after that operation, I had to be monitored for five years, but I didn't go … In France, I was considered a patient before being considered a human being. Whereas when I arrived in England, it was different. They spoke to me like a human first, explaining things to me, being very kind, very attentive and very caring, and I've never had any trouble getting an appointment. I've always had an extremely positive experience here, whereas in France that was not always the case. So, maybe I'm an exception, but I like the NHS and I feel relatively well-looked-after; I certainly wouldn't want to go to France for an operation or for after-care … The approach is definitely different, and I felt a lot more comfortable here than in France, and anyway, if I was to fall ill in France, I'd have time to come back to England for healthcare.

Robert's account is peppered with compassionate and quasi-religious terminology: *very kind, attentive, caring, well-looked-after, comfortable, blind faith* in the English system and *shameful* care in France, which substantiates his conversion to local beliefs and underlines the comparative humanity perceived in the NHS. It is noteworthy that Robert unintentionally inverts my initial question on whether, hypothetically, he would be tempted to return to France for medical treatment if ever he fell ill. On the contrary, he declares at the end of his diatribe, expressing an air of relief that the UK would be sufficiently close for him to 'come back' for treatment should the need arise. His wording suggests London is now 'home', medically speaking, and this inverted concept of 'return' counters the findings of Moreh *et al.* (2018) and Horsfall (2019). Similarly, Robert's trouble-free appointment-making rejects the (stereo)typically bemoaned 'waiting times associated with accessing care' (Horsfall, 2019: 11).

Significantly, Robert particularly appreciates being addressed on equal terms in London, as opposed to being spoken down to from the heights at which doctors are purportedly placed in the originary field, and, more importantly, place themselves. Their institutionalised symbolic capital awards them a distinctively elevated status in French society, which, like the male 'chef-cuisiniers' referred to by Bourdieu (1998) and the overly hierarchical society depicted by King *et al.*'s Italian migrants (2014), appears to be reproduced from generation to generation. It recalls the social reproduction that Hester links to healthcare (2018), which is arguably less acute in London than France, thanks to the effects of Anglo-American 'protocol feminism' (2018: 119). Such protocol has seeped into the everyday healthcare habits of the diasporic field, enabled by 'practices, manuals, and guidelines that explicitly sought to take note of how power, emotion, and bonding circulated within clinical settings so as to create less oppressive medical experiences and less pathologizing research' (Murphy, 2015: 3, cited in Hester, 2018: 119). It is precisely these 'more patient-focused practices of care' (Hester, 2018: 80) in the NHS that Robert values, and which contrast starkly with the anachronistic 'relationship between the providers and recipients of professionalized medical care' (2018: 79) in France, which, like in the Anglo-American model of the 1970s, is 'both highly gendered and deeply unequal' (2018: 79).

The inherent power dynamics and institutionalised patriarchism of French clinical practices are also noted by (straight, white, male) Bruno, who relates an unpleasant encounter with an ENT specialist in a private clinic in his 'hometown'. When debriefing Bruno post-tonsillectomy, the surgeon declared that Bruno had throat cancer, before exclaiming, several long seconds later, that it was nothing more than a quip. Bruno failed to appreciate the humour. For, as Smith contends, humour 'trades less on ambiguity than on attempts to essentialize human beings depending upon an easily accessed and potentially mutually understood metaphor or metonymic category' (Smith, 2012: 158). In this light, the doctor's reliance on humour is a 'mutually understood' mechanism for reaffirming the hegemonic medic–patient categories that prevail in the French social field. The anecdote also serves to support Charles's assertion 'that humour is always nasty in France, aggressive at the expense of other people'. It would appear, therefore, that while funds and time could be better spent in London hospitals, compassion and bedside manners could be improved in France. Even if English 'politenesses are so deeply ingrained as to be almost involuntary, and thus fairly meaningless', this 'negative politeness' (Fox, 2014: 556) serves the desired effect on the French migrants receiving it.

These testimonies have demonstrated that French imaginaries of the NHS as an outdated, ramshackle system to be avoided at all costs are ill-founded, with participants' lived experience of healthcare in London revealing it to be a place where unoppressive, empathetic habits prevail and the emphasis is on the 'care' in 'healthcare'. Their experiences in France, however, bring to bear an ideologically outmoded system, based on chronic patriarchal hegemonies and endemic over-medicalisation, with the emphasis on the 'health' in 'healthcare', at the expense of the human. Participants' performativity of an increasingly de-medicalised self in London serves to assert their embeddedness within the diasporic space and establishes their 'body as a potential locus of [transnational] emancipatory endeavour' (Hester, 2018: 137). Through the exchange of local knowledge, practices and habits, each nation can learn from the other. Consequently, mutually beneficial cultural dynamics ought to be encouraged, if they do not emerge organically, as in the case of Marie, who, since leaving London, has clung on to the habits that evolved during her time there, as a way of keeping that past alive. Aptly enough, she illustrates the point most compellingly with an eating habit: 'I've got a little [English] side; the things I like, well, I've adopted them. I mean I like my cup of tea, I like not necessarily having a big meal like the French; I can easily eat a little snack, and that's quite enough for me … A little sandwich isn't bad, and I make it in the English way, with a sandwich loaf, and I cut off all the crusts [she laughs].' Once again, the conversation turns to the culinary.

Conclusion

Over the course of this chapter, I have illustrated how habits and rituals instilled in the primary/secondary habitus interconnect my French research participants within the diasporic field in subtle yet powerful ways, without a consciousness on their part of their commonality in the collective migrant imagination. This, therefore, allows my participants to perceive themselves as agentive individuals, in possession of singular trajectories and practices within the diasporic field, rather than as a community per se, and as such gives the impression of defying the notion of a London-French habitus. However, shared rituals, such as eating certain foods, in certain ways, at certain times, in combination with the habituated adoption of local values and habits in the diasporic field, like the faith expressed in the national health system or the adoption of local cake-baking practices and resistance to local pub drinking habits, effectively resulted not only in a (partly) transformed individual habitus, but a 'common-unity' of practice, in other words, a London-French habitus, or a French community in London. Moreover, I have revealed how this community of practice (Wenger, 1998, 2004; Cox, 2005) is underpinned and informed by centuries of habits, which confirmed the multiple historicities, temporalities and spatialities of the migrant experience (Farrer, 2010).

On a micro-, individual level, I demonstrated that exposure to the habits of the diasporic space resulted in a particular form of 'Londonishness'. It was 'particular' in its sustainment of certain internalised aspects of performativity from the originary habitat, especially in relation to the primal, sensory dimensions of taste and physical well-being, which served to disconnect participants from the here and now of their mobility. In this light, therefore, it was not so much a question of a tertiary migratory habitus or 'third timespace' (Sprio, 2013: 61), succeeding the primary/secondary habitus chronologically, but rather an emergent habitus complex: a cultural fusion evolving over the transnational and translocal times and spaces of life, taking on new hues along the way, but retaining the fundamental palette of origin (Bourdieu, 1980a).

Constructed around the third 'habit prong' of my habitus triad, the chapter has illustrated that habits are subject to change, but that the originary gaze can be obstinately persistent. While enjoying the social drinking habits of the diasporic field, my participants remained detached, making a conscious decision to reject the excessive and/or gendered drinking habits thought to negatively dominate the migratory space. Similarly, eating habits from the homeland considered morally superior to the assumed informal and unhealthy eating habits of the adopted home were consistently maintained. Yet, habits were seen to be transformed in relation to healthcare and restaurant dining, where habituation to local attitudes and tastes resulted in an embodiment thereof. This proves the inherent dynamics of the habitus triad: the foodstuffs of the original habitats were translated into the eating and drinking habits of my participants in the same way that the multicultural restaurants prevalent in the external habitat of their London homes influenced their gustatory dispositions. Likewise, participants' habituation to local therapeutic practices altered their medical habits – purportedly for the better – and reinforced their sense of emplacement in the London field and simultaneous disembedding from the premigration space, where over-medicalised and pathologising practices were considered ideologically retrograde, particularly by women and gay interviewees. The majority of habits adopted by participants functioned as positive additions to their inherited dispositions, demonstrating a degree of agency over their cultural transformations and increasingly rich identities (Murphy-Lejeune, 2002).

Finally, through my emphasis on habits, I evinced how globalisation has given rise to a more culturally dynamic relationship between originary and diasporic spaces than ever before. The cultural remittances of French migrant populations, in the form of recipes transferred by physical, mediated and virtual means, led to their subsequent marketisation and adoption in the 'sending' society, having profound effects on everyday practices there. The way in which the internet is increasingly impacting on this process, reconfiguring habits, habitats, identity and emplacement in both pre- and postmigration contexts is hence the focus of the following two chapters.

Notes

1 The share of agriculture in the GDP of France and the UK is indicative of this difference. In 1970, agriculture accounted for 7.5 per cent of France's GDP, compared to only 2.9 per cent of the UK's. Although in significant decline, France's still outstripped the UK's in 2014, with 2.6 per cent, and 1.7 per cent (*Les Echos*, 2015).

2 François, the NHS surgeon, has been largely excluded from this evaluation, as his 'insider' experiences of the system are too long, complex and entangled in the struggles of the healthcare field to permit inclusion here. Moreover, as a provider of the care, rather than a recipient of the service, his is a partial, implicated perspective. That said, it is worth noting that hypothetically he would prefer to seek treatment overseas than in the UK.

5

Looking beyond:
blended understandings of symbolic forces in
London-French education on-land and on-line

Introduction

In this chapter and the next, I move from on-land research findings to an increasingly 'blended' ethnographic approach. In Chapter 4, we began to see the effects of the internet on transnational practices, as such, examining London-French on-line representations is a logical progression, adding another layer to my holistic ethnographic approach. A fundamental component of my research involved curating the London French Special Collection (LFSC; Huc-Hepher, no date), in the UK Web Archive (UKWA), hosted by the British Library. My blended approach, combining Bourdieusian ethnographic and Kressian semiotic principles, thus acknowledges the internet-based immersive insights that the curation process permitted (Huc-Hepher, 2015). The principal stimulus behind constructing a digital home for London-French web objects was to preserve the fragile (Strodl *et al.*, 2011; Taylor, 2012) and ephemeral (Day, 2006; Masanès, 2006; Gomes and Costa, 2014) digital cultural capital of the 'community' for posterity, thereby providing a lasting record of web objects deemed of intellectual and cultural value to current and future generations (Digital Preservation Coalition, no date; Pennock, 2007; Kitchin, 2014), whether migration scholars, internet historians or London-French community members eager to trace their online heritage. Beyond its pertinence as a stable consultative archive, however, the LFSC constitutes a rich and varied source of ethnographic material, whose value is only cemented by Britain's exit from the EU. Being a unique record of twenty-first-century London-French digital heritage, it provides a window onto the reflections and plans of a minority group directly affected by 'Brexit', for migrant 'archives are not only records of the past but are also maps for the future' (Appadurai, 2019: 558). Nevertheless, my focus in the following two chapters is not on the impact of the 2016 EU membership referendum (see the Epilogue for that discussion). Rather, I return to the themes of symbolic violence, cultural and social capital, habitus and home, doing so from a progressively digital perspective, using data sourced in the web archive and the 'live' internet.

Since the turn of this century, which saw the publication of Daniel Miller and Don Slater's *The Internet: An Ethnographic Approach* (2000) and later Jennifer Brinkerhoff's *Digital Diasporas: Identity and Transnational Engagement* (2009), together with Mirca Madianou and Daniel Miller's *Migration and New Media: Transnational Families and Polymedia* (2012), there has been increasing scholarly interest in the relationship between internet technologies, identity construction (trans)national belonging and relationships. In 2008, Dana Diminescu (2008, 2016) launched the ambitious e-Diasporas Atlas project, which sought to map and archive diasporic networks and territories across the web. A decade later, Jessica Retis and Roza Tsagarousianou's *Handbook of Diasporas, Media, and Culture* (2019), brought much of this contemporary thought together in a single edited volume, as did Sandra Ponzanesi's Special Issue, 'Migration and Mobility in a Digital Age: (Re)Mapping Connectivity and Belonging' (2019). However, what all these works have in common, bar Brinkerhoff's international relations' approach, is their predominantly media and communication studies' disciplinary perspective. Consequently, much of the emphasis is on large-scale flows of information and people across the globe and on the digital practices of 'forced' or economic migrants, as opposed to the lifestyle-leaning typology of my participants.

There is very little language or semiotics-based (ethnographic) work on diasporic digital representation in general, with the notable exception of Naomi Wells's research on the Latin American community in London (Huc-Hepher and Wells, 2021), and a dearth of critical thinking on the French online diasporic presence in particular. Indeed, William Berthomière's attempt to map the connected French diaspora, referred to by the author as a 'A French What?' (Berthomière, 2012: 1) bears witness to their perceived 'non-histoire' (2012: 1). As Retis and Tsagarousianou demonstrate, given that European policies have developed 'a hierarchy of suffering that distinguishes between migrants defined as *at* risk and therefore in need of protection and care, or *a* risk to the integrity of the territory, economy, and culture of European countries' (Retis and Tsagarousianou, 2019: 7; original emphasis), migrants such as the French, who are neither at risk or a risk, typically escape scholarly attention.

Furthermore, in spite of the appositeness of multimodal social semiotic approaches to online material, particularly the kind advocated by Myrrh Domingo and Gunther Kress (Kress, 2010, 2011; Domingo, 2011; Domingo *et al.*, 2014, 2015), involving ethnography alongside 'textual' digital analysis, there is little evidence of the application of such methodologies to digital diasporic output. Yet, the foregrounding of internet research that apprehends the web not as a place but as a text, where there is no participative interaction and 'the use of computer-mediated communications [functions] like the citation of or quotation from a published book' (Kozinets, 2010: 141), lends itself to ethnographic migration studies. Since 'the layering of modes' in internet-based diasporic texts acts as a 'resource for expressing social and cultural identities within digital communities' (Domingo, 2011: 227), it provides valuable insights into the 'blended' migration experience, which is precisely the approach I adopt in the following chapters. My analysis draws on the on-land/on-line 'blended ethnography' proposed by Androutsopoulos (2008: 4) and Tagg *et al.* (2017: 275), but differs from theirs, and from the ontologically embedded methodology proposed by Miller and Slater (2000), inasmuch as theirs involves interacting with on-line content producers in on-land spaces. I, however, use on-line and on-land sources in parallel; the on-line data enters into a dialogue with the previously gathered on-land data, but each dataset is sourced discretely. By not interacting with the creators of the web resources, I argue that the data – or texts – can be analysed in a more detached manner, thereby fulfilling a role of triangulation despite necessarily being interpreted within the social context of the wider on-land French community and generic/ discursive on-line 'diasberspace'. I opted for this 'combination of "objective" and "subjective" data' (Androutsopoulos, 2008: 16) precisely because the duality is seen as an advantage, with the different datasets requiring different methods of analysis and presenting different, but complementary, insights into the community as a blended whole.

Unlike Chapter 6, where web resources are my starting point, in this chapter I begin with on-land interview data for contextualisation, and, in an 'ethnosemiotic' turn (Huc-Hepher, 2015), subsequently test the findings against the semiotic affordances of the on-line data. The first section of the chapter is dedicated to on-land experiences and perceptions of French and British education models, within the framework of symbolic violence. The second section is devoted to the on-line representations of three schools/ colleges cited in my on-land interviews and attended by 'French' children in London. In the on-line case-study, I foreground the aspects of the UK education model that my on-land participants value most, including the practice-based approach, the emphasis on positive encouragement and participation, teacher–student equality, the valuing of the individual, and the development of oral, sporting and creative skills, alongside employability. By conducting this blended, ethnosemiotic analysis, I seek to understand why the majority of my research participants favour the English educational model (a preference which again dispels habituated myths), whether my on-land findings are translated into on-line educational contexts, and what such insights can offer French and UK education systems, which evidently has policy implications beyond the remit of this book. Since the education of participants' children is critical to their embedding within the diasporic field and has received relatively little attention in the literature, I also contend that it is important to problematise education comparatively and within the broader framework of transnational emplacement.

Several studies have investigated how education can help or hinder migrants' integration. Cornejo Torres and Rosales Ubeda (2015) have researched the role of habitus and symbolic violence among migrants in Santiago, and Lopez Rodriguez's study of Polish migrants' views on UK education adopts a similar Bourdieusian theoretical framework. She addresses how education can contribute to feelings of 'normalcy' but can also be a challenging field for 'outsiders' to navigate, ill-equipped with the necessary (habitus-conditioned) sociocultural insights to be aware of the complexities. Her participants are nonetheless 'relentless [in their ...] robust belief that the UK provides an ideal ground for practising meritocracy', which they hold in high esteem (Lopez Rodriguez, 2010: 344). Ryan and Sales (2013) also examine Polish migrants, emphasising the significance of children in pre- and postmigration decision-making. Their age is considered crucial, and the degree to which they are settled in UK education directly impacts longer-term family settlement, their progeny's 'education and friendships ... rooting them in London' (Ryan and Sales, 2013: 97).

Luchtenberg's volume (2004) goes a step further, highlighting the key role of education in postmigration integration and its profound effect on social cohesion. The authors underline the importance of a multicultural education policy and the criticality of 'host' language acquisition, a point reiterated by Ryan and Sales (2013). Zembylas (2012), on the other hand, turns to the dynamic power of affect in transnational and migrant educational contexts, but again interrogates how it can feed into a multicultural education policy. He asserts that 'pedagogical practices need to constantly provide learning opportunities for a historical and political understanding of the role of emotions in power relations [and ...] need to translate emotional understandings into relationships and new knowledge that benefit learning about multiculturalism and discrimination' (Zembylas, 2012: 174).

However, in none of these works is there detailed consideration of education 'close up', based on the lived experience of migrants' own educational pathways and their children's day-to-day practices within the classroom setting. Maïtena Armagnague and Isabelle Rigoni's special issue on migration and education in France (2018) gestures towards a more microscopic lens, offering multiscalar, multidisciplinary responses to the question and recognising its structuring dynamics, with the education system impacting the lives of the young migrants and the latter impacting educational policy. However, in the existing literature, the underscoring of education's role in the migrant experience detracts from attitudes *towards* education itself. As a result, education emerges largely in the abstract, its first-hand ontological dimensions overlooked, and critical migrant reflections on educational provision and pedagogies, in pre- and postmigration contexts, underdeveloped. In the analysis that follows, I address this shortcoming, asking precisely which aspects of the British education system act as a pull or emplacement factor and which elements of the French system operate the reverse function. Informed by the spontaneous and repeated London vs France comparisons of my participants, I redeploy Mulholland and Ryan's 'grounded comparative epistemology of place' (2017: 135) and explore the key themes that emerged from my on-land ethnographic data. I then reassess them through the prism of on-line multimodal social semiotics, thereby illustrating the credibility of my blended ethnosemiotic framework.

Crucially, I argue that the French and UK education systems – as apprehended by my participants – and the three schools representing them in the internet-based case-study, serve as microcosms for the respective societies' approaches to migration, nationalism and citizenship. As Armagnague and Rigoni (2018) postulate, France has been slow to conceive of itself as a land of immigration, which has delayed political recognition of the need to adapt education to suit its increasingly diverse student body. Consequently, we observe the dissemination of Republican values into the school system and the reproduction of the assimilationist citizenship model, 'whereby migrants are expected to give up their distinctive linguistic, cultural, and social characteristics and become indistinguishable from the majority population' (Koser, 2007: 23–4). In practice, this universalism translates into a positivist educational epistemology (Lea *et al.*, 2003), where conventional, didactic teaching methods persist, and where teachers and students are positioned as 'enemies' (Brandes and Ginnis, [1986] 2001: 38). Conversely, London has a multiculturalist social model, where migrant populations become communities and 'remain distinguishable from the majority population with regard to language, culture and social behaviour' (Koser, 2007: 24). Since the late twentieth century, this multiculturalism has been operationalised in London classrooms through the adoption of a student-centred 'neoliberal agenda' (Starkey, 2019: 375), embedded in constructivist (Lea *et al.*, 2003), humanist (Starkey, 2019) principles, which value students as individuals, respond to their diverse needs and backgrounds through co-created material, and encourage agency and empowerment (Brandes and Ginnis, [1986] 2001; Starkey, 2019). Paradoxically, although humanism is based on French thought, with 'its roots in the writing of Rousseau (1762/1979), who was critical of [French] educational practices which he believed stifled children's creativity and inquisitiveness' (Starkey, 2019: 380), it is precisely these humanistic ideals that are thought to be lacking in French education and are valued by French migrants in the UK system, as the following on-land and on-line empirical evidence will reveal.

On-land perceptions of French and English educational models

> Emmanuel Macron: It begins in early childhood, when you start getting answers wrong in class, you're stigmatised, marks are given back in order – you know how it goes. But if your children are in the English system, it's very different. They won't be stigmatised, the child's strengths will be pursued instead, so they can succeed with the abilities they have. As a result, we're a lot more afraid of failure [in France]. (En Marche, 2017, presidential campaign speech to French residents in London)

As Laura and I continue our discussion in the South Clapham French café, the conversation turns towards education. Although we met several years before Macron's 2017 campaign speech, she predicts much of what he proclaims. Instead of lamenting the poor academic standards of the English education system, the lack of discipline or the over-sized classes, as I anticipate, she is deeply critical of the French, state-run Wix school nearby. Laura identifies a communicational breakdown between parents and teachers, 'the teachers think we're attacking them all the time; and the parents think no one ever listens to them'. This results in 'an authority problem at the French school: they're always giving out orders, whereas in the English classrooms, the children are very calm, there's no unruliness whatsoever, the teachers never shout'.

The staff–student power imbalance noted at Wix corresponds to 'the incorporated form of domination, [which] makes this relationship seem natural' (Bourdieu, 1998: 55) and therefore only becomes noticeable to Laura through comparison with the UK model. It recalls the 'shouting and hushing' and consequent 'battle of wills', described by Brandes and Ginnis ([1986] 2001: 38), whose student-centred approach instead recommends teachers 'play the Waiting Game … sitting quietly until [they] have everyone's attention' ([1986] 2001: 38). The comparative serenity at Honeywell, the English state primary Laura's younger daughter attends, is thus attributable to the increased degree of teacher–pupil views being valued by teachers and the learning process seen as a collaboration rather than a top-down transfer of knowledge. It also concurs with field evidence I have collected from French students, who remark favourably on the value awarded to their opinion by academic staff, be it in the classroom or through institutional feedback surveys and course committees. Evidencing the impact of responding to students' needs and recognising their cultural situatedness (Starkey, 2019), Honeywell has gone so far as to introduce a French-language provision to cater directly for its high proportion of students from French-speaking migrant backgrounds.

Laura also notes a lack of enthusiasm among teachers at Wix: 'there's this kind of weight, you can feel the depressed side, whereas at Honeywell, you go there in the morning and all the teachers seem to be having a whale of a time, they're super happy.' Likewise, 63-year-old returnee, Marie contrasts the 'playful', nurturing approach of English teaching staff with the 'depressed and aggressive' teachers of the French system. Again, this discrepancy can be ascribed to the tenets of the UK child-centred model, because once they 'have been internalised by the teacher, each day in school can be fresh and new, and unpredictable' (Brandes and Ginnis, [1986] 2001: 6). This transforms teaching into a journey of discovery and hence contributes to staff happiness, which in turn fosters 'an atmosphere of unconditional positive regard [... where pupils] are individually and collectively valued' (Brandes and Ginnis, [1986] 2001: 16). By contrast, Laura affirms that 'in France, we're into punishment and frustration', and 'the narrative is a lot more "could do better", whereas at Honeywell, it's always "well done", "brilliant"'. Just as Macron declared, the English system is considered celebratory of pupils' achievement, while the French model's emphasis on (public) humiliation and failure recalls the legal definition of harassment as 'insidious violence' (Chapter 1), normalised to the extent of being transferred to French state schools in London.

Brandes and Ginnis assert that valuing and celebrating mistakes is consistent with the child-centred approach, which considers them 'learning points of a high order' (Brandes and Ginnis, [1986] 2001: 48). The authors contend that '[i]f we let mistakes stand and be aired, we are not damning the student to a whole life of wrongness. In fact, it can be useful to do away with the whole notion of right and wrong' ([1986] 2001: 48). However (in)correctness governs practices in the French system. When comparing her French Saturday school with her UK state primary, and explaining why she did not wish to apply for the secondary French Lycée, my daughter declared that 'they always make you feel like you're wrong'. Hélène, a former Lycée Français Charles de Gaulle (LFCG) student in her fifties, now a lawyer, whom I encountered in the field, exposed the historicity of the sentiment. Corroborating Macron's proclamation, she recounted how teachers handed back homework in order of 'merit', from the strongest to the weakest, thus giving the entire class a clear sense of each other's academic ranking. This outmoded practice reinforces the inevitability of pupils' positions as high or low achievers and compounds the reproductive characteristics of their relative status (Bourdieu, 1994: 48). Such painful pedagogies (Zembylas, 2012) therefore serve to attract French migrant parents to the British system for their children, where diametrically opposed practices encourage self-esteem:

if a student's 'opinions and ideas are valued, she must be a valuable person. If she is expected to take responsibility, she must be a responsible person … language change and the behaviour change are interwoven' (Brandes and Ginnis, [1986] 2001: 80). The favouring of UK teaching practices therefore has far-reaching implications for migrants, prolonging their London sojourn and reinforcing the family's sense of emplacement within the diasporic context (Lopez Rodriguez, 2010; Ryan and Sales, 2013).

Together with the more supportive framework identified in British schools, my respondents allude to a greater emphasis on 'learning through doing', as Antoine explains, contrasting it to France, where 'there is too much thinking about doing, more than doing and then thinking about it'. His observations relate to tertiary education, but Greenwich mother, Sarah, notes a similar phenomenon at primary level:

> I like the English system more for now. I find it a lot more participatory. I think they focus on engaging the children rather than cramming them … There's a lot more interaction, a lot of groups, it's not always the teacher explaining things. There's a lot of teamwork, student research, and they make everything lively.

The picture Sarah paints of English pedagogics corresponds with uncanny accuracy to Brandes and Ginnis's ([1986] 2001) conception of child-centred learning. Indeed, they toyed with the idea of naming the approach 'Active Learning' or 'Participatory Learning', but settled for Rogers's (1965) child-centred coinage because of its explicit foregrounding of the pupil, which gestures towards its emphasis on constructivism (Lea *et al.*, 2003).

Interviewees' overwhelming positivity regarding English education is initially surprising to me given the frequency with which the French model is praised in British political and media discourses.[1] The power of received knowledge is illustrated further by it being only participants with no first-hand experience of UK education who challenge the English model and endorse the French one (as was the case with the NHS). Thus, Paulette, of Beninese heritage, whose originary habitus was influenced by the vestiges of a French colonial narrative aimed at bolstering Republican values (Hulstaert, 2018), 'battled to send [her] son to a French primary school in London'. She seconds Lopez Rodriguez's Polish participants' 'readiness to compete in the rat race' (Lopez Rodriguez, 2010: 344) for the sake of increased academic capital, particularly valued in the premigration context (Thatcher and Halvorsrud, 2016: 101). Paulette nevertheless recognises that one of the benefits of the English system is 'to see the child more as an individual. For example, the English don't repeat an academic year … Maybe it's less academic here, more cultural, more sporty, more arty, which is also important for children's development.' The humanist approach and valuing of creative and non-academic learning do not, however, outweigh the advantages of the French system for Paulette. These include belonging to a worldwide network of schools teaching an identical curriculum, and therefore facilitating onward migration and potentially 'leaving the door open for … return' (Ryan and Sales, 2013: 99). The 'opportunity' for academically weaker pupils to repeat a year of schooling, as 'a way of filling in knowledge gaps', is also considered an advantage by Paulette, irrespective of its psychological effects, as is the transmission of the French language to her children.

Significantly, Paulette was denied such a legacy by her own father, who banned the Beninese mother tongue in the primary habitat, perceiving it to epitomise the inferiority of the colonised and as being counterproductive to future career opportunities. He believed his ascension through the ranks of the French (colonising) administration was due to his embracing of the French language, culture and education system:

> He was very geared towards culture. Actually, I think that might be why I don't speak the mother tongue. I think Dad enforced that because Mum hadn't received the same education as him. It's something I regret enormously, not being able to speak my mother's language, it's an absence, a void.

Paulette acknowledges her linguistic loss as the flipside of her father's academic and professional success: 'at the time my dad had a very good position and I think we were respected because of his status'. Yet, she fails to see his stance as an expression of the (post)colonial indoctrination to which he was exposed at the very *Ecole de la République* she is so keen for own children to attend (Simon, 2006; Hulstaert, 2018). As Puwar (2004) indicates, the 'association of European languages with rational thinking, the values of civilization and intelligence is part and parcel of the long routes of colonisation that make our post-colonial times today' (2004: 108–9). We therefore note how 'notions of hierarchy and social order framed the colonial imagination' and continue to inform 'the mundane routines of everyday interactions' (Leonard, 2010a: 1,260), including Paulette's educational decision-making. Despite migration to London, where differing symbolic capital systems and field struggles prevail, the reproductive cycle is maintained (Bourdieu and Passeron, 1970; Ingram and Abrahams, 2016; Thatcher and Halvorsrud, 2016). So powerful are the postcolonial forces of the premigration space, they tacitly cause Paulette to overlook the symbolic violence she underwent at school in France and the racist microaggressions her son is now facing at a French school in London:

> Oh yes, I really felt it [the discrimination]. I felt it through non-verbal communication and verbal as well, yeah, totally … I had a few teachers who sometimes made remarks, but perhaps not specially because I was of

African origin ... What I went through, I wouldn't wish it on my children, no way ... At my kids' [London] French school there are only two children of African origin, so the French mentality is still there, but that's life ... My son said there'd been several comments, but they're only kids, aren't they; I think it might have happened to him somewhere else as well. I think my son's happy.

While Paulette's testimony reignites evidently painful memories which – through their continuation beyond school – ultimately pushed her to London, in this extract she simultaneously endorses her teachers' prejudicial behaviour ('not specially because I was of African origin'). More surprisingly, she also vindicates the racism towards her child ('but they're only kids'). Habituated to this subordinate positioning ('that's life') being the 'natural' consequence of her ethnicity (Delphy, 2006; Simon, 2006; Senni, 2007), Paulette is at once aware of, and oblivious to, the discrimination. In denial about the seriousness of the microaggressions directed at her son ('I think my son's happy') and contradicting her desire to protect him from the symbolic violence she endured ('What I went through, I wouldn't want it for my own children, no way'), she is intent on defending the French education system, notwithstanding her acknowledgement of its discriminatory traits ('the French mentality is still there'). In this way, Paulette is unwittingly complicit in the oppressive process, actively reproducing the very criticisms she has of the French system. Thus, Garratt's observation that it is 'habitual schemas of perception that prevents racist behaviour being labelled as such by both perpetrator and victim' (2016: 77) is borne out by Paulette.

One of the few other interviewees critical of the English system is returnee, Moses. Of Senegalese descent and undoubtedly exposed to a similar postcolonial pro-French-education discourse in his primary habitat, he laments the English education system's failure to equip its students with basic general knowledge. He claims English students have 'no clue where to place China or Russia on a map' because 'they specialise early, too early'. The French system is thought to be academically more rigorous, providing students with solid intellectual grounding and a broad knowledge base, as 52-year-old surgeon, François, confirms. Born into a (white) privileged place in French society and having drawn on his inherited cultural capital to reap the benefits of the *Ecole de la République*, he reports being 'very proud' of 'such a powerful and organised education system', of which he is 'a pure product'. By contrast, he finds fault in the high cost of (private) education in the UK and yet, like Paulette, commends its emphasis on extra-curricular activities, if questioning their long-term benefits: 'All the surgeons I know here have done art, music or singing at school – but everything stops at 23 years old – not one of them has carried on.'

Meanwhile, François is particularly grateful for the linguistic capital acquired in the French system: 'I'm part of that generation who were lucky enough to have access to three languages during our education', but he regrets the lack of practical application. Gastronomic chef, Bruno reiterates the last point, describing how he was 'incapable of having a conversation in English' when he arrived in London and 'couldn't understand a thing', despite twelve years of language-learning. His current acquaintance with a regular flow of young, French, kitchen porters and commis chefs recruited via the Centre Charles Péguy, migrating for their ritual *années Londres*, bears witness to the perpetuation of this pedagogical shortfall. In his words, 'not one of them knows how to speak English well'. As François explains, 'teaching has nothing to do with learning ... All the emphasis has been placed on teaching [in France], but ... there's no feedback.' François juxtaposes this criticism of the didactic French positivist epistemology with esteem for English higher education: 'England has potentially the best education system in the world. And I'm being completely sincere, the universities and standards are of the highest level from the outset, and the educational tools given to doctors are the best in the world.'

In a similar vein, the teenagers in Focus Group One (at Newham Sixth Form College) refer to UK education as the main advantage of living in London, whereas the French schooling of Lycée students in Focus Group Two constitutes the main disadvantage. Despite both groups' contrasting socio-economic backgrounds and educational pathways, they reach equivalent conclusions. The 'hands-off' approach is criticised in Focus Group One: 'in France it was writing, writing, writing, and there was less practical work'. Focus Group Two students criticise Lycée mentalities and emphasis on institutionalised cultural capital (Bourdieu, 1979b). Their discontentment verges on the incriminatory: 'the teachers don't give a damn about us ... They don't give us any advice.' Even though François was experiencing the French education system some thirty-five years earlier, his objections to the lack of 'feedback and guidance' (Lea *et al.*, 2003: 332) are reiterated here. Moreover, since they are considered 'essential elements of what student-centred learning should be' (2003: 332), this gap in the French system is representative of its didactic shortcomings, undoubtedly the consequence of inadequate interim reform and the perpetuation of the status quo (Dubet, 2004) in 'a system which is highly resistant to change' (Brandes and Ginnis, [1986] 2001: 87).

In an age where factual knowledge is at learners' fingertips, able to tap into the online 'data deluge' (Kitchin, 2014: 130) at the click of a mouse or tap of a touchscreen, French schools' quest to impart vast quantities of general knowledge, and thereby nurture a population befitting the country's 'exception culturelle' (Poirier, 2006: 63–70), is a retrograde model.

Encouraging students to think independently and develop such social, cultural and practical skills as inter-student or inter-cultural collaboration, problem-solving, task-based activities, public speaking and active listening are, however, of increasing socio-professional value (Huc-Hepher and Huertas Barros, 2016). Indeed, the acquisition of large quantities of knowledge, while enhancing informed critical analysis competence, can serve as an impediment to creativity and invention. As seen in Chapter 4 regarding the culinary, the weight of students' cultural heritage, 'condemned by history' (Parisot, 2007: 13), might suppress their imaginations and contribute to an 'inclination to pessimism' (Hazareesingh, 2015; Parisot, 2007: 12).

Compounding the *lycéens'* disparagement of LFCG teachers is their purported self-satisfaction. According to one student, they are 'unbearable, arrogant ... the picture of France, but in London'. Another is more discerning in his criticism: 'there are teachers who are good', but 'the administration's lousy', and it is 'incredibly academic, everything's based on grades, competitive exams, etc. But in England, there are more dossiers, interviews, you have to put yourself into it, what you like, what you're good at' and 'it's based on personality a lot'. Through a process of epistemological comparison, students become aware that the humanistic valuing of individual traits (Starkey, 2019) is missing from the French model, which creates a sense of disempowerment and hence disengagement. It also adds to the sense of symbolic violence hinted at by Macron and perceived by the average pupil, who, 'having no other sign ... than academic success ... feels overcome by failure or anonymity' (Bourdieu and Passeron, 1964: 74). This explains why another student compared the Lycée to a factory, with students 'on a production line ... that the teachers have to process'. Demonstrating the cross-generational and reproductive relevance of the phenomenon, 80-year-old Suzanne, a former teacher at the school, laments the focus on academic capital: 'the French Lycée used to be really nice, it's become less nice. The students are completely preoccupied with marks. We can't do poetry anymore.' It is telling that Suzanne imputes the overly prosaic emphasis to the students rather than staff, and through this misplaced blame she is complicit in the symbolic violence. Her words therefore corroborate that the teachers 'create clans', as seen in Chapter 1, and collectively portray pupils in a negative light, which is in diametric opposition to the 'positive learning relationships' advocated in the humanist student-centred approach (Starkey, 2019: 381).

Consequently, although Focus Group Two students concede that there is 'quite a good atmosphere' at the Lycée, its pedagogical rigidity can drive them to English alternatives for GCSEs, A levels, the International Baccalaureate and/or university courses, as one participant, moving to City of London School for A levels, testifies: 'I'm not going back to France [for uni], no way'. Kensington-based Chantal expresses similar sentiments:

> in terms of human relationships, the lycée here's very pleasant for the children, but … what attracts them is an English-style education, with lots of sport, art and music: there's the possibility to do lots of things we don't have in the French system which is extremely academic. My eldest son left for his final two years. He's been at Sevenoaks in Kent for two years and his sister wants to go too, and my youngest wants to go to Harrow in a year. So, they'll all be in the English system.

This rejection of the French education system – despite its inherent 'conditioning' – and embracing of the London alternative bears witness to a sense of comfortableness in postmigration mentalities and practices that has evolved outside the school environment. The students' educational choices are thus a means of performing their belonging (Ryan and Sales, 2013; Levin, 2016) and asserting the 'Londonishness' of their identities, irrespective of the Frenchness of their schooling. It should be noted, however, that all the English schools for which these children are opting are the high-fee-paying independent schools alluded to by François above; only a select few will be sufficiently 'able' and financially secure to access them (costing around £35,000 per annum for boarding places). Laura acknowledges the exclusivity of her son's place at Whitgift as a privilege not available to everyone and not necessarily applicable to her other children:

> Private English schools are very, very expensive; but they said 'We want him, so we're giving him a bursary.' So, he got into this amazing school; he's in uniform in an all-boys school. He's as happy as can be, really, super fulfilled. But then my daughter, after three years at an English state school, we realised she wasn't that comfortable in French and not that comfortable in English either; it wasn't easy for her. And as we're French after all, we decided to put her back into the French system [Wix]. And the youngest has been at school for two years now and we put her into an English school [Honeywell].

Examples of affluent London-French children preferring English education, based on their knowledge of privately funded schools, could be perceived as non-representative of the broader London-French experience. However, arguably as a testament to their naivety and the failure of their UK education to equip them with a critical eye, the students involved in Focus Group One condone the system's two-tiered, maintained/independent, constitution: 'It's fair', exclaims one student, 'if your parents want to send you to private school, it's their choice, and if you accept, it's your choice as well'. They appear unaware of the likelihood of means taking precedence over desire and of the inherent inequity, again playing out the complicity conjectured by Bourdieu and Wacquant (1992). As Lopez Rodriguez posits, therefore, 'this limited class consciousness may in fact inhibit their understanding of how class structure can doom underprivileged (among these are migrants) individuals' social, professional and economic trajectories', meaning that, paradoxically, 'a lack of self-ascription can work as an enabler rather than a constraint' (Lopez Rodriguez, 2010: 351).

Thus, we observe the students expressing gratitude that their current English state education offers them flexibility and prepares them for the world of work: 'after your studies there are different places you can go with your qualifications. There'll be more opportunities here than in France.' Similarly, Laura claims that in the workplace 'the English perform a lot better orally, because of their education' and Brice explains that it is only on leaving the French education system that students will 'learn what company life's like, working in a team, with managers, things like that. Whereas here … you leave uni and you're able to work.' The interpersonal skills developed in the UK system are deemed conducive to employment, but 'in the French University tradition, the co-operative ideal is not encouraged at all and, from primary school up to scientific research, collective work is only supported by institutions on an exceptional basis' (Bourdieu and Passeron, 1964: 52).

While the British emphasis on developing employability is commended, some believe it comes at the cost of academic rigour. Laura asserts that those who have passed through the English system are 'very confident when it comes to speaking, but the underlying substance isn't that great; they're much less analytical … and a lot less technical than us.' This chimes with the disillusionment expressed by one of Lopez Rodriguez's 15-year-old Polish participants, who claimed that in the UK 'the teachers didn't test knowledge, only effort' (Lopez Rodriguez; 2010: 345). Brice, who completed his primary and secondary education in southwest France and his tertiary education in the UK, confirms that 'the theoretical side [of the French model] also has advantages because you can … go further … which, in exceptional cases, means you can go beyond just the formula, and know how to adapt it in a specific case'. Therefore, the deep theoretical knowledge of mathematics developed in France (to such an extent that Brice was excused from all maths classes on his UK undergraduate course), allows students to take ownership of the ideas and apply them autonomously and creatively in practical situations. Such an assertion undermines Bourdieu and Passeron's contention that learning is 'an end in itself' in France (1964: 66) and instead apprehends theory as the key to practical know-how. Significantly and somewhat ironically, mathematical and analytical skills are two attributes that London employers find highly attractive among French migrants, which casts doubt over the genuine workplace value of the student-centred, practice-based learning so venerated by my participants.

'They do the same class for everyone, so that very able students get bored out their minds and very weak ones do, too'

Regardless of the success, or otherwise, of each educational model to prepare students for working life, an unanticipated pattern of symbolic violence in the French system and of symbolic support in the English one has emerged. Surreptitious aggression is criticised in the former, but equally, and perhaps more fundamentally, so is the hypocrisy of the entire edifice, which serves to compound the violence felt. Epitomising an 'emperor's new clothes' phenomenon, the *Ecole de la République* is founded on France's core values of liberty, equality and fraternity, and yet it is in the name of equality itself that French education is able to mask the inequalities of the system. In the same manner that Bourdieu and Passeron (1964) draw attention to the illusion on which France's educational model is constructed, particularly as regards assessment, so Dubet (2004) argues that it is only through the construction of a complex illusion, in which all parties are duped, that France's values are seen to be upheld (Wolfreys, 2018). In place of the emperor's opulent attire, here, the people of France are persuaded to behold a meritocratic system that treats its students equitably, with underachievement blamed on the students themselves, as seen in Focus Group Two. For, as Brandes and Ginnis contend, 'the teacher feels that he has done his job once the information has been broadcast' and if 'the students do not receive the transmission, they have faulty equipment ... a screw loose somewhere' (Brandes and Ginnis, [1986] 2001: 69). The effect is to transform academic failure into an agentive act, that is, a perverse exercising of individual liberty (Dubet, 2004: 29).

Having been introduced to alternative models through her mobility to London, this illusion is beginning to wear thin for Laura, however. Migration has stripped the French education system of its fictitious, universalist apparel, and its underlying imperfections emerge before her eyes. She sums up her frustrations at this revelation, as follows:

> The English system is one where students never retake a year, but where there's streaming, which is of course unthinkable in the French system. In French schools, everyone's equal, so you're not allowed to say that some children do better than others; they do the same class for everyone so that very able students get bored out of their minds and very weak ones do, too. It's the result of the French system's equality of opportunity and equality of who you are. In English schools, students are split into different groups based on level, and can go from one level to another: I think it's quite a significant advantage. And there's support as well.

Laura's testimony lays bare the egalitarian deception at the core of the French education system, and one doing a disservice to the very students it is designed to serve, which is conceivable as institutionalised symbolic violence. Dubet echoes Laura's words when writing that 'students are placed at the heart of a fundamental contradiction: they are all considered fundamentally equal while being engaged in a series of tests whose purpose is to make them unequal' (Dubet, 2004: 28). By failing to treat students as individuals, with individual strengths and weaknesses (Starkey, 2019), which the streaming of the student-centred English model permits, the French system places all its students on an artificially equal footing. 'Equality' thus functions as a tacit differentiation mechanism, the 'one-size-fits-all' philosophy fitting only the few. Selective streaming is consequently perceived by Laura as a transparent way of addressing the intrinsic variability between students, whether this is due to inherited sociocultural or biological rates of capital, and is hence apprehended as intrinsically egalitarian. Conversely, by maintaining a masquerade of student equality, the French system covertly, and seemingly legitimately (Bourdieu *et al.*, 1993), perpetuates inequality, causing those students at the bottom of the 'class' (publicly relegated to the position through their low marks in formal assessments) to fail the year and to undergo the social humiliation of retaking it. This articulation of symbolic violence can lead to self-despair (1993: 133) and an ultimate rejection of schooling, if not mainstream society as a whole (1993: 128). We see, therefore, social reproduction in action, with students from disadvantaged backgrounds maintaining their positions at the base of the social ladder, as discussed in Chapter 1. While the UK system is by no means devoid of inequalities, it is significant that the 'social reform agenda' implicit in student-centred education 'challenges authoritarian models of education for being complicit in the perpetuation of economic and social inequality' (Starkey, 2019: 387). It is also edifying that many participants, like Lopez Rodriguez's, underline the UK system's comparative meritocratic characteristics, which correspond to 'their imaginings of normality and well-being' (Lopez Rodriguez, 2010: 340), as well as to their longer-term aspirations to realise the migratory dream (Benson and O'Reilly, 2009).

Beneath the veneer of equality adorning the French educational model lies a highly competitive system, its achievements built on punishment and a disingenuous 'ideal ... of individualistic competition' (Bourdieu and Passeron, 1964: 52). It is this institutionalised hypocrisy, together with the subtle yet damaging symbolic acts (Zembylas, 2012) experienced in the French education system, that has led many French Londoners to turn towards the English model for their own children, in whom they harbour their own ambitions (Lopez Rodriguez, 2010). Indeed, all those who responded to the survey I conducted at the beginning of my research indicated that they had opted for local English state primary schools for their children. A minority of others, however, continue to enact the myth, thereby contributing to the opening of new French state schools in the British capital, most recently the Lycée Winston Churchill in Wembley, founded in September 2015. It remains to be seen whether this 'international' *lycée*, named after one of Britain's most influential political leaders, will adopt an English pedagogy to match its name, devoid of the symbolic violence described at the Lycée Charles de Gaulle, thought to expunge the confidence from its students and nurture the disillusioned adults referred to by Macron (En Marche, 2017), who are taught to fear failure (Brandes and Ginnis, [1986] 2001) and hence entrepreneurship.[2]

It is with an air of satisfaction, tinged with surprise, that Miranda tells me: 'I'm doing my PhD here now; that's something I could never have done in France.' Her sentiments meet mine with respect to the differences that have emerged between the French and English pedagogic models in the minds of a number of my participants. The following analysis of on-line data will ascertain whether these on-land views are corroborated in the digital representations of the London-French educational structures featured in this section.

Semiotic meaning-making in on-line educational settings

The selection rationale behind this case-study was inspired by Laura's on-land experience. As shown, Laura has a privileged overview of the three core schooling options available to London-French migrants. One of her children attends Wix, a local French maintained primary, another attends Honeywell, a nearby English maintained primary, and a third, Whitgift, an independent English 'public' secondary school, with a dedicated bilingual French-English pathway. My ethnosemiotic analysis therefore follows this tripart French-state, English-state, English-private paradigm, but for increased parity and hence validity, I have chosen secondary institutions only. My multimodal on-line analysis is hence based on the landing pages of the state-funded secondary schools where I conducted on-land focus groups, namely the Lycée Français Charles de Gaulle (LFCG) in South Kensington and Newham Sixth Form College (NewVIc), with Whitgift in South Croydon serving as the UK-independent example.

By conducting a multimodal social semiotic analysis of each school's landing page(s) as an extension of my on-land fieldwork, I respond to Rowsell's call to braid ethnographic and multimodal approaches in order to 'lift out how materialities exist within modes' (Rowsell, 2011: 332).

Through my unpicking of the websites' various meaning-making modes, I am keen to discover what messages the schools implicitly project and whether they cohere with on-land educational practices and perceptions. The exercise has the potential to add 'objective' weight to participants' subjective views and is likely to be of intercultural-knowledge-exchange value to educational policy-makers and/or their webmasters. This holistic approach, as discussed in the Introduction, is consistent with Bourdieu's methodological recommendations, as well as the aspirations of socio-semiotic ethnographers (Vannini, 2007; Dicks *et al.*, 2006, 2011; Kress, 2011). If complementary results are obtained, the blended ethnosemiotic approach will prove an effective triangulation tool, of particular relevance in an age of increasing digitally mediated communication.

Branding exclusivity on the French Lycée website

As can be seen from Figures 9 and 10, the Lycée updated its website to coincide with its centenary celebrations in 2015. The now obsolete image retrieved from the UK Web Archive (Figure 9) is noticeably more text-heavy than the 2015 equivalent (Figure 10), which presents a sliding carousel of full-screen images. The modal change from the predominantly written, 'page-like' and static to the photographic and auto-rotating not only demonstrates advancements in the technological affordances of the site, but a shift in its underlying function. Fundamentally, we observe a development from the communicational to the representational (Kress, 2010), with the reader dominant in Figure 9, and the projection of the LFCG's 'brand' taking precedence in Figure 10.

Despite criticisms of auto-rotating homepage carousels, principally because the multiplication of images and movement between them detracts from the key content, causing 'banner blindness', and the lack of navigational intuitiveness undermines usability (Laja, 2019), their use by the LFCG is revealing of the (state-subsidised) school's drive towards marketised self-promotion. Significantly, the London-French code-switching found repeatedly in the pre-2015 landing page has been substituted for French text only, except for the 'British Section' reference targeting a high-fee-paying British/international audience. This linguistic segregation corroborates field evidence that students attending the British and French sections do not mix, a separation replicated in the physical layout of the school, which demonstrates the interplay between the on-line and on-land (Casilli, 2010) and undermines the school's egalitarian tenets.

The 2015 emphasis on representation over communication (Kress, 2010) recalls the staff hubris mentioned in Focus Group Two and the demographic shift undergone since the mid-twentieth century. In 1945–46, tradesmen,

Figure 9 LFCG landing page in LFSC (UKWA), captured 2014

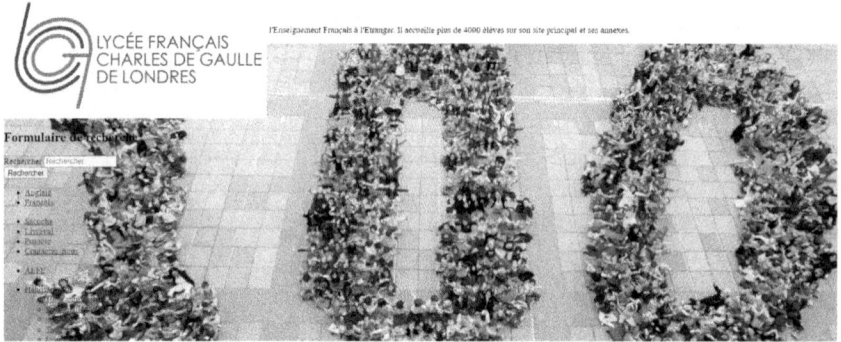

Figure 10 LFCG landing page, live Web, captured 2015

hoteliers and restaurateurs constituted the largest segment of parents, with bankers' children being the second smallest group (Faucher *et al.*, 2015). By 2014, however, stay-at-home parents were the largest segment and bankers had risen to third position, representing 600 children, against only four in the 1940s (Faucher *et al.*, 2015). This is a clear indication of the upward socio-economic shift in the student body, and could explain the website's representational reorientation, the motivated branding (Kress,

2010: 67; 2011: 334) aimed at elite migrant families to match the school's changing profile. Indeed, the admission criteria published on the website demonstrates the importance of social capital: priority goes first to the children of French civil servants in London and teachers at the school, while the third criterion prioritises children linked to the AEFE network (agency for French teaching abroad), whose significance is emphasised multimodally through the compositional prominence of the AEFE logo at the top of the screen. By contrast, in UK state schools, the mandatory principal admission criterion is 'children who are in care or being looked after' (GOV.UK, 2017). Looked-after children and those in care are absent from all seven LFCG criteria, exclusively centred on previous schooling and inclusion in professional, filial (fraternal links being the second criterion) or educational networks, bar the seventh, which is open to any other 'francophone'. These admission criteria shed light on the under-representation of minorities at the LFCG, attested to by several students in Focus Group Two, and confirm participants' claims that the UK system is more supportive (Lopez Rodriguez, 2010). They also demonstrate the transposition of premigration social capital to the postmigration space (Oliver and O'Reilly, 2010) and a socially 'distinctive' South Kensington presence, unrepresentative of the wider 'community'.

The second and third images in the Lycée's homepage carousel (Figures 11 and 12) are again student-focused and functionally representational. At first sight, the photographs convey a positive image: students engaged in entertaining activities outside the classroom, notably table-tennis. This coheres with the on-land finding that there are good interpersonal relationships among students at the Lycée but eclipses the teacher–student antagonism noted. Figure 11 is more effective at portraying the desired image of the congenial extra-curricular student experience, for the pupils' facial expressions appear spontaneous and unrehearsed, and their gazes are oriented towards other students or the table-tennis balls, indicating genuine immersion in the activity. In Figure 12, however, the students' bats lie flat on the table, the authentic action halted, an artificial composition replacing it. The students are lined up with regimented precision, countering the spontaneity of movement present in Figure 11. Their gazes, oriented directly at the camera/photographer, and smiles reflect social and photographic convention rather than sincere sentiments. The facial expressions thus suggest a staged causal relationship between smiling and happiness, which corresponds to the Lycée's self-crafted image as a cheerful institution but belies the underlying staff–student tensions related in my on-land discussions. Accentuating the light-hearted atmosphere intermodally is the natural sunlight cast over the students' faces, light functioning as a mode to imply lightness of mood. Yet, the tangible affectation of the students' smiles, implying convention as

Figure 11 LFCG landing page 2, live Web, captured 2015

Figure 12 LFCG landing page 3, live Web, captured 2015

opposed to spontaneity, ultimately undermines the shot's credibility and hence potentially the school's branding success.

Upon closer multimodal inspection of both images, additional unintended meanings become apparent. Beyond the socio-semiotic meanings of the students' attire as a marker of habitus (or class) and of 'global americanisation' (Miller and Woodward, 2012: 3), materialised through the 'MIAMI'-fronted 'hoody' and the dominance of denim (Miller and Woodward, 2012: 3; Huc-Hepher and Drake, 2013),[3] it is also a signifier of core Republican values. The lack of uniform is a material representation of the LFCG implementing freedom of expression, as stipulated in the 1789 *Déclaration des Droits de l'Homme et du Citoyen* (Article 11). Meanwhile the absence of religious symbols conveys the *Ecole de la République*'s secularist, egalitarian principles, which contrasts the social-levelling functionality of school uniform in the UK, where freedom of expression is performed precisely through the wearing of faith symbols. Compositionally, Figure 12 showcases the Lycée's gender equality, with a ratio of four boys to three girls, and there is little gender distinction between the sartorial choices of the male and female students. Almost all opt for the self-imposed uniform of jeans and T-shirt.

However, as problematised in Chapter 1, this perceived sartorial equality could mask underlying divides, because '[g]ender difference, like class, seems ... difficult to bridge' (de Backer, 2019: 11) and young (French) females often feel socially pressurised into rejecting a more 'feminine' dress code (de Backer, 2019: 11). Therefore, although Chantal purports that if 'you go into the Paris equivalent of the Lycée Charles de Gaulle, they're all dressed the same ... Here, there's more freedom, everyone has the right to their own style', the self-imposed uniformity displayed in these images in fact points to a transposition of originary habitus dispositions and mentalities. In terms of racial equality, the images fall even further short. People of Colour are not represented in any of the carousel photographs, which reflects the under-representation expressed on-land and the racially nuanced symbolic violence encountered in the French educational field more broadly (Lorcerie, 2004; Guénif-Souilamas, 2006).

The final two photographs in the rotating LFCG homepage (Figures 13 and 14) relay an image of the school as provider of academic and mathematical rigour, identified during a minority of interviews. In Figure 13, the gaze of the two students on the right is directed at their work, and the

Figure 13 LFCG landing page 4, live Web, captured 2015

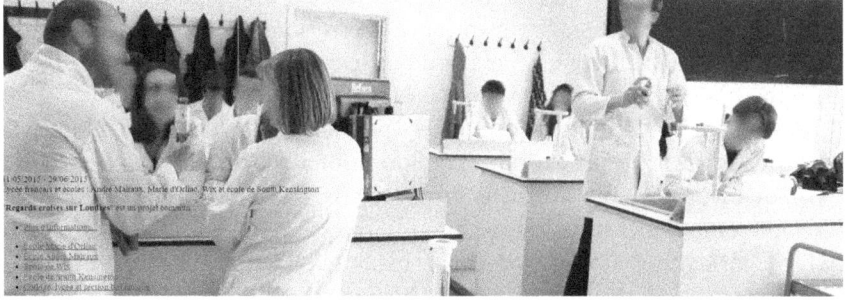

Figure 14 LFCG landing page 5, live Web, captured 2015

two on the left, at each other, seemingly having erupted into spontaneous laughter at being the centre of attention, the boy's raised hand covering his mouth as a gestural signifier of embarrassment. As in Figure 10, this disconnection from the onlooker and interpersonal peer connection creates a sense of authenticity that enhances the credibility of the shot and, by extension, that of the school's academic rigour, suggested by the academic objects occupying the foreground. This compositional centrality could be read as a motivated sign in itself, designed to reinforce the message that 'the standard of our maths is generally higher' and that 'the English are much less analytical than us', as reported by Sarah and Laura respectively. Likewise, the decision to include a photograph taken in the science laboratory (Figure 14) is a motivated one, showcasing the school's facilities, its high teacher–student ratio and commitment to a broad range of subjects, including the 'hard' sciences. As Bruno explains, in London, 'as soon as you say you're French ... people think you've had a good education', which, according to Moses, is largely due to the breadth of the curriculum: 'in France, the foundations are more general ... they specialise too early [in England]'.

However, a closer multimodal reading of Figure 14 reveals less favourable meanings, adding weight to the on-land symbolic violence argument. For instance, there is evidence to support interviewees' criticisms of French education's universalism, whereby all students, irrespective of achievements or (suit)ability, are placed in the same class. The shot also substantiates Hélène's assertions that deep competitiveness underlies the practices and structures of the purportedly egalitarian system. That is, again taking gaze and facial expression (smiling/laughing) as modes, the students positioned in the front row of the class – and thus dominating the photograph – appear to be included in a humorous exchange with the three staff members, whose stance embodies their authority over the seated students and didactic, positivist teaching methods (Lea *et al.*, 2003). By contrast, the facial expressions of students occupying the middle and back rows display no trace of amusement, nor is their gaze met by those involved in the 'exclusive' joke. This gives the impression that the female student on the left is on an equal footing with the teachers, in the privileged position of directly attracting the gaze of two of the three teachers and participating in the in-group laughter (Smith, 2012; Westcott and Vazquez Maggio, 2016).

According to Western stereotyping, spectacles have long been associated with academic prowess, as epitomised traditionally by the spectacle-wearing wise owl (for example, Cornelis Bloemaert's 1625 etching *The Wise Owl, or Owl with Glasses*) and more recently the so-called 'nerd face' emoji 🤓, which 'caricatures a nerd with thick, black glasses and buck teeth [... and is] used to signify learning, reading, being smart' (dictionary.com, 2019). The fact that the student in the 'exclusive' position at the front of the class and sharing a joke with the staff is wearing glasses could, therefore, be read as a motivated sign choice to relay the school's academic standards. More importantly here, however, as a multimodal orchestration, the image is indicative of the stratified status system evidenced in French education, with physical structures reflecting mentalities (Bourdieu *et al.*, 1993; Brandes and Ginnis, [1986] 2001). Ostensibly high achievers are set in a spatially distinct area of the classroom (and photograph) from the other apparently low(er) achieving students, excluded from 'insider' jokes, potentially believing such positioning to be the inevitable corollary of their habitus (Bourdieu and Passeron, 1964), and hence susceptible to becoming complicit in the symbolic violence tacitly articulated.

Furthermore, when decoding the image semiotically (Figure 14), its emphasis on the practical skills honed at the school (through the inclusion of the substances/receptacles, white coats, etc.) is undermined by it being only the teachers holding the scientific instruments; the students are but passive onlookers. Rather than illustrating practical work and student collaboration, the photograph thus confirms Bourdieu and Passeron's contention that 'absolutely non-directive teaching' (Bourdieu and Passeron, 1964: 58) is a utopia and nothing more than a myth in France (1964: 58). Similarly, though Figure 14 challenges gender stereotypes because the apparently highest-achieving science student is a young woman, the same cannot be said of social and ethnic equality. In both Figures 13 and 14, there is again a noticeable absence of people of Colour, confirming a Focus Group Two remark from an LFCG student that 'in Year Twelve, there's one Black student in the entire year, one student out of a hundred or 120'.

If hairstyle is apprehended as mode, capable of imparting socio-semiotic meaning (McMurtrie, 2010; Ravelli and van Leeuwen, 2018) the uniformly long, flowing, 'natural' coifs among four of the five girls are suggestive of their bourgeois backgrounds, since, according to Synnott, long hair is 'a status symbol ... It is the evidence of wealth and leisure' (Synnott, 1987: 384–5, cited in Eock Laïfa, 2016: 54). More importantly, it is the embodiment of the privilege of whiteness in French society (Beaman, 2018), where natural African hair types are experienced as a social stigma and the 'symbol of the black condition'; whereas 'hair hanging down loose like a white woman' is associated with advantage (Eock Laïfa, 2016: 483, 487).[4] The incorporated capital (Bourdieu, 1979b) visible in Figure 13, then, serves as a sign of social distinction and exclusivity rather than uniformity, as well as embodying the students' conformity to hegemonic gendered stereotypes (Synnott, 1987), as emerged from my interviews.

Having examined the five LFCG homepage slider images, the tacit meanings uncovered are ones of a socially and ethnically exclusive educational environment. It appears egalitarian in its gender balance, and academically rigorous, yet the photographs undermine the founding principles of the *Ecole de la République* as open to all, irrespective of background, and devoid of academic or social differentiation. Just as the demographic data published by Faucher *et al.* (2015) reveal a development in the student body from children of working-class backgrounds in the 1940s to the affluent sons and daughters of bankers in the 2010s, so the web images support Robert's claim that 'the French do have a class system in relation to education', despite the egalitarian rhetoric. Moreover, corroborating the interviews, there is no multimodal evidence to support a practice-based, student-centred pedagogical model. Traditional teacher–student power relations are conveyed compositionally, as are tacit forms of inter-student stratification, liable to be experienced as symbolic violence among those in physically subordinate positions. Finally, although there appear to be genuine positive interpersonal relationships among students (Figures 11 and 13), as confirmed in Focus Group Two and by Chantal ('in terms of human relationships, the *lycée* here's very pleasant'), there are no visual signs to suggest that individuals are valued for their personal (as opposed to academic) attributes, nor is there any representation of creative, artistic or non-recreational sporting pursuits being recognised as legitimate forms of cultural and educational capital.

Until now, therefore, the multimodal social semiotic meanings of the LFCG website substantiate my on-land findings. To test them further, my blended analysis now turns to Newham Sixth Form College's website, where I ascertain whether the same pattern is transferable to another educational context.

Communicating inclusivity and student-centred learning on the NewVIc website

As a multimodal ensemble, Newham Sixth Form College's (NewVIc) landing page (Figure 15) differs considerably from that of the LFCG. Instead of a (self-)representational auto-rotating image carousel, the visitor is presented with a static, modular composition (Domingo *et al.*, 2015), designed to frame meaning into allocated compartments on the screen. The homepage composition gives the visitor more obvious navigational choice (Laja, 2019), which in turn renders it more functionally communicational. With different informational areas framed by distinct modules, significantly of varying sizes, the very layout of NewVIc's homepage invites the visitor/reader to participate in the meaning-making process (Kress, 2010; Domingo *et al.*, 2015), rather than project a contrived set of self-promotional, full-screen images. It is pertinent that the first tab of the secondary navigation menu (if reading from left to right in accordance with Western

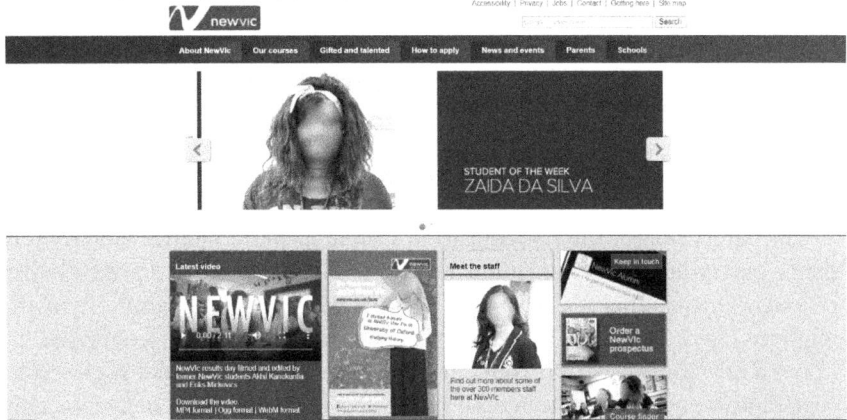

Figure 15 Newham Sixth Form College landing page, live Web, captured 2015

convention) is 'Accessibility'. This is an immediate indicator of inclusivity, consideration for disabled visitors and the importance of communicational effectiveness. Similarly, the use of the imperative tense in the modules in the bottom right-hand quarter of the homepage, directs the text unambiguously at readers and demands communicational engagement: 'Keep in touch', 'Meet the staff', 'Be inspired', and so on.

Although communicational in focus, the reliance on modules and images distinguishes the homepage from the text-heavy pre-2015 version of LFCG landing page. Here, the visual mode dominates, but does so in an interpersonal manner (Halliday, 1978; Adami, 2013). A large head-shot of the 'student of the week' dominates the page; being at least twice the dimensions of the other photographs, it effectively serves as a call to action. In (almost) central position, it compositionally affirms the college's ostensibly student-centred, humanist approach, designed 'to enhance each student's academic achievement' (Starkey, 2019: 379) and valued by my on-land research participants (Paulette: 'the English approach is to see the child more as an individual'). The portrait photograph (changing each week) and the large font size selected for the particular student's name is testament to the importance of the ethos. Rather than cloak inter-student competitiveness in a shroud of egalitarian rhetoric, embedded in the very structures (a single class/curriculum for all) and practices (e.g. returning homework in order of merit) of the French system, in Figure 15 the accomplishments of individual students are celebrated publicly, as prescribed by Brandes and Ginnis ([1986] 2001). The photograph – and the compositional importance assigned to it within the multimodal orchestration – thus corroborates the on-land assertion that the UK educational model is 'less punitive ... the positive is always foregrounded, so as to encourage rather than reprimand' (Charles). Moreover, the fact that the 'student of the week' is a young Black woman suggests a lack of sexually and racially motivated discrimination at NewVIc. As demonstrated by the 'Gifted and talented' tab above the headshot, it is precisely by not treating all students equally that equality is achieved: indiscriminate meritocracy trumps discriminatory universalism.

The perception of the UK education system as more meritocratic than in the originary habitat is also confirmed by Thatcher and Halvorsrud's Polish research participants (2016). The authors nevertheless attribute it to the migrants' lack of insight into British class barriers, a point confirmed by Lopez Rodriguez (2010). It could also be argued, however, that such scepticism refutes the power of inherited social and cultural capital in purportedly 'classless' Polish society (Thatcher and Halvorsrud, 2016: 91), where, as in France, mediated and politicised egalitarian rhetoric obscures inegalitarian practices noted in the field.

Reinforcing NewVIc's image as a diverse and inclusive learning environment, 'developing positive learning relationships, being culturally responsive and treating each student as a unique individual' (Starkey, 2019: 381), a three-quarter shot of another student, wearing a hijab and long skirt, occupies a central position in the bottom half of the page. The photograph bears witness to the college's openness to different faiths and its commitment to freedom of (religious and sartorial) expression, which in turn suggests an absence of symbolic violence. Significantly, an image such as this would, by law, be banned on a French state-school website, due to the garments' functioning as 'ostensible religious signs' (Beyer, 2015) and consequent incompatibility with France's secular values. Guénif-Souilamas postulates that opposition to the hijab, legitimated through the prohibitive legislation, 'offers contemporary racism a seductive mask, that of ordinary discrimination, the ultimate expression of condescending colonial concern' (Guénif-Souilamas, 2006: 110). However, at NewVIc, where Focus Group One students report feeling freer to practise their faith than in France, citing religious emancipation as a major mobility and settlement determinant, the headscarf goes virtually unnoticed and hence contrasts the 'virtuous racism' of France's education system (2006: 109). Likewise, in Figure 15, the student's achievements take precedence over her garments and any postcolonial struggles they could symbolise, since she is holding a cut-out 'speech bubble', reading: 'I studied A-levels at NewVIc. Now I'm at University of Oxford studying History.' Thus, the image implicitly challenges the popular stereotype of the subjugated woman hijab-wearer (Guénif-Souilamas, 2006). On the contrary, it connotes the determination and ultimate success of an independent young woman, potentially from a socio-economically disadvantaged background, since Newham has London's second-highest child poverty rate (41 per cent), highest overcrowding (25 per cent) and one of the highest unemployment rates (8.6 per cent) (London's Poverty Profile, 2015).

Another, smaller module in the bottom right-hand corner of NewVIc's homepage is suggestive of the 'teamwork' praised by Sarah. The quirky, diagonal framing of the shot imparts a blitheness consistent with my on-land findings, which underline the 'playful' (Marie), 'happy' (Laura) atmosphere of UK schools and the student-centred approach. The students – again of minority-ethnic heritage – are photographed working collaboratively and actively in pairs. Significantly, the teacher is out of shot and the low angle of the camera elevates the students' position, accentuating their influence. As a physical incorporation of practices (Bourdieu, 1996), the classroom's non-linear layout, is also indicative of the student-centred, collaborative teaching methods. The photograph, albeit comparatively small, summarises visually Sarah's words that UK state-sector education is 'a lot more participatory', with 'more interaction', 'it's not always the teacher explaining things'. Similarly, the adjacent 'Meet the staff' module and staff-member photograph implies an open and equitable relationship between staff, students and their families, where teachers 'build trust' and 'facilitate interpersonal communication' (Brandes and Ginnis, [1986] 2001: 47, 15).

The module at the bottom left of the page encapsulates interviewees' valuing of the task-based UK approach, together with the public-speaking and creative skills noted. It consists of an embedded, short video, 'filmed and edited by [an] A-level studies student'. As such, it signals the perceived UK emphasis on practice and employability, and contrasts 'the French system [which] is extremely theoretical, and not at all practical; you can leave with a very good qualification but not having learnt how to work', according to Brice. Here, NewVIc is seen to reap the benefits of the creative capital nurtured at the college, while posting the film on the homepage provides the student with valuable professional experience. This not only confirms Marie's observation that the system 'encourages creativity', but that the school publicly values the contribution of the (named) student making the film *and* the voices of those being filmed. In contrast to the LFCG landing page, it confirms Antoine's statement that in the UK, 'the objective of education is like teaching how to learn ... I don't know if that's the ideal in France ... [where] you're within this Republican ideal that education is a way to create good citizens.'

As opposed to developing abstract civic competences, the student's A-level course has provided practical skills directly transferable to the workplace, and by giving him the freedom and trust to make a film for the college's public-facing webpages, the staff are acting as a 'facilitator, rather than as a giver of knowledge', the aim being 'to equip the student to find out for himself' (Brandes and Ginnis, [1986] 2001: 19) from the experience of practice in a real-world setting. Through the still of a single modular frame, employability, creative capital, task-based learning, public-speaking skills and student-centred, collaborative pedagogics are multi-modally communicated.

Once again, therefore, on-line evidence validates my on-land observations, which could explain the high numbers of 'francophone' students choosing NewVIc over the LFCG and why the majority of my research participants have opted for the English model for their own progeny.[5]

Valuing culture(s) on the Whitgift website

The final homepage under scrutiny is Whitgift's, where representation outweighs communication. In common with the 2015 LFCG website, it has a rotating offer of five, full-screen, school-oriented images (Figure 16). Unlike the reds of the Lycée landing pages and in keeping with NewVIc's colour-scheme, greens and blues dominate, creating a 'mood' of serenity. The colour-inspired atmosphere recalls the calmness described by Laura in relation to her daughter's UK-state-sector school, and contrasts the aggression noted by Marie concerning French education, associable with the colour red (Wiedemann *et al.*, 2015). The principally representational function is demonstrated through the choice of a full-screen image carousel and by the motivated choices observable in the photographs themselves, all of which foreground the non-academic activities that represent the school's socioculturally distinctive ethos and brand (Figure 16).

The representational function of the slider is reinforced intermodally by the words framing the images in the primary navigation menu: 'Home', 'About Whitgift', 'Admissions', 'Boarding', 'Academic', 'Sports', 'Co-Curricular', 'Facilities', 'Events' and 'Contacts and Directions'. The words' informative and interactive affordances increase the site's communicative function relative to the Lycée's 2015 version, but it is telling that they are all, except 'Admissions', projections of the school and its USP. The order of the tabs (again, according to Western left-to-right reading) is also significant as regards (self-)representation, as information on boarding precedes the academic field, suggesting, as with 'admissions', that the school/website targets an affluent global audience able to invest in a traditional, live-in, public-school education. The subsequent tabs are indicative of the advantages such an education purveys, namely, sports, co-curricular pursuits and state-of-the-art facilities. There is an absence of this type of information on both the NewVIc and LFCG homepages, and

Figure 16a-e Whitgift School homepage auto-rotating image carousel, captured 2015

it is precisely this value-added factor that distinguishes the school from its counterparts in the French and, arguably to a lesser degree, UK state sector.

Creative capital is not only celebrated here, as displayed in the carousel photograph of the school orchestra, but constitutes an integral part of the education on offer. It is meaningful that the applicable tab is titled Co-Curricular, as opposed to extra-curricular, itself a connotation that music and the arts are not mere adjuncts to the academic curriculum, but essential components thereof. Sport occupies a position of even greater prominence, assigned two of the five slider images, and considered cultural capital worthy of £9 million investment, in the form of a new sports' centre. In fact, and contrasting both the NewVIc and LFCG homepages, the *academic* provision of the school is entirely absent from the visual resources that dominate the multimodal ensemble. As if Whitgift's first-class academic standards were self-evident, not warranting pictorial recognition, the school devotes the image carousel unreservedly to the *holistic* education it provides. For, just as the Ancient Greeks considered athleticism to be on a par with intellectual virtue, Plato himself taking part in the Olympic Games, so UK public schools are based on the classical model.

Continuing in the tradition of Anglo-Saxon humanist, Alcuin of York (*c.*732–804), whose liberal-arts approach to learning was ironically embraced by Charlemagne and adopted in medieval Frankish schools, British independent schools nurture the rounded, sporting, artistic individual. Indeed, it is this rounded education, which values students' creative and sporting capital, that attracts many young, well-heeled London-French residents. The Whitgift homepage thus multimodally supports Paulette's assertion that English education is 'more cultural, more sporty' and 'more arty'. While the irresistibility of such an all-inclusive offering is corroborated by Chantal: 'English private schools, they really are mind-blowing. When the kids go to Open Days, they only want one thing: to go.'

Significantly, however, it is not athletics or football that Whitgift's landing page showcases, but fencing and cricket. Beyond the co-curricular symbolic value of these two sports is their relevance as signs of sociocultural distinction, carrying the same semiotic weight as the comparison between tennis and football made by Bourdieu in *La Distinction* (1979a). Cricket being the quintessential English gentleman's game, this image situates the school geographically, culturally and socially, recalling the principle of the public-school tradition to transform boys into gentleman fit for positions of power in professional and social fields. Similarly, fencing is a sport predominantly practised by the British bourgeoisie. Like cricket, in a transnational cultural-capital exchange, the sport was initially introduced by historic waves of elite French migrants to London (Randall, 2013). Through a pro-longed process of social reproduction and gradual cultural appropriation, it continues to be an English elite who practise it.

Although an elite education is expressed multimodally on the Whitgift homepage, chiefly through the value awarded to cultural capital, this exclusivity does not translate into under-representation of ethnic minorities. On the contrary, the central figure in the fencing photograph is a Black pupil, and almost half the students featured in the final slider photograph have visible minority ethnic heritage. Consequently, despite the school's preclusion of children lacking the financial or academic means to attend, as a multimodal orchestration, the carousel projects an image of minority inclusivity and equality, in keeping with NewVIc's landing page and in contrast to the LFCG's. Laura's son is a case in point, since he represents a (French) minority and benefits from a full bursary thanks to the language capital he brings to the school's bilingual section. While not immediately obvious, the peacock in the first slider photograph illustrates Whitgift's capacity to fund a socio-economically disadvantaged minority of its ethnically diverse student body. Widely recognised as a symbol of wealth and royalty, and associated with renewal in the Christian faith and good luck in Hinduism, the peacock also makes more literal semiotic connections to the school. Aesthetically, the bird pleasingly emulates the greens and blues of the homepage colour scheme, thus contributing to its overall coherence and recalling the institutional appreciation for creative capital. More importantly, however, when considering the school's commitment to financially support academically, musically, artistically or sportively gifted children, the peacock is a semiotic reminder of its considerable estate, comprising forty-five acres of (London) parkland inhabited by the birds.

The final carousel photograph is also suggestive of legacy, not inherited wealth, but hereditary habitus and dispositions traditionally associated with Englishness: a sense of humour and eccentricity (Fox, 2014). This sentiment is evoked through the shot's incongruous composition. The high angle gives an air of theatricality, as if looking down onto a stage, whereas the dispersion of staff and students among the hedges of a maze, only their torsos and heads visible above the shrubbery, epitomises the self-derision admired as a 'national' trait by Charles. It also contrasts the humourlessness of the other two schools' landing pages. It is noteworthy that in 1954, France was referred to as 'perhaps the only country where … it is still not only respectable but highly enviable to be an intellectual' (Faucher *et al.*, 2015: 100–101), which chimes with Séverine's words regarding a *diametrically opposed* characteristic: 'in London, eccentricity is still allowed and respected'. In this light, the Whitgift landing page is arguably the most 'English' of the three schools; so confident in its ability to supply students with an exclusive education, it boldly prioritises the extra-curricular and conveys a somewhat absurd image of itself. It is precisely this cheerful atmosphere, where 'all the teachers seem to be having a whale of a time' (Laura), that the majority of my participants seek. And it is precisely the school's digital representation as a quintessentially English school, but where Englishness does not mean whiteness, unlike in the French system, where 'the links between whiteness and belonging to France are continually produced and reproduced' (Beaman, 2018: 2), that distinguish it from the LFCG.

Irrespective of the photograph's compositional light-heartedness, the student diversity and their cheery facial expressions, under closer inspection, the perceived equality begins to fade. The apparent sameness of the school uniform hides subtle symbolic meanings. Differences in pupils' ties are one example, where an additional stripe, a change in colour or another abstract symbol can signify division or merit. Acting as a more traditional equivalent to NewVIc's 'Student of the week' feature, the coded motifs of scholars' ties celebrate their academic or co-curricular accomplishments, supporting interviewees' assertions that the UK education system favours praise over reprimand, values non-academic pursuits and is more meritocratic. Other ties might symbolise belonging to a particular house within the school and, by extension, division from others. Such material signifiers of distinction directly contradict the purportedly egalitarian sartorial uniformlessness and morally charged pedagogic uniformity of the French educational model, yet they do not undermine the social levelling instilled by the uniform per se. This discreet symbolism, albeit semiotically loaded for those with sufficient 'insider' knowledge (Bourdieu, 1980b), defies the anonymity imposed by the uniform as a whole, but in so doing represents institutional esteem for the student as an individual, with individual talents, as observed by Paulette. Later in life, the semiotic affordances of school or house ties are intensified, potentially serving as markers of social capital and operationalised for entry into 'old boys' networks, thus facilitating employment opportunities, and so on. These various levels of meaning-making are indicative of the semiotic complexity inherent in a superficially straightforward, if somewhat frivolous, photograph.

Encapsulating this web of meaning and on-line/on-land dynamics, is my final observation that the shot is set against the school's performing arts centre, which highlights Whitgift's championing of creative capital and its preparation of students for their subsequent professional and social trajectories. Since, in the words of Shakespeare, 'All the world's a stage' (*As You Like It*, Act II, Scene VII).

Conclusion

On one hand, my blended ethnosemiotic approach has revealed a discrepancy between the French education system's egalitarian ideals and its exclusionary image. On the other, it has confirmed the application of student-centred learning in both maintained and fee-paying UK models, thereby shedding light on participants' educational choices and correlated long-term emplacement. Participants' verbal accounts have been borne out online, where semiotic comparison has allowed hidden meanings to be teased out of the public-facing multimodal ensembles. The ostensibly positive Lycée landing pages concealed more negative underlying messages, which coincided with participant claims regarding subtle forms of symbolic violence at the school and in French education more broadly. They tacitly demonstrated that while academic standards may be high and gender equality respected, there is a structural, epistemological and ontological lack of educational egalitarianism. Paulette's experiences of xenophobic microaggressions were thus corroborated online, with 'the French mentality', as she observed, 'still there' and minorities under-represented. Similarly, the homepage confirmed interviewees' convictions regarding the French system's shortcomings in preparing students for the world of work, in valuing their individual attributes and prizing creative capital, especially in artistic, sporting and musical forms. In this way, the findings confirmed the 'expatriate continuities' to which Fechter and Walsh refer (2010: 1,197), with France's (post)colonial legacy transposed to the London context, as well as its teaching methods and ideologies.

Conversely, and in keeping with the principles of student-centred learning, NewVIc's landing page relayed an image of gender, religious and ethnic-minority inclusion, with celebration of achievement dominating. Practical skills were seen to be valued, as were employability and students' individual attributes. No evidence of structural hierarchy emerged from the analysis. These characteristics again substantiated my on-land findings, where participants spontaneously associated them with the UK education system and looked upon them favourably. The final case in this study was Whitgift's homepage. Compositionally and functionally, it initially appeared to have more in common with the LFCG – arguably an indication of the latter's increasingly socially elevated student body – but on closer examination, the messages were noticeably divergent. Whereas the Lycée's auto-rotating carousel projected an image of academic rigour alongside recreational pursuits, Whitgift's prioritised sport and the creative arts as integral components of the curriculum. So confident in the school's heritage and well-rounded educational provision, the principal message of the landing page was not academic, but geared towards creative capital, English/cultural heritage and eccentricity. A finer-grained multimodal reading uncovered additional messages, such as the ethnic diversity of the student body and symbolic forms of distinction operationalised to demarcate individual achievement or collective identity. In both the UK maintained and independent internet examples, through processes of deliberate distinction and a constructivist epistemology (Lea *et al.*, 2003), they achieved equality, whereas in the French model, through its positivist epistemology (Lea *et al.*, 2003) and didactic application of ideological equality, a state of inequality was perceptible on-land and on-line.

The ethnosemiotic approach I adopted in this chapter therefore validated the comparative on-land/on-line method as an effective triangulation mechanism, adding a layer of credibility to the ethnography. It enabled a deeper understanding of the interrelatedness between the digital and physical, and of participants' reasons for favouring English pedagogics. Each educational system has emerged as a microcosm for British and French society, with the respective websites being microcosms of a yet smaller order. Migrants' decisions to turn towards the UK system – at least for primary education – therefore echo the rationale behind their initial migration to London, with perceived openness, meritocracy and opportunity serving as powerful pull factors (Lopez Rodriguez, 2010) in both cases. However, as seen in their international mobility, their 'repertoire of choices and actions' were also constrained by circumstance (Ryan and Sales, 2013: 92), for once inside the UK system, it is difficult to (re)integrate into French secondary education, because some will have never been in the French system and others may have. Given the formative effect of education (Lopez Rodriguez, 2010), moulding mentalities and building (or eroding) confidence in the long term, these semi-conscious decisions therefore have lifetime consequences. Starkey contends that '[s]tudent-centred learning is the antithesis of institutionalism in education, placing emphasis on an affective domain in which each student is recognised as an individual inquisitive, creative, culturally located human being' (2019: 380). As such, the student-centred learning I have shown to be at the heart of UK education diametrically opposes the institutionalism epitomising *l'Ecole de la République* and explains its dehumanising characteristics. Built on humiliation and stigmatisation, just as Macron claimed (En Marche, 2017), the French system risks inhibiting future success individually and societally. The mutually structuring dynamic between school and society is hence confirmed (Armagnague and Rigoni, 2018) and the urgency of educational 'empowerment through a social reform agenda … [which] challenges authoritarian models' is underlined (Starkey, 2019: 387).

Notes

1 However, the UK continues to outperform France in the PISA rankings in all areas, with an average score of 504 for reading comprehension, 502 for maths and 505 for science in 2018, against 493, 495 and 493 respectively for France (OECD, 2019).

2 The Lycée Winston Churchill has made a bold visual statement through its introduction of a conventional 'British' school uniform, which suggests a departure from Republican tradition, where freedom of expression translates into a uniformless dress code – again simultaneously in the name, and at the expense, of 'equality', particularly if the Muslim headscarf and long-skirt bans are taken into consideration (Wolfreys, 2018).

3 While denim today represents the global influence of North American culture, the words 'denim' and 'jeans' speak of the fabric's transnational past, having been initially 'imported [to London] "*de Nîmes*", from Nimes, by the Huguenots' (Janvrin and Rawlinson, 2013: 70), specifically from the town of Gênes (as in 'denim' and 'jeans'). It travelled to North America later, on another migratory route, the Levi's label being founded in 1873 by Bavarian Jewish migrant to San Francisco, Levi Strauss.

4 It is important to note that this social stigma is now actively resisted by some. See, for example, the French 'nappy' – natural and happy – hair movement.

5 The metal detectors greeting students at the entrance to NewVIc are testimony to the social challenges faced by the college, but they do not detract from the empowering teaching methods deployed there and identified on the website.

6

Digital representations of habitus: a multimodal reading of archived London-French blogs

Introduction

This chapter brings the ethnosemiotic paradigm (Fiske, 1990) into its own, taking internet data as the analytical starting point. I return to the notion of habitus, deconstructed in previous chapters, but seek its representations in the London-French blogosphere. By examining five blogs preserved in different web archives between 2009 and 2014, I assess how they have evolved in social semiotic terms and what such developments tell us about the London-French migration experience over time. My analysis seeks to understand how identity is performed in this technologically enabled but ontologically enacted in-between space, bridging – to a certain extent – France–London, physical–digital and private–public dichotomies (Collins, 2009). Rather than illustrating a cleft habitus (Bourdieu, 2004), I posit that the culturo-digital representations gesture towards hybridity (Hall, 1990; Huc-Hepher, 2016; Ponzanesi, 2019). Through the prism of my triadic habitat-habituation-habits conception of habitus, I argue that formal transformations common to the blogs, be they visual, textual or typographical, are indicative of an emergent London-French collective on-line/on-land habitus (Brinkerhoff, 2009), which supports the notion of a 'common-unity' of practice and hence community belonging (Vaisman, 2011, 2016; Sargeant and Tagg, 2014).

In an age where the digital has an ever-increasing presence in the everyday practices of the world's population (Pink and Mackley, 2013; Hine, 2015), ostensibly transcending national borders and physical boundaries, it comes as little surprise that the rise of the internet has brought a (re)turn to materiality in academic research (e.g. Basu and Coleman, 2008; Miller, 2010, 2012; Pahl and Rowsell, 2010; Ankerson, 2011; Rowsell, 2011; Wang, 2016; Asenbaum, 2019) and social spheres (e.g. community-led 'libraries of things'). As if in a desire to cling on to a fading past, where people once felt secure in the grounded reality of their physical world, immersed in a nauseating sea of limitless digital data (Kitchin, 2014), the solidity of the everyday is attractive (Ankerson, 2019). While the twenty-first-century look towards the material provides a counternarrative to nineties' cyber-discourses (Ankerson, 2019), there is a danger that it overlooks the fragility of the digital (Strodl *et al.*, 2011; Taylor, 2012) and the semiotic dimensions of socio-technical systems (Ankerson, 2019). I therefore argue that it is flawed to approach the digital and material dichotomously, since 'reality is relational' (Bourdieu, 1994: 17) and there is materiality in immaterial modes of digital expression (Kress, 2010; Jewitt, 2014). We need to dismantle barriers and embrace a 'technomaterialist', third-wave paradigm (Hester, 2018) which acknowledges the web's digital-material ephemerality (Masanès, 2006; Gomes and Costa, 2014), inherent hybridity and embodied subjectivity (Asenbaum, 2019). I hence embrace *digital new materialism* (Asenbaum, 2019) and posit that the London-French blogs under scrutiny in this chapter are intrinsically hybrid object-subjects in form, function and inferential force. As Hall contends, 'identity lives with and through, not despite, difference; by hybridity' (1990: 235). Accordingly, migrant blogs' material multimodality bears witness to their creators' 'double consciousness', their 'betwixt-and-between' selfhood and positioning (Werbner, 2018: 147).

However, the very duality of the blog *form*, being at once a private log and a public cultural product on the World Wide Web (Fazal and Tsagarousianou, 2002; Casilli, 2010; Vaisman, 2016), as the portmanteau term implies – (we)b log – is problematic. With 'homepages that we wear' (Badger, 2004, cited in Vaisman, 2016), blogs recall the inherent hybridity of clothing, functioning as a public statement of the wearer/blogger's internal frame of mind (Miller, 2012) and as an outward display of personal practices for pre- and postmigration audiences. They are at once self and other, individual and collective, as well as material and affective, social and cultural. None of these features exists in sterile isolation; they play off and feed into each other organically. The internet, as previously posited (Hine, 2000; Bräuchler, 2005; Kozinets, 2010), is not divorced from physical reality, it is a dynamic extension of migrants' everyday lived experience (Collins, 2009). The digital perforates their private, material worlds when 'connecting' to the web in a particular place and the personal spaces migrants' physically inhabit are reflected in the public cyberspaces they construct and 'furnish'. Constituting virtual apartments (Casilli, 2010) or bedrooms (Vaisman, 2016), combined with the 'characteristics of personal journals' (Collins, 2009; Yoon, 2013: 175), their blogs add individuated cultural colour to a space dominated by an anglophone US presence. Like the intimate habitats explored in Chapter 2, (archived) blog-homes therefore offer us both a privileged 'window into the past' (Yoon, 2013: 175, quoting O'Sullivan, 2005) and into the online identities and cultural positioning of the migrants who create them. However, and this is why they are ontologically and epistemologically problematic, blogs are also *functionally* hybrid.

Not only are we presented with the (self-)representation vs communication (Kress, 2010) tension observed in Chapter 5, but we find an increasingly hazy boundary between the cultural and the commercial, the expressive and the promotional. In turn, such functional blurriness impacts the blogs' form. Traditionally, hybridity has been welcomed as a positive concept and existential state that overcomes essentialist views of identity and belonging (Hall, 1990; Papastergiadis, 1998), but as Werbner asserts, 'hybridity is not essentially good' (2018: 151). In its privileging of the cultural, it negates the political and underplays asymmetric hegemonies and marginalisation (Anthias, 2018). Equally, in its normalised 'flattening of difference' (Hutnyk, 2018: 142), '[h]ybridity lulls us to sleep' (2018: 143) and 'serves the status quo' to the benefit of a cosmopolitan elite 'from the cosy comforts of magnanimity' (2018: 144).

While I acknowledge these criticisms, what is significant in the formal, and therefore socio-semiotic hybridity emerging from the London-French diasberspace, is precisely its rose-tinted connotations. The symbolic violence, microaggressions, exclusion, longing and displacement identified in the on-land environment and in the blended field of education (discussed in Chapter 5) are typically replaced by a *vie-en-rose* picture of mobility in the contemporary diasporic blogosphere. Whether in an attempt to promote themselves or their commercial services, or simply to sell their resettlement success story to relatives left behind or strangers envisaging the migration dream, the blogs package mobility as an enriching and life-affirming experience (Benson and O'Reilly, 2009; Benson, 2011), thus playing 'into the hegemony of a fabricated, and commercialised, diversity' (Hutnyk, 2018: 141). Instead of the 'imaginary homelands' nostalgically evoked by Salman Rushdie (2018: 227), we discover an illusory present, a carefully crafted depiction of individuated transnationalism that renders the migrant blog a 'living, aspirational archive' (Appadurai, 2019: 563), arguably 'displacing thought about problems "here" today onto fantasies of the future' (Hutnyk, 2018: 141).

It would nevertheless be an oversimplification to assert that the blogs paint a uniform picture of diasporic hybrid happiness which is 'unequivocally progressive' (Hutnyk, 2018: 139). Although lightness and optimism characterise the London-French diasberspace, my multimodal analysis unearths more complex meanings beneath the bright veneer, relating to migrant constructions of identity, culture, community, emplacement and (be)longing (Levin, 2016) on-line and on-land. In keeping with Anthias's contention that 'hybridity arguments need to stress the retention of part of a cultural heritage ... if they are able to identify the cultural identity which is then merged with other aspects to form an organic whole' (Anthias,

2018: 134), I explore the ways in which the blogs provide a platform for both explicit (self-)representations – the notion of 'design' in multimodal terms (Kress, 2010: 6) – and tacit expressions of Frenchness. Such Anglo-French cultural hybridity also involves the dynamics of language (Collins, 2009; Werbner, 2018), or what Li Wei refers to as 'translanguaging' (Li, 2011; 2018). Indeed, focusing on blogs preserved in internet archives has paradoxically enabled, unlike in a material, on-land setting or on the inherently transient live web (Gomes and Costa, 2014), the materialisation of words which would otherwise be lost to memory no sooner than they were uttered. Provided they are archived, messages produced in online environments, irrespective of mode and medium (written, spoken, photographed, etc.) are immortalised for posterity in the 'material' form and spatio-temporal context of their utterance.

This digitally materialised trace of a particular language community's, previously ephemeral, linguistic here-and-now is receiving increasing scholarly attention in the field of applied and sociolinguistics (for example, Blackledge, 2013; Androutsopoulos, 2014; Sargeant and Tagg, 2014; Schreiber, 2015; Zhu Hua *et al.*, 2015; Lyons and Tagg, 2019) and beyond, including social geography, cultural anthropology, media studies and modern languages (for example, Cheshire's geographical mapping of London's 'tweeted' languages, 2012a, 2012b; Adami and Kress, 2010; Madianou and Miller, 2012; Huc-Hepher, 2016; Pitman, 2018; and Wells *et al.*'s forthcoming interdisciplinary Special Issue). However, these studies often – and understandably – concentrate on communication via Social Networking Sites (SNS) and SMS messaging, rather than representation on blogs and/or websites. Collins's (2009) work on the personal homepages of Korean migrants in Auckland, and Vaisman's research on Israeli girls' blogs (2016) are notable exceptions. Yet, as Adami (2015) posits, the typical approach taken in the analysis of blogs is a content-based or textual one (Vaisman, 2016), using either discourse analysis or conversation analysis, or a combination of both (Adami, 2015). These approaches overlook the 'customizing features that bloggers can select and combine ... such as colour palette, layout, font type, animation and interactivity display, among others' (2015: 44) and hence crucially overlook the blog's aesthetics and related semiotic affordances, which position it in relation to audience and genre (Vaisman, 2011, 2016; Huc-Hepher, 2015), while constituting its material subjectivity (Asenbaum, 2019). Pitman (2018) bucks the trend, with her study of the subtle political messaging on indigenous Brazilian websites, but she admits to prioritising written poetics over visual aesthetics. Multimodality and translanguaging necessarily look beyond the linguistic, however, following the premise that 'there is in principle equity between all modes' (Jewitt, 2011: 13). Drawing on Kress's work (2010), Li Wei asserts that:

Translanguaging embraces the multimodal social semiotic view that linguistic signs are part of a wider repertoire of modal resources that sign makers have at their disposal and that carry particular socio-historical and political associations. It foregrounds the different ways language users employ, create, and interpret different kinds of signs to communicate across contexts and participants and perform their different subjectivities. (Li, 2018: 22)

Crucially, however, Li Wei affirms that translanguaging not only transcends conventional linguistic distinctions, such as code-switching and written vs spoken dichotomies, but also 'goes beyond hybridity theory' (2018: 23), functioning 'as a Thirdspace which does not merely encompass a mixture or hybridity of first and second languages' (2018: 24), but goes 'beyond language' itself, by 'transforming the present [... and] by reinscribing our human, historical commonality in the act of Translanguaging' (2018: 24). Just as cultural theorists are challenging hybridity and proponents of student-centred learning were seen to inject humanism back into teaching in Chapter 5 (Starkey, 2019), so sociolinguists are disrupting formerly stable notions of linguistic situatedness and nationally bounded codification systems.

By studying the London-French blogosphere, therefore, we again apprehend a microcosm of the transnational diasporic experience, seeing precisely how this cultural and linguistic in-between space is enacted through bloggers' multimodal translanguaging practices and what they tell us about their postmigration relationships and embedding. Miller posits that 'objects construct subjects' and provide insights 'into the everyday understanding of what it means to be human' (2010: 11). Through the multimodal materiality of London-French blogs, together with the artefacts and cultural 'stuff' incorporated within them, I use the following case-study to uncover subtle meanings pertaining to the individual, collective and – socially, culturally and geographically – situated human migrant experience (Appadurai, 1990; Smith, 2005; Walsh, 2012).

From big data to thick data: ethnosemiotics in practice

Building on lessons learnt in previous collaborative projects (notably, Analytical Access to the Domain Dark Archive [AADDA], and Big UK Data for the Arts and the Humanities [BUDDAH], using the 1996–2010 JISC UK Domain Dataset), my ethnosemiotic case-study tackles the *big* data of web archives from a purposefully small perspective (Huc-Hepher, 2015). I favour the 'thick description' (Geertz, 1973: 7) of 'thick data' (Wang, 2013b: 1) over a more proportionate but inherently 'thinner', quantitative one. This avoids the dangers of 'data fundamentalism' and the fallacy 'that massive data sets and predictive analytics always reflect objective truth'

(Crawford, 2013: 1). In addition, it plays to my disciplinary strengths and responds to Ponzanesi's call 'to develop useful integrations of newer digital methods' (2019: 551) and to resist 'succumbing to "digital positivism"' (Ponzanesi, 2019: 551, citing Fuchs, 2017). My ethnosemiotic, blog-based approach seeks the '"beautiful histories of small things"' (Winters, 2017: 241, citing Hitchcock, 2014), rather than 'the historian's macroscope' (Winters, 2017: 241), embracing the 'complexity and mess' of the web archive precisely 'because it reflects and records complex and messy human interactions' (2017: 241). Tricia Wang postulates that 'ethnographic work holds such enormous value in the era of Big Data', thanks to its power to 'bridge and/or reveal knowledge gaps' (Wang, 2013b: 1); my ethnosemiotic paradigm is designed to do just that. It reintroduces the subjective human to the ostensibly objective numbers in order to unearth the untold stories of a chronically overlooked migrant group.

As previously established (Huc-Hepher, 2015; 2016), the approach combines Bourdieusian ethnographic principles with Kressian social semiotics to produce a 'natural', ethnosemiotic union (Vannini, 2007). It also draws on Adami's (2013) redefinition of Halliday's metafunctional triad (1978) to understand the blogs' ideational, interpersonal and textual functions. Embedded in the textual function are notions of coherence and cohesion (Domingo and Kress, 2013: 2), which loosely correspond to intertextuality and intratextuality respectively, and which acknowledge multimodal blog design as contingent on audience perception and construction, with the blog visitor playing an active role in the meaning-making process (Domingo *et al.*, 2015). Considering the blogs' semiotic coherence therefore has far-reaching sociocultural implications. As Vaisman posits, blog 'designs are produced, reproduced, and circulated among ... bloggers who use blogs not only as texts but also as avatars, performing gender and [cultural] identities through blog iconography and signaling group identity and subcultural affiliations through engagement with specific blog design styles' (Vaisman, 2016: 294). Though often neglected by digital (diasporic) scholarship, the subtle design and language choices of blogs and other online media are hence of considerable ethnographic significance.

A la recherche de blogs perdus: methodological challenges

Archiving born-digital and digitised media poses considerable preservation challenges (Brügger, 2005, 2009; Brügger and Laursen; 2018; Ben-David, 2019), but once archived, they also present the researcher with a range of pragmatic challenges. That they are effectively reborn digital versions, rather than identical copies of the web objects, is one (Brügger, 2012; Huc-Hepher, 2015); the multiplicity of versions, rendering web archives 'too complete' is another (Brügger, 2012: 110; Cowls, 2017); and this over-completeness contrasts with the simultaneous '(in)completeness' noted by Winters (2017: 244) and Brügger, which leaves the researcher with a potentially visually and/or multimodally 'deficient' (Brügger, 2018) archived version. Images are sporadically present and absent – sometimes in the same blogpost – layouts, even fonts can be misrepresented compared to the live version, and on occasion 'the entire style sheet keeping the elements in place is not archived and the result is that only running text is shown, without any placeholders' (Brügger, 2012: 112), all of which occurs seemingly arbitrarily (Ben-David, 2019). It is conceded that incomplete and/or damaged objects of analysis are typical of the hurdles faced by historians in the physical world (Winters, 2017), but when conducting a multimodal analysis, these apparently minor deficiencies and inconsistencies present major obstacles, ultimately jeopardising the very validity of the multimodal social semiotic approach.

Provenance is another challenge posed by online research, with both temporal and spatial identification resisting precise qualification and hence raising questions over sample suitability. Unlike standard websites, blogs are hosted by external platforms (WordPress, Squarespace, etc.), which renders site-based postcode search tools unhelpful. Clues can be garnered from the (con)text, but accurate positioning is often left wanting. For instance, a comment posted by a blog visitor, 'te voici de nouveau en Angleterre' (so you're back in England; Nenesse, 2010), confirms the blogger's national whereabouts, but does not specify London as the ultimate destination or place of abode. Version deficiency, such as absent visual parameters and/or metadata (Winters, 2017) can make gleaning a sense of place yet more taxing. Fortunately, however, the geographical detective work required for this case-study was minimal, since all five blogs – preserved in the London-French Special Collection (LFSC) – contained an explicit reference to London in their name and/or (sub)header.

A more fundamental identification risk posed by analysing archived blogs over time and by their functional blurriness, is the potential for refurbishments to have been conceived and executed by an external webmaster (Domingo *et al.*, 2015). This would inevitably cast doubt over the validity of habitus transformation findings. However, I argue that the blogs' dependency on pre-publication blogger approval legitimates them as reliable sources. Indeed, this is insinuated by a statement on the Lost and Found in London blog, in which the combined efforts of the blogger and a Paris-raised London-based designer are accredited: 'The homepage banner was thought up by myself and Lili Bé, who executed it.' The multimodal design choices therefore embody London-French imaginings and identity, despite the involvement of a 'third party'. Moreover, Boyd conceptualises

Myspace sites as digital bodies (Boyd, 2008). Vaisman goes further, claiming blogs to be avatars representing 'both the body and the spirit' (2016: 307), while Haraway goes further still, positing that 'we are all chimeras, theorized, and fabricated hybrids of machine and organism; in short, we are cyborgs' (2006: 118). Apprehending blogs as constitutionally representative of habitus subjectivities and materialities is thus not without precedent and credibility, particularly within the framework of a *blended* ethnography. Just as Fuchs (2017) advocates a critical-realist approach to digital and social media research, striking a balance between quantitative positivism and ethics fundamentalism, so I advocate a rationalised approach to blogs. I recognise the risks, but do not consider them to outweigh the critical insights such analysis brings.

Another question posed by the historic study of blogs is the usefulness of institutional archives, since blogs are intrinsically archival. What can a macro archive offer that a blog's integral archive cannot? Clearly, in the case of obsolete blogs, many of whose creators have switched to social media platforms (Lobbé, 2018; Pitman, 2018), snapshots archived by memory institutions are ordinarily the only records available. Although only fleeting captures of cyberspace and cybertime, these 'instances' (to use UK Web Archive terminology) preserve *instants* that would otherwise be permanently lost. In the case of 'live' blogs, however, the value of institutionally archived versions is less obvious due to the blog's inbuilt archive, but as my inter-archival case-study demonstrates, the integrated archive is not as integral as it might first appear. Semiotically telling design modifications are often absent from the blog archive but present in web archives. Furthermore, 'looking for [mediated] traces of women's experiences in the realm of the invisible, ephemeral everyday life can open fruitful theoretical avenues ... shedding light not only on untold stories, but ... [on] how a mass medium develops in relation to its social context and how responses to this shape its cultural form' (Ankerson, 2011: 389).

Despite being only an *image* of a dead blog (Barthes, 1980; Lobbé, 2018) and by no means an identical copy (Brügger, 2018), suspended between the (multiple) there(s) of its taking and the here of its viewing (Ankerson, 2019), the archived web snapshot is an important object of study. It presents the researcher with a reborn object, whose 'strange stasis, the very essence of a stop' (Barthes, 1980: 142) constitutes its long-term worth, capturing the myriad spatio-temporalities of the (online) migrant experience and offering insights into the changing patterns and affordances of early twenty-first-century online cultural production.

This leads to the challenge of defining the analytical object itself (Bourdieu and Wacquant, 1992; Brügger, 2009, 2012). Early blogs were akin to a long and ancient scroll, requiring, as the verb suggests, continual scrolling down in order to reach the earliest blogpost, that is, the blog's beginning and its end. Beyond the temporal and manipulative inconvenience, it posed no challenge to accessing the material either in its born-digital (live) or reborn-digital (archived) forms. It does, however, present difficulties when attempting to re-present blog data within the body of a critical text (Fuchs, 2017). It demands the problematisation of both terminology and boundary-setting. Is it apposite to refer to the analytical object as a web 'page' (Brügger, 2012: 111) when it is not self-contained on a single page or screen? Screenshots of sections of web pages or of 'web elements' (2012: 111) are more accurate designations, but decidedly less elegant. Reducing the object of analysis to a spatio-temporally suspended screenshot is analytically adequate and easier to manage from presentational – especially in hard copy – and audit-trail perspectives. Yet, the time-space interruption is unfaithful to the live web object/subject (Asenbaum, 2019) *and* its archived reincarnation, which aims to maintain the original '"Internet" dynamics ... and to some extent the recipient-specific dynamics' (Brügger, 2005: 33). In relation to the blog's initial design, semiotic potentiality and navigational affordances, the doubly reborn screenshot therefore provides a substantially altered and inauthentic experience (Lyman, 2002; Bezemer and Mavers, 2011; Huc-Hepher, 2015).

Involving tensions between boundaries, the methodological challenges I have evoked in this section recall the conflict epitomising 'the relation between organism and machine' (Haraway, 2006: 118), referred to as 'a border war', the stakes of which are 'the territories of production, reproduction, and imagination' (Haraway, 2006: 118). Be they spatial–temporal, ontological–epistemological, digital–material or 'defining the boundaries of study' itself (Ankerson, 2011: 385), it is the divides that have dominated here. In the following multimodal analysis, while acknowledging these borderlands, and Barthes's distinction between (codified, hence removed) language and (authenticating, present-perfect-tense) photography (1980), I attempt to dismantle the borders between the visual and the written, the formal and the functional. Rather than 'style over substance', my case-study sees style *as* substance (Asenbaum, 2019). Following Ankerson's recommendation, I 'read against the grain of algorithmic logics of probability and prediction' (Ankerson, 2019) by '[r]ecognising the queer potential of web archives' (Ankerson, 2019), by reinjecting the socio-semiotic into the material (Ankerson, 2019) and by seeking out the meaning-making potential of intermodal relationships, all of which embraces 'a xenofeminist politics of technology' (Hester, 2018: 149). In this light, the process of researching the archived internet becomes not one of omnipresent borders and dichotomies, but – despite its critiques – one of progressive hybridisation.

Searching for home in the historic web: a multi-archival, multi-blog case-study of habitus transformation over time

Tea Time in Wonderland: Towards or beyond a hybrid habitus?

The first blog chosen for this case-study is Tea Time in Wonderland. Initially captured in 2009, it is one of the few blogs in the LFSC with a UK country-code Top-Level Domain (.co.uk cc-TLD), making the British Library's UK Web Archive its native 'home'. Created by Coralie, the blog bears witness to the predominance of women bloggers in the London-French blogosphere and hence mirrors on-land consulate figures (Bellion, 2005; see Chapter 4), as well as Israblog statistics, according to which 'the percentage of female bloggers has consistently risen, and by August 2011 had reached 80 percent' (Vaisman, 2016: 294). The gendered provenance of the blogs under scrutiny thus detracts from the traditionally male-dominated portrayal of technology and instead corresponds to the third-wave feminist contention that 'technology is not inherently male and can serve women equally well' (Haraway, 2006; Skowronsk, 2015: 27; Asenbaum, 2019). Indeed, these figures demonstrate that growing numbers of women 'find it empowering' and reject the notion that tech 'violates their true feminine nature' (Skowronsk, 2015: 27; Pitman, 2018).

Comparing the earliest 2009 version of the blog (Figure 17) and the 2014 version (Figure 18) archived in the public-facing LFSC, the contrast is obvious. In both instances, however, there appears to be a high degree of authenticity in relation to the born-digital resource. While a soft colour palette has been selected for each incarnation, maintaining a sense of representational consistency over time, there has been a significant change to the blog design. The banner has undergone the most substantial restyling, evolving from a (stereo)typical photographic shot of London, taken from the South Bank of the Thames, to a semiotically more complex graphic collage, akin to the banners of other London-French blogs of the period (see Huc-Hepher, 2016). We note a shift from the 'London Tourist' perspective to an increasingly 'French Londoner' one, which arguably reflects the transforming habitus of the blogger and a redefined London-French audience, confirming the assertion that '[a]s communities, digital diasporas may evolve a moving consensus on shared hybrid identity' (Brinkerhoff, 2009: 204).

The images in the updated banner improve the blog's intratextual and intertextual coherence, with the modal interplay between the blog

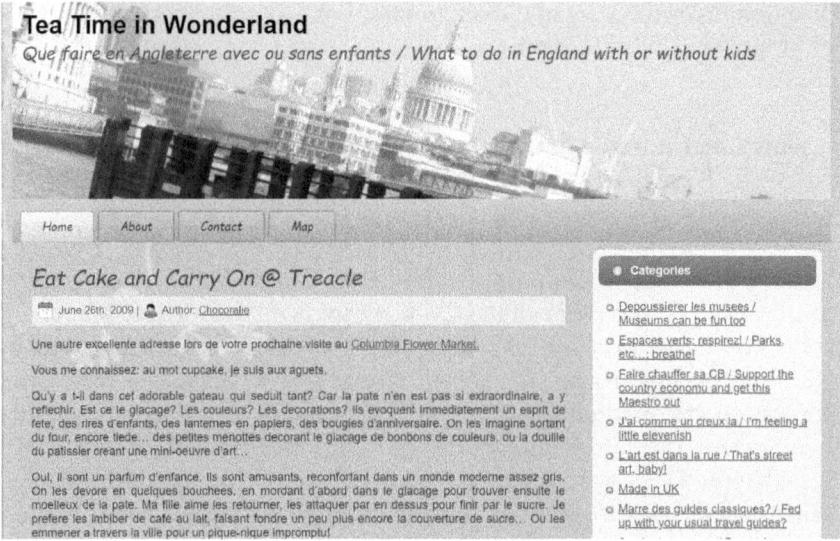

Figure 17 Tea Time in Wonderland, captured 2009

Figure 18 Tea Time in Wonderland, captured 2014

name – Tea Time in Wonderland – and banner iconography reinforcing the landing-page messaging. The White Rabbit from Lewis Carroll's classic *Alice's Adventures in Wonderland* (1865) is at once a nod to the well-known (on both sides of the Channel) literary work, and a symbol of London as a wonderland in its own right, which also coheres with the header tagline: 'La *magie* de Londres' (the *magic* of London – my italics). Both are suggestive of London's otherworldliness and mysterious allure, enchanting a continuous flow of French people through its quirky eccentricity and celebration of otherness, observed in my Apéro-blog London case-study (Huc-Hepher, 2016), and repeatedly confirmed on-land. For example, as discussed earlier, the creep of habituation to local mindsets was articulated by Séverine through her recognition of London being a place where 'eccentricity is still allowed and respected', unlike in France, which echoes Agnès Poirier's description of London as the epitome of 'imperfection and eccentricity' (Deen and Katz, 2008). Meanwhile, in the Lost and Found in London blog, the British capital is described as 'eccentric, dynamic and so endearing'. The motivated signs of the banner are thus testament to the blogger's increasing habituation to, and incorporation of, Londoners' perceived idiosyncrasy.

Although the reference to 'teatime' in the blog name reinforces the intertextual link to Carroll's work – particularly, and befittingly, the *Mad Hatter's* tea party – and increases the homepage's coherence as a multimodal text, 'le teatime' speaks equally vociferously of clichéd Franco-French associations with the imagined practices of 'les British'. This reliance on stereotypical evocations of London(ers) could be explained by Coralie's choice of blog name predating the redesign of the banner and doubtless corresponding temporally to her recent migration to the city, when still very much embedded in, and perceiving the world from, the perspective of the originary habitus. Her imaginings of the city and its practices were at that time informed by the mythologised tropes (Pitman, 2018) circulating in her premigration mediascape, and subsequently shaped the blog's initial conception. In this way, we observe the language and form of the archived blog serving as an aspirational map for the future as well as a record of the past (Appadurai, 2019).

Irrespective of the blog's exoticised name, comparing the 2009 and 2014 banners reveals a shift from the pedestrian and stereotypical to the playful and typical, mirroring the blogger's evolving sensibilities. The 2009 version constitutes a 'presence sheet' (Barthes, 1980: 142) characteristic of the photographic medium, a statement that the blogger 'was there' at that moment, with the shot's rakish angle providing the merest of hints of the magical mischievousness to come. In 2014, London's physical habitat is suggested, rather than photographically reproduced (Barthes, 1980: 142), and expects greater semiotic decoding. It is implied through the graphic representation of the double-decker bus, whose material, découpage quality – apparently a cut-out bus ticket – points to the blogger's movement through the capital on public transport and infuses an invented historicity through the ticket's outdatedness. This semiotic (re)construction of the London habitat is strengthened cohesively through the sidebar photograph of miniature models of decommissioned London buses and a taxi precariously piled on top. Verging on the absurd, the image recalls the disproportioned, London-Transport-laden iconography of Apéro-blog London (Huc-Hepher, 2016).

Such iconography thus situates the blog coherently within an online 'aesthetic community' (Werbner, 2018), representative of a London-French community of women digital practitioners.

As a multimodal ensemble (Kress, 2010) or material–digital, subject–object assemblage (Asenbaum, 2019), the 2014 banner tacitly articulates the nonconformity epitomising London in the eyes of many participants, considering it a liberating and appealing quality comparatively rarely encountered in France. Chantal conveys the sentiment: 'you have more freedom here; everyone has the right to have their own style. In France you're judged straight away.' Her words echo those of Mulholland and Ryan's participants, who define London as a place where one has 'the freedom to present oneself entirely as one wishes without judgement from others' (Mulholland and Ryan, 2017: 143). The blog(ger)'s self-appropriation of the idiosyncrasy permitted in London is further embodied by the subtle intertextual referencing of the hearts in the banner background. Operating as a pictographic gesture to the Queen of Hearts in *Alice*, their playful inversion, just perceptible on the right-hand side of the banner, coherently underlines the playing-card symbolism of the tale, while contributing to the blog's multimodal cohesion as a representation of London's 'magical' lure. Digging semiotically deeper, the hearts could also connote Coralie's fondness for the city, corresponding to an image sent to me by French-Canadian interviewee, Jacqueline. When asked what image represented 'her' London, she replied: 'I'd like to send you a photo of a heart; London's where my family is, where my love is, where my interests and passions are.'

Despite the clear transformative process displayed in the archived blog instances, semiotically, Tea Time in Wonderland is not an entirely 'anglicised' entity. Rather, it tends towards London-French hybridity (Brinkerhoff, 2009; Ponzanesi, 2019) and the 'translocational positionality' described by Anthias (2018: 136). Hinged 'on an apparently paradoxical combination of sameness and difference' (Lawler, 2008: 2), it is an expression of the blogger's 'continuously made and remade' identity (Anthias, 2018: 135). The process is illustrated in Figure 18 by the depiction of quintessentially British 'teatime' habits through fractal elements from the 'local' habitat: a 'teapot' and seat. Significantly, however, the shape of the former is more reminiscent of a French coffee pot than a British teapot, and the latter is not a traditional English wheelback chair or Chesterfield wing chair, but a Louis XV armchair. I therefore argue that the blog is undergoing a process of cultural hybridisation that mirrors the translocal emplacement of the blogger. As Collins asserts, 'the internet has stretched the everyday life-worlds of transnationals ... [but] remains always and necessarily grounded in and reliant upon offline spaces' (Collins, 2009: 857). The iconography is (inter/ra)textually coherent and cohesive, but, as observed in participants' on-land homes and practices, culturally plural, encompassing the habitat and habits of both France and London. Recalling the inflexible on-land coffee-drinking habits of Sprio's interviewees (2013) and Suzanne, the banner simultaneously embodies Coralie's persistent performativity of premigration habits and her habituation to the perceived quirkiness of the postmigration space.

Is the web object therefore a reflection of Coralie's 'identity slippage' (Mulholland and Ryan, 2011: 5) and 'destabilised' selfhood (Block: 2006: 27)? Or is it the product of an enriching process of 'interpenetration and translation … depicted through the concept of hybridity' (Anthias, 2018: 135)? While the ludic merging of cultural practices and paradigms implies the latter, closer attention to the evolving language practices belies such an assertion (Li, 2018). When scrolling down the page, we discover, outside the 2009 screenshot frame, an English (self-)translation of the French blogpost. It lacks the embedded photographs of the French text and its placing below is indicative of the English version's inferiority. Both French- and English-language versions are nonetheless present within the same web 'page', suggesting a combined 'intended audience' (Yoon, 2013: 181), French and (then) English. Epitomising the blog's integrated bilingualism in 2009, yet primacy of French, is the header tagline: 'Que faire en Angleterre avec ou sans enfants/What to do in England with or without kids'. Coralie supplies two iterations within the same tagline, separated (only) by a slash, but French(ness) comes first. When examining the 2014 capture, we note that this parallel bilingual approach has been replaced by two navigable sidebar options: 'Le blog en Français' (signalled through a photograph of a model Eiffel Tower, bearing a *tricolore* rosette) or 'The blog in English' (represented by the model modes of London Transport), their discrete framing connoting increasing compartmentalisation – of self and audience. However, when consulting the Internet Archive's 2016 version, all traces of its French-language identity have disappeared, and it has become an exclusively monolingual English web object. Could this be a reflection of Coralie surpassing hybridity and fully embodying Englishness? Is she now more comfortable in the English language than her native French? Is it a coincidence that the capture was taken in the same year as the UK's EU membership referendum? Or does it reflect Coralie's increasingly international audience, for whom English serves as a lingua franca?

The ideological implications of the (trans)languaging practices evinced in the blog are manifold and far-reaching. Yet, by turning to the US Internet Archive (IA), which – unlike the UK Web Archive (UKWA) and the Bibliothèque nationale de France (BNF) – trawls and harvests sites from the entire World Wide Web, regardless of cc-TLD affiliation, another important finding emerges: the creation of a .fr incarnation of the blog, this time, entirely in French. In 2016, we thus note a complete splitting of the blog into two discrete entities, aimed at two distinct language communities and spatially bordered on the 'worldwide' web by their nationally bounded Top-Level Domains and associated memory institutions (British Library and BNF). Beyond hybridity, therefore, we observe a return to the contested territories referred to by Haraway (2006) and what could be deemed a reflection of Coralie's cleft habitus. Equally, some might argue that this cyberspatial territorialisation and solidified language division (Webster, 2019) typify the nativism of the times (Richardson and Wodak, 2009; Looney, 2017; Lulle *et al.*, 2018). I contend, however, that they are in fact an expression of the neoliberal undercurrents, tacitly yet forcefully, shaping the blog.

Hutnyk (2018) encourages us to be suspicious of cultural hybridisation, claiming that 'diaspora and mixture do little more than confirm middle-class securities and draw others into the hegemony of a fabricated, and commercialised, diversity' (Hutnyk, 2018: 141). Building on this bold indictment, but diverting from it, I argue that the creation of two discrete .fr and .co.uk Tea Time in Wonderland blogs not only moves beyond the cotton-wool effects of hybridisation, but is indicative of Coralie's awareness of the workings of market forces, and an expression of her agency and business prowess. The bifurcated reconfiguration of the blog and repackaging of information to appeal to distinct French- and English-speaking audiences demonstrates that Coralie does not passively fall victim to commercial diversity hegemonies but manipulates them to her own ends. The prominence of an Ibis hotel advertisement in another 2014 UKWA capture of the site, taking central position across the page, is testimony to the blog's transforming functionality, developing from 'the most intimate and personal ... to the most public and collective' (Appadurai, 2019: 562) and, crucially, a revenue source if (re)packaged to meet the needs of the target audiences/ markets. In this sense, the French cc-TLD reincarnation of the blog could be 'considered a form of critical feminist repurposing' (Hester, 2018: 102); for, as Hester posits 'acts of strategic, technomaterial appropriation can take various forms', including the 'process of selective appropriation and recontextualisation' (Hester, 2018: 102).

Thus, beyond its playful portrayal of London life, Tea Time in Wonderland is the digital materialisation of the empowerment that mobility and blogging can bring women migrants (Wang, 2013a; Vaisman, 2016; Mulholland and Ryan, 2017). Beyond diasbserspaces for the performance of cultural identity and belonging, it is indeed credible to conceive of 'blogs as gendered avatars' (Vaisman, 2016: 293).

Visual 'geonarratives':
space-making and home-making in Lost and Found in London

Turning our attention to the Lost and Found in London blog, we can identify a significant transformation to its design between the 2010 (Figure 19) and 2014 captures (Figure 20). Given the blog's .com TLD, I needed to consult the nationally indiscriminate Internet Archive to locate the blog's earliest (re)incarnation. It is worthwhile noting that the Internet Archive also enabled the tracking of the blog beyond the 2014 capture, since at some point between 3 October 2016 and 7 February 2017, the https://lostandfoundinlondon.wordpress.com version of the blog became obsolete, but the blog was reborn as https://lostinlondon.fr (the date is again telling within the context of "Brexit").

Figure 19 Lost and Found in London blog landing page, captured 2010

Figure 20 Lost and Found in London blog banner, captured 2014

Consistent with Apéro-blog London (Huc-Hepher, 2016) and Tea Time in Wonderland blogs, the banner has undergone the most substantial restyling, again evolving from the photographic presence sheet (Barthes, 1980), depicting 'pragmatic truth' (Ravelli and van Leeuwen, 2018: 283), to an elaborate graphic patchwork. I therefore concentrate on the banner in this section. The instantly and globally recognisable London landmarks of the original incarnation, notably Big Ben and the London Eye, are transposed in the 2014 version, but the semiotic affordances of the latter provide greater insights into the space-making practices and emplace-ment of the blogger. We are presented with a carefully crafted semiotic orchestration in which naive, 'hand-drawn' caricatures of London's built environment are superimposed onto a bird's-eye view map of the city. Both elements are coded representations of space, but one is an objecti-vated overview following strict cartographic rules, while the other is a subjectivated, expressionistic sequence of close-ups, the multimodal mate-riality of which has sociocultural habitus implications that transcend the formal.

Superficially, the crude, green and blue 'sketches' in the foreground of the 2014 banner (Figure 20) denote trees, grass and waves. However, their manually drafted appearance is a motivated sign choice, consciously impos-ing the analogue on the digital and in so doing reminding the onlooker of the blog's humanity. Rather than Vaisman's 'gendered avatar' (2016: 293), this banner corresponds more closely to Haraway's 'cyborg' (2006: 118), providing a 'condensed image of both imagination and material reality' (2006: 118). A ludic quality is conveyed through the primary colours, recalling children's felt-tip scribbles or Picasso's deliberately and subver-sively naive one-line drawings. Importantly, Picasso's contrived pictorial simplicity had the benefit of capturing the essence of his subject. Similarly, these primal scrawls speak eloquently of London's green and blue spaces and their function as 'therapeutic landscapes' within the urban environment (Bell *et al.*, 2017: 93). As Bell *et al.* assert, by using personal 'geonarra-tives', the agency of individuals within their environment, as opposed to the agency of the places and spaces themselves, comes to the fore, demonstrat-ing their purposeful deployment of 'local green and blue spaces ... in a way that promotes their personal sense of well-being, within the social and cul-tural contexts specific to their daily lives' (Bell *et al.*, 2017: 94). Here, there-fore, the essentialising and affectedly unaffected depictions of waves, trees, bushes and grass relate not only to the River Thames and treelined streets mapped out in the monochrome banner background, and constituting the physical backdrop of the migrants' everyday postmigration existence, but to their agentive engagement with London's parkland, canal paths and their own back gardens.

The affective space between the migrant subject and their objectivated physical surroundings emerges from the pictographic juxtaposition of the bright rudimentary foreground doodles and the dull cartographic background. The banner emulates French migrants' active, present appreciation for London's verdure and its accommodation of nature, particularly in comparison to the relentlessly built-up Paris cityscape, as frequently recounted by on-land participants and reiterated by Mulholland and Ryan's (2017). Marie provides a condensed definition of her diasporic habitat which mirrors the distilled imagery of the blog banner, identifying London simply as 'squares with little gardens and parks'. Sarah, on the other hand, epitomises the comparative-moralist place-making alluded to by Mulholland and Ryan (2017: 138–9), 'where practices of judgement … construct moral geographies that … position, rank and rate cities in terms of their "worth"'. She describes her London habitat as preferable to Paris for the following reason: 'I don't live in a concrete suburb; I live in a suburb where there are lots of little two-storey houses, with a park, with trees.' Laura's testimony concurs with both Marie's concentrated leafy classification of London and Sarah's normative comparison:

> London, it is greenery. It's trees, flowers and parks; it's the joy English people get from being in their parks. It's not like that in France. In Parisian parks you're not allowed to walk on the grass. You go to the park to sit on a bench and look at the flowers; absolutely no ball-playing allowed!

These geonarratives corroborate Bell *et al.*'s (2017) contention that through agentive interaction with their local green spaces, individuals stimulate their therapeutic properties. We sense the salubrious effects of 'offsetting … the "buzz" of the urban experience' by accessing 'nature and seasonality without leaving the city' (Mulholland and Ryan, 2017: 148) and its conduciveness to long-term settlement. The sentiment is reiterated by Conradson and Latham's New Zealand interviewees, who underline the pleasure taken from 'walking, having picnics and playing informal sports' in London's parks' (Conradson and Latham, 2007: 243). As the authors explain, '[e]ngagement with green space and the accompanying sense of "slow time" were an important part of many respondents' rhythms of work, rest and play' (2007: 243). The respite from the megacity's oppressive pace and volume that migrants gain from their interaction with its green and blue spaces awards London a habitability unavailable in Paris. Indeed, average population density in each confirms participants' impressions: 21,200 residents per square kilometre in Paris, against 2,800 'within London city limits' and 6,000 in Greater London (World's Capital Cities, 2019a, 2019b).

Figure 21 David Hepher, study (1993)

Critically, however, London's green and blue spaces not only provide 'opportunities for *meaningful activity ... embodied restoration ... and ... sociality*', but also '*safety* ... offering a sense of security, inclusion, and belonging over time' (Bell *et al.*, 2017: 94–5; original italics). It is precisely migrants' deployment of these natural spaces, therefore, that contributes to their imagined postmigration 'securiscapes' (see Chapter 3) and ultimately provides them with a reassuring sense of feeling *at home* in London (Levin, 2016). In the 2014 blog banner, this comfortable, secure, embeddedness in the urban cityscape is connoted through its naive, childlike iconography. Indeed, the red and black 'drawings' of the houses to the left of the banner (Figure 20) are reminiscent of David Hepher's atavistic additions to his concrete-based paintings (Figure 21).

In both cases, the primary-coloured, purposefully wobbly, single-line depictions jump out against the earthy hues (Pitman, 2018) and linear geometry of their backgrounds, accentuating the innocent spontaneity of home as symbol and space. Glancey (1997) affirms the universality of the iconography, when describing Hepher's *Home Sweet Home* painting, on which is depicted:

> a child's drawing, big and splashy in yellow paint, of a house with four front windows, a centrally located front door, a pitched roof, corner chimneys, a garden and a big sunny sun. This is a telling detail: even the child brought up in a brutal, late-Sixties concrete megastructure depicts the idea of 'home' in exactly the same way as every child has before, whether from a smart house in the country, a semi-detached in suburbia or a local-authority tower block.

Just as the banner's lurid, childlike imagery jars with its understated, car-tographic background, so Hepher's naive houses are the antithesis of the brutalist towers on which they are painted. Likewise, participants' experiences of London's terraced houses, private gardens, sprawling parks and winding riverbanks are at the polar extreme of their lived or imagined experience of urban life in a Parisian 'concrete suburb'. Home and belonging in the postmigration space are thus reinforced by perceived opposition. In turn, a playful, optimistic sense of home is (self)consciously constructed in the digital habitat (Casilli, 2010) to counter the 'weight' (Robert) and pessimistic inclinations of the originary space (Parisot, 2007), while projecting an image of migration as fundamentally positive. For, as Benson and O'Reilly observe, participants' current state is informed by past experience and 'may not reflect objective reality; the presented advantages of life in the destination are often romanticised' (Benson and O'Reilly, 2009: 610).

Though semiotically complex compared to the earlier version of the banner, the 2014 incarnation (Figure 20) nevertheless functions effectively as a coherent and cohesive multimodal ensemble. Compositionally, the left/west–right/east directionality of the images is geographically coherent and graphically cohesive in relation to the background map (Tower Bridge straddling the Thames at the same point in both). The suburban terraced houses to the left of the 'Web element' (Brügger, 2018: 31) correspond to the trope that 'all London houses look alike' (fieldnotes, 5 July 2014), an essentialising observation which resonates with Flora Tristan's ([1840] 2008: 28) reference to London's 'long rows of uniform houses' almost two centuries' previously, suggesting continued outsiderness. However, their left/west positionality is also a clue as to the blogger's broader diasporic habitat and emplacement. The houses show a sensitivity to contrasting architectural features which implies an embeddedness in, and familiarity with, the (south)west London built environment incompatible with the contrived naivety of the 'sketches'. The Tudor-style edifices in the far left/west create a historic link to the Tudor stronghold, Hampton Court Palace, an area also home to Hampton Court House, an independent Anglo-French bilingual school, popular among the well-heeled ranks of the French community.

Moving right/east and more central (compositionally and geographically), the colour and form of the house differs from the others. Its classical rectangular symmetry, hidden roof and elegantly proportioned windows are suggestive of a Georgian townhouse, quite possibly in Kensington, given the banner's compositional–geographical coherence. In view of (South) Kensington's reputation as the 'home' of a certain – affluent – segment of the French community in London, these architectural details communicate a degree of insider knowledge consistent with embeddedness in the French 'community' proper. The blogger, Fabienne, identifies herself as a trained lawyer, which is not without socio-economic connotations, and the (south)west London habitat furnishing her blog is found across the

London-French blogosphere, suggesting an interwoven on-line and on-land network (Pitman, 2018; Asenbaum, 2019). The 'Fin d'automne à Richmond Park' blogpost (Delphine, 2014) and repeated visual and written allusions to Richmond Park, Parson's Green, Kew Gardens, Ravenscourt Park, and so on, are testimony to the community and, pertinently, to their agentive utilisation of the local habitat's green spaces. Equally revealing is how the residential properties depicted are restricted to the left/west of the banner and map, neither of which go further east than Tower Bridge. We are thus reminded of Miranda's allusion to 'les Français posh' in (south)west London and 'les Français hip' in the east, with Fabienne and the majority of London-French blog(ger)s appearing to correspond to the former.

While the photograph in the 2010 banner is equally evocative of London (Figure 19), the absence of Fabienne's (south)west London habitat and of London's financial centre, the City – represented by St Paul's Cathedral, the Swiss Re Tower (or 'Gherkin') and Tower Bridge in the 2014 instance – is significant. By omitting these habitat signs, we are denied insight into related habits. The 2010 photograph's exclusive focus on central London's West End again identifies the blogger as tourist more than resident, suggesting a habitus little altered by postmigration-field immersion at that stage. Whereas the inclusion of iconic City edifices in the 2014 banner implicitly sheds light on the professional habitat and habits of many highly skilled French migrants (Favell, 2006, 2008a; Mulholland and Ryan, 2011), indicating Fabienne's greater embeddedness in the broader diasporic space/community. Indeed, evidence from an article titled 'The French Phenomenon', harvested on 1 June 2007 and archived in the JISC UK Domain Dataset, triangulates this semiotic reading: 'BNP Paribas alone employs more than 400 French people in its Harewood Avenue office … French talent is underpinning London's leading position in the OTC derivatives markets … Another recruiter alleges that 80% of quants [quantitative analysts] at Goldman are French' (eFinancial Careers, 2007). Visually portraying the City in the updated banner is, therefore, an accurate reflection of the professional habitat and habits of a segment of London's high-skilled French population, providing insights into Fabienne's construction of place and her positioning within the wider London-French community. It also supports my on-land participants' contention, discussed in Chapter 5, that mathematical teaching is more rigorous in the French education system.

Another telling introduction to the 2014 banner is Tate Modern. Cohesively positioned relative to the map and 'hand-drafted' waves, and coherently emulating the gallery's physical location overlooking the River Thames, its inclusion is revealing of London-French leisure-time pursuits and performative homemaking. The migrants' appreciation for London's inclusive highbrow culture is articulated repeatedly in other blogs and on-land verbal accounts. Brice exclaimed that 'museums are free, so it's great' and Antoine mentioned the 'culture of free things, which is strange in a way'. Perhaps the strangeness is perceived because of the high cost of other activities in the capital – an observation made by Sadia – or in comparison to the entry fees of cultural institutions in France. The latter would corroborate Mulholland and Ryan's (2017) assertion that London's high-culture provision contributes to the normative place-making of London-French residents, with both its qualitative (breadth and depth) and ethical (cost-free policy) characteristics underscoring London's culturo-moral superiority in relation to Paris. The understated depiction of Tate Modern in the 2014 banner therefore has far-reaching socio-semiotic affordances. It not only depicts participants' quotidian habitat, offering insights into their leisure-time habits, but symbolises their affective relationship with, and positioning within, the migratory space. It also underscores the personal and civilising benefits of France–London migration and publicly validates private mobility decision-making.

My comparative, multi-archival analysis of the Lost and Found in London banner has identified an evolving digital habitus and, by extension, a changing on-land habitus, particularly regarding Fabienne's everyday habitat. Having designed the banner with the support of mutual French Londoner, Lili Bé, the shift from the literal, photographic outsider's recording of the city, to the more symbolic insiders' visual geonarrative is meaningful on individuated and collective levels. Messages encoded in the superficially light-hearted imagery (van Leeuwen, 2005; Vaisman, 2016) have provided profound insights into Fabienne's affective embedding and emplacement within the postmigration habitat, which emerges as a landscape of belonging, rather than one of 'unbelonging' (Conway and Leonard, 2014). The material-imagined (Haraway, 2006) digitised place-making supports my on-land findings, demonstrating coincidental community cohesion through shared praxis, together with a growing sense of safety and familiarity within the postmigration space, leading to an increased impression of London being 'home'. Since the banner design modifications are no longer visible in the dead .com TLD blog or its 'live' .fr reincarnation – not updated since summer 2017 and devoid of a banner – the importance of web archives as valuable contemporary historical (re)sources is also endorsed.

Interpersonal meaning in fine-grained reading: Londres Calling and Good Morning London

As demonstrated, far from keeping an authentic record (Lyman, 2002) of past posts, the in-built blog archive is open to unrecorded manipulation,

Figure 22 Londres Calling blog landing page, captured 2010

Figure 23 Londres Calling blog landing page, captured 2014

reflecting the transforming identity and positionality of the blogger. Design choices can also lock in meanings regarding interpersonal functionality and reach. The shift in cultural reference points contained in refurbished blogs necessarily narrows the accessibility of the multimodal text among those unfamiliar with the London-French experience and is thus indicative of a new audience being targeted and an emergent 'cybercommunity' (Brinkerhoff, 2009: 86). This audience reorientation is exemplified compellingly in the 2010 (Figure 22) and 2014 (Figure 23) captures of the Londres Calling blog, supported by the canalblog.com platform.

Once again, the most noticeable change relates to the banner. 'London calling' is no longer depicted through the representation of iconic Gilbert Scott K2 London telephone booths alone, but by a culturally sensitised suite of 'hand-drawn' images. As argued elsewhere (Huc-Hepher, 2016) and evinced here, this pictographic styling is a typical feature of the London-French blogosphere and situates the blog on multiple levels. Historically, it builds on France's long and respected *bande dessinée* tradition; generically, it engages in an intertextual dialogue within the blog genre (Huc-Hepher, 2015), and, interpersonally, it embeds the blog within a networked community of London-French bloggers and readers (Casilli, 2010). The *bande dessinée* quality is achieved through textual-visual intermodality, with one serving as anchorage for the other, 'so that both text and image work together to convey the intended meaning in a similar way to a comic strip' (Vaisman, 2016: 296–7, citing Barthes, 1977). We note this literal intermodal meaning-making in the blog name (Londres Calling) and its visual embodiment in the London 'phone-calling' kiosks in the 2010 banner. The more complex 2014 iteration, however, recalls the 'graphic design mashups of popular culture symbols decorating' other London-French blogs (Vaisman, 2016: 299), thus leading to the creation of a particular diasporic genre and, significantly, providing valuable insights into the performativity of 'subcultural identities and affiliations' (2016: 299).

Whereas the 2010 image of the K2 telephone booths is a universally recognisable representation of the London habitat, the symbolic significance of a Dalek would have been lost on a Franco-French audience at that time, generally unacquainted with the long-running BBC science-fiction series, *Doctor Who*. Consequently, the Dalek not only suggests a change in the TV-viewing habits of the blogger, Léa, but a reorientation away from an exclusively Franco-French audience, towards a predominantly London-French one, capable of decoding the (sub)culturally inflected imagery. In some ways, including the cyborg from *Doctor Who*, whose protagonist plays on the eccentric, English, 'mad scientist' figure, resonates with the ideational function of the White Rabbit in Coralie's blog, thereby connecting the two generically. Yet, given the Dalek's relative meaninglessness to a pre-Netflix Franco-French audience, unlike the widely known Lewis Carroll character, its interpersonal function is evidently geared towards a London-based French audience. This interpersonal narrowing is further emphasised by the other fractal habitus artefacts in the 2014 banner, such as several quintessentially British ice-creams (99 Flake, Twister, etc.), whose cultural embeddedness and childlike appeal illustrates Léa's increasing rootedness within the adoptive postmigration culture and community.

The addition of three 'paintings' to the 2014 banner, one of which includes an onlooker to imply a gallery space, connects it intertextually, interpersonally and temporally with the 2014 Lost and Found in London blog, recalling the latter's depiction of Tate Modern. In so doing, it supports my argument for a community of practice both on-line and on-land, with 'innovation and creativity [being] accorded high value' in both spaces (Werbner, 2018: 146) and serving as markers of ingroup identity. Other culturally meaningful features of the 2014 Londres Calling banner, indicative of Léa's mutating gustatory dispositions and affiliations, are the Victoria

sponge cake and jar of Marmite. This archetypal English comestible, ritualistically transported to the postmigration context by British migrants in
France (Benson, 2011), also speaks of less obvious, earlier migratory and
linguistic flows, thus embodying the double historicity evoked by Bourdieu
(Bourdieu and Wacquant, 1992). As the packaging suggests, the brand
name is in fact French, *une marmite* denoting a stockpot or cauldron. Yet,
being a beer-brewing by-product, Marmite is the material expression of
Britishness par excellence. So much so, owing to the seeping of advertising
into the mores of the British social field, 'Marmite' has become a recognised
adjective in the English language, signifying a love-or-hate relationship
(*Cambridge Dictionary*), and perhaps symbolising Léa's audience's mixed
feelings about London life. The fact that it features in the video pastiche,
Shit French People in London Say (Meard Street Productions, 2012), is
testament to its significance in the London-French collective imagination.
Consequently, its inclusion in the 2014 banner embeds the blog(ger) intertextually and interpersonally, as well as culturally (Parkhurst Ferguson,
2004; Bodomo and Ma, 2012).

However, while these semiotic readings confirm the banner's material-
imagined (Haraway, 2006) performance of belonging, they simultaneously
uncover 'internal boundaries framed in stereotypes' (Farrer, 2010: 1,225).
The Marmite, Wall's ice-creams, sponge cake, Dalek, mini-graffiti-ing
Banksy and 'high-art' gallery depictions all contribute to recreating the
'affective atmosphere' of the cosmopolitan London habitat (de Backer,
2019), and their inclusion in a French-language blog is illustrative of a
virtuous form of hybridisation (Ponzanesi, 2019). However, as Anthias
contends, such material–digital, French–English hybridisation necessarily
implies the continued reliance on 'residual elements of essentialization and
culturalism' (Anthias, 2018: 136) and therefore on less virtuous concep-
tions of sameness and difference. Through the objects' localised cultural
positioning and elusive codification, a 'targeted diasporic "ingroup"'
(Mitra, 1997: 158) is articulated, which necessarily excludes others, notably
'the indeterminate global "outgroup"' (Collins, 2009), among whom, are
the sedentary Franco-French. Beyond its function as a decorative feature
of the blog, therefore, the banner embodies normative interpersonal affect
and processual identity construction (Block, 2006) on both individual and
collective levels. On one hand, the shift in the banner's semiotic affordances
between 2010 and 2014 demonstrates a transforming blog(ger) habitus. On
the other, it lays bare the construction of 'invisible boundaries' (Abutbul-
Selinger, 2018), setting the London-French (blogging) community apart
from those left behind and paving the way for new, 'cosmopolitan affiliations' (Ponzanesi, 2019: 548). The semiotically sophisticated iconography
of the 2014 banner, tacitly targeting a London-based French audience, or

at least sensitive to the subtle materialities constitutive of British culture, places blog(ger) and audience in a position of metropolitan moral superiority. This audience compartmentalisation echoes that of the web itself, whose worldwide pretences are carved up by country-code Top-Level Domains (Webster, 2019) and entrenched by nationally circumscribed archiving memory institutions. Such territorialisation consequently raises questions over (trans)national identity and emplacement, both online and on-land, and the deterritorialisation associated with digital diasporas (Kele, 2016).

The Good Morning London blog, situated within the .fr ccTLD domain, but archived in the UK Web Archive's LFSC, thanks to curatorial intervention, also bears witness to metafunctional transformation indicative of London-French collective identity building and differentiation (Bourdieu, 1979a; Werbner, 2018). There are repeated indications in the blogposts and related comments that the blogger, Aurélie, targets and reaches a Franco-French audience in addition to the London-French community. However, under closer examination, subtle formal and/or typographical alterations suggest a shift away from the premigration habitus and audience over time. When placing a screenshot of the inaugural blogpost's first capture by the Internet Archive (Figure 24) alongside the 'same' blogpost in the blog's inbuilt 'micro archive' (Brügger, 2005: 10), accessed three years' later via the meso LFSC archive in the macro UKWA (Figure 25), ethnosemiotically meaningful modifications are detectable.

In addition to the font change in the 2014 version of the blogpost title, a telling blending of French and English typographic norms is evident, exemplifying the non-language-specific dimension of translanguaging (Li, 2018). The space before the colon typical of French standards is found in both instances, whereas the reliance on the exclamation mark – used far more liberally in French texts than their English counterparts – has been reduced, as its absence from the 2014 blogpost title confirms. Likewise, the non-standard placing, according to British writing conventions, of the sterling symbol (between the pounds and pence: '9£50', '15£65') in the 2011 instance, has been 'corrected' in the 2014 version ('£9.50', '£15.65'), thus corresponding to British orthographic norms and the expectations of readers habitually exposed to them. This suggests growing habituation to local writing practices over time and an agentive effort to 'assimilate' through self-appropriation of postmigration typographic customs and the retrospective masking of punctuated otherness. As Vaisman asserts, 'practices with orthography and typography demonstrate how people convey social meaning through form and not solely content' (2011: 179). By comparing the blogpost version archived institutionally in 2011 to the integrated-blog-archive version (enabled by a subsequent institutional capture), formal modifications ordinarily invisible are exposed. Punctuation

Figure 24 Inaugural Good Morning London blogpost, captured 2011

Figure 25 Inaugural Good Morning London blogpost, captured 2014

is seen to act as *mode*, its explicit and implicit semantic materiality providing an indication of the blogger's evolving habits, audience and sense of self.

The sidebar Welcome module also attests to a more targeted London-French identity and audience through typographical amendment and lexical economy. Punctuation again functions socio-semiotically, with the exclamation mark after the 2011 'Welcome!' replaced by a typed 'smiley face':) in the 2014 capture. The revision illustrates the blogger's praxial distancing from French writing conventions and her purposeful adoption of a more playful typographic form (Vaisman, 2011). Punctuation as mode therefore reflects Aurélie's normative performativity of perceived 'English' humoristic traits, alluded to repeatedly by my on-land participants, such as Charles's comment that 'the English have a sense of self-deprecation which the French don't have at all'. Aurélie's motivated punctuation choice

(Kress, 2010) thereby illustrates her attempt to position herself within a culturally delineated London-French diasberspace, rather than in 'a post-geographically bounded global' network (Alonso and Oiarzabal, 2018: 250). In this way, the blog plays out the chronotopic identity work alluded to by Blommaert and De Fina (2017), whereby identity construction is shaped by time–space specificity. Aurélie's ostensibly inconsequential playful typographic alteration consequently speaks of the spatio-temporal situatedness of her diasporic lived experience, but equally of profound belonging aspirations and a desire to script her own 'diasporic story' (Appadurai, 2019: 562).

Compounding the blog's functionality as a 'self-realisation narrative' (Benson and O'Reilly, 2009: 610) are the post-publication modifications made to the sidebar Welcome paragraph. The 2014 version is a considerably abbreviated iteration of its former self, again more characteristic of English rhetorical norms than French. Gone is the redundant use of synonym and adjectival description whose sole purpose is to add stylistic weight to the sentence. 'Ce blog est dédié au partage de bons plans divers et variés pour profiter au mieux de la superbe capitale british' (This blog is dedicated to sharing diverse and varied top tips to make the most of the superb British capital) is condensed down to 'Ce blog a pour objectif premier le partage de bons plans sur Londres' (The main aim of this blog is to share top tips about London), followed by several concrete examples. This discursive shift from the ornate and superlative to the streamlined and concrete is consistent with the types of changes made when translating and/ or adapting information from French into English (referred to as 'transduction' by Kress, 2010). In the 2014 instance, we therefore note a peculiar form of translanguaging, with semantic content coded in the French language, but the lexical and syntactic simplification expressing the incorporation of English communicative praxis. As such, the web element reflects both habitus transformation, regarding Aurélie's writing habits, as well as metafunctional repurposing. Although the text has not been translated into the 'official language' of the postmigration habitat, the stylistic adaptation towards English writing conventions is indicative of an interpersonal and ideational function now more directed towards a London-French audience than in 2011.

Accentuating this shift, the exaggerated Anglo-French lexical hybridisation of the 2011 text, brought about by liberal French-English code-switching, is gone. While superficially indicative of *less* culturo-linguistic blending over time, I argue, on the contrary, that the repeated integration of English lexical items in the 2011 French Welcome text was a self-conscious act to portray a fashionable and 'connected' blogger, au fait with the English terms used in the originary field, itself suggestive of Aurélie's initial prioritisation of a Franco-French audience. Therein lies the paradox. As observed previously (Huc-Hepher, 2016), the almost involuntary, habituated code-switching that occurs among long-standing French Londoners for the sake of efficiency or non-equivalence is very different from the code-switching practised by French non-movers. The former, according to Sadia, incorporate English in their French spontaneously, when 'the English word actually comes first, and then the equivalent ends up not coming at all'. The latter, however, voluntarily make use of English terms for stylistic effect, which explains why on-land participants are perceived to be 'snobbish' and contrived when pre-reflexively peppering French sentences with English words on return visits to France. The affectation is evidenced in the 2011 snapshot, where 'british' [*sic*] and 'enjoy' appear in French sentences, both of which have easily accessible alternatives in French, and therefore relay a manufactured evocation of 'cool Britannia' (Favell, 2008a: 143). Conversely, in the 2014 version, 'shopping' is the only English word used in the web element. Irrespective of the term's entry into standardised Franco-French vocabulary, here it is relied upon principally for efficiency rather than symbolic effect, as its French translation would be one of several three-word phrases. Thus, the affected linguistic 'style' of the 2011 instance has been replaced by sparser, British substance in the integrated – and updated – blog 'archive', again illustrating an interpersonal refocusing from Franco-French to London-French audiences, as well as a sense of the blogger being more culturally aware and linguistically 'at home'.

Focusing on visual and written form over message in the Londres Calling and Good Morning London blogs has therefore confirmed Vaisman's contention that 'digital texts could be regarded as objects to look at rather than to look through for their meaning' (Vaisman, 2011: 179) and that typography should not be apprehended 'as an abstract sign system, but as a situated code choice, which is always part of a specific genre in a specific communicative situation' (2011: 179). Similarly, the multimodal analysis has substantiated Li Wei's (2018) assertion that translanguaging functions as a 'Thirdspace' beyond the bilingual hybridity observed in the 2011 version of Londres Calling's Welcome paragraph. By exploring the semiotic depths of modal materiality, I have demonstrated how the diasberspace both reproduces and transcends territorialisation. Coded ingroup iconography inscribed 'a discrete field of taste and distinction' (Werbner, 2018: 146), whereas typographic translanguaging has surpassed the boundaries of affected binary code-switching and instead enabled the implicit articulation of habitus subjectivities (Collins, 2009). This sheds light on changing migrant embedding and interpersonal relationships with imagined London-French and homeland blogging communities. As Appadurai (2019: 563) eloquently asserts:

Operating outside the official spheres of both the home society and the new society, the migrant archive cannot afford the illusion that traces are accidents, that documents arrive on their own and that archives are repositories of the luck of material survival. Rather, the migrant archive is a continuous and conscious work of the imagination, seeking in collective memory an ethical basis for the sustainable reproduction of cultural identities in the new society.

This section has brought to bear the archival traces of intentional expressive choices and the identity narratives emerging from such residues. In the next and final section, I deliberately turn to the accidental, seeking meaning in the technological boundaries and fragments of memory in archived blogs.

Technological scope and limitations: Good Morning London – About and Home Sweet London

Just as form has been seen to take on semiotic weight, so developments in the technical and navigational affordances of blogs have meaning-making potential. In the 2011 snapshot of the Good Morning London 'About' page (Figure 26), the navigation menu options are limited to three: 'Accueil' (Welcome), 'A Propos' (About) and 'Contact'. By 2014 (Figure 27), they have more than doubled, with eight tab headers leading to other spaces deeper within the blog and digitally embodying the changing praxial and objectivated habitus of the blogger. Despite the About page, captured in 2014, being dated 30 September 2011, we are presented with features that did not exist in 2011, including 'Shopping', 'Food', 'Sorties' (Going Out), 'En dehors de Londres' (Outside London) and a 'Blogroll'.

The greater intratextual navigational scope of the 2014 version, enabled by the platform, bears witness to transformation in all three facets of the habitus triad. Aurélie's evolving dining and purchasing habits are materialised through the 'Food' and 'Shopping' pages. Her increasingly broad London habitat is represented by the 'Sorties' (Going Out), 'En dehors de Londres' (Outside London) tabs, the scope of which dispels myths about the French community's exclusive South Kensington positioning. Meanwhile, Aurélie's habituation to spontaneous London-French translanguaging is expressed through the navigation menu lexis: standard French lexical items ('A propos', 'Sorties') are juxtaposed with standardised Franco-French anglicisms, such as 'Shopping' and, importantly, the non-standard use of arguably 'London-French' anglicisms, such 'Food'. Regardless of publications such as *Le Fooding* guide (Kelly, 2016), launched in 2000 and now competing with Michelin, 'Food' remains a somewhat alien anglicism in standard French. Phonetically shorter and semantically broader than its French-language counterpart (*nourriture*), 'Food'

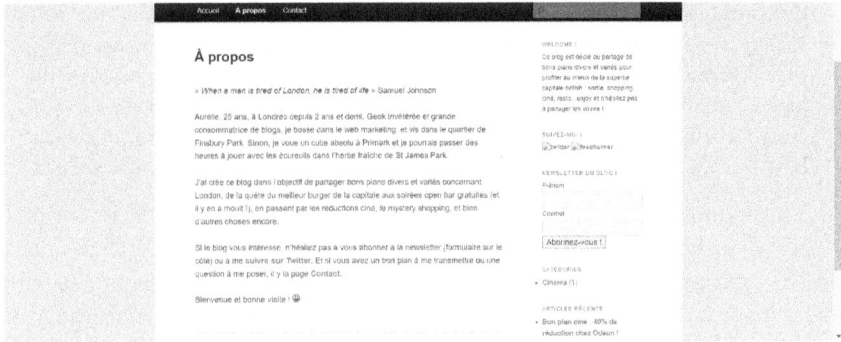

Figure 26 The Good Morning London 'About' page, captured 2011

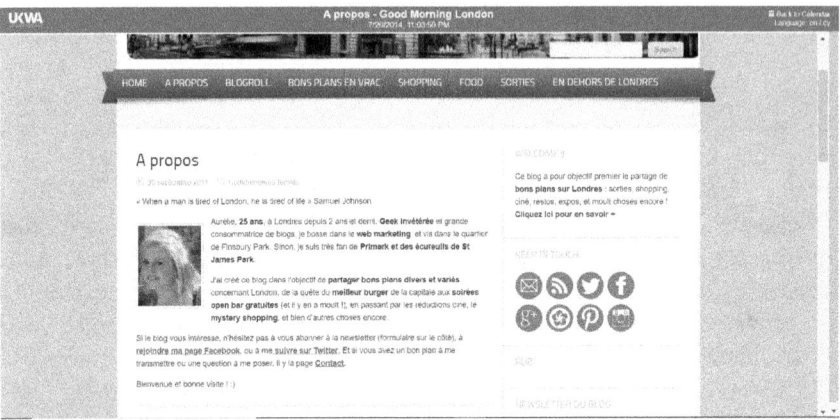

Figure 27 The Good Morning London 'About' page, captured 2014

corresponds to the economy-based code-switching characteristic of the London-French on-land linguistic space. Moreover, it is telling that Aurélie did not use the inflected and affected term 'fooding', whose gerund form ('ing') positions it in a decidedly Franco-French context, as Léa confirms in a blogpost dedicated to 'false anglicisms': 'The French seem particularly fond of -ing words' (Teuscher, 2014). Conversely, highly colloquial and idiomatic Franco-French wording, such as 'Bons plans en vrac' (Loads of top tips) would elude and therefore exclude most non-native French speakers. As such, we note that 'the (re)production of these imagined communities *online* is characterised by the very practices of inclusion and exclusion that haunt the imagining and performing of national, ethnic and other affiliations *offline*' (Collins, 2009: 842; original emphasis). Structural changes to the blog have thus instigated greater sociolinguistic complexity, attesting to Aurélie's continued attachment to, and self-identification with, her premigration Frenchness, alongside London-French community embedding.

Further alterations to the technical affordances of the 2014 capture (Figure 27) are noticeable in the more explicitly modular layout of the web object. Written information is now framed by visible lines, signifying an additional departure from a traditional, physical diary page (Domingo *et al.*, 2015), but the most patent difference in the 2014 orchestration is the photograph. Placed in 'prime' reading position on the left of the text, it gives Aurélie a physical presence denied in the original version, either through former technological limitations or blogger design. Its inclusion suggests Aurélie's increasingly settled sense of self within the diasporic space and her conception of the blog as a 'digital harbor' (Alonso and Oiarzabal, 2018: 247; Appadurai, 2019), where identity can be agentively, yet securely performed (Asenbaum, 2019). The headshot therefore confirms the blog's function as a digital 'safe house', 'where groups can constitute themselves as horizontal, homogenous, sovereign communities with high degrees of trust' (Pratt, 1991: 40) and relative protection from anti-French microaggressions in the broader postmigration space (Huc-Hepher, 2019). Accordingly, it testifies to blogs' operationalisation as diasberspaces where community members can 'construct shared understandings, knowledges, claims on the world that they can then bring into the contact zone' (Pratt, 1991: 40; de Backer, 2019), underlining the importance of preserving such voices in national web archives (Huc-Hepher and Wells, 2021).

A final, technologically motivated, development on the About page is the increased number of extratextual (hyper)links to social media platforms, a manifestation of their growing interpersonal and ideational roles in on-line and on-land environments. The icons' prominence – emphasised by the colour red – is tantamount to the very real risk they pose to the 'life expectancy' of the blog, as convincingly demonstrated by Quentin Lobbé's research on 'dead' diasporic blogs (2018; forthcoming) and evidenced by the 'live' but dormant state of Good Morning London, Lost in London and Home Sweet London blogs, apparently not updated since 2017. The module heading, which has shifted from a somewhat dogmatic 'Suivez-moi' (Follow me) to a more genial 'Keep in Touch', is also testimony to Aurélie's habituation to postmigration politeness codes (discussed in Chapter 3), comfortableness in the English language and reoriented audience. Finally, the module's unfaithfulness to the born-digital object, owing to the absence of an icon in the 2014 reborn-digital version, indicates the deficiency to which web archives often fall victim. While the 'link rot' (Ben-David, 2019: 317) is not overly detrimental in this instance, such omissions are potentially critical in multimodal web analyses, where every detail has the potential to carry meaning.

The impact of such visual incompleteness is demonstrated unequivocally in the Home Sweet London blog's founding post. As Winters asserts, '[i]mages are one of the elements of a web page which the crawl process is more likely to fail to capture, and the absence of metadata or alternative text confers invisibility' (2017: 243). While some visibility is provided by the blogpost title, the effects of the visual lacunae are severe. In the 2011 Internet Archive capture (Figure 28), the compositionally dominant set of five Carter Steam Fair photographs has been preserved, affording the multimodal sign-recipient a tangible sense of the funfair's material reality, tinged with an air of nostalgia produced by the monochrome shades. In the 2014 UK Web Archive capture of the same blogpost, however, all traces of the photographs have disappeared (Figure 29).

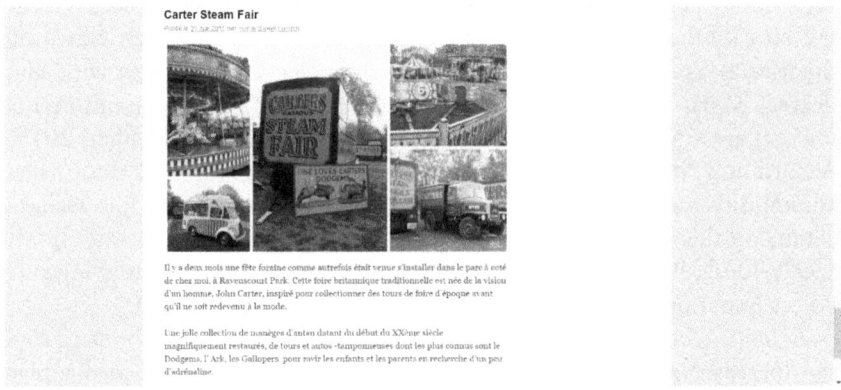

Figure 28 Inaugural Home Sweet London blogpost, captured 2011

Figure 29 Inaugural Home Sweet London blogpost, captured 2014

According to the blogpost, John Carter was a collector of early twentieth-century fairground trappings, so the choice to present the image-grid photographs in black-and-white plays into the antiquated ambience. Functioning as a mode within the visual mode (Ravelli and van Leeuwen, 2018), the monochrome hues operate intermodally with the iconography and written text, whose semantic field is predominantly 'old'. Lexis such as 'autrefois' (yesteryear), 'traditionnelle', 'd'époque' (vintage) and 'd'antan' (of old) peppers the seven-line post, reinforcing its historic messaging in the same way that the black-and-white images convey the wistful quaintness of the bygone fair. The enigmatic mood orchestrated by these multimodal dynamics creates a temporality and affective atmosphere (de Backer, 2019) redolent of Jeff Hall's photographic world. Serving as a visual oxymoron, the immobile funfair therefore embodies Barthes's conceptualisation of a photograph as the living image of something dead and transports the visual here-and-now back to a frozen, lifeless then (Barthes, 1980). The photographs' multiple reborn incarnations in the web archive and infinite semiotic potential (Kress, 2010; Ankerson, 2019) only intensify their haunting effects. Unlike moving images, the still photographs 'throttle' time (Barthes, 1980: 142), imparting an inherent melancholy (1980: 142). It is this melancholic quality of the colourless and motionless fairground that infuses the blogpost with nostalgia, a nostalgia which also speaks of the blogger's 'placial' migratory experience (Gieles, 2009: 276) and displaced longing (Appadurai, 2019). Reigniting living memories of a temporally and spatially remote childhood (Collins, 2009), the mournful funfair imagery reflects the migrant's present dislocated state, torn between suppressed regret for a dead past and the rose-tinted aspirations of the inspired mover, connoted through the pink blog background, sugary cup-cake-and-rose-ornamented 2014 banner and the blog name: Home Sweet London.

Underlining the memory-laden imagery's affective potency, when asking on-land participants what they miss most about the homeland, it is not places that are evoked, but people (Walsh, 2018), as Brice encapsulates: 'What do I miss most? Not a lot … Friends, family.' The emotional pulls and time–space tensions of the blog therefore challenge the spatio-temporal collapsing commonly associated with diasporic digital media production (Kele, 2016; Alonso and Oiarzabal, 2018) and instead confirm Retis and Tsagarousianou's underlining of the situatedness and ethnospecificity of contemporary migrant media use, 'grounding them in translocal spaces' (2019: 6). These spatio-temporal tensions also support Appadurai's contention that migrant archives are 'site[s] of negotiation between … memory and desire' (2019: 563), which should be apprehended 'not only as storehouses of memory but also as aspirational maps' (2019: 564).

In view of the semiotic vibrancy of the 2011 capture of the blogger's snapshots, the disappearance of the photographic ensemble from the 'same' blogpost preserved in the LFSC in 2014 is negatively significant. In the 2014 instance, all that remains of this telling, intermodally meaningful, set of images is an absence, reminiscent of the absence of people in the fairground photographs and of absent loved-ones in the premigration space. A geographical sense of place is specified through the reference to the fairground being set up 'dans le parc à côté de chez moi à Ravenscourt Park' (in the park near where I live in Ravenscourt Park). Yet, this useful textual clarification as to the blogger's external habitat (non-South-Kensington, but west London again) is *missing* the silent meanings conveyed through the images, relating to the blogger's internalised habitus and sense of (be)longing (Levin, 2016). The importance of a macro-archiving system that can preserve the micro-modal detail of the born-digital web objects is thus substantiated.

Conclusion

Taking a multi-archival, cross-temporal, comparative approach, and concentrating on form rather than content, my fine-grained socio-semiotic analysis has succeeded in confirming habitus transformation. Teasing out the multimodal meaning-making of the five London-French blogs revealed a shift from Franco-French outsider to London-French insider, in a matter of only three to five years. Subtle changes in the webpages or web elements uncovered the progressive targeting of a like-minded audience, capable of tapping into the same unsaid, habituated, culturo-linguistic references as the bloggers, and therefore connoting the existence of a particular London-French community identity (Collins, 2009). The blogs' intertextual coherence and analogous reconfigurations implied a community of London-French blogging practice that mirrored the commonality of the bloggers' on-land environment and subjectivities. Articulated visually and textually, their multimodal geonarratives spoke of (south)west London material habitats and consequently of a more affluent sub-category of the London-French community than the 'hip', to borrow Miranda's wording, East-End French or London-wide hospitality employees. Confirming Asenbaum's contention that the internet is intrinsically corporeal, and hence gendered, classed and raced (2019), the blogs' exclusive geographic positioning reflected the social positioning of the bloggers, arguably possessing the luxury of time needed to update their blogs. However, the narrow typology may also have been a corollary of the prevalence of their freelancing in media-related fields, suggesting the manipulation of blogs as (self-)promotional tools.

This leads to one of the most striking patterns that emerged: the blogs, without exception, belonged to women. Reflecting the on-land gender imbalance noted by Bellion (2005), it was a discovery that allowed me to draw conclusions about the women's empowered use of technology and repurposing of their blogs. The functional reconceptualisation, from personal log to commercial device, was, I posited, a form of xenofeminist expression, entirely consistent with the agency required to migrate internationally. Another pattern observed was a predilection for 'hand-drafted' imagery in blog banners, testifying to the status and embeddedness of the *bande dessinée* (comic strip) in French culture and blogger habitus.

However, beyond the collective-memory and sub-community bonding functionality of such pictographics, they served as outlets for 'identity expression, contributing to integration and … security' (Brinkerhoff, 2009: 203). Fixed within the imagery were messages about the bloggers' place-making practices, their increased ownership of the city and, importantly, their engagement with London's green and blue spaces. These emerged as sites not only of well-being, but as spaces embodying London's habitability and security (Bell *et al.*, 2017), the affective and normative affordances (Mulholland and Ryan, 2017) of which ultimately contributed to a sense of safety, belonging and feeling at home (Collins, 2009). Food was also a symbolic leitmotif running across the LFSC blogs, from the teapot of Wonderland or the Marmite and ice-creams of Londres Calling to the 'Food' tab in Good Morning London and the Home Sweet London cupcake. The culinary presence was consistent with its place in French culture, but equally illustrative of the cultural dynamics occurring in the diasporic field (Bodomo and Ma, 2012). Constituting a celebration of *English* rather than French comestibles, the banner iconography pointed to the bloggers' habituated adoption of London eating habits and the materialisation of a hybrid habitus, embodied most literally by the food blog entitled 'Pauline à la crème anglaise' (which escaped analysis in this chapter).

In short, 'thinking small' effectively bridged some of the 'knowledge gaps' (Wang, 2013b: 1) between Big Data and sociocultural meaning-making. My ethnosemiotic unpicking of the multimodal materiality knitted into a modest corpus of archived blogs provided a qualitative alternative to the numeric data fundamentalism (Crawford, 2013) and digital positivism (Fuchs, 2017) to which the sprawling web archives could easily lend themselves. It was also fruitful in revealing the interplay between internalised and externalised lived experience, with the London-French subjectivities and objectivities materialised in the blogs (Asenbaum, 2019) testifying to increasing embeddedness in London. Yet, as Bourdieu (1980a) asserts, their habitus transformation was shown to be incomplete, giving rise to a 'certain permanence in … self-identification even if the multilocal context increases

[the] possibilities of identification, experiences and assignations' (Duchêne-Lacroix and Koukoutsaki-Monnier, 2016: 137). Thus, while acknowledging the limits and implications of hybridity, overall the 2014 blog snaphsots incarnated a common hybrid London-French habitus, where a shared repertoire of English and French languages, identities and understandings were performed. Through the coded sign systems of their blogs and the evolving language practices observed, moving from affected code-switching to more organic translanguaging, the migrants were not seen to be torn between two cultures, but to embody both through a merging of French and British habits, habitats and attitudes. This gave rise to a sense of community and personal growth. At least, that is the message the bloggers constructed. For, as Kress (2010) reminds us, all signs are motivated, and they are motivated by interest (Bourdieu, 1994). Wittingly or not, the affective atmosphere created in the London-French blogosphere was increasingly hybrid, mirroring the on-land experience of my participants, as Catherine epitomises: 'I don't feel torn between the two countries, I have integrated both now, I've found a good balance.'

Conclusion

Through the chapters of this book, I hope to have taken the reader on a journey that has provided insights into the lived experience of French residents in London in the 2010s, but significantly in the years preceding the 2016 EU membership referendum. With all that has come to pass politically since then, my original fieldwork now looks and feels disproportionately distant, so much so that these pages read more as a contemporary history than a present-day ethnography. Capturing and recording the appeal of London at a time when it was perceived to be the multicultural capital of Europe, open to its neighbours who looked on with admiration, is thus all the more valuable. For, as I write this conclusion, Boris Johnson has taken his 'Brexit' project to completion and the voices that shouted for 'Remain' outside the Houses of Parliament for three years following the Referendum have fallen ominously silent. Nobody knows what the future holds, but net migration from the EU fell dramatically in 2019 (ONS), rendering this book a snapshot of a time I suspect is irretrievably lost.

A distinctive mobility

As I posited in the opening pages of this monograph, the French are a chronically under-researched migrant group, leading a collective double life as both highly visible and invisible players in the postmigration space. Their distinctive privilege, as 'old' migrants (Lulle *et al.*, 2018: 2) in possession of extensive cultural capital, masks the complexity of their mobility, which, as these chapters have demonstrated, is messy, heterogeneous, ambiguous and processual. Semi-agentively suspended between 'home' and 'host' cultures, the performativity of their emplacement has also emerged as distinctive, normative even (Mulholland and Ryan, 2017). Homeland practices deemed more authentic (Benson, 2011) and thus morally superior, such as eating homemade foods according to prescribed rituals, were shown to be maintained, whereas excessive 'host' drinking habits were rejected, due to 'a fundamental lack of fit [... with French] drinking practices' (2011: 144). Similarly, 'host' habits considered to morally outstrip those of the premigration space, like politeness codes, demedicalised healthcare or multicultural restaurant dining were selected as worthy substitutes for insensitive, outmoded or overly conservative originary alternatives. In this way, participants were seen to 'cherry pick' aspects of their identity they wished to reinvent (Conradson and Latham, 2007) and to cherish those they felt provided a stable sense of premigration 'French' selfhood within a shifting diasporic space.

Equally distinctive was the book's theoretical contribution to migration literature. Though Bourdieusian thought has been repeatedly deployed to address changing rates of (cultural/symbolic/social) capital across pre- and postmigration fields (Erel, 2010; de Haas, 2010; Ryan, 2011; Carlson, 2018; Wessendorf, 2018) or to explain a propensity for migration through mobility capital (Murphy Lejeune, 2001, 2002; Scott, 2006), and habitus has been used to understand migrant positioning and identity within the diasporic space (Kelly and Lusis, 2006; Benson and O'Reilly, 2009; Oliver and O'Reilly, 2010; Benson, 2011; Cohen, 2014; Duchêne-Lacroix and Koukoutsaki-Monnier, 2016), the concepts of symbolic violence and hysteresis have been drawn on less frequently, with some notable exceptions (Lopez Rodriguez, 2010; Noble, 2013; Cornejo Torres and Rosales Ubeda, 2015; Wessendorf and Phillimore, 2018). Clearly, and intentionally, there is overlap between all these concepts, and I have explicitly embraced this theoretical breadth and dynamism within these chapters, while exploring the conceptual depth of each. For example, to account for the full reach of Bourdieu's habitus construct, I subdivided it into three interconnecting component parts: habitat, habituation and habits. This allowed me to drill down into the materiality of the migration environment, but also to probe internalised homemaking and settlement practices, while acknowledging the subconscious dimension of mobility, emplacement and identity. Through this triadic habitus lens, several key themes emerged, notably, a coincidental 'common-unity' of practice (Wenger, 1998, 2004; Cox, 2005) which belied consciously individuated narratives; a tension between agency and passivity; the processual nature of mobility and settlement; together with spatial ambivalence and cultural hybridity.

Moreover, by apprehending the microaggressions to which participants testified within a wider framework of symbolic violence (Huc-Hepher, 2019), the detrimental effects of explicit negation and implicit complicity were revealed, as were underlying migration and emplacement forces. Similarly, as a by-product of habituation, the relevance of hysteresis to the sense of unease experienced by respondents was evinced. Contrary to previous applications, the disquieting sensation rarely emerged in relation to 'the disruption between *habitus* and *field*' (Hardy, 2012: 127; original emphasis) in the postmigration space (Huc-Hepher and Lyczba, forthcoming), but during encounters with the homeland. Thus, through hysteresis, an unthinking embeddedness in pre-2016 London was brought to light. Consulting the Epilogue completing this book will confirm whether that persists in a post-EU-membership referendum context.

Intimate subjectivities, temporalities and spatialities

In response to Walsh's call for a more holistic approach to 'intimate subjectivities and the collective cultural discourses about intimacy that shape our everyday lives' (2018: 145), I homed in on individual friendships and families to gain a broader understanding of how such relationships influence embedding and settlement (Ryan, 2018). Humour and language were found to be key in the creation of affective bonds, serving to exclude participants from local friendship groups (Westcott and Vazquez Maggio, 2016) and strengthen ties with other French Londoners, whose common primary habitus functioned as a barrier to integration and diver of community formation. Similarly, children's schooling proved decisive in longer-term emplacement processes. Migrant parents' preference for the constructivist epistemology (Lea *et al.*, 2003) of the UK education system, based on confidence-building individualism, over the positivism of the didactic French model, experienced as dehumanising institutionalism, coupled with their desire not to disrupt the educational trajectories of their progeny once settled in either system, resulted in unintended settlement within the diasporic space.

The creep of habituation and its mobilising potency also emerged earlier in participants' migration journeys. By assessing migration over multiple temporalities and spatialities, looking back at the premigration educational, professional and social spaces, and subsequently focusing on the postmigration present, I uncovered both explicit and, more uniquely, implicit drivers stemming from symbolic violence in France. Beneath the typical migration pulls, such as English language acquisition or job opportunities, participants' narratives exposed potent ideological pushes, including the downside of Republican universalism, rigid hierarchical workplace stratification, the grip of nepotism, social and symbolic capital, together with racialised and gendered microaggressions. Countering neo-classical structuralist and functionalist migration discourses (Wang, 2013a), my findings thus foregrounded the affective influences underpinning French mobility to London, as well as the pre-reflexive forces that planted the migration seed and paved the way for longer-term settlement, emerging, as an 'undeliberate determinacy' (McGhee *et al.*, 2017).

Prefacing my examination of the here-and-now of participants' everyday lived experience with the there-and-then of their premigration habitus also allowed localised belonging to surface. The 'habitus-turned-habitat' prism (Bourdieu, [1972] 2000; Friedmann, 2005: 328) effectively opened a view on to 'transnational' subjectivities and ambivalent belonging (Benson, 2011). However, the materiality of London-French homes foregrounded spatial specificity, with particular regions, cities, homes or lands emplacing participants in a translocal environment rather than a transnational one per se (Smith, 2001; White, 2011). Examining homemaking practices in various sites, from the intimate and mediated spaces of participants' London abodes to the online 'diasberspaces' of the London-French blogosphere, confirmed both the stubborn durability of the originary habitus (Bourdieu, 1980a) and the normative geographies configured in collective London-French imaginings (Mulholland and Ryan, 2017). Respondents' mobility aspirations were impressed upon the diasporic space such that France, and particularly Paris, emerged as hostile, unsafe, judgemental and segregated, whereas London was perceived to be open, secure, liberated and (super)diverse. An affective sense of settlement therefore produced a sensation of embeddedness and, crucially, feeling at home in London.

Blended meanings

An important finding of my on-land fieldwork was how participants bridged the spaces of postmigration here/now and premigration there/ then through the construction of mediascapes (Appadurai, 1990) and soundscapes (Schafer, [1977] 1994). Facilitated by the rise of the internet, which coincided with the implementation of the Maastricht Treaty (1992), granting free movement of people across EU member states, the inauguration of the Eurostar and Channel Tunnel (1994), and the introduction of budget airlines such as easyJet and Ryanair (1995), connectivity with the homeland was without precedent. By the 2010s, London had been elevated to global-city status and migration from France was administratively, logistically and technologically routine. Participants were observed filling their everyday lives with the sounds, language, laughter and culturo-historic references of France by using immersive communication technologies in a manner capable of challenging their very mobility. Alonso and Oiarzabal claim that on 'the Internet, all of us are "immigrants"' (2018: 251); yet, the opposite is equally true: through the internet, none of us are immigrants, for movers remain closely connected to the premigration space, letting it imbue their quotidian lives and using web-based technologies to transcend physical time-space divides (2018: 251). Consequently, the internet, as a 'digital ... harbor for contemporary immigrants' (2018: 247), was afforded an important place in this book. British culinary practices were seen to impact the on-land premigration space through the mediated transfer of recipes, thereby challenging France's place as the world's gastronomic leader and illustrating the cultural reach of contemporary migration (Cohen and Sirkeci, 2011). Likewise, London's French 'digital diaspora' were observed creating a community of bloggers, who exploited the platforms 'to re-create identities, share opportunities, spread their culture, [and] influence homeland and host-land' audiences (Alonso and Oiarzabal, 2018: 251). Embedding the digital within this ethnography was thus central to my research objectives and has allowed the book to make an important contribution to the field of ethnography more broadly, crossing disciplinary boundaries through its innovative ethnosemiotic framework.

Notwithstanding Bourdieu's rejection of the deterministic *structuralist* semiotics characteristic of the French School, my blended analysis of London-French institutional websites and personal blogs demonstrated the compatibility of ethnography and semiotics (Kress, 2011). Adopting the *social* semiotics advocated by Hodge, van Leeuwen and Kress (Hodge and Kress, 1988; Kress and van Leeuwen, 1996, 2001; van Leeuwen, 2005; Kress, 2010; Ravelli and van Leeuwen, 2018) and combining it with the ethnographic holism prescribed by Bourdieu (Bourdieu and Wacquant, 1992), enabled the acknowledgement of 'indigenous orders of signification and genres of representation' (Atkinson, 2005: 9), together with the 'material order ... encoded in systems of places and spaces [... which] ethnographic reportage seems oddly lacking in' (2005: 9). As Vannini (2007) contends, the marriage between ethnography and social semiotics is a natural union owing to both sets of researchers' shared sensibilities regarding empiricism, induction, empathy, reflexivity and subjectivity. And as Dicks *et al.* reiterate, 'ethnographers and social semioticians are interested in examining the diversity of resources that people use in their everyday worlds, and both do so from a perspective that favours social over cognitive explanation' (2011: 228), recognising 'socially meaningful practices' and 'systems of doings, not of beings' (Lemke, 2002: 2, 3). It is my hope, then, that the 'analytic tactics' (Sassen, 2013: 211) used in this book, geared towards on-land and on-line 'doings', serve as an ethnosemiotic template applicable to other studies, cultures, practices and (digital) materialities.

It is important to note that, whether school websites or personal blogs, these internet-based diasporic spaces functioned as microcosms for the wider London-French experience. The xenophobic microaggressions and 'immigration au féminin' (Salcedo Robledo, 2019: 174) observed in the on-land environment, were reconfigured on-line, with quasi egalitarian inequalities subtly reproduced on the French Lycée website and third-wave feminist practices, such as agentive repurposing and technological empowerment (Hester, 2018), evidenced in the all-women London-French blogs. Both the pull of London, through its confidence-building individualism, meritocracy and opportunity, and the push of France, through its symbolic exclusivity and (post)colonial 'expatriate continuities' (Fechter and Walsh, 2010: 1,197), were seen to be replicated in the diasberspace. Similarly, the 'affective atmosphere' (de Backer, 2019) of London as a destination place (Atkinson, 2005) was (re)presented digitally, whether in terms of its green and blue spaces acting as 'security landscapes' (Bell *et al.*, 2017; Hopkins *et al.*, 2019;) or its rich cultural offering, denoted stylistically and substantially. The multimodal analysis also revealed the migrants' habituation to local practices and mindsets over time, with bloggers blending into the local environment and 'able to escape their migrant status through the demonstration of their cultural fluency' (Benson, 2011: 141). However, as seen in their on-land habitat, their 'repertoire of choices and actions' (Ryan and Sales, 2013: 92) were also defined by circumstance, and the bloggers' cultural and linguistic situatedness ultimately constrained the hybridisation noted in the London-French blogosphere. My blended ethnosemiotic methodology therefore constituted a compelling triangulation tool, substantiating on-land findings, while proffering more nuanced insights into migrant positioning, belonging and community-making.

Future avenues

This book has paved the way for several future lines of enquiry, beginning with a return to the phenomenon of symbolic violence. In the shadow of the 2016 EU membership referendum and Britain's exit from the European Union in 2020, a logical step would be to re-evaluate my findings and assess the impact of the transformed sociopolitical climate on return migration levels and on migrants' sense of belonging, safety and feeling welcome in the city they once called home. I make a small-scale attempt at this in the Epilogue which follows this Conclusion, but the seriousness, perniciousness and relative obscurity of anti-EU-resident xenophobia warrants a larger, possibly pan-EU-27 migration study. Second, should 'Brexit' anxieties be causing a return migration phenomenon (as the *French Morning London* podcast series 'Moi Impat' suggests) an investigation into returnee 'destablized habitus' (Ingram and Abrahams, 2016: 148) and the 'reverse hysteresis' effect I proposed in Chapter 3 would be sociopolitically edifying. Redeploying the ethnosemiotic methodology successfully applied here, the research could examine the on-line and on-land 'impatriate' spaces of France, with field positioning and adjustments assessed in situ.

The formal confines of this monograph prevented the inclusion of link analysis findings, so a third exploratory pathway could be the application of these innovative, semi-quantitative methods to the school websites examined in Chapter 5 and potentially to other London-French community resources. Alternative link analysis ideas include an appraisal of the inward and outward links connected to French-domain and UK-domain food blogs, for example, or a comparison of London-French church websites, to ascertain which has more links, and hence closer ties, with the pre- or post-migration space. A fourth and final extension of the ethnosemiotic work presented here would be to target London-French sub-communities, such as migrants of Colour, faith minorities (Jewish, Muslim and/or Christian – Catholic and Evangelical), LGBTQ+ groups, or recent mothers, all of whose presence became apparent during the course of my fieldwork, but who each warrant more dedicated scholarly attention.

With these future projects in mind and the satisfaction of having given the city speech (Sassen, 2013) through the voices of my on-land and on-line participants, 'making presence to rescue [… them] from the silence of absence, invisibility, [and] the virtual/representational eviction from membership of the city' (2013: 217) and from much migration scholarship, it is now necessary to bring this monograph to a close. To that end, it is fitting to recall a statement by Bourdieu and posit that the study has been successful in conveying 'an empirical reality, historically located and dated' (Bourdieu: 1996: 8), and one that transcends the reductionist prisms through which migrant communities are so often apprehended. Rather than conclude with a sentence that condenses this culturally nuanced and multifaceted London community to 'an anonymous mass of people' (Mazzara, 2015: 449), as is so often the case in today's purposefully 'hostile environment' (Home Office), I therefore return to the final words of my research participants themselves. For them, in response to my final 'London-in-a-nutshell' interview question, London was ultimately an 'exciting', 'dynamic', 'diverse' and 'free' city, where you could be yourself and do so with the 'solidarity' of the community at large. It remains to be seen whether this is still the case.

Epilogue: 'Brexit blues'

Since beginning my research on the French community in London and drafting much of this book, the city and its habitants have been struck by a major quake. Not a geological seism, but a political tremor of a magnitude many Londoners had not predicted and that shook them to their core. I refer, of course, to the 2016 EU membership referendum. Carving deep chasms between family members, friends, neighbours and political parties, the aftershocks of the referendum remain active. As the British wife of a French migrant in London and mother of two children who wear their dual British-French heritage with pride and affection, the impact of the referendum was particularly powerful and inescapably personal. Importantly, its repercussions also extended to the findings presented in this book. I have asked myself whether my participants' rose-tinted view of London and their normative criticisms of France still ring true today. Or have the tables been turned? Could the effects of one fateful day have shattered their sense of belonging to such an extent that they no longer feel welcome in London and have sought refuge in sociopolitically more clement climes?

To begin answering these questions, I returned to the field, reconnecting with my original research sites and participants. Some were quick to respond positively, others were willing but not forthcoming, and many, in keeping with Rzepnikowska's experience (2019), did not respond at all. Time has moved on, email addresses have changed and the hostile climate may have taken its toll. In addition to the handful of participants able to contribute, I therefore drew on a variety of other primary sources. Echoing the mixed-methods approach I took in the first wave of this research, I began by distributing a short, open-ended questionnaire at a Settlement Scheme Public Briefing organised by the French consulate and hosted by the French Institute. I then invited several respondents of my original survey to take part in an email interview. Subsequently, I conducted four, semi-structured interviews in person or by telephone and, finally, I returned to my blog corpus in search of explicit and implicit 'Brexit' musings.

Given the 'seismic socio-political' proportions of the 2016 referendum result (Gawlewicz and Sotkasiira (2019: 3), there has been a multiplication of research outputs related to the phenomenon. In 2017, the BrExpats: Freedom of Movement, Citizenship and Brexit in the Lives of Britons Resident in the European Union project was launched to explore the affective and material impact of Brexit on migrants outside the UK. One arm of the project investigates those based in France and has resulted in a paper which usefully conceptualises Brexit as a process, according to which 'hierarchies of European belonging' (Benson, 2019: 513) are established 'by a politics of bordering that sorts "deserving Europeans" from "undeserving Europeans" (2019: 505). In 2019, an edifying 'Negotiating Brexit' Special Issue was published in *Population, Space and Place*, covering a range of diasporas and locations, from 'old' and 'new' UK-based EU migrants, to British migrants in Spain. Most relevant to my work, however, is Brahic and Lallement's (2018) research on French residents in Manchester. Focusing on the concept of resilience and participants' coping strategies, such as flexibility, they underscore the emotional impact of the referendum, the intensity of which is associated with length of stay, degree of embeddedness in the postmigration space and time elapsed since 2016.

The work of Lulle *et al.* (2018) on Irish, Italian and Romanian migrants in the London region, and McGhee *et al.* (2017) on the UK's Polish population, is more explicitly oriented towards the future and offers several convincing conceptual tools. The former apprehends 'Brexit' as a 'rupture' within the framework of previously 'liquid' intra-EU migration (Lulle *et al.*, 2018: 1); whereas the latter, quantitative in approach, notes a transformation from 'deliberate indeterminacy' (McGhee *et al.*, 2017: 2,111), as discussed in Chapter 3, to 'undeliberate determinacy' (2017: 2,124), with migrants' settlement plans 'solidified' by external political forces in both studies. Gawlewicz and Sotkasiira focus on 'specific timescapes', arguing that 'feelings about Brexit are not only fixed *in* but also fixed *on* time' (Gawlewicz and Sotkasiira, 2019: 7; original emphasis); whereas Rzepnikowska's (2019) pre- and post-referendum research on 'xeno-racism' (2019: 63) against Polish migrants in Manchester concurs with my own (Huc-Hepher, 2019). She ascertains that anti-EU-migrant discrimination predates the 2016 referendum, but that 'racism and xenophobia have intensified in the context of Brexit' (Rzepnikowska, 2019: 72), with the political rhetoric surrounding it emboldening 'individuals to carry out acts of hate and intimidation' (Looney, 2017: 29); for example, Lycée students physically assaulted for speaking French in public (Lamnaouer, 2018). Whereas prejudice was often muted in the past, the 2016 referendum has legitimated it.

Consequently, while the referendum result was initially 'felt and narrated as a "punch," a "hit," an "earthquake," or a "shock"' (Lulle *et al.*,

2018: 9), its progressive concretisation – through the parliamentary invoking of Article 50, the implementation of the discriminatory EU Settlement Scheme, the 'hardening' of the Brexit 'deal' under Prime Minister Johnson and the daily airing of Brexit Party leader, Nigel Farage, as an affable talk-show host on primetime radio – has reinforced the 'solidification' process (Lulle *et al.*, 2018: 9). EU nationals living in the UK can no longer turn a blind eye to the othering that has persisted for decades (Fox *et al.*, 2012; Looney, 2018; Huc-Hepher, 2019; Rzepnikowska, 2019), for they are now confronted with its tangible and unwavering everyday validation (Anderson and Wilson, 2018). In this sense, the referendum and its aftermath are the ultimate materialisation of symbolic violence. Having developed from mediated (Fox *et al.*, 2012) and socially accepted micro-aggressions, often disguised as humour (Huc-Hepher, 2019) or 'teasing/banter and minor comments (mainly on their French accents)' (Brahic and Lallement, 2018: 9), the discrimination has hardened into state-inflicted, and hence legitimised, hostility (Bourdieu and Wacquant, 1992; Bourdieu *et al.*, 1993; Schubert, 2012). Lulle *et al.* contend that the 'unfair treatment is perpetuated politically and becomes internalised individually, reducing the possibilities to resist such hierarchies' (Lulle *et al.*, 2018: 7), which resonates with Schubert's definition of symbolic violence, whereby the 'social origins of this suffering are often misrecognised and internalised by members of society, a fact which only serves to exacerbate suffering and perpetuate symbolic systems of domination' (Schubert, 2012: 180).

Denied a vote, voiceless, yet profoundly affected, these self-motivated individuals, who agentively chose to make London their home, have been stripped of their agency, held 'hostage' to external decision-making (Brahic and Lallement, 2018: 5). Bourdieu posits that 'this soft violence is active' (Bourdieu and Wacquant, 1992: 141) and it is precisely this external agency that compounds the painful helplessness of those no longer in control of their destiny (Gawlewicz and Sotkasiira, 2019). Whenever Leave voices speak of 'taking back control', for EU migrants it signifies losing control. Theresa May's 'strong and stable' soundbite equates to 'insidious insecurity' and instability for migrants (Lulle *et al.*, 2018: 8; Benson, 2019). Similarly, Amber Rudd's 2017 Conservative Party Conference allusion to foreign workers 'taking jobs that British people could do' not only echoes Gordon Brown's *Labour* Party Conference slogan, 'British jobs for British people', ten years' earlier (Rzepnikowska, 2019), but also – and more disconcertingly – the 1925 British Fascists' mantra, 'Britain for the British' (Richardson and Wodak, 2009: 256; Huc-Hepher, 2019). In 2020, proposals for 'Big Ben' to ring out to mark Britain's exit from the EU and plans to stage a 'Festival of Brexit' in 2022 are experienced by London's EU residents not as celebrations but as vindictive public humiliations. In addition to normalising discourses and practices of 'hate' (Gawlewicz and Sotkasiira, 2019: 6), such rhetoric bears witness to a profound lack of empathy. As a result, 'Brexit' is experienced both as a rejection, taken personally (Brahic and Lallement, 2018; Lulle *et al.*, 2018), and a betrayal, the mask having finally fallen (Remigi and Martin, 2017: 223).

By returning to my original research sites and participants, I aim to discover the personal repercussions of this 'politics of othering' (Looney, 2017: 2), this democratically validated xenophobia. I shall afford them a voice suppressed at the 2016, 2017 and 2019 ballot boxes. Underlining 'the affect of Brexit' (Lulle *et al.*, 2018: 2), I seek to understand whether its destabilising force triggered a hysteresis effect, causing participants' 'migrancy habitus' (Lulle *et al.*, 2018: 2) to become unsettlingly out of kilter with the external field (Bourdieu, 1972[2000]; Hardy, 2012). If so, I ask whether it was intensified by the realisation that the free, 'open and meritocratic system' (Brahic and Lallement, 2018: 4) which had initially drawn the French to London (Remigi and Martin, 2017; Mulholland and Ryan, 2017), meaning hysteresis was not experienced on arrival (Thatcher and Halvorsrud, 2016) but on return (Noble, 2013), no longer exists. Just as Brahic and Lallement note a transformation in how French migrants are perceived in the postmigration social space, going from 'global citizens supporting open-mindedness, culture sharing and cosmopolitanism ... to ... aliens ... responsible for growing political and economic concern and uncertainty' (Brahic and Lallement; 2018: 4), might my participants' perceptions of the place they once called home now be fundamentally subverted, their believed settlement emerging as nothing more than imagined stability and belonging? And what do participants' reactions to the referendum tell us about their (trans)national identity and positioning within the postmigration social space?

Replicating the structure of this book, to answer these questions, I first 'look back', exploring participants' memories of June 2016 and their initial reaction to the referendum result. I then endeavour to 'look in', seeking insights into their feelings on the situation in 2019. Finally, I 'look beyond', reflecting on participants' future intentions in the wake of Brexit's 'un-settling' of their home (Miller, 2018).

Looking back: sorrow, solace and hysteresis

In the days and weeks following the referendum, my participants' overwhelming response to the result was unexpectedness. Although a trip to the Lake District in the Easter preceding the referendum sent a warning signal to Séverine, she was in the minority and nonetheless reported a period of 'panic' in the aftermath of the vote, frantically filling out the eighty-five-page permanent residency form, before ultimately discarding it. In addition to 'a strong feeling of disgust towards the political class', reported by email interviewee Anne (a pseudonym for a respondent to my original survey) among others, more common reactions were 'surprise', 'frustration' and 'sadness'. One of the most succinct responses to my 2019 questionnaire was: 'Disappointed, furious, sad', condensing the range of negative emotions felt. For another survey respondent, the emotional impact was stronger, perhaps attributable to the longevity of her migrancy (Brahic and Lallement, 2018). Having arrived in the UK in 1972, she described being 'totally ripped apart' and experiencing the referendum result as 'a major humiliation'. The affective intensity of her words resonates with that of an email interviewee, Martine, who recounted a feeling of 'absolute shock, as if numbed or paralysed, emptied of all substance, suddenly deprived of identity, incredulous, a feeling that it wasn't real. A violent experience, like when you discover you have a serious illness or a loved-one has just died'. This painful testimony recalls 'the process of grieving' reported by other French migrants (Brahic and Lallement, 2018: 8), although, as the authors warn, the metaphor should not be extended too liberally, since recent movers' reactions are less affectively charged than longer-term residents (2018: 8).

However, I argue that recent movers' pragmatism is also informed by their premigration possession of the 'facts'. As Bruno explains,

> if it had been like that from the outset, I would've chosen to come here in the knowledge of the consequences; but you come to England for like the free side, that's always how we've thought of England, there's this freedom you don't necessarily have in France … but now we find ourselves in a different situation which didn't exist before.

It is precisely this extrinsic transformation that destabilises London's pre-2016 French residents and triggers a sense of loss and grieving. As Lulle *et al.* contend, 'Brexit came as a political rupture … threatening not only the positivity of a mindset of intentional unpredictability but also the aspiration for a longer-term stability in the United Kingdom in the future' (2018: 9). Habituated to the city's openness, the isolationism of the referendum – fought and won on anti-migration rhetoric – rendered the field the migrants had considered home inhospitable and alien overnight, transfiguring the diasporic space and their place within it. The result effectively made participants feel disoriented, out of place, like 'fish out of water' (Bourdieu and Wacquant, 1992). Bruno illustrates this unanticipated 'Brexit' hysteresis effect with lucidity:

> Having felt so integrated, never having any problems and feeling that there were a lot of opportunities, all of a sudden, you feel the opposite. I was even grateful towards England to be able to do things here I might not have been

able to do in France, and then in the end it's like going backwards, like a U-turn; it's quite sad to have got to this point.

The aspirations that the migrants had projected onto London, allowing them to 'realise the dream' (Benson and O'Reilly, 2009) through their everyday practices (Conradson and Latham, 2005a) and on which they had built lives, raised families and forged identities, were now abruptly called into question. As Professor Pollet wrote in poignantly simple terms, '[m]y home has been taken away' (Remigi and Martin, 2017: 18). The irretrievability of the(ir) pre-referendum state and status gave rise to a profound sense of loss and yearning. They were not mourning the death of a loved one, but the death of their dream and the life they had led prior to 23 June 2016. Rather than the familiar settlement process from longing to belonging (Levin, 2016), the 2016 referendum instigated a reverse motion from belonging to longing, longing for a present now irredeemably relegated to the past. Rocking the very foundations of their diasporic existence, the referendum result caused these 'pioneers of European integration' (Favell, 2008: x), whose European citizenship automatically conferred them a right to UK residency, to feel 'displaced', as Sadia recounted and, in the words of blogger, Fabienne, 'foreign for the first time' (Lost in London, 2016a). Like other major 'life events – such as divorce or bereavement' (Ryan, 2018: 248), the referendum therefore activated 'reverse embedding (disembedding)' (2018: 248), or inverse hysteresis. It rapidly metamorphosed participants from 'good citizens' to 'unworthy', 'undeserving Europeans' (Benson, 2019: 504, 505), and '[f]rom "Expats" to "Migrants"' (Brahic and Lallement, 2018: 2).

Coupled with feelings of loss and disorientation, came anger and frustration. Anne, who, anecdotally and ironically, had taught Jacob Rees-Mogg French during his gap year in France, was deeply frustrated at being denied a vote in the referendum, particularly because she saw a contradiction in UK-based EU citizens being able to vote *in* EU elections but not *on* EU membership. Others, having been politically silenced, were keen to vent their anger online, thereby countering Gawlewicz and Sotkasiira's affirmation that to '"keep calm and carry on" … is an attempt to domesticate Brexit … and … is the right (i.e., the rational) thing to do in the longer run' (Gawlewicz and Sotkasiira, 2019: 5). For, as Fabienne's Brexit blog trilogy testifies, defiance is more typical of the London-French reaction:

I don't want to 'keep calm and carry on'. Why? Because I'm in the same boat as you. A boat that's off-course. And, unlike you, I'm not at the helm (actually, nobody is … iceberg ahead … somebody, somebody? …). I have a right to be angry and I don't give a damn if it makes you Brits feel uncomfortable. (Lost in London, 2016b)

Provocatively flouting the politeness codes to which she, like other participants, had become accustomed in the postmigration space (see Chapter 3),
the void created by Fabienne's lack of voting rights was filled by her self-
assigned right to cynicism and anger. In the same way that the French
have 'a particular fondness for defeatism' (Hazareesingh, 2015: 301) and
are well-known for being 'capable of turning out in their millions ... to
reaffirm their republican values' (2015: 326), Fabienne's 'Brexit blues'
blogpost (Lost in London, 2016b) crystallises the 'progressive pessimism'
(2016b: 300) and 'Gallic contestation' (2016b: 326) ('iceberg ahead ... I
have a right to be angry') that typifies her premigration identity. As such,
the blogpost is simultaneously a mouthpiece for her anger and an assertion
of her Frenchness. As Poirier writes, rebellion is France's 'motor' (Poirier,
2006: 103) and when discontented, 'we shout out our anger' (2006: 102).
Fabienne's agentive vocalisation of her rage thus distinguishes her from the
wider UK social space. The blog, now devoid of its socio-semiotically telling
banner (see Chapter 6), serves instead as a 'demonstration banner', uniting
Fabienne with her fellow London-French protestors in their opposition to
'My Mate Brexit' (the title of her 24 June 2016 blogpost).

At this point, therefore, we observe the 'rupture' (Lulle *et al.*, 2018: 1),
instigated by the referendum in the postmigration on-land space reflected in
the blog. There is a move away from hybridity (back) to French essential-
ism and exclusionism, a regressive optimism that inverts Hazareesingh's
'progressive pessimism' (2015: 300) through its community-constructive
performativity. In the face of division, Fabienne seeks (comm)unity; for at
8.29 a.m. on 24 June 2016 she resolves to 'shut [her]self off from the media
and social media' because she 'can't handle it anymore', but by 9.10a.m.
her strategy is 'to meet [likeminded] friends in Soho, late morning' (Lost in
London, 2016a). I therefore extend Lulle *et al.*'s argument that encounters
with the 'other' breed 'homegrown' nationalism and are 'embodied in specific events' (Lulle *et al.*, 2018: 6), by postulating that a particular political
event can also pave the way for 'affective nationalism' (2018: 6) on the
side of disenfranchised migrant 'Remainers', seeking solace and empathy
in nationalistic fraternity. As Brahic and Lallement recount, a 'feeling of
rejection experienced by some movers led to further rejection on their part'
(2018: 10) and this is borne out yet more explicitly by Fabienne's comment
at 7.16 a.m.: 'what if I got British nationality? Oh wait, do I want to cosy
up to a nation that rejects me?' (Lost and Found, 2016a).

The initial 'affective impact' (Gawlewicz and Sotkasiira, 2019: 3) of the
referendum is therefore characterised by deep sadness and a sense of loss,
which, as Martine explains, translated into 'several well-known stages of
grieving, particularly, enormous anger and an obsessive need to understand'.
However, and consistent with the grieving metaphor, the mourners also

endeavour to overcome these emotions through mutual support. Fabienne's small-scale on-line outpouring and spontaneous on-land networking was also embodied in large-scale post-referendum groupings, such as the3million collective, a campaign 'organisation *for and of migrants*' from the EU (the3million, 2019; original emphasis) and the 'In Limbo' project, a digital 'safe haven' to share their 'difficult and painful stories' (In Limbo, 2019), which began as a Facebook group and expanded into a blog, two published volumes and subsequently a website. Although such initiatives corroborate Appadurai's contention that 'the electronic archive becomes a doubly valuable space for migrants, [... where] some of the indignity of being minor or contemptible in the new society can be compensated, and the vulnerability of the migrant narrative can be protected in the relative safety of cyberspace' (2019: 562), they also serve the opposite function of entrenching the schism that the referendum prompted, deepening the space between 'us' and 'them'.

Looking in: (un)settlement as symbolic violence

In 2019, three years since the referendum, I am struck by the resoundingly self-contradictory sense of denial and resignation emanating from participants' testimonies. This consistent inconsistency mirrors the migrants' paradoxical positioning as those most influenced by Britain's exit from the EU with the least influence over it. Accordingly, they feel 'rejected' (Bruno) by society and inclined to reject the outcome of the referendum. Many, like Martine 'still don't accept Brexit could happen, even though [they] share numerous criticisms of the EU'. Recalling Brahic and Lallement's (2018) informants, none have yet applied for 'settled status', but all are reconciled to doing so at some point. Detachment from events is deployed as a mechanism for minimising their emotional clout. Thus, Séverine, Anne, Bruno and Sadia all slip spontaneously into political analysis, despite my explicit quest for affective responses. This supports Gawlewicz and Sotkasiira's (2019) stance on UK-based EU nationals becoming more rational and less emotional over time. Yet, beyond the appeasing effect of time alone, I posit that participants' analytical detachment and denial are operationalised more or less agentively as 'defence tactics' (de Backer, 2019: 11) that counter the lack of control over external forces.

However, these negational narratives can also be apprehended within the framework of symbolic violence (Huc-Hepher, 2019). After considerable probing, and coming only in the final moments of our discussion, Séverine reveals two cases of xenophobic microaggression experienced since the referendum. The first involved an altercation with a motorist, which resulted in Séverine – a pedestrian – being shouted at by the driver who, having detected her French accent, bellowed 'maybe the highway code is different in your country, but here, it's my right of way'. Rather than condemn the motorist, Séverine dismisses the 'microinsult' (Sue *et al.*, 2007: 277) and is keen to blame it on her 'strong French accent' and own insecurities: 'these incidents happen when I lack self-assurance ... When I don't care, there's never a problem.' The other episode involved Séverine's house 'mates' suggesting she should 'go back to where [she's] from'. Again bearing witness to misplaced magnanimity, Séverine assures me 'it's not very nice, but because there was a context, I attributed it to something else. I didn't really take it seriously.' Likewise, in a conversation I had with cycling commuter Bruno in 2017, he recounted being told to go back to where he came from by a driver near his South London 'home' of twenty-five years, his 'foreign accent mark[ing him] ... as the Other' (Rzepnikowska, 2019: 70). By 2019, he has only the faintest memory of the incident, implying a non-reflexive process of denial.

Sadia conjectures that 'the country has changed, and not for the better ... When I came here, there was a kind of curiosity ... a kind of admiration actually, towards me ... There was a simplicity, humility even, that I saw in the English'; whereas today, people are 'closed up to the outside'. To illustrate the point, she describes the division between colleagues at a recent workplace: 'in the French team, we were all together, we were always having a laugh, always smiling, it was great, but the English staff didn't speak to us. There was a distance ... it was them and us.' Recalling the 'spontaneous symbolisation' defined by Bourdieu (1993: 251), whereby social structures are 'hazily' inscribed in physical spaces and emerge as implicit fields of struggle (1993: 251), Sadia's account suggests that the workplace openness and equality that so impressed Paulette during my first wave of research (see Chapter 1) have been replaced by more complex office encounters, 'including various forms of conviviality, friendships, but also prejudice and racism' (Rzepnikowska, 2019: 72). Significantly, however, Sadia does not impute this workplace rift to Brexit, despite it dating back to *2016*.

In all these testimonies, then, we note the insidious workings of symbolic violence and its capacity to act on social agents with their complicity (Bourdieu and Wacquant, 1992). Just as most blogs in my corpus revealed little trace of 'Brexit' other than their lack of updating since 2017 or disappearance from the UK domain (itself telling), so my participants negate or minimise post-referendum xenophobic microaggressions. This is typical of 'the implicitness/complicity paradigm' (Sue *et al.*, 2007; Huc-Hepher, 2019: 5), and compounds both their perniciousness and the resentment caused (Lilienfeld, 2017). Tellingly, the process of negation extends to Brexit-related 'formalities'. Unlike McGhee *et al.*'s Polish participants,

72 per cent of whom 'were aiming for civic integration over the next five years', with longer stayers having a preference for British citizenship (McGhee *et al.*, 2017: 2,123), my participants, who arguably occupy a more privileged position due to their status as '"old" EU migrants' (Lulle *et al.*, 2018: 2), prove resistant to such procedures. Despite being resigned to applying for 'settled status', Bruno's umbrage was unequivocal:

> It annoys me. I don't want to [apply] because I've been here for over twenty-five years and I've always paid, always worked, I've paid taxes for those who don't work ... not necessarily immigrants, maybe more for people, like English people, who don't want to work, and then the same people vote for Brexit, so, it annoys me. It annoys me because I have a right *not* to have to register on a list saying I'm French. Why should I be separate? It's a bit like I've been rejected, it's weird; I know it's not the same but it's a bit like we've gone back to the Second World War, when there were lists for Jewish people. I shouldn't exaggerate, it's not the same, but it's like, strange ... because it didn't exist before.

Bruno's frustration at being suddenly relegated from a position of citizenship, enjoying full rights through his European identity, to being branded an outsider whose same identity is now a discriminating factor, is manifested by his repetition of the word 'annoy' and his impulsive recourse to 'boomerang' prejudice (Brahic and Lallement, 2018: 11). Far from being a formality, the EU Settlement Scheme is perceived as an institutionalised enactment of 'xeno-racism' (Rzepnikowska, 2019: 63). Authorised by the state, the ultimate wielder of 'legitimate symbolic violence' (Bourdieu *et al.*, 1993: 1,425), it is experienced as an affront whose toxicity surpasses that of the everyday microaggressions undergone in the social space. As one survey respondent wrote,

> we are being treated like second-class citizens. British people's attitude stems from xenophobia and their 'dominance' in the world. We can't forget what they did to the Windrush generation. It's not acceptable! Calling us 'EU migrants' is an indication of their desire not to be part of Europe and its objective of sharing.

Having always been on the margins of the European Project, the UK and its Leave-leaning population appear unfamiliar with the notion that EU membership signifies citizenship across the entire zone. As such, it is not just the transformation from 'expat' to 'migrant' that unsettles French residents (Brahic and Lallement, 2018), but the stripping of their common (European) citizenship. Granting 'settled status' simultaneously robs participants of their rights and formally invalidates their belonging, a point corroborated by Benson's British migrants in France (2019). As Anne confides, 'it's unpleasant to be considered different by the authorities', particularly when, as she expressed in my initial survey, 'immigrants are other people'.

The introspection imposed by the 'Brexit' agenda and EU Settlement Scheme is therefore not benign, quite the opposite. So-called 'settled status' sees 'participants' privileges suddenly ... unsettled' (Lulle *et al.*, 2018: 5); it is central to 'processes of (un)settling home' (Miller, 2018: 1); it prompts an 'unsettling feeling of ... suspended life' (Mata Codesal, 2008: 15, footnote 29) or hysteresis, engendered by the 'dislocation of habitus' (Hardy, 2012: 126) within the changing postmigration field; and, crucially, it reawakens imperialist discourses and 'settler imaginaries' (Higgins, 2019: 86), reasserting 'normative geographies of who is "in" and "out of place"' (2019: 101). Consequently, the EU Settlement Scheme not only undermines presumed certainties regarding (founding EU-member-state) citizenship and belonging, confronting participants with an 'impasse' (survey response) and 'wall of uncertainty' ('Anonymous – France', in Remigi and Martin, 2017: 90), but constructs a postcolonial hegemony founded on symbolic violence and headed by an ailing Britannia, who no longer 'rules the waves', being a mere shadow of the 'cool Britannia' that had once seduced them (Favell, 2008a: 143).

Looking beyond: habitus subjectivities in flux

Given that participants find themselves in a dead-end street, their trajectories having been blocked by a wall of uncertainty for over three years, it is a challenge for them to predict what is waiting on the other side. Contrasting 'the antithetical habitus of "undeliberate determinacy"' hypothesised by McGhee *et al.* (2017: 2,124), many of my participants remain resolutely undecided. Notwithstanding the passage of time and the UK's final acceleration towards 'Brexit', in autumn 2019 they still struggle to imagine it materialising, perhaps hoping their refusal to do so will have a preventive effect. They favour the status quo and embrace its 'liquidity' (Lulle *et al.*, 2018: 2), with structural 'Brexit' preparations not having altered or 'solidified' (2018: 3) any of their plans as yet. In (stereo)typical defiance of state-led change, they have 'resumed [their] habits' (Séverine), performing their belonging through routine practices (Conradson and Latham, 2005a), if not administratively or politically. Contemptuous of the notion of British citizenship, they instead reap 'the stress-reducing benefits of the muted emotional experiences associated with habit performance' (Wood *et al.*, 2002: 1,295). Indeed, 'the disconnection between habitual behavior and the self' (2002: 1,294) is a useful source of personal resilience (Brahic and Lallement, 2018; Gawlewicz and Sotkasiira, 2019) and conducive to 'Brexit' denial.

I note, however, a spectrum of 'deliberate indeterminacy' (McGhee *et al.*, 2017: 2,112), ranging from 'apathy' (Brahic and Lallement, 2018: 11) to agentive negation. Bruno is at the apathetic end: 'we have no power, so we're just waiting ... so I don't even want to make an effort ... I say to myself, "after all, if they don't want me here, why should I stay?" ... Even though I've built my life here ... I've become a bit disengaged.' Leaving the UK is contemplated, but Bruno's testimony is reactive rather than active, and ultimately disenfranchised. Anne, who is comparably indifferent, takes stasis for granted, '[o]f course, I'll stay in England', while juxtaposing it with reluctant pragmatism: '[a]t worst, one day I could also become British ...'. For Martine, who already has dual citizenship, the picture is understandably less binary:

> I don't feel less English or more French. But my dual nationality is now problematical. A few days' ago, a well-meaning gentleman, a wholehearted Brexiter, wanted to reassure the Frenchwoman I am by insisting I really had nothing to fear ... Unfortunately, it had the opposite effect. For the Englishwoman I've become, the anxiety is just as great, although for different reasons. My life remains here, for the time being at least, if only to continue to defend the values of openness in which I believe.

The identity challenges posed by Martine's hybrid subjectivities have forced her out of apathy into a position of reflective agency. However, the internal conflict between the principled Englishwoman, determined to engage in the struggle of the postmigration field, and her now vulnerable French habitus, has resulted in tensions. Rather than a cleft habitus, which implies disjuncture (Ingram and Abrahams, 2016), Brexit has inflicted a 'destabilized habitus' (2016: 150). Her once contentedly 'reconciled habitus' (2016: 150), which successfully incorporated both pre- and postmigration field forces, has been replaced by one which remains conjunctive in itself (2016: 150), united by unease, but disjunctive in relation to the post-referendum London field. Hysteresis-induced apprehension therefore engulfs Martine's selfhood and restricts her future plans to the short term.

Meanwhile, Sadia is towards the other end of the spectrum, with repudiation and a reluctance to remain in London dominating her narrative. Regarding British citizenship, she declares that 'as a matter of principle, it's out of the question ... I don't feel English at all. That's really something I'd have trouble doing, totally.' Having struggled to make friends in London, Sadia is affectively not 'at home' in the UK and Brexit has cemented her sense of dislocation. 'Picture a plant or a tree planted in fertile earth', she explains, 'for me, this earth, here, isn't fertile because it doesn't actually bring me much joy. My heart still wants to go back to France. I know France isn't perfect, I know the mentalities ... but the people I have a heartfelt affinity with are French.' In diametric opposition to the green and fertile image of London depicted in Fabienne's 2014 blog banner or the hearts of Teatime in Wonderland and Londres Calling (see Chapter 6), as well as the hospitable securiscape alluded to by Sadia, Séverine, Charles, Suzanne and Miranda (see Chapters 1 and 3), her description corroborates the centrality of friendship in 'transnational geographies of the heart' (Walsh, 2018). It also demonstrates Brexit's capacity to recalibrate the normative geographies articulated repeatedly in my original research, where Paris was typically conceptualised as the place where the grass was not greener (Mulholland and Ryan, 2017). So 'displaced' in London, Sadia – originally from Paris – semi-humorously welcomes the possibility of post-Brexit 'deportation': 'it'd be great, I'd leave, I'd have no choice. Laters! ... And the kids wouldn't have a choice anymore either, because they're all French', despite being born in the UK. Instead of resisting the external agency of Brexit (McGhee *et al.*, 2017; Gawlewicz and Sotkasiira, 2019), Sadia welcomes it, deploying it as a pretext to rebuff her 'host' city, freed from the ties of motherhood that have begrudgingly embedded her (Ryan and Sales, 2013; Ryan and Mulholland, 2015; Ryan, 2018) in this barren environment.

She continues,

> I want to leave, but I've got kids; and I've been here twenty years, I've got relationships, you create a life ... I might be happy right now, but deep down, I'm not 'content'. It's as if there's something missing ... I feel uprooted and I don't want to uproot my children ... But I don't see myself ending my days here.

Sadia's account reminds us of the importance of children and family in the mobility and settlement process (see Chapter 5); their education and happiness trumps hers. Yet, while such affective forces are powerful enough to have immobilised Sadia in London for two decades, they are insufficiently strong to cultivate belonging. On the contrary, her account is permeated by a sense of longing that is painful to hear, though not entirely unexpected, since she had spoken of relocating to Marseille almost ten years' earlier. Today, return migration remains the dream, reinforced by the growing 'small-mindedness' of 'Brexit Britain'. In many respects, Sadia's imaginings of life in France replicate the elusive desires of Benson's *British* migrants in the Lot, who 'believed that their entry into this idyllic social landscape ... would provide them with the antidote to their malaise with life in contemporary Britain' (Benson, 2011: 45). However, through Sadia's prior knowledge of the 'poor quality of life' in Paris and 'the mentalities ... that repel' her in the south of France, cracks begin to appear in the image. Her future path may yet lie in London.

To draw this Epilogue to a close, which I write on a cold, wet December day that sees the British people returning to polling stations for the second general election since the 2016 referendum, I wish to turn towards hope. For within my participants' narratives of pain, rejection and, most consistently, sadness, there are glimmers of consolation, reminding us why they initially chose to make London home. While Bruno 'really [does] not know' where the future will take him, his indecisiveness is underpinned by deep fondness:

> I don't know because I like England, I appreciate being here and I don't want to reject everything I've got from being here, for my children, who are getting a great education; I'm really pleased with it … I take things as they come … I hope [Brexit] doesn't cause more violence, not necessarily physical violence, but psychological, like between people. Creating divides is never very good, instead of uniting.

Martine's words echo Bruno's, gratitude tinged with apprehension colouring the prose, but she restores the impression of London as a safe and welcoming space: 'The country is deeply divided, more than ever, but I feel protected by London's great diversity, cultural richness and international links which I have benefited from for as long as I've lived here.' Thus, both Bruno and Martine confirm the positive aspects of London life uncovered in my pre-Referendum research and explored within the chapters of this book, whether concerning the opportunities provided by local pedagogies or London's cosmopolitan openness to the world.

Ultimately, however, the testimonies shared in the Epilogue illustrate that, just as I affirmed in the opening pages of this monograph, migration is messy. They show that identity is fluid and transnational subjectivities are intimately entangled with the neighbours' geographies, histories and ontologies. Epitomising these intertwined relationships, which the European Union celebrates and 'Brexit' voices distrust and drown out, are the words of a respondent to my 2019 survey, fittingly bringing the book to its end:

> My grandmother was English, and she married my French grandfather in 1920, in London. Having been raised by her, when I came here at the age of fifty-nine, I wanted to become English. I did so two months after the Brexit referendum … I will reside here until my death, but my ashes are to be scattered in the Channel. When one is French and English, it is up to the sea to decide. *Vive l'entente cordiale.*

Appendix: Participant profiles

Table 1 Interviewee profiles

Alias	Occupation	Age	Gender	Ethnicity	Premigration residence	London residence	Time in London
Bruno	Head chef	37	Male	White	Bordeaux (33)	West Norwood (SE27)	19 years
Jacqueline	Human resources	42	Female	White	Quebec, Canada	Bromley (BR1)	19 years
Sarah	Head of Investment Risk Framework	37	Female	White	Lyon (69)	Greenwich (SE10)	10 years
Arthur	Hotel food & beverage manager	34	Male	Minority Ethnic (Reunionese)	Reunion Island (97)	Docklands (E16)	11 years
Charles	UK correspondent	34	Male	White	Brittany, west-northwest region	Crystal Palace (SE19) (& Oxford)	11 years
Antoine	Urban designer/ architecture lecturer	52	Male	White	Marseille (13)	Archway (N19)	22 years
Marie	Retired import-export administrator	63	Female	White	Aix en Provence (13)	Wandsworth Bridge Road (SW6, in 1960s & 70s)	6 years
Sadia	Recent French & Spanish graduate, PGCE student	32	Female	Minority Ethnic (Franco-Algerian heritage)	Paris (75)	Beckenham (BR3)	12 years
Brice	Financial/IT consultant & amateur actor	33	Male	White	Carcassonne (11)	Tower Hamlets (E1)	14 years

Table 1 Continued

Alias	Occupation	Age	Gender	Ethnicity	Premigration residence	London residence	Time in London
François	Surgeon in inner-city NHS hospital	52	Male	White	Eastern France	Richmond (TW10)	5 years
Brigitte	Post-doctoral molecular neuroscientist	35	Female	White	Lyon (69)	Bethnal Green (E1)	3 years
Moses	Commercial exports representative	24	Male	Black (Senegalese heritage)	Paris suburbs (93)	Dartford (DA1), Abbey Wood (SE2), Leyton (E10) & Arsenal (N5)	2 years (recent returnee)
Catherine	English as a Foreign Language Teacher	53	Female	White	Bordeaux (33)	South Woodford (E18) & Acton (W3) (in 1980s)	5 years (returnee)
Robert	French as a Foreign Language Lecturer	40	Male	White	Northern France (village)	East Dulwich (SE22)	17 years
Suzanne	Retired teacher from Lycée Français Charles de Gaulle and writer	80	Female	White	Dijon (21)	Holland Park (W11)	47 years (first school-exchange visit in 1948)
Laura	Singer-songwriter	41	Female	White	Paris (75)	Clapham (SW4)	5 years
Chantal	Housewife, formerly in marketing	48	Female	White	Paris (75)	South Kensington (SW7)	22 years
Paulette	International logistics manager	35	Female	Black (Beninese heritage)	Normandy (town/ village), northern France	Chiswick (W4)	8 years
Miranda	Doctoral linguistics student	28	Female	White	Aube (village near Troyes) (10), eastern France	Brick Lane (E1)	10 years
Séverine	Lawyer	50	Female	Minority Ethnic	Paris (75)	Nunhead (SE15)	26 years

Table 2 Focus Group 1: Newham Sixth Form College students (E13)

Age	Gender	Heritage	Time in London
18	Female	Martinique + Ivory Coast	18 years
16	Female	Ivory Coast	7 months
18	Female	Africa/France	3 years
17	Female	Sri Lanka	2½ years
17	Male	Mauritius	5½ years
16	Male	Rwanda	5½ years
18	Male	Pakistan	3 years
(26 – teacher)	Female	France	4 years

Table 3 Focus Group 2: Lycée Français students (South Kensington)

Age	Gender	Heritage	Time in London
16	Male	France	13 years
16	Male	France	16 years (born in London)
16	Male	France	11 years
17	Male	Italy/France	1 year
17	Male	France	10 years
17	Female	France (but grew up in Morocco)	6 years

References

Abel, E. L. (2001) 'The Gin Epidemic: Much Ado About What?', *Alcohol and Alcoholism* 36:5, 401–5.

Abutbul-Selinger, G. (2018) 'Invisible Boundaries Within the Middle Class and the Construction of Ethnic Identity', *Identities*, DOI: 10.1080/1070289 X.2018.1520448.

Adami, E. (2013) 'A Social Semiotic Multimodal Analysis Framework for Website Interactivity' – MODE Working Paper: http://eprints.ncrm.ac.uk/3074/4/web site_interactivityAdami.pdf.

Adami, E. (2015) *Aesthetics in Digital Texts Beyond Writing* (Leiden, Netherlands: Brill), DOI: 10.1163/9789004297197_004.

Adami, E. and Kress, G. (2010) 'The Social Semiotics of Convergent Mobile Devices', in G. Kress, *Multimodality: A Social Semiotic Approach to Contemporary Communication* (London and New York: Routledge).

von Ahn, M. *et al.* (2010) 'Languages, Ethnicity and Education in London', DoQSS Working Paper No. 10–12 (London: Institute of Education): http://repec.ioe. ac.uk/REPEc/pdf/qsswp1012.pdf (accessed 23 May 2015).

Al-Ali, N. and Koser, K. (2002) *New Approaches to Migration?* (London: Routledge).

Albert, E. (2013) 'Les Britanniques malades de leur système de santé', *Le Monde* (13 June): www.lemonde.fr/sante/article/2013/06/13/les-britanniques-malades-de-leur-systeme-de-sante_3429774_1651302.html.

Albouy, V. and Wanecq, T. (2003) 'Les inégalités sociales d'accès aux grandes écoles', *Economie et Statistique*, 361: www.insee.fr/fr/statistiques/1375870?som maire=1375876&q=Albouy+Wanecq (accessed 15 January 2017).

Alonso, A. and Oiarzabal, P. (2018) 'The Immigrant Worlds' Digital Harbors', in K. Stierstorfer and J. Wilson (eds) *The Routledge Diaspora Studies Reader* (London and New York: Routledge).

Anderson, B. and Wilson, H. (2018) 'Everyday Brexits', *Area* 50:2, 291–95.

Androutsopoulos, J. (2008) 'Potentials and Limitations of Discourse-centred Online Ethnography', *Language@Internet* 9:8, URN: nbn:de:0009-7-16100.

Androutsopoulos, J. (2014) 'Moments of Sharing', *Journal of Pragmatics* 73, 4–18. DOI: 10.1016/j.pragma.2014.07.013.

Ankerson, M. S. (2011) 'Writing Web Histories with an Eye on the Analog Past', *New Media and Society* 14:3, 384–400, DOI: 10.1177/1461444811414834.

Ankerson, M. S. (2019) 'Zombies, Robots and Time Machines', *The Web that Was*, RESAW Conference, University of Amsterdam, 19–21 June 2019.

Anthias, F. (2018) 'New Hybridities, Old Concepts', in K. Stierstorfer and J. Wilson (eds) *The Routledge Diaspora Studies Reader* (London and New York: Routledge).

Appadurai, A. (1990) 'Disjuncture and Difference in the Global Cultural Economy', *Theory, Culture and Society* 7: 295–310, DOI: 10.1177/026327690007002017.

Appadurai, A. (1995) 'The Production of Locality', in R. Fardon (ed.) *Counterworks: managing the diversity of knowledge* (London: Routledge).

Appadurai, A. (1996) *Modernity at Large* (Minneapolis: University of Minnesota Press).

Appadurai, A. (2019) 'Traumatic Exit, Identity Narratives, and the Ethics of Hospitality', *Television & New Media* 20:6, 558–65, DOI: 10.1177/15274764 19857678.

Armagnague, M. and Rigoni, I. (2018) 'Éditorial: Expériences scolaires des mineurs migrants', *Revue européenne des migrations internationales* 34:4, 7–11: http://journals.openedition.org/remi/11532 (accessed 16 January 2021).

Asenbaum, H. (2019) 'Rethinking Digital Democracy', *Communication Theory*, DOI: 10.1093/ct/qtz033.

Ash, L. (2012) 'London, France's Sixth Biggest City', *BBC News*: www.bbc.co.uk/news/magazine-18234930 (accessed 16 January 2021).

Atkinson, P. (2005) 'Qualitative Research – Unity and Diversity', *Forum: Qualitative Social Research*, 6:3, 26: www.qualitative-research.net/index.php/fqs/article/view/4/9 (accessed 16 January 2021).

Atkinson, R. (2012) 'The Life Story Interview as a Mutually Equitable Relationship', in J. F. Gubrium *et al.* (eds) *The Sage Handbook of Interview Research* (London: Sage).

de Backer, M. (2019) '"Being Different Together" in Public Space', *Social & Cultural Geography*, DOI: 10.1080/14649365.2019.1594352.

Badger, M. (2004) 'Visual Blogs', in L. Gurak *et al.* (eds) *Into the Blogosphere* (University of Minnesota): blog.lib.umn.edu/blogosphere/visual_blogs.html (accessed 10 December 2005).

Barac, M. and McFadyen, L. (2007) 'Connected Space', *Home Cultures* 4:2, 109–16, DOI: 10.2752/174063107X216877.

Barthes, R. (1977) 'Rhetoric of the Image', in S. Heath (ed.) *Image-Music-Text* (New York: Hill and Wang).

Barthes, R. (1980) La chambre claire: notes sur la photographie (Paris: Gallimard).

Basu, P. and Coleman, S. (2008) 'Introduction: Migrant Worlds, Material Cultures', *Mobilities* 3:3, 313–30, DOI: 10.1080/17450100802376753.

Beaman, J. (2015) 'Boundaries of Frenchness', *Identities* 22:1, 36–52, DOI: 10.1080/1070289X.2014.931235.

Beaman, J. (2018) 'Are French People White? Towards an understanding of whiteness in Republican France', *Identities* 1–17, DOI: 10.1080/1070289X.2018.154 3831.

Beauchemin, C., Hamel, C. and Simon, P. (2010) *Trajectoires et Origines: Enquête sur la diversité des populations en France: Documents du Travail 168* (Paris: TeO, INED and INSEE): www.ined.fr/fichier/s_rubrique/19558/dt168_teo.fr.pdf (accessed 16 January 2021).

de Beauvoir, S. (1979) *Le sexisme ordinaire* (Paris: Le Seuil).

Beaverstock, J. (2005) 'Transnational Elites in the City', *Journal of Ethnic and Migration Studies* 31, 245–68, DOI: 10.1080/1369183042000339918.

Bell, S. L., Wheeler, B. and Phoenix, C. (2017) 'Using Geonarratives to Explore the Diverse Temporalities of Therapeutic Landscapes', *Annals of the American Association of Geographers* 107:1, 93–108, DOI: 10.1080/24694452.2016.121 8269.

Bellion, G. (2005) *French Business in The UK – A Survey*. MSc Project. Université de Franche-Comté: www.reloburo.com/fr/features/projetGB0905.pdf (accessed 30 July 2015).

Ben-David, A. (2019) '2014 Not Found: a cross-platform approach to retrospective web archiving', *Internet Histories*, 3:3–4, 316–42, DOI: 10.1080/247014 75.2019.1654290.

Benson, M. (2011) *The British in Rural France* (Manchester: Manchester University Press).

Benson, M. (2019). Brexit and the Classed Politics of Bordering: The British in France and European belongings, *Sociology* 54:3, 501–17. DOI: 10.1177/0038 038519885300.

Benson, M. and O'Reilly, K. (2009) 'Migration and the Search for a Better Way of Life', *The Sociological Review* 57:4, 608–25, DOI: 10.1111/j.1467–954X. 2009.01864.x.

Benson, M. and O'Reilly, K. (2016) 'From Lifestyle Migration to Lifestyle *in* Migration', *Migration Studies* 4:1, 20–37, DOI: 10.1093/migration/mnv015.

Berthomière, W. (2012) *"A French What?" A la recherche d'une diaspora française* (Paris: e-Diasporas Atlas): www.academia.edu/3530034/_A_French_ what_ percentC3percent80_la_recherche_d_une_diaspora_franpercentC3percen tA7aise._Premiers_percentC3percentA9lpercentC3percentA9ments_d_enquper centC3percentAAte_au_sein_de_l_espace_internet_2012 (accessed 16 January 2021).

Beyer, C. (2015) 'Après le voile islamique, la jupe', *Le Figaro*: www.lefigaro.fr/ actualite-france/2015/05/03/01016–20150503ARTFIG00169-apres-le-voile-is lamique-la-jupe.php.

Bezemer, J. and Mavers, D. (2011) 'Multimodal Transcription as Academic Practice', *International Journal of Social Research Methodology* 14:3, 191–207.

Bezemer, J. *et al.* (2014) 'Holding the Scalpel', *Journal of Contemporary Ethnography* 43:1, 38–63, DOI: 10.1177/0891241613485905.

Bilecen, B. and Van Mol, C. (2017) 'Introduction: international academic mobility and inequalities', *Journal of Ethnic and Migration Studies* 43:8, 1,241–55, DOI: 10.1080/1369183X.2017.1300225.

Birch, M. and Miller, T. (2000) 'Inviting Intimacy', *International Journal of Social Research Methodology* 3:3, 189–202, DOI: 10.1177/1077800412462978.

Blackledge, A. (2013) 'Investigating Digital and Social Media', *Cultural Dynamics and Creativity in Digital Europe* Conference, King's College London, 31 May 2013.

Block, D. (2006) *Multilingual Identities in a Global City* (London and New York: Palgrave Macmillan).

Blommaert, J. and De Fina, A. (2017) 'Chronotopic Identities', in A. De Fina and J. Wegner (eds), *Diversity and Super-Diversity*. Washington, DC: Georgetown University Press.

Blunt, A. (2005) 'Cultural Geography', *Progress in Human Geography* 29:4, 505–15, DOI: 10.1191/0309132505ph564pr.

Blunt, A. and Varley, A. (2004) 'Geographies of Home', *Cultural Geographies*, 11:1, 3–6, DOI: 10.1191/1474474004eu289xx.

Blunt, A. and Dowling, R. (2006) *Home* (New York: Routledge).

Bodomo, A. and Ma, E. (2012) 'We Are What We Eat', *African Diaspora* 5, 3–26, DOI: 10.1163/187254612X646198.

Bonnerjee, J. *et al.* (2012) *Connected Communities: Diaspora and Transnationality* (London: Queen Mary, University of London): www.geog.qmul.ac.uk/docs/research/61819.pdf (accessed 8 September 2015).

Bosio, A. (2015) 'Le restaurant de Maïté ferme ses portes', *Le Figaro* (21 April): www.lefigaro.fr/gastronomie/2015/04/21/30005-20150421ARTFIG00136-le-restaurant-de-maite-ferme-ses-portes.php.

de Bourbon, T. (2018) 'Le système de santé britannique en plein chaos', *La Croix* (11 January): www.la-croix.com/Monde/Europe/Le-systeme-sante-britannique-plein-chaos-2018-01-11-200905013.

Boucher, K. (2015) 'Audience: Petit bilan pour "Qui sera le prochain grand pâtissier?" saison 3', *Pure Médias* (29 July): www.ozap.com/actu/audiences-petit-bilan-pour-qui-sera-le-prochain-grand-patissier-saison-3/473678 (accessed 16 January 2021).

Bourdieu, P. ([1972] 2000) *Esquisse d'une théorie de la pratique* (Paris: Le Seuil).

Bourdieu, P. (1979a) La Distinction – critique sociale du jugement (Paris: Minuit).

Bourdieu, P. (1979b) 'Les trois états du capital culturel', *Actes de la recherche en sciences sociales* 30, 3–6: www.persee.fr/web/revues/home/prescript/article/arss_0335–5322_1979_num_30_1_2654 (accessed 16 January 2021).

Bourdieu, P. (1980a) *Le sens pratique* (Paris: Minuit).

Bourdieu, P. (1980b) 'Le capital social', *Actes de la recherche en sciences sociales* 31, 2–3: www.persee.fr/doc/arss_0335-5322_1980_num_31_1_2069 (accessed 16 January 2021).

Bourdieu, P. (1986) 'The Forms of Capital', in J. Richardson (ed.) *Handbook of Theory and Research for the Sociology of Education* (New York: Greenwood Press).

Bourdieu, P. (1989) *La Noblesse de l'Etat* (Paris: Minuit).

Bourdieu, P. (1994) *Raisons pratiques* (Paris: Le Seuil).

Bourdieu, P. (1996) *Physical Space, Social Space and Habitus, Rapport 10* (Oslo: Institutt for sosiologi og samfunnsgeografi): www.sv.uio.no/iss/forskning/aktuelt/arrangementer/aubert/tidligere/dokumenter/aubert1995.pdf (accessed 25 January 2016).

Bourdieu, P. (1998) *La Domination masculine* (Paris: Le Seuil).

Bourdieu, P. (1999) 'Preface', in A. Sayad *La double absence* (Paris: Le Seuil).

Bourdieu, P. (2004) *Esquisse pour une auto-analyse* (Paris: Raisons d'agir).

Bourdieu, P. (2005) 'Habitus', in J. Hillier and E. Rooksby (eds) *Habitus: A Sense of Place* (2nd edition) (Aldershot: Ashgate).

Bourdieu, P. and Passeron, J.-C. (1964) *Les Héritiers* (Paris: Minuit).

Bourdieu, P. and Passeron, J.-C. (1970) *La Reproduction* (Paris: Minuit).

Bourdieu, P. and Wacquant, L. (1992) *Réponses* (Paris: Le Seuil).

Bourdieu, P. *et al.* (1993) *La Misère du monde* (Paris: Le Seuil).

Bovill, C. *et al.* (2016) 'Addressing Potential Challenges in Co-creating Learning and Teaching', *Higher Education* 71:2, 195–208, DOI: 10.1007/s1073.

Brahic, B. and Lallement, M. (2018) 'From "Expats" to "Migrants"', *Migration and Development*, DOI: 10.1080/21632324.2018.1503486.

Brandes, D. and Ginnis, P. ([1986] 2001) *A Guide to Student-centred Learning* (Cheltenham: Thornes).

Bräuchler, B. (2005) 'Researching the INTERNET e-Seminar Statement', in *EASA Media Anthropology Network Series*: www.media-anthropology.net/braeuchler_eseminar.pdf (accessed 8 September 2015).

Braun, M. and Arsene, C. (2009) 'The Demographics of Movers and Stayers in the European Union', in E. Recchi and A. Favell (eds) *Pioneers of European Integration* (Cheltenham: Edward Elgar).

Brettell, C. B. (1986) *Men Who Migrate, Women Who Wait* (Princeton: Princeton University Press).

Brettell, C. B. (2008) 'Theorizing Migration in Anthropology', in C. B. Brettell and J. F. Hollifield (eds) *Migration Theory: Talking across Disciplines* (New York: Routledge).

Brinkerhoff, J. M. (2009) *Digital Diasporas: Identity and transnational engagement* (Cambridge: Cambridge University Press).

Brügger, N. (2005) *Archiving Websites* (Aarhus: Centre for Internet Research): http://cfi.au.dk/fileadmin/www.cfi.au.dk/publikationer/archiving_underside/archiving.pdf (accessed 16 January 2021).

Brügger, N. (2009) 'Website History and the Website as an Object of Study', *New Media and Society* 11:1&2, 115–32, DOI: 10.1177/1461444808099574.

Brügger, N. (2012) 'When the Present Web is Later the Past', *Historical Social Research* 37:4, 102–17, DOI: 10.12759/hsr.37.2012.4.102–117.

Brügger, N. (2018). *The Archived Web: Doing History in the Digital Age* (Cambridge, MA: The MIT Press).

Brügger, N. and Laursen, D. (2018) 'Historical Studies of National Web Domains', in N. Brügger and I. Milligan (eds) *The Sage Handbook of Web History* (London: Sage).

Burke, C. (2016) 'Bourdieu's Theory of Practice', in J. Thatcher *et al.* (eds) *Bourdieu: The Next Generation* (London and New York: Routledge).

Cambridge Dictionary (2021) 'Habit Definition': from http://dictionary.cambridge.org/dictionary/english/habit (accessed 22 January 2021).

Carlson, S. (2011) 'Just a Matter of Choice? Student Mobility as a Social and Biographical Process', University of Sussex Centre for Migration Working Paper Series, No. 68: www.sussex.ac.uk/webteam/gateway/file.php?name=mwp68.pdf&site=252 (accessed 15 January 2017).

Carpenter, K. (2013) 'The Novelty of the French Émigrés in London in the 1790s', in D. Kelly and M. Cornick (eds) *A History of the French in London* (London: University of London).

Casilli, A. (2010) *Liaisons numériques* (Paris: Le Seuil).

Cavico, F., Muffler, S., Mujtaba, B. (2013) 'Appearance Discrimination in Employment', *Equality, Diversity and Inclusion: An International Journal* 32:1, 83–119, DOI: 10.1108/02610151311305632.

Chamberlain, A., Zhao, D. and Stansell, A. (2019) 'Progress on the Gender Pay Gap: 2019' (Mill Valley: Glassdoor): www.glassdoor.com/research/app/uploads/sites/2/2019/02/Gender-Pay-Gap-2019-Research-Report.pdf (accessed 16 January 2021.

Chauvin, S. (2005) 'Honte', in L.-G. Tin (ed.) *Dictionnaire de l'Homophobie (Revised Version)* (Paris: Presses universitaires de France).

Chauvin *et al.* (2019) 'Class Mobility and Inequality in the lives of Same-Sex

Couples with Mixed Legal Statuses', *Journal of Ethnic and Migration Studies*, DOI: 10.1080/1369183X.2019.1625137.

Cheshire, J. (2012a) 'Mapped: Twitter Languages in London', *Spatial.ly*: http://spatial.ly/2012/10/londons-twitter-languages/ (accessed 27 April 2015).

Cheshire, J. (2012b) 'Languages in the London Twittersphere: The Complete List': https://docs.google.com/spreadsheets/d/1ODe56EStO4VpPT_tjUhkd7fno3xO0y3TizzIVJaQ9N4/edit#gid=0 (accessed 16 January 2021).

Cheshire, J. and Manley, E. (2012) 'Twitter Tongues: A Multilingual Social City – The Languages of Tweets in London in Summer 2012', *Twitter Mapping London*: http://twitter.mappinglondon.co.uk/ (accessed 16 January 2021).

Chiswick, B. (2008) 'Are Immigrants Favorably Self-Selected?', in C. B. Brettell and J. F. Hollifield (eds) *Migration Theory: Talking across Disciplines* (New York: Routledge).

Cohen, J. H. and Sirkeci, I. (2011) *Cultures of Migration: The Global Nature of Contemporary Mobility* (Austin: University of Texas Press).

Cohen, J. H. (2014) 'Migration and Culture', in B. Anderson and M. Keith (eds) *Migration: A COMPAS Anthology* (Oxford: COMPAS).

Collectif 'Levons l'omerta' (2016) 'Harcèlement et politique: "Pour que l'impunité cesse"', *Libération* (9 May): www.liberation.fr/france/2016/05/09/harcelement-et-politique-pour-que-l-impunite-cesse_1451542/.

Collins, F. (2009) 'Connecting "Home" With "Here"', *Journal of Ethnic and Migration Studies* 35:6, 839–59, DOI: 10.1080/13691830902957668.

Colquhoun, G. (2012) *Jumping Ships* (Wellington: Steele Roberts).

Conradson, D. (2005) 'Freedom, Space and Perspective', in J. Davidson, L. Bondi and M. Smith (eds) *Emotional Geographies* (Aldershot: Ashgate).

Conradson, D. and Latham, A. (2005a) 'Transnational Urbanism', *Journal of Ethnic and Migration Studies* 31:2, 227–33, DOI: 10.1080/1369183042000339891.

Conradson, D. and Latham, A. (2005b) 'Friendship, Networks and Transnationality in a World City', *Journal of Ethnic and Migration Studies* 31:2, 287–305, DOI: 10.1080/1369183042000339936.

Conradson, D. and Latham, A. (2007) 'The Affective Possibilities of London', *Mobilities*, 2:2, 231–54.

Consulat général (2013) 'Qu'est qu'un consulat?', *Consulat général de France à Londres* (11 July): www.ambafrance-uk.org/Consulat-general-et-consulats (accessed 23 April 2015).

Conway, D. and Leonard, P. (2014) *Migration, Space and Transnational Identities* (London: Palgrave Macmillan).

Cooke T. (2001) '"Trailing Wife" or "Trailing Mother"?', *Environment and Planning A*. 33:3, 419–30.

Cordier, V. (2005) Enfin un Boulot! Ou le parcours d'un jeune chômeur français à Londres (London: eVault First Publishing).

Cornejo Torres, R. and Rosales Ubeda, A. (2015) 'Objective Structures and Symbolic Violence in the Immigrant Family and School Relationships', *Social Sciences* 4, 1243–68, DOI: 10.3390/socsci4041243.

Cowls, J. (2017) 'Cultures of the UK Web'. In N. Brügger and R. Schroeder (eds) *The Web as History* (London: University College London Press).

Cox, A. (2005) 'What are Communities of Practice?' *Journal of Information Science* 31:6, 527–40, DOI: 10.1177/0165551505057016.

Crawford, K. (2013) 'The Hidden Biases in Big Data', *The Harvard Business*

Review Blog (1 April): http://blogs.hbr.org/2013/04/the-hidden-biases-in-big-data/ (accessed 16 January 2021).

Crenshaw, K. (1989) 'Demarginalizing the Intersection of Race and Sex', *University of Chicago Legal Forum* 1:8, 139–67.

Cross, M. (2013) 'The French in London During the 1830s', in D. Kelly and M. Cornick (eds) *A History of the French in London* (London: University of London).

Curtis, C. (2018) 'Brits still Love the NHS, But They Are Nervous About its Future': https://yougov.co.uk/topics/politics/articles-reports/2018/07/04/brits-still-love-nhs-they-are-nervous-about-its-fu (accessed 16 January 2021).

Declaration of the Rights of Man (1789): www.conseil-constitutionnel.fr/conseil-constitutionnel/francais/la-constitution/la-constitution-du-4-octobre-1958/dec laration-des-droits-de-l-homme-et-du-citoyen-de-1789.5076.html (accessed 16 January 2021).

Decree no. 2014–610 (2014): www.legifrance.gouv.fr/affichTexte.do;jsessionid=15 AF62D8375F3994D6B6AC291BF4E44C.tpdila16v_2?cidTexte=JORFTEXT00 0029072267&dateTexte=&oldAction=rechJO&categorieLien=id&idJO=JORF CONT000029072219 (accessed 16 January 2021).

Deen, M. and Katz, A. (2008) 'French Making Themselves at Home in London, *New York Times* (5 February): www.nytimes.com/2008/01/25/style/25iht-afrench.1.9495133.html.

Delphine (2014) 'Fin d'automne à Richmond Park', *From the Riviera to the Smog* (15 December): https://fromtherivieratothesmog.wordpress.com/2014/12/15/fin-dautomne-a-richmond-park/ (accessed 16 January 2021).

Delphy, C. (2006) 'Antisexisme ou antiracisme?', in N. Guénif-Souilamas (ed.) *La République mise à nu par son immigration* (Paris: La Fabrique).

Demossier, M. (2001) 'Territoires, produits et identités en mutation', *Ruralia*: https://ruralia.revues.org/220 (accessed 16 January 2021).

Demossier, M. (2011) 'Beyond *terroir*', *Journal of the Royal Anthropological Institute* 17, 685–705: https://foodethics.univie.ac.at/fileadmin/user_upload/inst_ethik_wiss_dialog/Demossier__Marion_2011._Beyond_terroir.pdf (accessed 16 January 2021).

Deschenaux, F. and Laflamme, C. (2009) 'Réseau social et capital social', *Sociologies, Théories et Recherches*: https://sociologies.revues.org/2902 (accessed 16 January 2021).

Deseine, T. (no date) 'About Biography', *Trist Deseine*: www.tristdeseine.com/ (accessed 30 July 2015).

Dhoest, A. (2018) 'Complicating Ethno-Cultural and Sexual Connections Among Gay Migrants', *Popular Communication* 16:1, 32–44, DOI: 10.1080/154057 02.2017.1413190.

Diallo, R. (2015) 'Fighting Denial and Suspicion in France', *Newsweek* (31 January): http://europe.newsweek.com/fighting-denial-and-suspicion-france-303452 (accessed 16 January 2021).

Dicks, B., Soyinka, B. and Coffey, A. (2006) 'Multimodal Ethnography', *Qualitative Research* 6:1, 77–96.

Dicks, B. *et al.* (2011) 'Multimodality and Ethnography: working at the intersection', *Qualitative Research* 11, 227–37.

Dictionary.com (2019) 'All the Words': www.dictionary.com/e/emoji/nerd-face-emoji/ (accessed 16 January 2021).

Digital Preservation Coalition (no date) 'UK Web Archiving Consortium (UKWAC)', *Digital Preservation Coalition*: www.dpconline.org/advice/web-archiving (accessed 6 March 2015).

Diminescu, D. (2008) 'The Connected Migrant', *Social Science Information* 47:4, 565–79.

Diminescu, D. (2016) 'Traces numériques', *Plein droit* 110, 3–6: www.cairn.infore vue-plein-droit-2016–3-page-3.htm (accessed 16 January 2021).

Divita, D. (2019) 'Discourses of (Be)Longing', in R. Piazza (ed.) *Discourses of Identity in Liminal Places and Spaces* (London and New York: Routledge).

Dinkwater, S. and Garapich, M. (2015) 'Migration Strategies of Polish Migrants', *Journal of Ethnic and Migration Studies* 41:12, 1,909–31, DOI: 10.1080/13691 83X.2015.1027180.

Domingo, M. (2011) 'Analyzing Layering in Textual Design', *International Journal of Social Research Methodology* 14:3, 219–30, DOI: 10.1080/13645 579.2011.563619 (accessed 16 January 2021).

Domingo, M. *et al.* (2014) 'Development of Methodologies for Researching Online Communication. Working Paper', *National Centre for Research Methods*: http:// eprints.ncrm.ac.uk/3704/4/food_blogs.pdf (accessed 16 January 2021).

Domingo, M., Jewitt, C. and Kress, G. (2015) 'Multimodal Social Semiotics', in K. Pahl and J. Rowsell (eds) *The Routledge Handbook of Literary Studies* (London: Routledge).

Draitser, E. A. (1998) *Taking Penguins to the movies* (Detroit: Wayne State University Press).

Drake, H. and d'Aumale, X. (no date) 'Regards sur la France depuis Londres', *Franco-British Council*: www.francobritishcouncil.org.uk/data/files/reports/Reg ards-sur-la-France-depuis-Londres.pdf (accessed 25 January 2021).

Dubet, F. (2004) *L'école des chances* (Paris: Le Seuil).

Dubet, F. (2014) *La préférence pour l'inégalité* (Paris: Le Seuil).

Dubucs *et al.* (2017) 'Je suis un Italien de Paris', *Journal of Ethnic and Migration Studies* 43:4, 578–95, DOI: 10.1080/1369183X.2016.1249051.

Dudley S. (2011) 'Feeling at Home', *Population, Space and Place* 17:6, 742–55, DOI: 10.1002/psp. 639.

Dyke, S. (2013) 'Utilising a Blended Ethnographic Approach to Explore the Online and Offline Lives of Pro-Ana Community Members', *Ethnography and Education* 8:2, 146–61, DOI: 10.1080/17457823.2013.792505.

Eade, J., Drinkwater, S. and Garapich, M. (2007) 'Class and Ethnicity: Polish Migrant Workers in London', End of Award Research Report (Swindon: ESRC).

Ehrenreich, B. and English, D. ([1973] 2011) *Complaints and Disorders* (New York: Feminist Press).

Elgesem, D. (2002) 'What is Special About the Ethical Issues in Online Research?', *Ethics and Information Technology* 4, 195–203.

Elliott, A. (2008) *Concepts of the Self* (Cambridge: Polity).

En Marche (2017) *Discours de Londres*: https://en-marche.fr/articles/discours/ meeting-macron-londres-discours (accessed 16 January 2021).

Engel, M. (2014) *Engel's England* (London: Profile Books).

English Oxford Dictionaries (2017) 'Habit Definition': https://en.oxforddictionaries. com/definition/habit (accessed 15 January 2017).

Eock Laïfa, E. (2016) 'Le Traitement des cheveux crépus dans les processus de socialisation et d'intégration en France et au Cameroun' (doctoral thesis,

Université de Strasbourg): https://www.theses.fr/2016STRAG031 (accessed 16 January 2021).

Equality Act, 2010, c.15: www.legislation.gov.uk/ukpga/2010/15/section/26 (accessed 16 January 2021).

Erel, U. (2010) 'Migrating Cultural Capital', *Sociology* 44:4, 642–60, DOI: 10.1177/0038038510369363.

Escafré-Dublet, A. and Simon, P. (2014) 'Ce qu'il y a derrière l'identité nationale', in C. Husson-Rochcongar and L. Jourdain (eds) *L'Identité nationale: instruments et usages* (Amiens: CURAPP).

Escafré-Dublet, A. (2019) 'The Whiteness of Cultural Boundaries in France', *Identities: Global Studies in Culture and Power* 1–16, DOI: 10.1080/10702 89X.2019.1587906.

Eurostat (2015a) 'Crimes Recorded by the Police: homicide in cities', *Eurostat*: http://appsso.eurostat.ec.europa.eu/nui/show.do?dataset=crim_hom_city&lang=en (accessed 27 July 2015).

Eurostat (2015b) 'Crimes Recorded by the Police by Offence Category', *Eurostat*: http://appsso.eurostat.ec.europa.eu/nui/show.do?dataset=crim_gen&lang=ena (accessed 27 July 2015).

Farrer, J. (2010) '"New Shanghailanders" or "New Shanghainese"', *Journal of Ethnic and Migration Studies* 36:8, 1,211–28.

Fassin, E. (2012) 'Au-delà du consentement: pour une théorie féministe de la séduction', *Raisons politiques* 44, 47–66.

Fassin, E. (2015) 'L'Homosexualité dans la famille', *Mouvements* 82, 81–9.

Fassin, E. (2018) 'Politiques de la (non-)représentation', *Sociétés & Représentations* 45:1, 9–27, DOI: 10.3917/sr.045.0009.

Faucher, C. *et al.* (2015) *Le Lycée Français Charles de Gaulle de Londres 1915–2015* (London: Association des Anciens du Lycée Français de Londres).

Favell, A. (2006) 'London as Eurocity', in M. P. Smith and A. Favell (eds) *The Human Face of Global Mobility* (New Brunswick: Transaction).

Favell, A. (2008a) *Eurostars and Eurocities* (Oxford: Blackwell).

Favell, A. (2008b) 'Rebooting Migration Theory', in C. B. Brettell and J. F. Hollifield (eds) *Migration Theory* (New York: Routledge).

Favell, A. and Nebe, T. (2009) 'Internal and External Movers', in E. Recchi and A. Favell (eds) *Pioneers of European Integration* (Cheltenham: Edward Elgar).

Fazal, S. and Tsagarousianou, R. (2002) 'Diasporic Communication', *Journal of the European Institute for Communication and Culture* 9:1, 5–18, DOI: 10.1080/13183222.2002.11008790.

Fechter, A. M. (2005) 'The Other Stares Back', *Ethnography* 6:1, 87–103, DOI: 10.1177/1466138105055662.

Fechter, A. M. and Walsh, K. (2010) 'Examining "Expatriate" Continuities', *Journal of Ethnic and Migration Studies* 36:8, 1,197–210, DOI: 10.1080/13 691831003687667.

Fielding, H. ([1749] 1985) *Tom Jones* (London: Penguin Classics).

Findlay, A. M. and Li, F. L. N. (1997) 'An Autobiographical Approach to Understanding Migration', *Area* 29:1, 34–44.

Fiske, J. (1990), 'Ethnosemiotics: Some personal and theoretical reflections', *Cultural Studies* 4:1, 85–99.

Flick, C. (2016) 'Informed Consent and the Facebook Emotional Manipulation Study', *Research Ethics* 12:1, 14–28, DOI: 10.1177/1747016115599568.

Flusty S. (2004) *De-Coca-Colonization* (New York: Routledge).

Fortier, A. M. (2002) 'Queer Diasporas', in D. Richardson and S. Seidman (eds) *Handbook of lesbian and gay studies* (London: Sage).

Fox, K. (2014) *Watching the English* (2nd edition) (London: Hodder & Stoughton).

Fox, J. E., Moroşanu, L. and Szilassy. E. (2012) 'The Racialization of the New European Migration to the UK', *Sociology* 46:4, 680–95, DOI: 10.1177/00380 38511425558.

Francis, B. and Wong, B. (2013) 'What is Preventing Social Mobility? A review of the evidence', Leicester: ASCL.

French Data Protection Act, 1978, c.2: www.legifrance.gouv.fr/affichTexteArticle. do?cidTexte=JORFTEXT000000886460&idArticle=LEGIARTI000006528072 &dateTexte=&categorieLien=cid (accessed 25 June 2016).

Friedman, S. (2016) 'Habitus Clivé and the Emotional Imprint of Social Mobility', *The Sociological Review* 64:1, 129–47, DOI: 10.1111/1467–954X.12280/ full.

Friedmann, J. (2005) 'Place-making as Project?', in J. Hillier and E. Rooksby (eds) *Habitus: A Sense of Place* (2nd edition) (Aldershot: Ashgate).

Frosh, S. (1997) *For and Against Psychoanalysis* (London: Routledge).

Fuchs, C. (2014) 'From Digital Positivism and Administrative Big Data Analytics towards Critical Digital and Social Media Research!', *European Journal of Communication* 10:2, 37–49, DOI: 10.1177/0267323116682804.

Fusch, P. I. and Ness, L. R. (2015) 'Are We There Yet? Data Saturation in Qualitative Research', *The Qualitative Report 2015* 20:9, 1,408–16: www.nova. edu/ssss/QR/QR20/9/fusch1.pdf (accessed 16 January 2021).

Gabaccia, D. R. (2006) 'Pizza, Pasta And Red Sauce: Italian or American?', *History in Focus*: www.history.ac.uk/ihr/Focus/Migration/articles/gabaccia.html (accessed 16 January 2021).

Garratt, L. (2016) 'Using Bourdieusian Scholarship to Understand the Body', in J. Thatcher *et al.* (eds) *Bourdieu: The Next Generation* (London and New York: Routledge).

Guardian (2015) 'Ocado Reports Rise in Shoppers After Drive to Shed Posh Image', *Guardian* (30 June): www.theguardian.com/business/2015/jun/30/ online-grocer-ocado-sharp-rise-shoppers-shed-posh-image.

Gauthier, J. and Jobard, F. (2018) *Police: Questions sensibles* (Paris: Puf-La Vie des idées).

Gawlewicz, A. and Sotkasiira, T. (2019) 'Revisiting geographies of temporalities', *Population, Space and Place*, DOI: 10.1002/psp. 2275.

Geertz, C. (1973) The Interpretation of Cultures: selected essays (New York: Basic Books).

Germain, F. and Larcher, S. (2018) 'Introduction: Marianne Is Also Black', in F. Germain and S. Larcher (eds) *Black French Women and the Struggle for Equality, 1848–2016* (Lincoln and London: University of Nebraska Press).

Gielis, R. (2009) 'A Global Sense of Migrant Places', *Global Networks* 9:2, 271–87, DOI: 10.1111/j.1471–0374.2009.00254.x.

Glancey, J. (1997) 'Reach for the Sky', *Independent* (3 January): www.independent. co.uk/arts-entertainment/art/news/reach-for-the-sky-1281372.html (accessed 16 January 2021).

Glick Schiller, N., Basch, L. and Blanc-Szanton, C. (1992) 'Transnationalism', *Annals of the New York Academy of Sciences*, 645: 1–24.

Glick Schiller, N. and Çaglar, A. (2013) 'Locating Migrant Pathways of Economic Emplacement', *Ethnicities* 13:4, 494–514, DOI: 10.1177/1468796813483733.

Gomes, D. and Costa, M. (2014) 'The Importance of Web Archiving for the Humanities', *International Journal of Humanities and Arts Computing* 8:1, DOI: 10.3366/ijhac.2014.0122.

Grenfell, M. (2012) 'Methodology', in M. Grenfell (ed.) *Pierre Bourdieu – Key Concepts* (2nd edition) (Durham: Acumen).

Grill, J. (2018) '"In England, They Don't Call You Black!"', *Journal of Ethnic and Migration Studies* 44:7, 1136–55, DOI: 10.1080/1369183X.2017.1329007.

Guénif-Souilamas, N. (2006) 'La Française voilée, la beurette, le garçon arabe et le musulman laïc', in N. Guénif-Souilamas (ed.) *La République mise à nu par son immigration* (Paris: La Fabrique).

Guiliano, M. (2007) *French Women Don't Get Fat* (New York: Vintage Books).

de Haas, H. (2010) 'The Internal Dynamics of Migration Processes', *Journal of Ethnic and Migration Studies* 30:10, 1,587–617, DOI: 10.1080/1369183X.2010.489361.

Hage, G. (1997) 'At Home in the Entrails of the West', in H. Grace *et al.* (eds) *Home/World* (Annandale, NSW: Pluto Press).

Halliday, M. (1978) *Language as Social Semiotic* (Maryland: University Park Press).

Hammersley, M. (2005) 'Ethnography and Discourse Analysis', *Polifonia* 10, 1–20: www.academia.edu/3722291/Ethnography_and_Discourse_Analysis (accessed 16 January 2021).

Haraway, D. (2006) 'A Cyborg Manifesto', in J. Weiss *et al.* (eds) *The International Handboook of Virtual Learning Environments* (Dordrecht: Springer).

Hardwick, S. W. (2008) 'Place, Space and Pattern', in C. B. Brettell and J. F. Hollifield (eds) *Migration Theory* (New York: Routledge).

Hardy, C. (2012) 'Hysteresis', in M. Grenfell (ed.) *Pierre Bourdieu – Key Concepts* (Durham: Acumen).

Hazareesingh, S. (2015) *How the French Think* (London: Allen Lane).

Hecht, A. (2001) 'Home Sweet Home', in D. Miller (ed.) *Home Possessions* (Oxford: Berg).

Heller, M. (2006) *Linguistic Minorities and Modernity* (London and New York: Continuum).

Hester, H. (2018) *Xenofeminism* (Cambridge: Polity).

Higgins, K. W. (2019) 'The Migrancy of Racial and Settler Imaginaries', *Social & Cultural Geography* 20:1, 86–106, DOI: 10.1080/14649365.2017.1347956.

Hillier, J. and Rooksby, E. (2005) *Habitus: A Sense of Place* (2nd edition) (Aldershot: Ashgate).

Hine, C. (2000) *Virtual Ethnography* (London: Sage).

Hine, C. (2015) *Ethnography for the Internet* (London: Bloomsbury).

Hitchcock, T. (2014) 'Big Data, Small Data and Meaning', *Historyonics Blog* (09 November): http://historyonics.blogspot.com/2014/11/big-data-small-data-and-meaning_9.html (accessed 16 January 2021).

Ho, E. and Hatfield, M. (2011) 'Migration and Everyday Matters', *Population, Space and Place* 17:6, 707–13.

Hodge, R. and Kress, G. (1988) *Social Semiotics* (Cambridge: Polity Press).

Hoerder, D. (2013) 'Transregionalism', in *The Encyclopedia of Global Human Migration* (Oxford: Blackwell), DOI: 10.1002/9781444351071.wbeghm546.

Hogarth (1751) *Beer Street and Gin Lane* [image]: https://commons.wikimedia.org/wiki/File:Beer-street-and-Gin-lane.jpg (accessed 16 January 2021).

Hopkins, P. *et al.* (2019) 'Young People's Everyday Landscapes of Security and Insecurity', *Social & Cultural Geography* 20:4, 435–44, DOI: 10.1080/14649365.2018.1460863.

Hörschelmann, K. (2011) 'Theorising Life Transitions', *Area* 43:4, 378–83, DOI: 10.1111/j.1475–4762.2011.01056.x.

Horsfall, D. (2019) 'Medical Tourism from the UK to Poland', *Journal of Ethnic and Migration Studies*, DOI: 10.1080/1369183X.2019.1597470.

Horton, S. and Cole, S. (2011) 'Medical Returns', *Social Science and Medicine* 72:11, 1,846–52, DOI: 10.1016/j.socscimed.2011.03.035.

Huc-Hepher, S. (no date). London French Special Collection. *UK Web Archive, British Library*: www.webarchive.org.uk/en/ukwa/collection/309 (accessed 16 January 2021).

Huc-Hepher, S. (2015) 'Big Web data, small focus', *Big Data & Society*, DOI: 10.1177/2053951715595823.

Huc-Hepher, S. (2016) 'The Material Dynamics of a London-French Blog', *Modern Languages Open*, DOI: 10.3828/mlo.v0i0.91.

Huc-Hepher, S. (2018) 'Hidden Histories in the Archived Web', Multilingual Digital Authorship Symposium, University of Lancaster, 8 March 2018.

Huc-Hepher, S. (2019) 'Sometimes There's Racism Towards the French Here', *National Identities*, DOI: 10.1080/14608944.2019.1649250.

Huc-Hepher, S. and Drake, H. (2013) 'From the 16ème to South Ken?', in D. Kelly and M. Cornick (eds), *A History of the French in London* (London: University of London): https://sas-space.sas.ac.uk/6460/1/FrenchLondonKellyCornick.pdf (accessed 16 January 2021).

Huc-Hepher, S. and Huertas Barros, E. (2016) 'Up-skilling Through e-Collaboration', in E. Corradini, K. Borthwick and A. Gallagher-Brett (eds) *Employability for Languages: A handbook*: https://research-publishing.net/publication/chapters/978–1–908416–38–4/475.pdf (accessed 16 January 2021).

Huc-Hepher, S. and Wells, N. (2021) 'Exploring online diasporas: London's French and Latin American Communities in the UK Web Archive', in D.Gomes *et al.* (eds) *The Past Web: Exploring Web Archives* (Heidelberg, London and New York: Springer).

Huc-Hepher, S. and Lyczba, F. (forthcoming) 'A French Home?', in C. Wang and T. Lamb (eds) *Bridging Borders, Creating Spaces* (Bristol: Multilingual Matters).

Hulstaert, K. (2018) '"French and the School are One" – the Role of French in Postcolonial Congolese Education', *Paedagogica Historica* 54:6, 822–36, DOI: 10.1080/00309230.2018.1494203.

Hutnyk, J. (2018) 'Hybridity', in K. Stierstorfer and J. Wilson (eds) *The Routledge Diaspora Studies Reader* (London and New York: Routledge).

Ilcan, S. (2002) *Longing in Belonging* (Westport, CT: Praeger).

Ingram, N. and Abrahams, J. (2016) 'Stepping Outside of Oneself', in J. Thatcher *et al.* (eds) *Bourdieu: The Next Generation* (London and New York: Routledge).

Inhorn, M. (2011) 'Diasporic Dreaming', *Reproductive Bio-Medicine Online*, 23:5, 582–91, DOI: 10.1016/j.rbmo.2011.08.006.

In Limbo Project (2019) 'About Us'. *In Limbo*: www.inlimboproject.org/# (accessed 16 January 2021).

Iriarte, R. (2014) 'Top 12 des stars de la télé … des années 1990!', *Le Figaro TV Mag* (19 September): http://tvmag.lefigaro.fr/le-scan-tele/people/2014/09/19/28

008–20140919ARTFIG00241-top-12-des-stars-de-la-tele-des-annees-1990.php (accessed 16 January 2021).

Jansson, A. (2016) 'How to Become an "Elite Cosmopolitan"', *European Journal of Cultural Studies* 19:5, 465–80, DOI: 10.1177/1367549416631549.

Janvrin, I. and Rawlinson, C. (2013) *Les Français à Londres* (Paris: Bibliomane).

Jean Michel Brun Ltd. (no date) 'About Us', *Jean Michel Brun Ltd* (UK Web Archive): www.webarchive.org.uk/wayback/archive/20150912220108/ http://www.jeanmichelbrunltd.com/about-us.html. (accessed 16 January 2021).

Jenkins, R. (2002) *Pierre Bourdieu* (rvd edition) (London: Routledge).

Jewitt, C. (2011) *The Routledge Handbook of Multimodal Analysis* (1st edition) (London: Routledge).

Jewitt, C. (2014) *The Routledge Handbook of Multimodal Analysis* (2nd edition) (London: Routledge).

Johnson, J. and Rowlands, T. (2012) 'The Interpersonal Dynamics of In-Depth Interviewing', in J. F. Gubrium *et al.* (eds) *The Sage Handbook of Interview Research* (London: Sage).

Jourdain, A. and Naulin, S. (2011) *La Théorie de Pierre Bourdieu et ses usages sociologiques* (Paris: Armand Colin).

Kele, J. (2016) 'Digital Diaspora and Social Capital', *Middle East Journal of Culture and Communication* 9:3, 315–33.

Kelly, D. (2016) 'A Migrant Culture on Display', *Modern Languages Open*: www.modernlanguagesopen.org/index.php/mlo/rt/printerFriendly/148/165 (accessed 16 January 2021).

Kelly, D. and Cornick, M. (2013) *A History of the French in London: liberty, equality, opportunity* (London: University of London): https://sas-space.sas.ac.uk/6460/1/FrenchLondonKellyCornick.pdf (accessed 16 January 2021).

Kelly, P. and Lusis, T. (2006) 'Migration and the Transnational Habitus', *Environment and Planning A* 38, 831–47, DOI: 10.1068/a37214.

King, R. and Christou, A. (2008) 'Cultural Geographies of Counter-Diasporic Migration', in University of Sussex Centre for Migration Working Paper Series, No. 45: www.sussex.ac.uk/webteam/gateway/file.php?name=mwp45.pdf&site=252 (accessed 8 September 2015).

King, R. *et al.* (2008) '"Turks" in London', in University of Sussex Centre for Migration Working Paper Series, No. 51: www.sussex.ac.uk/webteam/gateway/file.php?name=mwp51.pdf&site=252 (accessed 8 September 2015).

King, R. and Raghuram, P. (2013) 'International Student Migration', *People, Space & Place* 19:2, 127–37, DOI: 10.1002/psp. 1746.

King, R. *et al.* (2014) 'The Lure of London', in University of Sussex Centre for Migration Working Paper Series, No. 75: www.sussex.ac.uk/webteam/gateway/file.php?name=mwp75.pdf&site=252 (accessed 8 September 2015).

Kitchin, R. (2014) *The Data Revolution* (London: Sage).

Kivisto, P. (2003) 'Social Spaces, Transnational Immigrant Communities, and the Politics of Incorporation', *Ethnicities* 3, 5–28, DOI: 10.1177/1468796803003 001786.

Kneafsey, M. and Cox, R. (2002) 'Food, Gender and Irishness', *Irish Geography* 35:1, 6–15, DOI: 10.1080/00750770209555789.

Kofman, E. (2004) 'Gendered Global Migrations', *International Feminist Journal of Politics* 6:4, 643–65, DOI: 10.1080/1461674042000283408.

Korpela, M. (2010) 'A Postcolonial Imagination? Westerners Searching for

Authenticity in India', *Journal of Ethnic and Migration Studies* 36:8, 1,299–315, DOI: 10.1080/13691831003687725.

Korpela, M. (2014) 'Lifestyle of Freedom? Individualism and lifestyle migration', in Benson, M. and Osbaldiston, N. (eds) *Understanding Lifestyle Migration* (Basingstoke: Palgrave Macmillan).

Koser, K. (2007) *International Migration: A Very Short Introduction* (Oxford: Oxford University Press).

Kozinets, R. (2010) Netnography – Doing Ethnographic Research Online (London: Sage).

Krausova, A. and Vargas Silva, C. (2013) *London: Census Profile* (Oxford: The Migration Observatory): www.migrationobservatory.ox.ac.uk/briefings/london-census-profile (accessed 16 January 2021).

Kress, G. (2010) Multimodality. A Social Semiotic Approach to Contemporary Communication (London and New York: Routledge).

Kress, G. (2011) 'Partnerships in Research: multimodality and ethnography', *Qualitative Research* 11:3, 239–60, DOI: 10.1177/1468794111399836.

Kress, G. and van Leeuwen, T. (1996) *Reading Images* (London: Routledge).

Kress, G. and van Leeuwen, T. (2001) *Multimodal Discourse* (London: Arnold).

Kron, R. (1907) *The Little Londoner: A Concise Account of the Life and Ways of the English* (Freiburg: J. Bielefelds Verlag): https://archive.org/details/littlelondonerco00kron/page/n3 (accessed 16 January 2021).

Kross, E. *et al.* (2011) 'Social Rejection Shares Somatosensory Representations with Physical Pain', *Proceedings of the National Academy of Sciences of the United States of America* 108:15, 6,270–5, DOI: 10.1073/pnas.1102693108.

Laja, P. (2019) 'Image Carousels and Sliders: Don't use them (here's why)', *Conversion XL*: https://conversionxl.com/blog/dont-use-automatic-image-sliders-or-carousels/ (accessed 16 January 2021).

Lamnaouer, L. (2018) 'Des élèves du Lycée Charles de Gaulle victimes d'agressions xénophobes', in *French Morning London* (22 May): https://london.frenchmorning.com/2018/05/22/brexit-eleves-lycee-de-gaulle-agressions-xenophobes/.

Landry, J.-M. (2006) 'La Violence symbolique chez Bourdieu', *Aspects Sociologiques*, 13, 1, 85–92: www.fss.ulaval.ca/cms_recherche/upload/aspectssociologiques/fichiers/landry2006.pdf (accessed 15 January 2021).

Laplace, L. *et al.* (2002) 'Les systèmes de santé français et anglais: évolution comparée depuis le milieu des années 90', *Santé Publique* 1:14, 47–56: www.cairn.inforevue-sante-publique-2002-1-page-47.htm (accessed 15 December 2019).

Larcher, S. (2018) 'The End of Silence', in F. Germain and S. Larcher (eds) *Black French Women and the Struggle for Equality, 1848–2016* (Lincoln and London: University of Nebraska Press).

Law, L. (2001) 'Home Cooking', *Hong Kong Ecumene* 8: 264–83.

Lawler, S. (2008) *Identity: Sociological Perspectives* (Cambridge: Polity).

Lazarus (1994) 'What Do Women Want?', *Medical Anthropology Quarterly* 8:1, 25–46, DOI: 10.1525/maq.1994.8.1.02a00030.

Lea, S., Stephenson, D. and Troy, J. (2003) 'Higher Education Students' Attitudes to Student-centred Learning', *Studies in Higher Education* 28:3, 321–34, DOI: 10.1080/03075070309293.

Leach, N. (2005) 'Belonging', in J. Hillier and E. Rooksby (eds) *Habitus: A Sense of Place* (2nd edition) (Aldershot: Ashgate).

Leavey, G., Sembhi, S. and Livingston, G. (2004) 'Older Irish MIGRANTS LIVING in London', *Journal of Ethnic and Migration Studies* 30:4, 763–79, DOI: 10.1080/13691830410001699603.

Le Collectif 'Levons l'omerta' (2016) 'Harcèlement et politique: "Pour que l'impunité cesse"', *Libération* (09 May): www.liberation.fr/france/2016/05/09/harcelement-et-politique-pour-que-l-impunite-cesse_1451542.

Ledain, E. (2010) *Les Oubliés de Saint Pancras* (London: Consulat Général de France à Londres/Centre Charles Péguy).

Leeuwen (van), T. (2005) *Introducing Social Semiotics* (London and New York: Routledge).

Lehmann, W. (2013) 'Habitus Transformation and Hidden Injuries', *Sociology of Education* 87:1, 1–15, DOI: 10.1177/0038040713498777.

Le Monde (2010) '88 per cent de Français pensent que le piston prime sur le talent', *Le Monde Blog, Economie et entreprises* (27 October): http://lemonde-emploi.blog.lemonde.fr/2010/10/27/88-des-francais-pensent-que-le-piston-prime-sur-le-talent/.

Lemke, J. L. (2002) 'Discourse, Dynamics, and Social Change', *Cultural Dynamics*: http://static1.1.sqspcdn.com/static/f/694454/12424843/1306519848297/Discourse-Dynamics (accessed 16 January 2021).

Leonard, P. (2008) 'Migrating Identities', *Gender, Place and Culture* 15:1, 45–60, DOI: 10/1080/09663690701817519.

Leonard, P. (2010a) 'Work, Identity and Change?', *Journal of Ethnic and Migration Studies* 36:8, 1,247–63, DOI: 10.1080/13691831003687691.

Leonard, P. (2010b) 'Old Colonial or New Cosmopolitan?, *Social Politics* 17:4, 507–35.

Leonard, P. and Walsh, K. (2019) *British Migration: Privilege, Diversity and Vulnerability* (Abingdon and New York: Routledge).

Levin, I (2016) Migration, Settlement, and the Concepts of House and Home (Abingdon and New York: Routledge).

L'Express (2007) 'Sarkozy drague les expatriés', *L'Express* (31 January): www.lexpress.fr/actualite/politique/sarkozy-drague-les-expatries_462610.html.

L'Express (2010) 'La France, pays du piston?', *L'Express Emploi* (26 October): www.lexpress.fr/emploi/la-france-pays-du-piston_931262.html.

Li, W. (2011) 'Moment Analysis and translanguaging space', *Journal of Pragmatics* 43:5, 1,222–35, DOI: 10.1016/j.pragma.2010.07.035.

Li, W. (2018) 'Translanguaging as a Practical Theory of Language', *Applied Linguistics* 39:1, 9–30, DOI: 10.1093/applin/amx039.

Lilienfeld, S. (2017) 'Microaggressions: Strong Claims', *Perspectives on Psychological Science* 12:1, 138–69, DOI: 10.1177/1745691616659391.

Lobbé, Q. (2018) 'Archives, fragments Web et diasporas' (Doctoral thesis, Université Paris-Saclay): https://hal.inria.fr/tel-01963548/file/these.pdf www.lexpress.fr/emploi/la-france-pays-du-piston_931262.html

London's Poverty Profile (2015) 'Newham', *London's Poverty Profile – Trust for London and New Policy Institute*: www.londonspovertyprofile.org.uk/indicators/boroughs/newham/ (accessed 19 April).

Longhurst, R., Johnston, L. and Ho, E. (2009) 'A Visceral Approach: cooking "at home"', *Transactions* 34, 333–45, DOI: 10.1111/j.1475-5661.2009.00349.x/full.

Looney, S. (2017) 'Breaking Point? An examination of the politics of othering in Brexit Britain', *TLI Think!* King's College London Research Paper Series,

69: https://papers.ssrn.com/sol3/papers.cfm?abstract_id=3014638 (accessed 16 January 2021).

Lopez Rodriguez, M. (2010) 'Migration and a Quest for "Normalcy"', *Social Identities* 16:3, 339–58, DOI: 10.1080/13504630.2010.482422.

Lorcerie, F. (2004) 'Discovering the Ethnicized School: the case of France', in S. Luchtenberg (ed.) *Migration, Education and Change* (Abingdon and New York: Routledge).

Lost in London (2016a) 'Brexit mon pote', *Lost in London* [Blog]: https://lostinlondon.fr/2016/06/24/brexit/ (accessed 16 January 2021).

Lost in London (2016b) 'Brexit Blues', *Lost in London* [Blog]: https://lostinlondon.fr/2016/06/30/brexit-blues/ (accessed 16 January 2021).

Lozanovska, M. (2008) 'Resisting Assimilation', in SAHANZ 2008: History in Practice, 25th International Conference of the Society of Architectural Historians, Australia and New Zealand. Geelong, Vic., 1–20: http://hdl.handle.net/10536/DRO/DU:30018103 (accessed 16 January 2021).

Luchtenberg, S. (2004) 'Introduction', in S. Luchtenberg (ed.) *Migration, Education and Change* (Abingdon and New York: Routledge).

Lulle, A., Moroşanu, L. and King, R. (2018) 'And Then Came Brexit', *Population, Space and Place*', 1–11, DOI: 10.1002/psp. 2122.

Lycée Français Charles de Gaulle Londres (no date) 'Procédures d'inscription', *Lycée Français*: www.lyceefrancais.org.uk/inscription/procedures (accessed 17 July 2016).

Lyman, P. (2002) 'Archiving the World Wide Web', *Building a National Strategy for Preservation: Issues in Digital Media (Part 4)*, Washington DC: Council on Library and Information Resources/Library of Congress: www.clir.org/pubs/reports/pub106/web.html (accessed 16 January 2021).

Lyons, A. and Tagg, C. (2019) 'The Discursive Construction of Mobile Chronotopes in Mobile-phone Messaging', *Language in Society* 48:5, 657–83, DOI: 10.1017/S004740451900023X.

Maddox, K. and Perry, J. (2017) 'Racial Appearance Bias', *Policy Insights from Behavioural and Brain Sciences*, 5:1, 57–65, DOI: 10.1177/2372732217747086.

Madianou, M. and Miller, D. (2011) 'Mobile Phone Parenting', *New Media and Society* 13:3, 457–70, DOI: 10.1177/1461444810393903.

Madianou, M. and Miller, D. (2012) *Migration and New Media* (Abingdon and New York: Routledge).

Malka, S. and Malka, V. (2016) *Le Grand Desarroi* (Paris: Albin Michel).

Mandel, R. (1989) 'Ethnicity and Identity among Guestworkers in West Berlin', in N. Gonzalez and C. McCommon (eds) Conflict, Migration, and the Expression of Ethnicity (Boulder: Westview Press).

Marcoux, J. (2001) 'The Refurbishment of Memory', in D. Miller (ed.) *Home Possessions* (Oxford: Berg).

Markham, A. and Buchanan, E. (2012) 'Ethical Decision-Making and Internet Research (Version 2.0)', *Association of Internet Researchers*: http://aoir.org/reports/ethics2.pdf (accessed 16 January 2021).

Masanès, J. (2006) *Web Archiving* (Berlin, Heidelberg: Springer-Verlag).

Massey, D. (1995) 'The Conceptualization of Place', in D. Massey and P. Jess (eds) *A Place in the World?* (Oxford: Oxford University Press).

Mata Codesal, D. (2008) 'Rice & Coriander, Sensorial Recreations of home through food', University of Sussex Centre for Migration Working Paper Series No. 50:

www.sussex.ac.uk/webteam/gateway/file.php?name=mwp50.pdf&site=252 (accessed 18 September 2015).

Maton, K. (2012) 'Habitus', in M. Grenfell (ed.) *Pierre Bourdieu – Key Concepts* (2nd edition) (Durham: Acumen).

Mayer-Schönberger, V. and Cukier, K. (2013) *Big Data* (London: John Murray).

Mazzara, F. (2015) 'Spaces of Visibility for the Migrants of Lampedusa', *Italian Studies* 70:4, 449–64, DOI: 10.1080/00751634.2015.1120944.

McGhee *et al.* (2017) 'An "Undeliberate Determinacy"?' *Journal of Ethnic and Migration Studies* 43:13, 2,109–30, DOI: 10.1080/1369183X.2017.1299622.

McKee, H. and Porter, J. (2009) *The Ethics of Internet Research* (New York: Peter Lang).

McMurtrie, R. (2010) 'Bobbing for Power', *Visual Communication* 9:4, 399–424, DOI: 10.1177/1470357210382182.

Meard Street Productions (2012) 'Shit French People in London Say', YouTube: www.youtube.com/watch?v=wX32dW1bf3Y (accessed 16 January 2021).

Michel, H. (2014) 'On ne pleure pas la fin de "Kitchen Nightmares" de Gordon Ramsay, c'est les oignons', *Slate* (1 July): www.slate.fr/story/89217/gordon-ramsay (accessed 16 January 2021).

Miller, D. (2001) 'Behind Closed Doors', in D. Miller (ed.) *Home Possessions* (Oxford: Berg).

Miller, D. (2005) 'Introduction', in S. Küchler and D. Miller (eds) *Clothing as Material Culture* (Oxford: Berg).

Miller, D. (2010) *Stuff* (Cambridge: Polity).

Miller, D. (2012) 'Social Networking Sites', in H. Horst and D. Miller (eds) *Digital Anthropology* (London: Berg).

Miller, D. and Horst, H. A. (2012) 'The Digital and the Human', in H. Horst and D. Miller (eds) *Digital Anthropology* (London and New York: Bloomsbury).

Miller, D. and Sinanan, J. (2017) *Visualising Faceboook* (London: UCL Press).

Miller, D. and Slater, D. (2000) *The Internet: An Ethnographic Approach* (Oxford: Berg).

Miller, D. and Woodward, S. (2012) *Blue Jeans: The Art of the Ordinary* (Berkley, LA and London: University of California Press).

Miller, R. (2018) '(Un)settling Home During the Brexit Process', *Population, Space and Place* 25, 1–11, DOI:10.1002/psp. 2203.

Mitchell, R. (2018) 'Shaking the Racial and Gender Foundations of France', in F. Germain and S. Larcher (eds) *Black French Women and the Struggle for Equality, 1848–2016* (Lincoln, NE and London: University of Nebraska Press).

Moore, R. (2012) 'Capital', in M. Grenfell (ed.) *Pierre Bourdieu – Key Concepts* (2nd edition) (Durham: Acumen).

Moores, S. and Metykova, M. (2010) '"I Didn't Realise How Attached I Am"', *European Journal of Cultural Studies* 13:2,171–89, DOI: 10.1177/136754940 9352278.

Moriarty, E. *et al.* (2010) 'Putting Work Back in Mobilities', New Migrations, New Challenges Conference, Trinity College Dublin, 29 June–3 July.

Mulholland, J. and Ryan, L. (2011) 'French Capital: A Study of French Highly-Skilled Migrants – Preliminary Findings Report' (ESRC/Middlesex University).

Mulholland, J. and Ryan, L. (2014) 'Doing the Business', *International Migration* 52:3, 55–68, DOI: 10.1111/imig.12120.

Mulholland, J. and Ryan, L. (2015) 'Londres Acceuil', in L. Meier (ed.) *Migration of Professionals and the City* (London: Routledge).

Mulholland, J. and Ryan, L. (2017) 'London is a Much More Interesting Place than Paris', in M. Van Riemsdijk and Q. Wang (eds) *Rethinking International Skilled Migration* (London: Routledge).

Murphy, J. P. (2018) 'Foie gras in the freezer', *Food and Foodways*, 26:2, 146–69, DOI: 10.1080/07409710.2018.1454774.

Murphy-Lejeune, E. (2001) 'Le Capital de mobilité: Genèse d'un étudiant voyageur', *Mélanges CRAPEL*. 26, 137–65.

Murphy-Lejeune, E. (2002) *Student Mobility and Narrative in Europe* (London and New York: Routledge).

Murthy, D. (2008) 'Digital Ethnography', *Sociology* 42:5, 837–55, DOI: 10.1177/0038038508094565.

Nadal, K. L. (2013) 'Introduction', in K. L. Nadal (ed.) *That's So Gay! Microaggressions and the lesbian, gay, bisexual, and transgender community* (Washington, DC: American Psychological Association).

National Childbirth Trust (no date) 'NCT History', *National Childbirth Trust*: www.nct.org.uk/about-us/history (accessed 16 January 2021).

Nenesse (2010) 'Ma chronique – Radio Paris ment, Radio Paris ment …', UK Web Archive: http://web.archive.org/web/20100714051717/ http://nenesse1.blog.co.uk:80/2010/07/09/radio-paris-ment-radio-paris-ment-8943311/ (accessed 16 January 2021).

Neto, F. (2019) 'Acculturation, Adaptation and Saudade Among Portuguese Migrants', *The Journal of Psychology*, DOI: 10.1080/00223980.2019.1590298.

Noble, G. (2013) 'It is Home, But it is not Home', *Journal of Sociology*, 49:2–3, 341–56, DOI: 10.1177/1440783313481532.

Oberon Garcia, C. (2018) 'Remapping the Metropolis', in F. Germain and S. Larcher (eds) *Black French Women and the Struggle for Equality, 1848–2016* (Lincoln, NE and London: University of Nebraska Press).

O'Brien, O. (2013) *Tube Tongues: Second languages at tube stops* [Interactive Map]: http://vis.oobrien.com/tube/#metric=tongues&year=2013&layers=TTTT TF&zoom=12&lon=-0.1194&lat=51.5089 (accessed 6 May 2015).

Office for National Statistics (2012) *2011 Census: Country of birth (detailed), local authorities in England and Wales* (Titchfield: Office for National Statistics): www.nomisweb.co.uk/census/2011/qs203ew (accessed 16 January 2016).

O'Grady, S. (2011) 'The NHS Is a Religion and We'll All Have to Pay "Church Tithes" to Support its Existence', *Independent* (17 July): www.independent.co.uk/news/business/comment/sean-ogrady-the-nhs-is-a-religion-and-well-all-have-to-pay-church-tithes-to-support-its-existence-2315557.html (accessed 16 January 2021).

Oliver, C. and O'Reilly, K. (2010) 'A Bourdieusian Analysis of Class and Migration', *Sociology* 44:1, 49–66, DOI: 10.1177/0038038509351627.

O'Reilly, K. (2012) *Ethnographic Methods* (2nd edition) (London and New York: Routledge).

O'Sullivan, C. (2005) 'Diaries, On-line Diaries, and the Future Loss to Archives; or Blogs and the Blogging Bloggers who Blog Them', *American Archivist* 68:1, 53–73.

Owen, J., Tao, K., and Rodolfa, E. (2010) 'Microaggressions and women in short-term psychotherapy', *The Counseling Psychologist* 38, 923–46, DOI: 10.1177/0011000010376093.

Ozouf, M. (1995) *Les mots des femmes* (Paris: Fayard).

Pahl, K. and Rowsell, J. (2010) *Artifactual Literacies* (New York: Teachers College Press).

Papastergiadis, N. (1998) *Dialogues in the Diasporas* (London: Rivers Oram).

Parisot, L. (2007) 'Preface', in H. Senni *De la Cité à la City* (Paris: L'Archipel).

Parker, D. (2000) 'The Chinese Takeaway and the Diasporic Habitus', in B. Hesse (ed.) *Un/Settled Multiculturalisms* (London: Zed).

Parkhurst Ferguson, P. (2004) *Accounting for Taste* (Chicago and London: University of Chicago Press).

Pauline (no date) 'Welcome', *Pauline à la Crème anglaise* [blog]: www.paulineala creme.com/ (accessed 16 January 2021).

Pennock, M. (2007) 'Digital Curation: a life-cycle approach', *Library and Archives*: www.ukoln.ac.uk/ukoln/staff/m.pennock/publications/docs/lib-arch_curation. pdf (accessed 16 January 2021).

Percebois, L. (no date) 'La remise en question du concours dans la fonction publique'. Conference paper: http://colloque-grh.univ-lille2.fr/intervenants/pdf/ Texte-Laurent-Percebois.pdf (accessed 21 April 2016).

Peters, S. (2014) 'Chasms, Bridges and Borderlands', in B. Perry, S. Docket and A. Petrivskyj (eds), *Transitions to School* (Heidelberg, New York and London: Springer).

Petridou, E. (2001) 'The Taste of Home', in D. Miller (ed.) *Home Possessions* (Oxford: Berg).

Phillimore, J. (2019) 'Symbolic Violence and Refugees'. YouTube: www.youtube. com/watch?v=rDQSWX0nCkM (accessed 16 January 2021).

Pile, S. (2005) 'Spectral Cities: Where the Repressed Returns and Other Short Stories', in J. Hillier and E. Rooksby (eds) *Habitus: A Sense of Place* (2nd edition) (Aldershot: Ashgate).

Pink, S. (2004) Home Truths: gender, domestic objects and everyday life (Oxford: Berg).

Pink, S. and Mackley, K. L. (2013) 'Saturated and Situated', *Media, Culture & Society* 35:6, 677–91, DOI: 10.1177/0163443713491298.

Pitman, T. (2018) 'Warriors and Weavers', *Modern Languages Open* 1–14, DOI: 10.3828/mlo.v0i0.207.

Poirier, A. (2006) Le Modèle anglais – une illusion française (Paris: Alvik).

Polanyi, M. (1975) 'Personal Knowledge', in M. Polanyi and H. Prosch (eds) *Meaning* (Chicago: University of Chicago Press).

Pollard, S. (2014) 'Anti-Semitism Rears its Ugly Head', *The Sunday Times* (27 July): www.thesundaytimes.co.uk/sto/news/focus/article1439260.ece?shareToken=fa6 3cf384938ca33ba8414401f2b6a44 (accessed 16 January 2021).

Ponzanesi, S. (2019) 'Migration and Mobility in a Digital Age', *Television and New Media* 20:6, 547–57, DOI: 10.1177/1527476419857687.

Population Data (2014) 'France: Aires Urbaines 2014', *Population Data*: www. populationdata.net/pays/france/ (accessed 23 July 2015).

Portes, A. (2003) 'Theoretical Convergencies and Empirical Evidence in the Study of Immigrant Transnationalism', *International Migration Review* 37, 847–92.

Pratt, M. (1991) 'Arts of the Contact Zone', *Profession*, 33–40: www.jstor.org/ stable/25595469 (accessed 16 January 2021).

Puwar, N. (2004) Space Invaders: Race, Gender and Bodies out of Place (Oxford: Berg).

Puwar, N. (2009) 'Sensing a Post-colonial Bourdieu', *The Sociological Review* 57:3, 371–84.

Randall, E. (2013) 'A Special Case? London's French Protestants', in D. Kelly and M. Cornick (eds) *A History of the French in London* (London: University of London): https://sas-space.sas.ac.uk/6460/1/FrenchLondonKellyCornick.pdf (accessed 16 January 2021).

Ravelli, L. and van Leeuwen, T. (2018) 'Modality in the Digital Age', *Visual Communication* 17:3, 277–97, DOI: 10.1177/1470357218764436.

Reitz, J. G., Simon, P. and Laxer, E. (2017) 'Muslims' Social Inclusion and Exclusion in France, Québec, and Canada', *Journal of Ethnic and Migration Studies* 43:15, 2473–98, DOI: 10.1080/1369183X.2017.1313105.

Remigi, E. and Martin, V. (2017) *In Limbo: Brexit Testimonies from EU Citizens in the UK* (London: Byline Books).

Retis, J. and Tsagarousianou, R. (2019) 'Diasporas, Media, and Culture', in J. Retis and R. Tsagarousianou (eds) *The Handbook of Diasporas, Media, and Culture* (1st edition) (Hoboken, NJ: Wiley).

Richardson, J. E., and Wodak, R. (2009) 'Recontextualising Fascist Ideologies of the Past', *Critical Discourse Studies* 6:4, 251–67, DOI: 10.1080/17405900903 180996.

Robbins, D. (2005) 'The Origins, Early Development and Status of Bourdieu's Concept of "Cultural Capital"', *The British Journal of Sociology* 56:1, 13–30, DOI: 10.1111/j.1468–4446.2005.00044.x.

Robertson (1995) 'Glocalisation: time-space and homogeneity-heterogeneity', in M. Featherstone *et al.* (eds) *Global Modernities* (London: Sage).

Rogers, C. (1965) *Client Centred Therapy* (Boston: Houghton Mifflin).

de Roquemaurel, J. (2014) *La Reine, la City et les grenouilles* (Paris: Éditions Albin Michel).

Roudaut, C. (2009) *France, je t'aime je te quitte* (Paris: Fayard).

Rowsell, J. (2011) 'Carrying My Family with Me', *Qualitative Research* 11:3, 331–46. DOI: 10.1177/1468794111399841.

Rubenstein, P. (2011) 'Why (and How) the Growth of Social Media has Created Opportunities for Market Research', in *GreenBook – The Guide for Buyers of Marketing Research*: www.greenbook.org/marketing-research/social-media-opportunities-for-market-research-37076 (accessed 16 January 2021).

Rushdie, S. (2018) 'Imaginary Homelands', in K. Stierstorfer and J. Wilson (eds) *The Routledge Diaspora Studies Reader* (London and New York: Routledge).

Ryan, L. (2011) 'Migrants' Social Networks and Weak Ties', *The Sociological Review* 59:4, 707–24. DOI: 10.1111/j.1467–954X.2011.02030.x.

Ryan, L. (2015) 'Another Year and Another Year', Summary Report (London: Middlesex University): http://sprc.info/wp-content/uploads/2012/07/Polish-Mig rants-in-London-extending-the-stay.pdf (accessed 16 January 2021).

Ryan, L. (2018) 'Differentiated Embedding', *Journal of Ethnic and Migration Studies* 44:2, 233–51, DOI: 10.1080/1369183X.2017.1341710.

Ryan, L. and Mulholland, J. (2013) 'Trading Places', *Journal of Ethnic and Migration Studies* 40:4, 584–600, DOI: 10.1080/1369183X.2013.787514.

Ryan, L. and Mulholland, J. (2014a) 'French Connections', *Global Networks* 14:2, 148–66, DOI: 10.1111/glob.12038.

Ryan, L. and Mulholland, J. (2014b) '"Wives are the Route to Social Life"', *Sociology* 48:2, 251–67.

Ryan, L. and Mulholland, J. (2015) 'Embedding in Motion', in L. Ryan, U. Erel and A. D'Angelo (eds), *Migrant Capital* (Basingstoke, New York: Palgrave Macmillan).

Ryan, L., Mulholland, J. and Agoston, A. (2014) 'Talking Ties', *Sociological Research Online* 19:2, 1–12: www.socresonline.org.uk/19/2/16.html (accessed 16 January 2021).

Ryan, L. and Sales, L. (2013) 'Family Migration', *International Migration* 51(2): 90–103, DOI: 10.1111/j.1468–2435.2010.00652.x.

Rzepnikowska, A. (2019) 'Racism and Xenophobia Experienced by Polish Migrants in the UK Before and After Brexit Vote', *Journal of Ethnic and Migration Studies* 45:1, 61–77, DOI: 10.1080/1369183X.2018.1451308.

Said, E. (1994) *Orientalism* (London: Penguin).

Salcedo Robledo, M. (2019) 'Chantier de recherche: Genre et sexualité en migration', *Hommes & migrations* 1,322, 171–8: http://journals.openedition.org/hommesmigrations/6817 (accessed 16 January 2021).

Sargeant, P. and Tagg, C. (2014) *The Language of Social Media* (London and New York: Palgrave Macmillan).

Sassen, S. (2002) 'The Repositioning of Citizenship', *Berkeley Journal of Sociology* 46, 4–25.

Sassen, S. (2006) *Territory, Authority, Rights* (Princeton: Princeton University Press).

Sassen, S. (2013) 'Does the City have Speech?', *Public Culture* 25:2, 209–21, DOI: 10.1215/08992363–2020557.

Saul, J. (2013) 'Implicit Bias, Stereotype Threat, and Women in Philosophy', in J. Hutchison and F. Jenkins (eds), *Women in Philosophy* (Oxford: Oxford University Press).

Sayad, A. (1999) *La double absence* (Paris: Le Seuil).

Schafer, M. R. ([1977] 1994) *The Soundscape* (Vermont: Destiny).

Schmitter Heisler, B. (2008) 'The Sociology of Immigration', in C. B. Brettell and J. F. Hollifield (eds), *Migration Theory* (New York: Routledge).

Schreiber, B. R. (2015) '"I am what I am": Multilingual identity and digital translanguaging', *Language Learning & Technology* 19:3, 69–87, DOI: 10125/44434.

Schubert, J. D. (2012) 'Suffering/Symbolic Violence', in M. Grenfell (ed.) *Pierre Bourdieu – Key Concepts* (2nd edition) (Durham: Acumen).

Scott, S. (2004) 'Transnational Exchanges Amongst Skilled British Migrants in Paris', *Population, Space and Place* 10:5, 391–410, DOI: 10.1002/psp. 345.

Scott, S. (2006) 'The Social Morphology of Skilled Migration', *Journal of Ethnic and Migration Studies* 32:7, 1,105–29, DOI: 10.1080/13691830600821802.

Scotto, G. (2010) 'Italiani a Londra tra tradizione e meritocrazia', in F. Migrantes (ed.) *Rapporto Italiani nel Mondo 2010* (Rome: Edizioni Idos), 399–408.

Senni, H. (2007) *De la Cité à la City* (Paris: L'Archipel).

Service Public (no date) 'Harcèlement moral au travail', *Service Public – Site officiel de l'administration française*: www.service-public.fr/particuliers/vosdroits/F2354 (accessed 16 January 2021).

Shahrokni, S. (2019) 'The Transnational Career Aspirations of France's High-achieving Second-generation Maghrebi Migrants', *Journal of Ethnic and Migration Studies* 45:3, 437–54. DOI: 10.1080/1369183X.2017.1394179.

Simon, P. (2006) 'L'arbre du racisme et la forêt des discriminations', in N. Guénif-Souilamas (ed.) *La République mise à nu par son immigration* (Paris: La Fabrique).

Simon, P. (2012) French National Identity and Immigration: Who Belongs to the National Community? (Washington, DC: Migration Policy Institute).

Simon, P., and Tiberj, V. (2016) 'Les registres de l'identité: Les immigrés et leurs descendants face à l'identité nationale', in C. Beauchemin *et al.* (eds) *Trajectoires et Origines* (Paris: INED).

Skowronsk, G. A. (2015) 'Pain Relief in Childbirth', *Anaesthesia and Intensive Care – History Supplement* 25–8, DOI: 10.1177/0310057X150430S106.

Skulte-Ouaiss, J. (2013) 'Home is Where the Heart is; Citizenship is Where it is Safe', *Identities* 20:2, 133–48, DOI: 10.1080/1070289X.2012.763166.

Smith, M. P. (2001) *Transnational Urbanism* (Oxford: Blackwell).

Smith, M. P. (2005) 'Transnational Urbanism Revisited', *Journal of Ethnic and Migration Studies* 31, 235-44, DOI: 10.1080/1369183042000339909.

Smith, K. (2012) Fairness, Class and Belonging in Contemporary England (London: Palgrave Macmillan).

Snel, E., Faber, M. and Engbersen, G. (2015) 'To Stay or to Return?', *Central and Eastern European Migration Review*, 4:2, 5–24: www.ceemr.uw.edu.pl/vol-4-no-2-december-2015/articles/stay-or-return-explaining-return-intentions-central-and-eastern (accessed 16 January 2021).

Soysal, Y. (1994) *Limits to Citizenship* (Chicago: University of Chicago Press).

Sprio, M. (2013) *Migrant Memories* (Bern: Peter Lang).

Starkey, L. (2019) 'Three Dimensions of Student-centred Education', *Critical Studies in Education* 60:3, 375–90, DOI: 10.1080/17508487.2017.1281829.

Statistiques Mondiales (2015) 'Taux de chomage dans l'Union européenne': www.statistiques-mondiales.com/ue_chomage.htm (accessed 7 May 2015).

Stockdale, A. (2016) 'From "Trailing Wives" to the Emergence of a "Trailing Husbands" Phenomenon', *Population, Space and Place* 23:3, 1–18, DOI: 10.1002/psp. 2022.

Streeck, J., Goodwin, C. and LeBaron, C. (2011) *Embodied Interaction* (Cambridge: Cambridge University Press).

Strodl, S., Petrov, P. and Rauber A. (2011) *Research on Digital Preservation Within Projects Co-funded by the European Union in the ICT Programme* (Brussels: European Commission): www.ifs.tuwien.ac.at/~strodl/paper/Reportpercent20-percent20Researchpercent20onpercent20Digitalpercent20Preservation.pdf (accessed 23 March 2015).

Sue, D. W. *et al.* (2007) 'Racial Microaggressions in Everyday Life', *American Psychologist* 62, 271–86, DOI: 10.1037/0003–066X.62.4.271.

Sue, D. W. (2010) *Microaggressions in Everyday Life* (Hoboken, NJ: Wiley).

Sutton, D. E. (2001) *Remembrance of Repasts* (Berg: Oxford).

Synnott, A. (1987) 'Shame and Glory: A sociology of hair', *The British Journal of Sociology* 38:3, 381–413, DOI: 10.2307/590695.

Tacchi, J. (1998) 'Radio Textures', in D. Miller (ed.) *Material Cultures: Why some Things Matter* (Chicago: University of Chicago Press).

Tacchi, J. (2009) 'Radio and Affective Rhythm in the Everyday', *Radio Journal: International Studies in Broadcast and Audio Media* 7:2, 171–83, DOI: 10.1386/rajo.7.2.171/1.

Tagg, C. *et al.* (2017) 'The Ethics of Digital Ethnography in a Team Project', *Applied Linguistics Review* 8:2–3, 271–92, DOI: 10.1515/applirev-2016–1040.

Tate, S. A., and Page, D. (2018) 'Whiteliness and Institutional Racism', *Ethics and Education* 13:1, 141–55, DOI: 10.1080/17449642.2018.1428718.

Taylor, D. (2012) 'Save as. "On the Subject of Archives"', *E-misférica*. 9:1–2: www.hemisphericinstitute.org/hemi/en/e-misferica-91/taylor (accessed 16 January 2021).

Thatcher, J. and Halvorsrud, K. (2016) 'Migrating Habitus', in J. Thatcher *et al.* (eds) *Bourdieu: The Next Generation* (London and New York: Routledge).

The3million (2019) 'About Us', *The3million*: www.the3million.org.uk/about-us.

Théry, I. (2011) 'Un féminisme à la française', *Le Monde* (11 May): www.lemonde.fr/idees/article/2011/05/28/un-feminisme-a-la-francaise_1528802_3232.html.

Thompson, A. (2010) 'Migratory Drift: Why Temporary Migrants Stay', Bangor School of Social Sciences Seminar Series. Bangor (27 October 27).

Thomson, P. (2012) 'Field', in M. Grenfell (ed.) *Pierre Bourdieu – Key Concepts* (2nd edition) (Durham: Acumen).

Tolia-Kelly, D. (2004) 'Locating Processes of Identification', *Transactions of the Institute of British Geographers* 29, 314–29, DOI: 10.1111/j.0020–2754.2004.00303.x.

Tombs, R. and Tombs, I. (2007) *That Sweet Enemy* (London: Pimlico).

Tristan, F. ([1840] 2008) *Promenades dans Londres (extraits)* (Paris: Gallimard).

Trouillot, M. (1995) *Silencing the Past* (Boston, MA: Beacon Press).

Tyler, K. (2003) 'The Racialised and Class Constitution of English Village Life', *Ethnos* 68:3, 391–412, DOI: 10.1080/0014184032000134504.

Tzeng, R. (2012) 'Middle Class International Migration', *Advances in Applied Sociology* 2, 120–6, DOI: 10.4236/aasoci.2012.22016.

UK Crime Stats (2015) 'Neighbourhood Crime League Table', *UK Crime Stats*: www.ukcrimestats.com/Neighbourhood/3243#League (accessed 27 July 2015).

UNESCO (2010) 'The Gastronomic Meal of the French', YouTube: https://youtu.be/6nKBBb72J4k (accessed 16 January 2021).

UNSA (2019) 'PISA 2018, la France championne des inégalités sociales et scolaires: une fatalite?': www.unsa-education.com/PISA-2018-la-France-championne-des-inegalites-sociales-et-scolaires-une (accessed 16 January 2021).

Valentine, G. (1993) 'Desperately Seeking Susan', *Area* 25:2, 109–16: www.jstor.org/stable/20003237 (accessed 16 January 2021).

Valentine, G. (2001) *Social Geographies* (London: Pearson Hall).

Valentine, G. (2008) 'Living with Difference', *Progress in Human Geography* 32, 323–37, DOI: 10.1177/0309133308089372.

Van Hear, N., Bakewell, O. and Long, K. (2018) 'Push–Pull Plus: reconsidering the drivers of migration', *Journal of Ethnic and Migration Studies* 44:6, 927–44, DOI: 10.1080/1369183X.2017.1384135.

Van Mol, C. (2013) 'Intra-European Student Mobility and European Identity', *Population, Space and Place* 19, 2, DOI: 10.1002/psp. 1752.

Vaisman, C. (2011) 'Performing Girlhood Through Typographic Play in Hebrew Blogs', in C. Thurlow and K. Kroczek (eds) *Digital Discourse: Language in the New Media* (Oxford: Oxford University Press).

Vaisman, C. (2016) 'Pretty in Pink vs. Pretty in Black', *Visual Communication* 15:3, 293–315, DOI: 10.1177/1470357216643909.

Vannini, P. (2007) 'Social Semiotics and Fieldwork', *Qualitative Inquiry* 13:1, 113–40, DOI: 10.1177/1077800406295625.

Veolia (2016a) 'Veolia in the UK', *Veolia*: www.veolia.co.uk/about-us/about-us/veolia-uk (accessed 11 June 2016).

Veolia (2016b) 'The History of Veolia: 1853–1900', *Veolia*: www.veolia.com/en/veolia-group/profile/history/1853–1900 (accessed 11 June 2016).

Vertovec, S. (2001) 'Transnationalism and Identity', *Journal of Ethnic and Migration Studies* 27:4, 573–82, DOI: 10.1080/13691830120090386.

Vertovec, S. (2007) 'Super-Diversity and its Implications', *Ethnic and Racial Studies* 30:6, 1,024–54, DOI: 10.1080/01419870701599465.

Vogue Paris (2012) 'Les 40 femmes de la décennie (8/40)', *Vogue Paris*: www.vogue.fr/culture/en-vogue/diaporama/les-40-femmes-de-la-dcennie/6562#091231-les-40-femmes-de-la-decennieaspx72795imagejpg_image8 (accessed 16 January 2021).

Walsh, K. (2006) 'British Expatriate Belongings', *Home Cultures* 3:2, 123–44, DOI: 10.2752/174063106778053183.

Walsh, K. (2012) 'Emotion and Migration: British Transnationals in Dubai', *Environment and Planning D: Society and Space* 30, 43–59, DOI: 10.1068/d12409.

Walsh, K. (2018) *Transnational Geographies of the Heart* (Chichester/Oxford: Wiley).

Wang, C. (2013a) 'Place of Desire: Skilled migration from mainland China to post-colonial Hong Kong', *Asia Pacific Viewpoint* 54:3, 388–97, DOI: 10.1111/apv.12032.

Wang, C. (2016) 'Introduction: The "Material Turn" in Migration Studies', *Modern Languages Open*, DOI: 10.3828/mlo.v0i0.88.

Wang, C. (2017) 'Heritage as Theatre', *China Information*, 31:2, 195–215. DOI: 10.1177/0920203X17709916.

Wang, T. (2013b) 'Big Data Needs Thick Data', *Ethnography Matters*: http://ethnographymatters.net/2013/05/13/big-data-needs-thick-data/#more-4782.

Warhurst, C. *et al.* (2012) 'Great Expectations: Gender, looks and lookism at work', *International Journal of Work Organisation and Emotion* 5:1, 72–90, DOI: 10.1504/IJWOE.2012.048593.

Warin, M. and Dennis, S. (2005) 'Threads of Memory', *Journal of Intercultural Studies* 26:1–2, 159–70, DOI: 10.1080/07256860500074367.

Waterson, R. (2005) 'Enduring Landscape, Changing Habitus', in J. Hillier and E. Rooksby (eds) *Habitus: A Sense of Place* (2nd edition) (Aldershot: Ashgate).

Webster, P. (2019) 'Understanding the Limitations of the ccTLD as a Proxy for the National Web', in N. Brügger and D. Laursen (eds) *The Historical Web and Digital Humanities* (London and New York: Routledge).

Wenger, E. (1998) *Communities of Practice* (Cambridge: Cambridge University Press).

Wenger, E. (2004) 'Knowledge Management as a Doughnut', *Ivey Business Journal*: https://iveybusinessjournal.com/publication/knowledge-management-as-a-doughnut/.

Werbner, P. (2018) 'The Limits of Cultural Hybridity', in K. Stierstorfer and J. Wilson (eds) *The Routledge Diaspora Studies Reader* (London and New York: Routledge).

Wessendorf, S. (2007) '"Roots Migrants": Transnationalism and "Return" among Second-Generation Italians in Switzerland', *Journal of Ethnic and Migration Studies* 33:7, 1,083–102. DOI: 10.1080/13691830701541614.

Wessendorf, S. (2018) 'Pathways of Settlement Among Pioneer Migrants in Super-diverse London', *Journal of Ethnic and Migration Studies*, 44:2, 270–86, DOI: 10.1080/1369183X.2017.1341719.

Wessendorf, S. and Phillimore, J. (2018) 'New Migrants' Social Integration, Embedding and Emplacement in Superdiverse Contexts', *Sociology* 53:1, 123–38, DOI: 10.1177/0038038518771843.

Westcott, H. and Vazquez Maggio, M. L. (2016) 'Friendship, Humour and Non-native Language', *Journal of Ethnic and Migration Studies* 42:3, 503–18, DOI: 10.1080/1369183X.2015.1064764.

White, A. (2011) 'The Mobility of Polish Families in the West of England', *The Central European Journal of Social Sciences and Humanities* 37:1, 11–32.

Wiedemann, D. *et al.* (2015) 'Red Clothing Increases Perceived Dominance, Aggression and Anger', *Biology Letters* 11:5, 1–4, DOI: 10.1098/rsbl.2015.0166.

Wimmer, A. and Glick Schiller, N. (2003) 'Methodological Nationalism, the Social Sciences, and the Study of Migration', *International Migration Review* 37:3, 576–610.

Winters, J. (2017) 'Coda: Web Archives for Humanities Research', in N. Brügger and R. Schroeder (eds), *The Web as History* (London: University College London Press).

Wolfreys, J. (2018) *Republic of Islamophobia* (London: Hurst).

Wood, W., Quinn, J. and Kashy, D. (2002) 'Habits in Everyday Life', *Journal of Personality and Social Psychology* 83:6, 1281–97, DOI: 10.1037//0022–35 14.83.6.1281.

Woodward, S. (2005) 'Looking Good: Feeling Right', in S. Küchler and D. Miller (eds) *Clothing as Material Culture* (New York: Berg).

World's Capital Cities (2019a) 'Capital Facts for Paris, France': www.worldscapi talcities.com/capital-facts-for-paris-france/ (5 January 2020).

World's Capital Cities (2019b) 'Capital Facts for London, United Kingdom': www. worldscapitalcities.com/capital-facts-for-london-england/ (5 January 2020).

Yoon, A. (2013) 'Defining What Matters When Preserving Web-Based Personal Digital Collections', *The International Journal of Digital Curation* 8:1, 173–92: www.ijdc.net/index.php/ijdc/article/view/8.1.173 (accessed 16 January 2021).

Zembylas, M. (2012) 'Transnationalism, Migration and Emotions', *Globalisation, Societies and Education* 10:2, 163–79, DOI: 10.1080/14767724.2012.647403.

Zhu Hua, Li Wei and Lyons, A. (2015) 'Language, Business and Superdiversity in London', *Working Papers in Translanguaging and Translation* (WP. 5): www. birmingham.ac.uk/generic/tlang/index.aspx (accessed 15 January 2017).

Index

Lightning Source UK Ltd.
Milton Keynes UK
UKHW051528010721
386446UK00002BA/135